# Race, Ethnicity, Crime, and Justice

D1569885

# Race, Ethnicity, Crime, and Justice

Edited by

## Matthew B. Robinson

CAROLINA ACADEMIC PRESS
Durham, North Carolina

Library of Congress Cataloging-in-Publication Data

Race, ethnicity, crime, and justice / edited by Matthew B. Robinson.
    pages cm
  Includes bibliographical references and index.
  ISBN 978-1-61163-637-6 (alk. paper)
  1. Crime and race--United States. 2. Discrimination in criminal
justice administration--United States. 3. Criminal justice,
Administration of--United States.  I. Robinson, Matthew B., editor.

  HV9960.U55R33 2015
  364.973'089--dc23

                    2015025603

CAROLINA ACADEMIC PRESS
700 Kent Street
Durham, North Carolina 27701
Telephone (919) 489-7486
Fax (919) 493-5668
www.cap-press.com

Printed in the United States of America

# Contents

# Author Biographies

**Tammatha Clodfelter** is Assistant Professor in the Department of Government and Justice Studies at Appalachian State University. Dr. Clodfelter's current research and teaching interests include effective policing strategies, crime analysis and crime prevention, intimate partner violence, and sexual victimization. She received her PhD in Public Policy from the University of North Carolina at Charlotte and has published articles in *Addiction, Crime and Delinquency*, *Aggression and Violent Behavior*, and *Contemporary Drug Problems*.

**Beverly Crank** is Assistant Professor of Criminal Justice in the Department of Government and Justice Studies at Appalachian State University. Her research interests include crime and the life-course and serious adolescent offending.

**Rhys Hester** is a Sentencing Law and Policy Research Fellow at the University of Minnesota Law School. His primary research interests are in criminal sentencing, incarceration policy, and criminal procedure. Hester's research examines sentencing practices across a variety of jurisdictions. He holds a JD and a PhD, both from the University of South Carolina.

**Jefferson E. Holcomb** received his PhD from Florida State University and is Associate Professor of Criminal Justice in the Department of Government and Justice Studies at Appalachian State University. His research interests include the community supervision of offenders, the exercise of criminal justice discretion, capital punishment, and asset forfeiture by the police. His research has appeared in journals such as *Criminology*, *Justice Quarterly*, and the *Journal of Criminal Justice*.

**Catherine D. Marcum** is Associate Professor in the Department of Government and Justice Studies at Appalachian State University. She received her PhD in Criminology from Indiana University of Pennsylvania in 2008. She is currently the associate editor for *Corrections: Policy, Practice and Research*. Her research interests include criminological theory testing, cybercrime, and correctional issues.

**Bethany Poff** is originally from the Blue Ridge Mountains of southwestern Virginia, and is a graduate student at Appalachian State University. She will graduate with her Master's degree in Public Administration with a concentration in Administration of Justice.

**Matthew Robinson** is Professor of Government and Justice Studies at Appalachian State University. Robinson is the author of more than fifteen books on varied topics including criminological theory, crime prevention, corporate crime, criminal justice, capital punishment, the drug war, and social justice. He is Past President of the North Carolina Criminal Justice Association and Past President of the Southern Criminal Justice Association.

**Jason Williams** is a graduate of New Jersey City University (NJCU) with a Bachelor's and Master's degree in Criminal Justice. He subsequently earned his Doctorate in Administration of Justice from Texas Southern University. Aside from doing research for the academic audience, he is also involved in many public research and information forums, such as the Hampton Institute, where he serves as chair/editor of the Criminal Justice Department. His areas of expertise are race, ethnicity and crime, criminological/criminal justice theory, critical criminology, social control, criminal justice policy, and the sociology of knowledge.

**Marian Williams** is Professor of Criminal Justice at Appalachian State University. Williams has published in the journals *Criminology*, *Justice Quarterly*, and *Journal of Criminal Justice*. Her research interests include race, class, and gender in court processes, constitutional law, and criminal procedure.

**Barbara Zaitzow**, Professor of Criminal Justice at Appalachian State University, conducts research projects in men's and women's prisons and has been involved in local, state, and national advocacy work for prisoners and organizations seeking alternatives to imprisonment. Zaitzow has served on various editorial boards for nationally recognized journals and has published a co-edited book, articles, and book chapters on a variety of prison-related topics, including HIV/AIDS and other treatment needs of women prisoners and the impact of prison culture on the "doing time" experiences of the imprisoned. These works appear in *Criminal Justice Policy Review*, *International Journal of Offender Therapy and Comparative Criminology*, *Journal of Correctional Health Care*, *Journal of Crime and Justice*, *Journal of Gang Research*, *Journal of Prisoners on Prisons*, *Journal of the Association of Nurses in AIDS Care*, *Justice Policy Journal*, *Names*, *The Prison Journal*, and *Women's Studies Quarterly*.

# Preface

If you've seen the news at all in the past year, you are likely at least aware that the US criminal justice system has a serious *race* problem. Among the many cases of unarmed black men being killed by the police are these:

- Michael Brown in Ferguson, Missouri (who was shot dead after being warned about walking in the middle of a street);
- Jonathan Ferrell in Mecklenburg County, North Carolina (who was shot dead after surviving a car accident and merely trying to seek help);
- Tamir Rice in Cleveland, Ohio (who was shot dead by two officers seconds after they arrived on the scene of a call from a person who told the police a male was pointing a pistol at people but that it was "probably fake" [it was]);
- John Crawford in Beavercreek, Ohio (who was shot dead in Walmart while holding a toy gun); and
- Eric Garner (who was strangled to death on camera with an illegal chokehold maneuver in New York City).

Similarly, issues of *ethnicity* have regularly been in the news, as well. One prominent example is that of immigration in the US—and especially *illegal immigration*—an issue highly relevant to criminal justice. For example, more than 60,000 people each year are convicted for immigration crimes such as illegal entry into the country (Kirkham, 2013), burdening courts and swelling prison populations.

**Race** is a descriptive term used to refer to a group of people that share, or are perceived to share, common hereditary traits such as skin color, hair texture, or eye shape. In the US, we use terms like "Black" and "White" or "African American" or "Caucasian" when referring to different racial groups. **Ethnicity** is more broadly defined as having shared cultural traits like language, food, religion, customs, and traditions. In the US, data on ethnicities are gathered in a more limited way—for example, in the US Census we are asked to identify as "Hispanic or Latino" or "Not Hispanic or Latino."

For about as long as the disciplines of criminology and criminal justice have existed, scholars have studied relationships between race and ethnicity and crime and justice processing. Key questions include who is most processed by agencies of criminal and juvenile justice, and why? Data from the US Census Bureau (US Census, 2014) and The Sentencing Project (2014) show that, in 2012, for example, African Americans and Latinos collectively made up about 30% of the US population (13% African American, 17% Latino), yet 58% of all people incarcerated in the United States (36% African American, 22% Latino). Why is this so? Is it because African Americans and Latinos commit more crime? Is it because there is discrimination in policing and courts? Could both be true?

An enormous amount of evidence also points to huge disparities by race and ethnicity in juvenile justice practices, as well. For example, a report by The Sentencing Project (2008) shows that, while African Americans only comprise about 17% of juveniles in the US, they account for more than 45% of arrests of juveniles, almost one-third of referrals to juvenile courts, and more than 40% of waivers to adult court. And a report by the National Council on Crime and Delinquency found that residential placement is about four times higher for African Americans, three times higher for Native Americans, and two times higher for Latinos than for Whites, while racial and ethnic disparities in rates of imprisonment are even greater (Hartney & Vuong, 2009).

The problem has been around so long that it even has a term: **disproportionate minority contact**, a term that refers to the fact that people of color are more likely than Whites to come into contact with agencies of juvenile and criminal justice (Office of Juvenile Justice & Delinquency Prevention, 2012). In fact, reviews by the Office of Juvenile Justice and Delinquency Prevention show evidence that the problem has existed at least since 1989 (Hsia, Bridges, & McHale, 2004; Pope, Lovell, & Hsia, 2012).

Importantly, studies show that different levels of offending do *not* explain disproportionate minority confinement (Huizinga, Thornberry, Knight, Lovergrove, Loeber, Hill, & Farrington 2007). The significance of these data are explained by The Leadership Conference on Civil and Human Rights (2014), one of the most important civil rights organization in the US: "Racially skewed juvenile justice outcomes have dire implications, because the whole point of the juvenile justice system is to head off adult criminality."

*Race, Ethnicity, Crime, and Justice* allows us to provide answers to questions related to why disparities exist in criminal and juvenile justice practices, using empirical data and published studies to inform our conclusions. The goal of the book is provide a thorough, yet brief, summary of what is known about relationships between race, ethnicity, crime, and the practice of justice.

The authors of the book provide exhaustive coverage of race and ethnicity as they pertain to delinquency and crime, and summarize the most recent studies on race and ethnicity and juvenile and criminal justice practices. This includes how race and ethnicity impact the law, policing, courts, and corrections (including a separate chapter on capital punishment). In the book, the reader learns that there are indeed serious problems in the United States of not only individual discrimination but also institutionalized discrimination; that is, biases against different racial and ethnic groups have become part of American institutions (including criminal law and the mainstream media). The final chapter not only summarizes the entire book, but also offers needed reforms to bring the realities of justice practice more in line with American ideals.

# References

Hartney, C. & Vuong, L. (2009). *Created equal: Racial and ethnic disparities in the US criminal justice system.* Retrieved from: http://www.nccdglobal.org/sites/default/files/publication_pdf/created-equal.pdf.

Hsia, H., Bridges, G., & McHale, R. (2004). *Disproportionate minority contact: 2002 update.* Retrieved from: https://www.ncjrs.gov/pdffiles1/ojjdp/201240.pdf.

Huizinga, D., Thornberry, T., Knight, K., Lovergrove, P., Loeber, R., Hill, K., & Farrington, D. (2007). Disproportionate minority contact in the juvenile justice system: A study of differential minority arrest/referral to court in three cities. Retrieved from: https://www.ncjrs.gov/pdffiles1/ojjdp/grants/219743.pdf.

Kirkham, C., (2013). War on undocumented immigrants threatens to swell US prison population. *Huffington Post*, August 23. Downloaded from: http://www.huffingtonpost.com/2013/08/23/undocumented-immigrants-prison_n_3792187.html.

Leadership Conference on Civil and Human Rights (2014). *Justice on trial.* Chapter five: Race and juvenile justice system. Retrieved from: http://www.civilrights.org/publications/justice-on-trial/juvenile.html.

Office of Juvenile Justice and Delinquency Prevention (2012). *Disproportionate minority contact.* http://www.ojjdp.gov/pubs/239457.pdf.

Pope, C., Lovell, R., & Hsia, H. (2012). *Disproportionate minority contact:* A review of the research literature from 1989 through 2001. Retrieved from: http://www.ojjdp.gov/dmc/pdf/dmc89_01.pdf.

Sentencing Project (2014). Factsheet. Trends in U.S. corrections. Retrieved from: http://sentencingproject.org/doc/publications/inc_Trends_in_Corrections_Fact_sheet.pdf.

Sentencing Project (2008). *Reducing disparity in the criminal justice system.* Retrieved from: http://www.sentencingproject.org/doc/publications/rd_reducingracialdisparity.pdf.

US Census (2014). State & county QuickFacts. Retrieved from: http://quickfacts.census.gov/qfd/states/00000.html.

# Race, Ethnicity, Crime, and Justice

# Chapter 1

# Introduction to
# Race and Ethnicity

*by Matthew Robinson, PhD*

## Introduction

Americans are a just people. From the founding of the United States, we put our ideals on paper—terms like *liberty*, *equality*, and *happiness* appear in the Declaration of Independence and US Constitution. These terms and the documents themselves signify to contemporary Americans that their country continues to stand for freedom, equality, and happiness of all people. Yet freedom, equal rights, and happiness were not only *not* granted or assured to all people from the founding of our country, but they were expressly denied to many. For example, European settlers in America wiped out Native Americans, enslaved Africans, subjugated women, and oppressed young people. Much of this treatment was due to views of superiority and inferiority pertaining to race, ethnicity, gender, and age (Caravelis-Hughes & Robinson, 2015).

In this book, we examine the impact that race and ethnicity have on delinquency, crime, and juvenile and criminal justice. Given the strong connections between race and ethnicity and gender and age—the US largely incarcerates young, poor men of color—throughout the book the authors also pay attention to the impact of gender, social class, and age on crime and criminal justice. The major reason why gender, social class, and age are important for this book is because of the reality of **intersectionality**, or the reality that our identities and how others treat us are impacted by all of the statuses we hold in society—and that these statuses often interact to impact us (Omi & Winant, 2014). In this first chapter, the author defines key terms to be used throughout the book, including *race* and *ethnicity*, examines the demographic makeup of the US population today and in the past, and illustrates differences between *disparities* and *discrimination*.

# Key Terms: Race and Ethnicity

This book is about how race and ethnicity impact delinquency, crime, and juvenile and criminal justice. We begin by defining key terms used throughout the book—including *race* and *ethnicity*—along with offering a brief discussion of why these terms are important. Before we examine those terms, be aware that the term **extra-legal factors** refers to things outside the law that are not supposed to influence criminal justice policy, things such as race, class, gender, religion, sexual orientation, and so forth. Outcomes in criminal justice practice (e.g., arrests, convictions, punishment) can only legally be impacted by legal factors such as *offense seriousness* and *prior record* (so that people who commit more serious crimes and who commit them more often are worthy of greater attention by police, tougher sentences by courts, and longer and more severe forms of punishment by corrections). It is not legally permissible for people to be targeted and more severely sanctioned by criminal justice agencies because of their skin color, social class, gender, religion, sexual orientation, etc. (Caravelis-Hughes & Robinson, 2014).

## *What Is Race?*

**Race** is a descriptive term used to refer to a group of people that share, or are at least perceived to share, common traits passed down from parent to child through genetics (e.g., skin color, hair texture, eye shape). According to Templeton (2013): "Many human societies classify people into racial categories. These categories often have very real effects politically, socially, and economically."

In the US, we use terms like "Black" and "White" or "African American" or "Caucasian" when referring to different racial groups (Caravelis-Hughes & Robinson, 2015).

The US Census Bureau (US Census, 2014a) collects data on race and notes that:

> An individual's response to the race question is based upon self-identification. The Census Bureau does not tell individuals which boxes to mark or what heritage to write in.... People who identify with more than one race may choose to provide multiple races in response to the race question. For example, if a respondent identifies as "Asian" and "White," they may respond to the question on race by checking the appropriate boxes that describe their racial identities and/or writing in these identities on the spaces provided

Options for the Census Bureau's questions pertaining to race are included in Table 1.1.

---

### Table 1.1. Definitions of Race in the US Census

White—A person having origins in any of the original peoples of Europe, the Middle East, or North Africa.

Black or African American—A person having origins in any of the Black racial groups of Africa.

American Indian or Alaska Native—A person having origins in any of the original peoples of North and South America (including Central America) and who maintains tribal affiliation or community attachment.

Asian—A person having origins in any of the original peoples of the Far East, Southeast Asia, or the Indian subcontinent including, for example, Cambodia, China, India, Japan, Korea, Malaysia, Pakistan, the Philippine Islands, Thailand, and Vietnam.

Native Hawaiian or Other Pacific Islander—A person having origins in any of the original peoples of Hawaii, Guam, Samoa, or other Pacific Islands.

Source: http://census.gov/topics/population/race/about.html

---

The different racial categories of the US Census are *not* thought to reflect biological (i.e., genetic) differences between groups of people. The Census Bureau (US Census, 2014a) explains that these "racial categories … generally reflect a *social definition of race* recognized in this country and not an attempt to define race biologically, anthropologically, or genetically" (emphasis added). Further, the Census Bureau (US Census, 2014a) notes that the racial categories include not only race but also "national origin or sociocultural groups." Finally, respondents are allowed to select more than one race to indicate their racial background and those who identify their origin as Hispanic, Latino, or Spanish can be of any race (e.g., White, Black or African American).

With regard to the issue of biology and race, Fuentes (2014) clarifies:

> There is a biological basis (measurement and definition) for race. We can measure it by comparing populations within a species—and by that measure, the entire species (all populations) of Homo sapiens (us) currently falls into just one biological race. This does not mean that what most refer to as "races" ("White," "Black," "Asian," etc.) don't matter. They do. These are real categories in our social and political lives. But the ways these categories are created and defined are not scientifically valid biological categories; they are constructs that are put together based on social, historical, economic, and political features, and then superficially and erroneously linked with certain selected biological features (skin color, facial form, clusters of alleles, etc.). This does not mean that they are not socially relevant and a real part of our society; it just means that they are not biological categories (and thus are not the products of evolutionary histories).

There is thus a reason we refer to the *human race* as a singular entity.

From this discussion, it is clear that the term "race" has serious problems. Most importantly, it must be understood that race is a term that is a **social construct**, meaning that is it created or constructed by members of a society based on their own values and biases. Its meaning thus varies across societies and thus does not have universal meaning based on empirically demonstrable facts (Gallagher, 2011). When you hear a person say that race is *socially constructed*, this is what he or she means.

Merriam-Webster (2014) clarifies, writing that the term race was "once commonly used … to denote a division of humankind possessing traits that are transmissible by descent and sufficient to characterize it as a distinct human type (e.g., Caucasoid, Mongoloid, Negroid)." That is, the term race once was used to refer to biologically distinct groups based on nothing more than form of hair and differences in body measurements (which are actually impacted by environmental conditions), going back as far as the 1500s. Yet Merriam-Webster (2014) notes that "the term has little scientific standing" today "[b]ecause all

## Figure 1.1. Early Migrations out of Africa

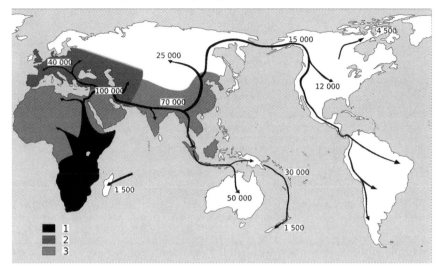

Source: http://en.wikipedia.org/wiki/File:Spreading_homo_sapiens.svg

human populations … are extremely similar genetically." As such many scientists now use the term **cline** rather than race, which refers to

> a graded series of differences occurring along a line of environmental or geographical transition. This reflects the recognition that human populations have always been in a state of flux, with genes constantly flowing from one gene pool to another, impeded only by physical or ecological boundaries. While relative isolation does preserve genetic differences and allow populations to maximally adapt to climatic and disease factors over long periods of time, all groups currently existing are thoroughly "mixed" genetically, and such differences as still exist do not lend themselves to simple typologizing. (Merriam-Webster, 2014)

Thus, there is *clinal variation* in peoples based on their past movements around the globe, resulting in different living conditions including climate, exposure to sunlight, nutritional intake, and so forth. For example, Figure 1.1 depicts the migration of Homo sapiens (depicted as number 1 in the figure), Neanderthals (depicted as number 2 in the figure), and other early hominids (depicted as number 3 in the figure). Among humans, people who migrated into sunny tropical regions would develop darker skin to protect them against the sun; whereas in colder regions in the North, people would have developed lighter skin to absorb sunlight to assure better health through absorption of vitamin D. Body build would also change based on climate to either reduce heat loss or maximize heat (Shane, 1999).

All this suggests that what we currently define as race may largely reflect differences in skin color and other physical differences produced by evolutionary adaptations stemming from diversity in past experiences. This is supported by Templeton (2013): "Adaptive traits, such as skin color, have frequently been used to define races in humans, but such adaptive traits reflect the underlying environmental factor to which they are adaptive and not overall genetic differentiation, and different adaptive traits define discordant groups" (where *discordant* means different).

Templeton (2013) explains that all species on the planet, including humans, "adapt to many environmental factors, not just one. Frequently, different adaptive traits display discordant geographical distributions because the underlying environmental factors have discordant geographical distribution." One example of this is skin color, which is the "adaptive trait most commonly considered by European cultures as a 'racial trait' in humans. Skin color is an adaptation to the amount of ultraviolet (UV) radiation in the environment: dark skins are adaptive in high UV environments in order to protect from radiation damage that can kill and burn cells and damage DNA if not protected by melanin, and light skins are adaptive in low UV environments in order to make sufficient vitamin D, which requires UV." According to Templeton (2013): "The geographical distribution of skin color follows the environmental factor of UV intensity. Skin color differences do not reflect overall genetic divergence. For example, the native peoples with the darkest skins live in tropical Africa and Melanesia. The dark skins of Africans and Melanesians are adaptive to the high UV found in these areas. Because Africans and Melanesians live on opposite sides of the world, they are more highly genetically differentiated than many other human populations … despite their similar skin colors." Thus, Templeton concludes: "Skin color differences in humans are not a reliable indicator of overall genetic differentiation or evolutionary history. Moreover, skin color varies continuously among humans in a clinal fashion rather than categorical ecotypes … Hence, there is a compelling biological reason to exclude skin color as the racially-defining adaptive trait under the ecotype concept of race."

Even with this fact, lifestyle differences between groups did emerge over time (e.g., preferences for certain types of foods, music, extra-curricular activities), reinforcing the perception that there are true differences between races. None of this, however, stems from innate, biological differences. Instead, as noted earlier, these differences reflect adaptations to different environmental conditions.

Templeton (2013) adds that it "is possible with modern DNA technology to infer the geographical ancestry of individuals by scoring large numbers of genes," suggesting to some that race is related to genetics. Further, it is possible to differentiate different human populations from one another if one has "enough genetic markers." Incredibly, a White supremacist by the name of Craig Cobb—who was working to convert a small North Dakota town into a place where only Whites could live—found out on a daytime talk show that his DNA showed genetically he was "86 percent European" and "14 percent sub-Saharan African" (Thompson, 2013). This should not be surprising because almost everyone alive shows "significant genetic inputs from two or more populations, indicating that most human individuals have mixed ancestries and do not belong to a 'pure' group" (Templeton, 2013).

Still, as explained by Templeton (2013): "Human populations certainly show genetic differences across geographical space, but this does not necessarily mean that races exist [biologically] in humans." Further, "genetic differentiation alone is insufficient to define a subspecies or race ... genetic differentiation [must exist] across sharp boundaries and not as gradual changes, with the boundaries reflecting the historical splits." This is not the case in human beings. Templeton's review of the evidence shows that "the five major 'races' of humans account for only 4.3% of human genetic variation" and the vast majority of genetic differences between people are unique to individuals rather than to races.

So, Templeton seems to favor the term **ecotype**, which he says "refers to a group of individuals sharing one or more adaptations to a specific environment." Thus, inner-city Blacks might be considered one type of ecotype, and they can be differentiated not only with inner-city Whites (based on skin color), but also rural Blacks, rural Whites, etc. (based on the specific environments in which different people live). As you read this book, please try to remember that race is a socially constructed reality, wherein clinal variations across different ecotypes are real and reflect not biological differences but instead different environmental impacts.

## What Is Ethnicity?

**Ethnicity** is more broadly defined as having shared cultural traits such as language, religion, food preferences, and other customs and traditions. Whereas race is socially constructed, ethnicity signifies a sense of connection or belonging between people based usually on country of origin (Cornell & Hartmann, 2006). When people refer to *ethnicity*, they are usually referring to a person's original place of origin. USA.gov, the official website of the US government (US, 2014), recognizes the following ethnicities within the US, at the broadest level of analysis: Hispanic and Latino; Asian American; Native American. Other categories related to ethnicity include Native American and Alaska Native, Asian American, and Native Hawaiian and Other Pacific Islander. To these categories one could add literally dozens of other categories from the broad (e.g., European American) to the specific (e.g., Italian American, Spanish American, Irish American, French American, German American, etc.). Each of these groups has its own unique history and experiences specific to that ethnicity and /or nationality.

As noted earlier, the largest ethnic group in the United States is Latinos or Hispanics. According to the US Census (2014c):

> Hispanics or Latinos are those people who classified themselves in one of the specific Spanish, Hispanic, or Latino categories listed on the Census 2010 questionnaire—"Mexican," "Puerto Rican," or "Cuban"— as well as those who indicate that they are "another Hispanic, Latino, or Spanish origin." People who do not identify with one of the specific origins listed on the questionnaire but indicate that they are "another Hispanic, Latino, or Spanish origin" are those whose origins are from Spain, the Spanish-speaking countries of Central or South America, or the Dominican Republic. The terms "Hispanic," "Latino," and "Spanish" are used interchangeably.

Thus, the Latino ethnicity is comprised of a large number of people from many different places and very divergent backgrounds. These groups will be illustrated later in this chapter.

The US Census is currently considering revising the annual census forms to include in its race category Latinos and Hispanics, meaning this would no longer be counted as an ethnicity. This shows the arbitrary nature of these terms. Twenty-three-year-old Elizabeth Zamora, who is a Dallas native and the daughter of Mexican immigrants, reacted to the news from the proposed census changes this way: "We're not just White or Black or Asian. Our parents may be coming from Jamaica, Mexico, Argentina, Europe…. You can't put us in one category" (El Nasser, 2013).

Many historical and contemporary political issues and social problems relate to ethnicity. Take the Holocaust of Nazi Germany as an historical example, where about six million Jews were slaughtered because of their perceived inferiority to Germans. A contemporary example is the debate about immigration in America, especially illegal immigration by Latinos or Hispanics. These issues inevitably end up involving criminal justice agencies in one way or another, making ethnicity highly relevant for understanding criminal justice practice.

## *Other Terms Related to Race and Ethnicity*

Historically, racial and ethnic groups in American society have been referred to as **minority groups**, a term meant to denote the small size of the groups relative to the dominant majority group made up of Caucasian or Whites. According to Schaeffer, minority groups can be identified based on five characteristics, shown in Table 1.2. Stated simply, they not only have distinguishing physical or culture traits (e.g., non-white skin, different language or religion), but they also tend to be treated unfairly, thereby having fewer opportunities for success through legitimate means such as education and work. The key determinant of minority group membership is less power or privilege than the members of the dominant or majority group (Schaeffer, 2011).

---

### Table 1.2. Characteristics of Minority Groups

1) *Unequal treatment.* Members of minority groups often have fewer opportunities for education, wealth, success, and power than members of dominant groups. They also have less power over their own lives. This is primarily due to discrimination, prejudice, segregation, and isolation, which perpetuate social, economic, and political inequality.

2) *Distinguishing physical or cultural traits.* Minority group members possess physical traits (skin color, hair texture, eye shape) or cultural traits (language, religion) that differentiate them from members of the dominant group. The distinguishing characteristics that are most important in defining dominant group membership are unique to each society and are further mediated by time and place.

3) *Involuntary membership.* An individual cannot choose whether he or she belongs to a dominant or minority group. Instead, people are involuntarily born into the group.

4) *Awareness of subordination.* Members of minority groups are aware of their level of "otherness" from the dominant group. They have a strong sense of solidarity within the group and the longer the prejudice and discrimination continues, the more concrete their feeling of outsider status.

5) *In-group marriage.* Primarily, in-group marriage occurs because a member of the dominant group does not want to decrease their social status by joining themselves with a member of the minority group. Secondly, minority group members are encouraged to marry within their own group to maintain the social solidarity of the group.

Source: Schaeffer, R. (2011). *Racial and Ethnic Groups.* Upper Saddle River, NJ: Prentice Hall.

---

Increasingly, minorities are being referred to by a different term—**people of color**—which is a broader and potentially less offensive term meant to capture all non-White people in American society. The major problem with this term is it does not differentiate between the large number of different racial and ethnic groups in the United States, each of which is unique in its history and culture. As you'll see in this book, it is people of color—especially minority groups—who most often come into contact with juvenile and criminal justice agencies.

# Demographic Makeup of the US Population: Past and Present

According to the US Census (US Census, 2011), the United States remains a White-majority country. That is, Caucasians make up the largest share of the US population. Table 1.3 shows the racial and ethnic breakdown of the US population from the 2010 Census. As you can see, nearly all Americans report only one race (97.6%), and most Americans are Caucasian (75.1%). The largest *minority group* in the US is Hispanic or Latino (12.5%), followed closely by African Americans (12.3%).

---

**Table 1.3. Demographics of the US Population (2010).**

| | |
|---|---|
| One race | 97.6% |
| Caucasian | 75.1% |
| African American | 12.3% |
| Asian | 3.6% |
| American Indian and Alaska Native | 0.9% |
| Native Hawaiian and Other Pacific Islander | 0.1% |
| Some other race | 5.5% |
| Two or more races | 2.4% |
| Hispanic or Latino | 12.5% |
| Not Hispanic or Latino | 87.5% |
| White Alone | 69.1% |

Source: http://www.census.gov/prod/cen2010/briefs/c2010br-02.pdf

---

According to the US Census (2011), of those who classified themselves as Hispanic or Latino, 53% described themselves as White, 2.5% said they were Black, 1.4% identified as American Indian and Alaska Native, 0.4% said they

Figure 1.2. Changing Demographic Population of the United States

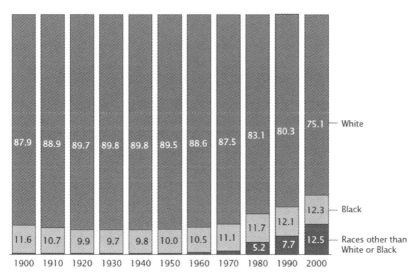

Note: In 2000, the percent distribution is based on the reporting of race alone for Whites and Blacks.
Source: U.S. Census Bureau, decennial census of population, 1900 to 2000.

Source: http://www.census.gov/prod/2002pubs/censr-4.pdf

were Asian, and 0.1% called themselves Native Hawaiian and Other Pacific Islander, while 36.7% indicated they were from some other race and 2% said
two or more races.

America has always been a predominantly White country. Yet Figure 1.2
shows that, over time, the portion of America that is identified as White is declining over time. According to Hobbs and Stoops (2002, p. 71):

> The United States population was much more racially diverse in 2000
> than in 1900. At the beginning of the century, 1 out of 8 Americans was
> of a race other than White; at the end of the century, the ratio was 1
> out of 4. The increased diversity in the United States was largely a phe-
> nomenon of the latter part of the century. Both the White population
> and the Black population represented a slightly smaller share of the
> U.S. total population in 1970 than they did in 1900. From 1970 to
> 2000, the population of races other than White or Black grew consid-
> erably and, by 2000, was comparable in size to the Black population.

An examination of Figure 1.2 illustrates that the decline in the White population occurred between 1980 and 2000.

## Figure 1.3. The Increasing Hispanic or Latino Population

Source: U.S. Census Bureau, decennial census of population, 1980 to 2000.

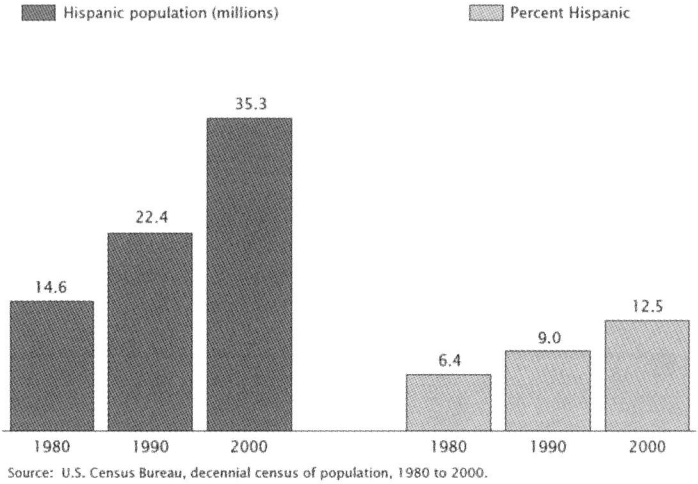

Source: http://www.census.gov/prod/2002pubs/censr-4.pdf

Figure 1.3 shows that it is increases in Hispanic or Latino populations which explain why America is becoming "less White." In 1980, Hispanics or Latinos made up 6.4% of the population, but by 2000, this number had increased to 12.5% (Hobbs & Stoops, 2002). This population is growing for two reasons: a higher rate of immigration into the US, and a higher birth rate. The US Census projects that between 2040 and 2050, Whites will be a minority in the US (Yen, 2013).

One period in US history stands out as having great relevance for the disciplines of criminology and criminal justice, for it was during this period that the roots of the discipline of American criminology emerged. This period is the late 1800s and early 1900s and the place of significance is the city of Chicago. According to Bernard, Snipes, and Gerould (2010): "Chicago was at that time a massive city of over 2 million; between 1860 and 1910 it had doubled in population every 10 years, with wave upon wave of immigrants" (p. 134). Scholars from the University of Chicago used theories and methods from fields such as sociology and ecology to first describe changes occurring in the city over time, and then to create theories such as *social disorganization* to explain why rates of crime and delinquency tended to be higher in some areas of the city than others (the theory is discussed later in this chapter as well as in Chapter 4).

Incredibly, even when the ethnic composition of the inner-city changed from German and Irish to Italian and Polish as immigrants flocked to American and the city of Chicago for jobs, rates of delinquency remained highest in the same areas of the city. According to Bernard et al. (2010), in 1884, about 90% of the population of the *zone in transition* (the highest crime area in the city of Chicago) was German, Irish, English, Scottish, or Scandinavian, but by 1930, about 85% of the population was either Czech, Irish, Polish, Slavic, or other. As the social and economic situation of each group improved, it would move out of the zone in transition and into more desirable areas of the city, "leaving space for the new immigrant groups" in the least desirable areas of the city in what would become seen as the "breeding ground for the city's criminal population" (Figlio, Hakim & Rengert, 1986, p. xii).

Thus, it was not individual characteristics unique to one's biology or psychology—and it was not race or ethnicity per se—that explained higher crime rates in some areas of the city, but instead conditions that were found to be linked to crime included *urbanization, immigration, poverty, culture conflict,* and similar factors (Jeffery, 1990, p. 256). If anything, it was social class conditions and the environmental realities that accompany poverty which explain higher crime rates in some areas of the city. For example, high crime areas were found to be characterized by high levels of welfare and rental properties rather than home ownership. According to Figlio, Hakim and Rengert (1986, p. xii), delinquency areas were "specialized habitation niches for *low income migrants* into the city" that were "used by a succession of immigrant groups from different ethnic backgrounds at different time periods" (emphasis added).

At the heart of what would become known as **social disorganization theory** is the argument that residents of a given area of the city were not intimately connected and integrated into a collective of people to naturally prevent crime in their neighborhood through means of knowing their neighbors, supervising their children, and looking out for each other's property. In such places, residents did not care about or care for the physical conditions of buildings and blocks, and thus they would deteriorate and possibly attract crime. Further, the level of "neighborliness" declines, thereby reducing informal social controls that naturally act to prevent crime (Robinson & Beaver, 2009).

Interestingly, whereas race seemed to be largely irrelevant to the original Chicago School scholars and earliest statements of social disorganization theory, contemporary tests of social disorganization theory often include measures of race and suggest race plays an important role in explaining outcomes such as crime rates, fear of crime, perceptions of disorder, among others (e.g., see Drakulich, 2013; Pitner, Tu & Brown, 2013; Price-Spratlen & Santoro,

2011; Sampson & Raudenbush, 2004). Possible relationships between race, social disorganization and crime will be discussed in Chapter 4.

## A Snapshot of the Major Races and Ethnicities in the United States

There are numerous racial and ethnic groups within the United States, too many in fact to be able to examine in this text, especially when you consider the number of countries from which contemporary Americans originated. Even within the ethnicity of Latino or Hispanic, there are dozens of countries from which people come. Table 1.4 illustrates the top countries with which people identifying as Latino identify. As you can see, the top country of origin for American Latinos is Mexico, followed by Puerto Rico, El Salvador, Cuba, the Dominican Republic, Guatemala, Colombia, Spain, Honduras, Ecuador, Peru, Nicaragua, Venezuela, and Argentina.

### Table 1.4. Country of Origin for American Latinos

| Country | % of all Latinos |
| --- | --- |
| Mexico | 64.6% |
| Puerto Rico | 9.5% |
| El Salvador | 3.8% |
| Cuba | 3.6% |
| Dominican Republic | 2.9% |
| Guatemala | 2.3% |
| Colombia | 1.9% |
| Spain | 1.4% |
| Honduras | 1.4% |
| Ecuador | 1.2% |
| Peru | 1.1% |
| Nicaragua | 0.8% |
| Venezuela | 0.5% |
| Argentina | 0.5% |

Source: http://www.pewhispanic.org/2013/06/19/diverse-origins-the-nations-14-largest-hispanic-origin-groups/

In this book, we focus primarily on the following minority groups or people of color: African Americans (or Blacks), Latinos, and Native Americans; other groups receive some focus but not in as much depth, since the groups just mentioned are most likely to come to the attention of criminal justice agencies. We focus on Blacks because they have, since the founding of this country, been subjected to the worst and most pronounced forms of discrimination of any group in American history (Loewen, 2007; Zinn, 2005). Starting with their enslavement, Blacks have always been treated as second-class citizens, including literally so in matters of law for several centuries. Further, as will be illustrated throughout this book, they continue to suffer from disproportionate involvement with juvenile and criminal justice agencies, which is only partially explained by greater involvement in some forms of delinquency and crime.

Similarly, we focus on Native Americans because it is this minority group that was virtually eliminated from the United States once White European cultures were established and came to dominate (Loewen, 2007; Zinn, 2005). Today, as will be demonstrated later, Native Americans are also disproportionately involved in some acts of delinquency and crime, as well as juvenile and criminal justice system processing.

Our focus on Latinos stems from the fact that they are the largest and fastest growing minority group in the country. Further, there are unique issues related to crime and criminal justice that pertain to Latino populations, including but not limited to illegal immigration into the United States. Detention facilities for adult and child immigrants have been created to deal with this issue, including private, for profit prisons and jails.

Finally, we focus on Asians because, as a group, Asians have among the lowest rates of delinquency and criminality in America, as well as among the lowest levels of involvement with juvenile and criminal justice agencies. Why this is so is quite relevant for our analysis.

# Relationships Between Race, Ethnicity, and Social Class

It is important to note that, in the United States, there is a close relationship between race, ethnicity, and social class, consistent with the reality of *intersectionality* defined earlier. Specifically, it is people of color who tend to have the lowest levels of income and wealth, and who also tend to suffer from higher rates of poverty and unemployment in the US. Table 1.5 illustrates this clearly.

As you can see in the table, Whites do better on nearly all economic measures than do people of color. Asians tend to have slightly higher levels of household income and lower rates of unemployment than Whites, but their poverty

Table 1.5. Economic Prosperity by Race and Ethnicity

|  | Asian | White | Hispanic/ Latino | Black |
|---|---|---|---|---|
| Household Income (2011) | $65,100 | $55,400 | $38,600 | $32,200 |
| Wealth (2010) | —— | $97,000 | $1,300 | $1,300 |
| Poverty rate (2011) | 12.3% | 9.8% | 25.3% | 27.6% |
| Unemployment rate (2010) | 6.8% | 7.5% | 10.8% | 13.4% |
| Rate of non-insurance | 16.8% | 11.1% | 30.1% | 19.5% |

Sources: US Census (2012). Income, poverty, and health insurance coverage. Downloaded from: http://www.census.gov/newsroom/releases/pdf/20120912_ip_%20slides_noplot-points.pdf; US Census (2014). Table 627. Unemployment and employment rates by educational attainment, sex, race, and Hispanic origin: 2000 to 2010. Downloaded from: http://www.census.gov/compendia/statab/2012/tables/12s0627.pdf; Wolff, E. (2012). *The asset price meltdown and the wealth of the middle class.* New York: New York University.

rate is higher than Whites. Whites have higher levels of household income and wealth than Hispanics/Latinos and Blacks, and have lower rates of poverty, unemployment, and non-health insurance coverage.

These empirical realities are important for at least two reasons. First, there are criminological theories that suggest that people living in tougher economic conditions should be more likely to commit acts of street crime. For example, **strain theories** assert that frustration and other negative emotions produced by not being able to achieve one's goals (including economic goals) are significant sources of crime (Robinson & Beaver, 2009). If people of color suffer from higher levels of *strain* or frustration, we ought to expect them to commit more than their fair share of crime; this issue is examined further in Chapter 3.

Second, if *discrimination* or *bias* in criminal justice exists, it will be hard to determine if this is due to racial and ethnic prejudice or social class biases. That is, a system biased against people of color would be expected to catch a large number of poor people. Further, a system that targets the poor will undeniably catch a large percentage of people of color (Reiman & Leighton, 2013). Each role in society occupied by a person—race, class, gender—is associated with some degree of privilege; in America, it is Whites, the wealthy and men who enjoy the most privileges, benefits that are largely unseen but nevertheless known to be real. One clear example of such a privilege is the absence of discrimination directed against the groups; another is the lack of focus by criminal justice agencies on especially wealthy White men relative to other groups in society (e.g., poor, Black men) (Barak, Leighton & Flavin, 2010). These issues are addressed further in several subsequent chapters of this book.

# Disparities versus Discrimination

For about as long as the disciplines of criminology and criminal justice have existed, scholars have studied relationships between race and ethnicity and crime and criminal justice processing. Key questions include who is most processed by agencies of criminal and juvenile justice, and why? Data from the US Census Bureau (US Census, 2014b) and The Sentencing Project (2014) show that, in 2012, for example, African Americans and Latinos collectively made up about 30% of the US population (13.1% African American, 16.9% Hispanic or Latino), yet 58% of all people incarcerated in the United States (36% African American, 22% Latino). Why is this so? Is it because African Americans and Latinos commit more crime? Or because there is *discrimination* in policing and courts? Both?

An enormous amount of evidence points to huge *disparities* by race and ethnicity in juvenile justice practices. The term **disparity** merely refers to a difference between groups (Walker, Spohn & DeLone, 2012). There are, and always have been, major disparities in criminal justice and juvenile justice outcomes. For example, a report by The Sentencing Project (2008) shows that, while African Americans only comprise about 17% of juveniles in the US, they account for more than 45% of arrests of juveniles, almost one-third of referrals to juvenile courts, and more than 40% of waivers to adult court. And a report by the National Council on Crime and Delinquency found that residential placement is about four times higher for African Americans, three times higher for Native Americans, and two times higher for Latinos than for Whites, while racial and ethnic disparities in rates of imprisonment are event greater (Hartney & Vuong, 2009).

The problem has been around so long that it even has a term: **disproportionate minority contact**, a term that refers to the fact that people of color are more likely than Whites to come into contact with agencies of juvenile and criminal justice (Office of Juvenile Justice & Delinquency Prevention, 2012). In fact, reviews by the Office of Juvenile Justice and Delinquency Prevention show evidence that the problem has existed at least since 1989 (Hsia, Bridges & McHale, 2004; Pope, Lovell & Hsia, 2012). The issue of racial disparities within juvenile justice will be examined in Chapter 10.

Incredibly, Attorney General Eric Holder, the highest ranking law enforcement official in the US, recently stated that,

> in our criminal justice system, systemic and unwarranted racial disparities remain disturbingly common. One study released last year by the US Sentencing Commission indicated that in recent years, African American men have received sentences that are nearly 20 percent longer than those imposed on White males convicted of similar crimes. Another report showed that American Indians are often sentenced even more harshly.... Like a growing chorus of lawmakers across the political spectrum, we recognize that disparate outcomes are not only shameful and unacceptable—they impede our ability to see that justice is done. And they perpetuate cycles of poverty, crime, and incarceration that trap individuals, destroy communities and decimate minority neighborhoods. (Reilly, 2014)

Holder's comments were made as part of a commencement speech and were in response to recent high profile examples of racist statements by public officials in the US (including an NBA team owner in Los Angeles and a police commissioner in New Hampshire).

Importantly, studies show that different levels of offending cannot explain disproportionate minority confinement (Huizinga, Thornberry, Knight, Lovergrove, Loeber, Hill & Farrington 2007). The significance of these data are explained by The Leadership Conference on Civil and Human Rights (2014), one of the most important civil rights organization in the US: "Racially skewed juvenile justice outcomes have dire implications, because the whole point of the juvenile justice system is to head off adult criminality."

This book will allow us to provide answers to questions related to why disparities exist in criminal and juvenile justice practices, using empirical data and published studies to inform our conclusions. The goal of the book is provide a thorough, yet brief summary of what is known about relationships between race, ethnicity, crime, and justice practice.

## Types of Discrimination

When people think about discrimination, they probably tend to think of an individual harming another or standing in the way of another, based on factors such as race, ethnicity, social class, gender, etc. In fact, there are other types of discrimination besides individual discrimination. Table 1.6 shows the "discrimination continuum" from Walker, Spohn, and DeLone (2012).

## Table 1.6. The Discrimination Continuum

| | |
|---|---|
| Systematic | Discrimination at all stages of the criminal justice system, at all times and places |
| Institutionalized | Racial and ethnic disparities in outcomes that are the result of the application of racially neutral factors such as prior criminal record, employment status, demeanor, etc. |
| Contextual | Discrimination found in particular contexts or circumstances |
| Individual | Discrimination that results from the acts of particular individuals but is not characteristic of entire agencies or the criminal justice system as a whole |
| Pure justice | No racial or ethnic discrimination at all |

Source: Walker, S., Spohn, C. & DeLone, M. (2014). *The Color of Justice*. Beverly Hills, CA: Wadsworth.

When it comes to criminal justice in the US today, we can pretty confidently rule out *pure justice*, for the condition of "no racial or ethnic discrimination at all" has not yet been achieved. Yet we can also confidently state that *systematic discrimination* also probably does not exist (because is there really "discrimination at all stages of the criminal justice system, at all times and places"?). An examination of US history *and* criminal justice outcomes concludes that systemic discrimination has been eliminated after centuries of struggle and especially due to changes in the law (Caravelis-Hughes & Robinson, 2015).

This leaves three types of discrimination that are found to exist within criminal justice practice:

- *Individual*—Discrimination that results from the acts of particular individuals but is not characteristic of entire agencies or the criminal justice system as a whole;
- *Contextual*—Discrimination found in particular contexts or circumstances; and
- *Institutionalized*—Racial and ethnic disparities in outcomes that are the result of the application of racially neutral factors such as prior criminal record, employment status, demeanor, etc.

Contemporary studies of police, courts, and corrections find evidence that these forms of discrimination do still exist (Walker et al., 2012). Most significant is contextual discrimination:

> Racial minorities are treated more harshly than whites at some stages
> of the criminal justice process ... but no differently than whites at
> other stages ... The treatment accorded racial minorities is more puni-
> tive than that accorded whites in some regions or jurisdictions ...
> Racial minorities who commit certain types of crimes ... or who have
> certain types of characteristics ... are treated more harshly than whites
> who commit these crimes or have these characteristics. (Walker et al.,
> 2012, p. 493)

According to the authors, contextual discrimination is documented by the
following findings:

- Police in some jurisdiction use race and ethnicity to profile people (p. 156).
- African Americans and Hispanics are more likely to be stopped, questioned, searched, and arrested by the police than Whites; they are also more
  likely to have force used against them, including excessive force and lethal
  force (p. 181).
- In some places, race and ethnicity impact pre-trial decision-making including bail, charging by prosecutors, and plea bargaining in the courts
  (p. 231).
- People of color are, in many jurisdictions, denied the right to serve on
  trial juries through the use of peremptory challenges based solely on their
  race (p. 273), even though this practice is explicitly illegal.
- African Americans and Hispanics who are convicted of certain types of
  crimes (e.g., drug crimes and violent crimes against Whites) are treated
  more harshly than Whites for those crimes (p. 274).
- Tougher sentences tend to be handed down to racial minorities than to
  Whites in "borderline cases" where prosecutors and judges tend to have discretion about whether to pursue probation or a term of incarceration (p. 333).

Evidence from studies of police and race will be examined in Chapter 5,
from studies of courts and race in Chapters 6 and 7, and from studies of race
and corrections in Chapter 8; the findings above are revisited in these chapters.

There are also serious disparities based on race in capital punishment practice. Here, Walker et al. (2012) suggest the evidence is consistent with *systematic discrimination*:

> Racial discrimination in the capital sentencing process is not limited
> to the South, where historical evidence of racial bias would lead one
> to expect different treatment, but is applicable to other regions of the
> country as well. It is not confined to one stage of the decision-making
> process, but affects decisions made by prosecutors as well as juries. It

is also not confined to the pre-*Furman* period, when statutes offered little or no guidance to judges and juries charged with deciding whether to impose the death penalty or not, but is found, too, under the more restrictive guided discretion statutes enacted since *Furman*.[1] Moreover, this effect does not disappear when legally relevant predictors of sentence severity are taken into consideration. (p. 391)

Evidence from studies of race and the death penalty will be examined in Chapter 9.

The final type of discrimination found in criminal justice is *institutionalized discrimination*. This type of discrimination is common in American criminal justice, especially during the phases of arrest and sentencing (Walker et al., 2012, p. 492). For example, poor minorities are more likely to be arrested, convicted, and sentenced to correctional punishment for some crimes, especially those crimes that are more likely to happen in the neighborhoods in which they tend to live. Disparities in criminal justice will be found in police and court processes if police focus on certain areas and/or types of people more than others and if the law calls for harsher sentences for some types of crimes, suggestive of institutionalized discrimination. Whether this is so will be examined in Chapter 3 of this book.

Social class is also relevant for institutionalized discrimination. For example, when a criminal defendant is unemployed and thus poor, he or she is more likely to be detained in **preventive detention**, meaning he or she will be held in jail prior to trial rather than being released to his or her family. This leads to disparities in criminal justice (e.g., in jail populations) that are caused by factors related to social class even though the practice of preventive detention is not intended to discriminate against people based on extra-legal factors such as class or race.

# Conclusion

The United States is an increasingly diverse nation. America is increasingly become more "brown" as the portion of the population that is White continues to decline, especially since the 1980s, as immigration and high birth rates among one ethnic group in particular—Latinos and Hispanics—are leading to a near future where "minorities" will constitute a majority of the population.

Although race is a socially constructed term, there is little doubt among criminologists that there are meaningful relationships between race, ethnic-

---

1. *Furman* refers to the US Supreme Court case, *Furman v. Georgia* 408 US 238 (1972), which struck down capital punishment statutes across the US (new statutes were approved by the Court in *Gregg v. Georgia* 428 US 153 [1976]).

ity, delinquency, crime, and criminal justice. While some disparities in juvenile and criminal justice outcomes (e.g., intake, arrest, convictions) are likely attributable to different levels of involvement in delinquency and criminality among different racial and ethnic groups, there is also evidence that various forms of discrimination continue to plague juvenile and criminal justice practice. Individual, contextual, institutional, and even systematic discrimination must be examined to fully understand why some racial and ethnic groups are overrepresented among juvenile and criminal justice populations.

# Discussion Questions

1. What is race?
2. What is ethnicity?
3. What does it mean that race is socially constructed?
4. To what does the term cline refer? How does clinal variation help us understand differences in groups of people?
5. Describe the demographic makeup of the US population. How has this changed over time?
6. What is a minority group? What are the major minority groups in the US?
7. What are the major reasons why the percentage of Whites in the US population is decreasing over time?
8. Explain the theory of social disorganization.
9. Compare and contrast the terms disparity and discrimination.
10. Define the major forms of discrimination according to Walker, Spohn, and DeLone (2012). Provide an example of each type.
11. Define disproportionate minority confinement.

# References

Barak, G., Leighton, P. & Flavin, G. (2010). *Class, race, gender & crime.* Lanham, MD: Rowman & Littlefield.

Bernard, T., Snipes, J. & Gerould, A. (2010). *Vold's theoretical criminology.* New York: Oxford University Press.

Caravelis-Hughes, C. & Robinson, M. (2015). *Social justice criminal justice: How American law effects and prevents social change.* Cincinnati, OH: Anderson.

Cornell, S. & Hartmann, D. (2006). *Ethnicity and race: Making identity in a changing world.* Thousand Oaks, CA: Pine Forge Press.

Drakulich, K. M. (2013). Perceptions of the local danger posed by crime: Race, disorder, informal control, and the police. *Social Science Research, 42*(3), 611–632.

El Nasser, H. (2013). Census rethinks Hispanic on questionnaire. *USA Today*, January 4. Downloaded from: http://www.usatoday.com/story/news/nation/2013/01/03/hispanics-may-be-added-to-census-race-category/1808087/.

Figlio, R., Hakim, S. & Rengert, G. (1986). *Metropolitan crime patterns*. Boulder, CO: Lynne Rienner.

Fuentes, A. (2014). A troublesome response: Nicholas Wade still avoids the debate about race and genetics. *Huffington Post*, June 1. Downloaded from: http://www.huffingtonpost.com/agustin-fuentes/a-troublesome-response-ni_b_5419505.html.

Gallagher, C. (2011). *Rethinking the color line: Readings in race and ethnicity*. Columbus, OH: McGraw Hill.

Hartney, C. & Vuong, L. (2009). *Created equal: Racial and ethnic disparities in the US criminal justice system*. Retrieved from: http://www.nccdglobal.org/sites/default/files/publication_pdf/created-equal.pdf.

Hobbs, F. & Stoops, N. (2002). Demographic trends in the 20th Century. Downloaded from: http://www.census.gov/prod/2002pubs/censr-4.pdf.

Hsia, H., Bridges, G. & McHale, R. (2004). *Disproportionate minority contact: 2002 update*. Retrieved from: https://www.ncjrs.gov/pdffiles1/ojjdp/201240.pdf.

Huizinga, D., Thornberry, T., Knight, K., Lovergrove, P., Loeber, R., Hill, K. & Farrington, D. (2007). Disproportionate minority contact in the juvenile justice system: A study of differential minority arrest/referral to court in three cities. Retrieved from: https://www.ncjrs.gov/pdffiles1/ojjdp/grants/219743.pdf.

Jeffery, C. (1990). *Criminology: An interdisciplinary approach*. Upper Saddle River, NJ: Prentice Hall.

Leadership Conference on Civil and Human Rights (2014). *Justice on trial*. Chapter five: Race and juvenile justice system. Retrieved from: http://www.civilrights.org/publications/justice-on-trial/juvenile.html.

Loewen. J. (2007). *Lies my teacher told me: Everything your American history textbook got wrong*. New York: Touchstone.

Merriam-Webster (2014). Race. Downloaded from: http://www.merriam-webster.com/dictionary/race.

Office of Juvenile Justice and Delinquency Prevention (2012). *Disproportionate minority contact*. http://www.ojjdp.gov/pubs/239457.pdf.

Omi, M. & Winant, H. (2014). *Racial formation in the United States*. New York: Routledge.

Pitner, R., Yu, M. & Brown, E. (2013). Which factor has more impact? An examination of the effects of income level, perceived neighborhood disorder, and crime on community care and vigilance among low-income African American residents. *Race and Social Problems, 5*(1), 57–64.

Pope, C., Lovell, R. & Hsia, H. (2012). *Disproportionate minority contact*: A review of the research literature from 1989 through 2001. Retrieved from: http://www.ojjdp.gov/dmc/pdf/dmc89_01.pdf.

Price-Spratlen, T. & Santoro, W. (2011). Neighborhood disorder and individual community capacity: How incivilities inform three domains of psychosocial assessment. *Sociological Spectrum, 31*(5), 579–605.

Reilly, R. (2014). Eric Holder: Systemic, subtle racism much more damaging than high-profile rants. Retrieved from: http://www.huffingtonpost.com/2014/05/17/eric-holder-racism-speech_n_5342010.html?ncid=fcbklnkushpmg00000013.

Reiman, J. & Leighton, P. (2013). *The rich get richer and the poor get prison: Ideology, class, and criminal justice.* Upper Saddle River, NJ: Prentice Hall.

Robinson, M. & Beaver, K. (2009). *Why crime? An interdisciplinary approach to explaining criminal behavior.* Durham, NC: Carolina Academic Press.

Sampson, R. & Raudenbush, S. (2004). Seeing disorder: Neighborhood stigma and the social construction of "broken windows". *Social Psychology Quarterly, 67*(4), 319–342.

Sentencing Project (2014). Factsheet. Trends in U.S. corrections. Retrieved from: http://sentencingproject.org/doc/publications/inc_Trends_in_Corrections_Fact_sheet.pdf.

Sentencing Project (2008). *Reducing disparity in the criminal justice system.* Retrieved from: http://www.sentencingproject.org/doc/publications/rd_reducingracialdisparity.pdf.

Shane, S. (1999). Genetic research increasingly finds "race" a null concept. *The Baltimore Sun*, April 4, pp. 1A, 6A.

Templeton, A. (2013). Biological races in humans. *Studies in History and Philosophy of Biological and Biomedical Sciences.* Advanced copy. Downloaded from: http://lesacreduprintemps19.files.wordpress.com/2013/08/biological-races-in-humans.pdf.

Thompson, C. (2013). White supremacist Craig Cobb is told a DNA test shows he's part African. Downloaded from: http://talkingpointsmemo.com/livewire/white-supremacist-submits-to-dna-test-learns-he-s-14-percent-black-video.

US (2014). Culture and ethnic groups. Downloaded from: http://www.usa.gov/Citizen/Topics/History-Culture.shtml.

US Census (2014a). Race. About. Downloaded from: http://census.gov/topics/population/race/about.html.

US Census (2014b). State & county QuickFacts. Retrieved from: http://quickfacts.census.gov/qfd/states/00000.html.

US Census (2014c). State & county QuickFacts. Hispanic origin. Retrieved from: http://quickfacts.census.gov/qfd/meta/long_RHI825212.htm.

US Census (2011). Overview of race and Hispanic origin: 2010. Downloaded from: http://www.census.gov/prod/cen2010/briefs/c2010br-02.pdf.

Walker, S., Spohn, C. & DeLone, M. (2014). *The color of justice: Race, ethnicity, and crime in America.* Belmont, CA: Wadsworth.

Yen, H. (2013). Census: White majority in U.S. gone by 2043. Downloaded from: http://usnews.nbcnews.com/_news/2013/06/13/18934111-census-white-majority-in-us-gone-by-2043?lite.

Zinn, H. (2005). *A people's history of the United States: 1492 to present.* New York: Harper.

# Chapter 2

# Introduction to Criminal and Juvenile Justice

*by Beverly Crank, PhD*

# Introduction

In order to understand issues involving race, ethnicity, and crime in the United States, it is important to have a background on the justice systems that govern behavior. In the United States, both the criminal justice system and the juvenile justice system uphold the law and respond to violations of the law. When a violation of the law occurs, which specific system responds—the **criminal justice system** or the **juvenile justice system**—depends on a number of factors such as age of the offender, seriousness of offense, and specific state laws.

This chapter begins by defining crime and delinquency, and explaining the nature and extent of crime and delinquency in the United States. In addition, this chapter includes a discussion comparing and contrasting the criminal justice system and the juvenile justice system, in order to understand how the two systems operate and differ from one another.

# What Is Crime?

Although, the term *crime* may seem simple enough to understand, scholars have long debated the precise definition of this term. For example, who determines what crime is? Is the definition of crime consistent and stable across time and space? For the sake of simplicity, many scholars employ a **legalistic definition** of crime, looking to statutory definitions of criminal behavior. According to the legalistic view, "a crime is a crime because the law says so" (O'Connor, 2011, para. 1).

Conversely, a **normative definition** conceptualizes crime as deviant behavior that violates **norms** (standards of behavior that govern our actions). One advantage of a normative definition is that it takes into consideration how definitions of crime change based on current social, political, and economic conditions. In comparison, using a legalistic definition, a crime in one jurisdiction may not be a crime in another jurisdiction. For example, *prostitution* is considered legal in some parts of Nevada, but nowhere else in the United States. Further, some states have legalized marijuana possession and use, although most have not. Even more broadly, importing chewing gum into Singapore is illegal (unless you have a doctor's prescription), but it is certainly not a crime in the United States.

Crime in the United States can cover a range of behaviors in terms of severity. Acts such as armed robbery, illegally downloading music, and injecting heroin are all considered crimes. Using a legalistic definition, **crime** can be defined as any action that is classified as illegal according to local, state, or federal law. Crimes are illegal and punishable under criminal law. Punishments can range in severity from a monetary fine to the death penalty. Which punishment a person receives depends on a number of factors, such as who committed the crime, the damage caused by the crime, and the legal classification of the crime.

In terms of legal classification, crimes may fall into a number of different categories. These categories usually include *infractions, misdemeanors,* and *felonies.* Legislators are charged with determining the classification of specific crimes, based on the degree of seriousness of the offense. For example, **infractions** are the least serious crimes and are usually punishable by monetary fines, instead of jail time. One of the most common forms of infractions is a traffic violation, such as speeding, failure to yield, or following too closely. Almost all automobile drivers in the United States have committed some form of infraction, regardless if these infractions were detected by the police.

The next level of crime in terms of seriousness is **misdemeanors**. These crimes are considered to be of greater severity than infractions, but less serious than felonies. Misdemeanors typically carry a punishment of up to one year in jail, but these punishments do not involve prison time. In addition, individuals may be required to pay a fine, perform community service, or be placed on probation in lieu of jail time. For example, in North Carolina, it is considered a misdemeanor to possess an ounce of marijuana, which may result in some jail time or the payment of a fine.

Finally, the most serious offenses are considered felonies. Based on the severity of these types of crimes, **felonies** can range in punishment from one year in prison to the death penalty. An example of a felony crime in all states is murder. This offense is seriousness enough to warrant much time spent in prison (or perhaps death), but is too serious of an offense to be punishable by jail time, probation, or a monetary fine.

## A Few Words on Other Kinds of Crimes

There is another class of harmful behavior that is generally ignored by the criminal justice system, and it has great importance for this book because it informs how we think about race, ethnicity, and crime. Stated simply, the focus of our nation and justice systems is on **street crime**—crimes committed on the streets of America, generally by the poor and disadvantaged (e.g., theft, robbery). Other forms of harmful behaviors receive far less attention by our justice systems—often because the behaviors are legal—but also even when they are illegal! For example, the criminal justice system rarely targets and successfully prosecutes white-collar and corporate offenders.

**White-collar crime** is usually defined as a crime committed by an employee against the business for which the employee works, while **corporate crime** can be understood as illegal acts of corporations against shareholders, customers, or citizens (Robinson, 2013). An example of white-collar crime is an employee embezzling money from his employer. *Embezzlement* is a form of theft that occurs after a person has rightful possession of property. So, for example, if an employee has legal access to the money of a business (e.g., as a book keeper or accountant), and then steals it, that is embezzlement.

An example of corporate crime is a company committing *fraud* against consumers. **Fraud** is also a form of theft, but it occurs when the taking of property is done through deceit or trickery. For example, when a company is legally selling a product, but makes knowingly false claims about the product, that is a form of fraud called *false advertising.*

White-collar and corporate crimes are not defined as serious crimes by the federal government even though data gathered by researchers demonstrate that direct harms caused by white-collar and corporate crimes are much greater than those caused by street crimes (Reiman, & Leighton, 2009). Incredibly, acts of corporations even injure and kill more people each year than street crime. Consider injuries and deaths caused by hazardous working conditions, hospital error, and unsafe and defective merchandise, which clearly dwarf injuries and deaths caused by street crimes (Robinson & Murphy, 2009). Table 2.1 shows the relative costs of street crime and white-collar and corporate crimes.

### Table 2.1. Costs of Street Crime versus White-Collar and Corporate Crimes

MONETARY LOSSES:

| | |
|---|---|
| *Property street crimes* | *$15.7 billion (2010)* |
| Unnecessary medical tests | $200 billion+ |
| Consumer fraud | $190 billion |
| Health care fraud | $100 billion |
| Insurance fraud | $85 billion |
| Computer fraud | $67 billion |
| Identify fraud | $53 billion |
| Securities fraud | $40 billion |
| Automotive fraud | $22 billion |
| Medicare/Medicaid fraud | $20 billion+ |
| Telemarketing fraud | $20 billion+ |
| Worthless medical products | $20 billion+ |
| Credit card/check fraud | $13 billion |
| Cellular phone fraud | $1 billion |

DEATHS:

| | |
|---|---|
| *Murder* | *14,612 (2011)* |
| **Tobacco use** | **443,000** |
| Medical treatment & infection | 325,000 |
| Poverty & income inequality | 291,000 |
| Adverse reactions to prescriptions | 100,000 |
| Hospital error | 98,000 |
| Air pollution | 55,000 |
| Occupational disease & injury | 54,000 |
| Lack of health insurance | 45,000 |
| Defective products | 20,000 |

Source: Robinson, M. (2015). *Criminal injustice: How politics and ideology distort American ideals.* Durham, NC: Carolina Academic Press.

---

What is the relevance of these acts for this book? Simply stated, these acts are committed disproportionately by the powerful, who happen to be overwhelmingly White. Thus, scholars studying all forms of crimes, including white-collar and corporate crimes, would undoubtedly conclude that most crimes are committed by White people rather than people of color. However, the criminal justice system is largely focused on street crimes, which unquestionably impacts how we think about race, ethnicity, and crime—because, as you will see in this book, these acts are disproportionately committed by people of color.

# What Is Delinquency?

Although sometimes used interchangeably, crime and delinquency are not necessarily the same. Some delinquent acts can be considered crimes, while others cannot. Further, some people can commit delinquent acts, while others cannot. If all of this seems confusing, remember that the key to defining delinquency is the age of the offender. **Delinquency** is defined as acts committed by juveniles that are illegal according to local, state, or federal law. In most states, individuals are considered juveniles if they are under the age of 18 years. However, in some states, the individual is considered a juvenile if under the age of 17 or even 16 years.

Some specific delinquent acts may be illegal for juveniles, but not for adults. Known as **status offenses**, these offenses are illegal based on the juvenile status of the offender. For example, breaking curfew, running away from home, and truancy are all considered status offenses. Applying this logic, drinking an alcoholic beverage as a juvenile may be illegal, but this action is not illegal for an adult of 21 years or older.

Although the term delinquency has a negative connotation, readers will humble themselves by realizing that they too were, most likely, delinquent. In fact, self-report studies show over 90% of juveniles have engaged in some form of delinquency. This could be something as small as sneaking into a movie theater, or as serious as breaking into people's homes.

Also important to keep in mind is that juvenile delinquents are viewed and treated differently than adults (Agnew & Brezina, 2012). For example, the results from one national survey show that 62% of respondents "opposed giving juveniles the same sentences as adults" (Schwartz, Guo, & Kerbs, 1993, p. 8). This finding supports the view that the public is more likely to view juveniles as amenable to treatment compared to adults.

This idea that juveniles are viewed and treated differently than adults is extended into sentencing decisions, as adults typically receive more punitive sentences than juveniles for the same action. If you think this is an unfair practice, consider current research on the adolescent brain. We know through this research that the *prefrontal cortex*, the portion of the brain that is responsible for decision-making, is not fully developed until we reach our mid-20s or later. This portion of the brain is responsible for regulating emotions, so adolescents may be less able to exercise self-control when compared to adults. Those with still developing prefrontal cortexes are more likely to make irrational decisions and participate in risky activities. Most of us can think back to some embarrassing action we committed during adolescence, and we have our underdeveloped brain to thank for our behavior.

## How Much Crime and Delinquency Exists?

Now that we know what crime and delinquency are, we can examine how much crime and delinquency exists. According to the Federal Bureau of Investigation (FBI), in 2012, a violent crime occurred every 26 seconds. Further, a property crime occurred every 3.5 seconds (FBI, 2013a). These statistics may lead you to believe that crime is a serious problem in the US, and perhaps that it is on the rise. However, in order to fully understand the nature and extent of crime and delinquency in the United States, we must first evaluate the different sources of data.

## Measurements of Crime and Delinquency

There are three major ways of measuring both crime and delinquency: official statistics, self-report data, and victimization data. Each of these measurements has its own advantages and disadvantages when it comes to evaluating the extent of crime and delinquency in the United States. Because of the different strengths and weaknesses of these data, estimates of crime and delinquency, especially those reported in the media, can be problematic.

**Official statistics** are those derived from the police, the courts, and the correctional system. Thus, official statistics come from "official agencies." The most common type of official statistic is arrest data. Most of our arrest data come from the FBI's *Uniform Crime Reports* (UCR). This report provides information on crimes known to the police, crimes cleared (or closed) by arrest, and the characteristics of persons arrested. These data have been collected by the FBI since 1930. In 2012, more than 18,000 law enforcement agencies across the nation (including college and universities, county, state, tribal and federal law enforcement agencies) voluntarily reported crime data to the FBI. Because of the high participation rates by law enforcement agencies, approximately 98% of the total United States population is represented by the UCR (FBI, 2013b).

There are a number of advantages of the UCR. Because these data have been collected since 1930, we have long-term information on crime trends. So we can see how rates of crime have changed across time. Further, the UCR provides moderately accurate estimates of serious crime in the United States (Gove, Hughes, & Geerken, 1985). So, for example, murder rates reported in the UCR are very accurate in terms of how many murders were committed in a given year.

At the same time, there are disadvantages in relying on the UCR to estimate the extent of delinquency. First, most forms of minor crime and delinquency are underestimated because these crimes typically fail to become known to the police. Second, sometimes the data reported to the FBI are inaccurate. The police may accidently or intentionally misreport crime. One example is that a local agency may want to portray that crime is down in their jurisdiction—even if it is not. Third, the UCR only includes data on the most serious offense for which an individual was arrested. Thus, if an individual were to break into someone's home (*unlawful entry*), steal a few items (*burglary*), kill the homeowner (*murder*), all while under the influence of methamphetamine (*under the influence of an illegal substance*), the only crime that is reported to the FBI is murder.

The second measurement of crime and delinquency is **self-report data**. This type of data is compiled by asking offenders (both adults and juveniles) about their involvement in criminal and delinquent activities through the use of interviews and questionnaires. Many self-report surveys are predominately focused on juveniles, and when these surveys are used on adult populations, they frequently use the same questions asked of juveniles (which may not be appropriate for adults) (Weitekamp, 1989). Popular examples of self-report surveys include the *National Youth Survey* (NYS) (Elliott, Huizinga, & Ageton, 1985), and the *Monitoring the Future* survey (Bachman, Johnston, & O'Malley, 2014).

Self-report data also has its advantages and disadvantages. One of the primary advantages of self-report data is that it provides a more comprehensive estimate of crime and delinquency than official statistics, because it includes crimes known to the police and crimes *unknown* to the police. However, there are few long-term, nationwide self-report data sources, so our ability to examine trends in crime and delinquency using this measure is limited. Also, samples of self-report surveys are sometimes small, and may not be representative of the population. As noted above, most of these surveys target juveniles, and further, these studies tend to under-sample serious juvenile offenders. For example, many times these surveys are administered in schools, and usually the most serious delinquents are either truant or have dropped-out of school. This is concerning because self-report studies may underestimate juvenile delinquency based on this limited sample. Further, juveniles may be less likely to report serious offenses; thus, self-report data underestimates the extent of serious delinquency.

The third measure of crime and delinquency is **victimization data**. Typically in the form of interviews or surveys, these measures ask adults and juveniles about their experiences as crime victims. One of the most well-known victimization surveys is the **National Crime Victimization Survey** (NCVS). Approximately 90,000 households, comprising nearly 160,000 individuals in the United States ages 12 years and older, are interviewed for the NCVS. Adults and juveniles are asked if they have been victims of crimes such as assault, rape, robbery, burglary, and motor vehicle theft. The benefits of victimization data are that crimes known and unknown to the police are included, and, because the NCVS started collecting data in 1973, we can look at some trends in victimization rates over time; these trends are thought to be the most valid crime trends available.

One disadvantage of victimization data is that information on victimless crimes are not received (such as drug use). Also, the sample of those interviewed may be limited, for example, individuals who are homeless may not be interviewed. Finally, some victims do not wish to report their victimizations to interviewers due to embarrassment, viewing the matter as a personal issue, or for other reasons.

Each of the three measurements of crime and delinquency have advantages and disadvantages. Being aware of the benefits and challenges of each measurement is important, especially when evaluating sources providing information on trends in crime and delinquency. Thus, the best way to evaluate the prevalence and trends of crime and delinquency is to examine all three measurements.

## Extent and Trends of Crime and Delinquency

Now that we know the different measurements of crime and delinquency, we can discuss how much crime and delinquency actually exists. We begin with official police data from the Uniform Crime Reports (UCR). The UCR tells us about crimes known to the police as well as arrests in the US.

### Official Statistics: Arrest Data

According to the UCR in 2012, there were approximately 1,214,462 violent crimes involving both juveniles and adults. In addition, there were 8,975,438 property offenses, which resulted in losses calculated at $15.5 billion. Table 2.2 shows the number of crimes known to police in 2012.

| Table 2.2. Crimes Known to the Police, 2012 | |
| --- | --- |
| Murder | 14,827 |
| Rape | 84,376 |
| Robbery | 354,520 |
| Aggravated Assault | 760,739 |
| Burglary | 2,103,787 |
| Theft | 6,150,598 |
| Motor Vehicle Theft | 721,053 |

Source: http://www.albany.edu/sourcebook/pdf/t31062012.pdf

Overall, for juveniles and adults combined, approximately 12.2 million arrests (excluding traffic violations) were made in 2012. The largest number of arrests (approximately 1,552,432) were made for drug abuse violations, followed by driving under the influence arrests (approximately 1,282,957), and then larceny-theft arrests (1,282,352). In 2011, for violent crime index offenses, 87.3% of all arrests were adults ages 18 and over. Further, 79.6% of all arrests for property crimes were adults (NCJJ, 2014). Table 2.3 shows the number of arrests made by the police in 2011.

This all seems like bad news. Yet consider that, in America, there are more than 300 million people, all of whom could be victimized by crime.

Table 2.3. Arrests Made by the Police, 2011

| | |
|---|---|
| Murder | 10,832 |
| Rape | 19,491 |
| Robbery | 106,674 |
| Aggravated Assault | 397,707 |
| Burglary | 296,707 |
| Theft | 1,264,986 |
| Motor Vehicle Theft | 66,414 |

Source: http://www.albany.edu/sourcebook/pdf/t412011.pdf

With only about nine million property crimes and only about one million violent crimes (known to the police), it is clear that the vast majority of Americans are not victimized by serious street crime. With millions of crimes being committed in a given year, and with news media reporting more and more violent incidents, surely crime is on the rise? Fortunately, one of the advantages of the UCR is that we can look at crime trends. Figure 2.1 presents the number of violent crimes and the number of property crimes in the United States from 2007 to 2011, including both juveniles and adults. When viewing these graphs, you can see that crime has actually *decreased* since 2007.

Figure 2.1. Trends in Violent and Property Crime
in the United States, 2007–2011

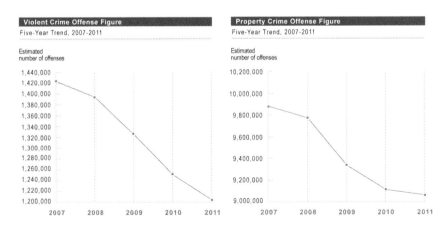

Source: http://www.fbi.gov/about-us/cjis/ucr/crime-in-the-u.s/2011/crime-in-the-u.s.-2011/offenses-known-to-law-enforcement/offenses-known-to-law-enforcement

Figure 2.2. Trend in Drug Possession/Use Arrest Rates in the
United States for Adults and Juveniles, 1990–2010

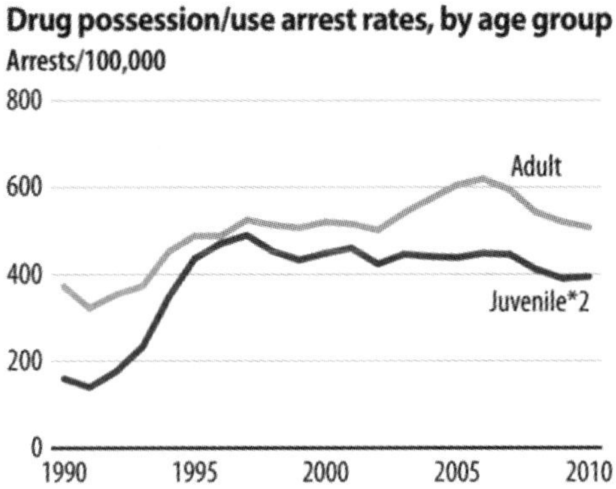

**Drug possession/use arrest rates, by age group**
Arrests/100,000

*Arrest rate for juveniles have been multiplied by 2.
Source: http://www.bjs.gov/content/pub/pdf/aus9010.pdf

If we look prior to 2007, we find that the overall trend is that, for many crimes, arrests are at an all-time low. For instance, arrests for murder, forcible rape, and robbery are lower now (for both juveniles and adults) than they were in 1980. The overall trend in violent crime (excluding the crime of assault) is that violent crime increased from the late 1980s to the mid-1990s, when these crimes reached an all-time high; violent crime then decreased since the mid-1990s. The overall trend for property crime is that property crime was fairly stable from the 1980s to early 1990s, and there was a modest increase in the rate of arrests in the mid-1990s. Since the mid-1990s, the property crime arrest rate for both juveniles and adults decreased.

We also can look at trends of drug arrests. The number of drug possession/use arrests increased from 1990 to 2006, and has declined somewhat between 2006 and 2010. The arrest rate for drug possession/use was still higher in 2010 (1,336,530 total arrests) than in 1990 (741,600 total arrests). Figure 2.2 shows trends in drug possession/use arrests for both juveniles and adults from 1990 to 2010.

Many times, especially when discussing trends in adult crime, we refer to official statistics. The UCR is representative of approximately 98% of the population, and is a fairly accurate measure of serious crime. But at the same time, what about crimes unknown to the police? We must turn to self-report and victimization data for this answer. We begin with self-report data. Recall that self-report surveys have been criticized for being overly focused on juveniles. Given this focus, the discussion on self-reported crime trends is largely based on juveniles.

## Self-Report Data

The Monitoring the Future survey provides us with rates of self-reported delinquency from high school seniors across the nation. A total of 107 public schools, 20 private schools, and 14,343 students participated in the 2012 survey (see Bachman, Johnston, O'Malley, 2014). Approximately 5.6% of these students indicated that they had been arrested or taken to the police station within the past year.

As far as violent offenses, 11.1% of the students in the Monitoring the Future survey admitted they had been in a serious fight at school or work, and 14.3% admitted they had taken part in a fight with a group of friends against another group. Further, 2.7% indicated they had used a knife, gun, or other weapon to take something from an individual. As far as property offenses, 22.1% indicated they had taken something of value under $50, and 7.3% indicated they had taken something worth more than $50 in the past year. Approximately 22.1% admitted to taking something from a store without paying for it. Further, 3.9% had taken a car without the owner's permission, and 21.1% had gone into a house or building they were not supposed to enter (see Bachman, Johnston, O'Malley, 2014).

These data give us a sense of the prevalence of some acts of delinquency among 8th, 10th, and 12th graders in U.S. schools, because the Monitoring the Future survey interviews these high school students, as well as college students and young adults (aged 19–28). In 2013, 50.4% of 12th graders in the survey indicated using an illicit drug at some point in their lifetime. In addition, 51% of college students and 60.5% of young adults also indicated illicit drug use at some point in their lifetime. But what about illicit drug use other than marijuana? For this category, only 24.7% of 12th graders, 26.7% of college students, and 24.2% of young adults indicated use of an illicit drug other than marijuana at some point in their lives (see Johnston, O'Malley, Bachman, Schulenberg, & Miech, 2014).

Does self-report data show that delinquency is increasing? When reviewing the overall trends from the Monitoring the Future survey, we find similar trends to those reported in the arrest data. Property crime increased somewhat during the late 1980s and 1990s, but then began to decline during the 2000s. Further, violent crime increased during the late 1980s and mid-1990s, and then began to decline during the late 1990s. Further, illicit drug use declined during the 1980s and early 1990s, and then increased from 1992 to the early 2000s. Illicit drug use has fluctuated since the early 2000s with a slight increase in 2008.

## Victimization Data

The third measure we can use to examine the prevalence of crime and delinquency is victimization data. According to the National Crime Victimization Survey (NCVS), there were 6,126,423 violent victimizations in 2013. Again, this is a nation of more than 300 million people, showing you that the odds you'll be the victim of a serious street crime are actually quite small. Only 1.2% of individuals 12 and older experienced at least one violent victimization. In addition, 9% of all households experienced at least one property victimization during this same year. Because the NCVS measures victimization rather than offending, we do not have data on drug use (because it is a **victimless crime**, not meaning there is no harm or no victim, but instead meaning that the "victim" willingly participates in the offense).

How many juveniles were victimized in comparison to adults? Again, remember the NCVS only collects data for individuals 12 years and older, so we do not have information on youth younger than 12 years. However, we know that approximately 21.3% of all violent victimizations reported in the NCVS were committed against youth between the ages of 12 and 17. Further, the age group with the highest rates of violent victimization was 12- to 14-year-olds (65.1 per 1,000), followed by 15- to 17-year-olds (39.2 per 1,000). The age group with the lowest number of violent victimizations were those 65 years and older (3.1 per 1,000). Further, for personal thefts and larcenies, 17.5% of these offenses were committed against youth between the ages of 12 and 17 (statistics retrieved from the Bureau of Justice Statistics, NCVS Victimization Analysis Tool).

### Figure 2.3. Trend in Violent and Property Crime Rate in the United States, 1993–2013

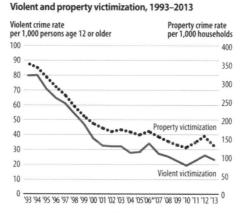

Source: http://www.bjs.gov/content/pub/pdf/cv13.pdf

We also can use the NCVS to estimate trends in victimization across time. Data from the NCVS indicate that the rate of violent and property crime has been decreasing since 1993, with property crime actually down since the 1970s. This is fairly consistent with the trends we see in arrest data and self-report data. From 2003 to 2013, there have been slight fluctuations in the amount of violent and property crime; however, the levels of both property and violent crime in 2013 are significantly lower than they were in 1993. Figure 2.3 illustrates trends in violent and property victimization from 1993 to 2013.

# Who Engages in Crime and Delinquency?

Now that we know how much crime and delinquency exists, and what these trends look like across time, we can discuss who is responsible for committing these offenses. We can use the characteristics of offenders and delinquents to better understand who, if anyone, is responsible for the majority of crime and delinquency, and if there are any biases within the criminal justice and juvenile justice systems. The characteristics discussed in this section include age, biological sex, and race.

## Age and Crime and Delinquency

The two characteristics that are most strongly associated with offending are age and biological sex. Let's begin with age. Self-report, arrest, and victimization data all show similar patterns when discussing age and offending. This general pattern is that individuals tend to peak in their leveling of offending in mid- to late-adolescence. More specifically, for property crimes, arrest rates tend to peak in mid- to late-adolescence and then decline rather quickly. For violent crimes, rates tend to peak a little later than property crime (mid-adolescence) and then decline more slowly. Drug use tends to peak in late adolescence and early adulthood, but the peak is also dependent on the specific drug.

Figure 2.4 illustrates the relationship between age and offending over the past few decades. Looking at this graph, you can see that the age-crime curve remains the same, despite the different number of arrests. So regardless of the fact that crime was higher in the mid-1990s and lower in 2010, the age-crime curve remains fairly consistent. Individuals tend to increase their levels of offending in mid- to late-adolescence, and then decrease their offending upon entering adulthood.

Those who follow this pattern of an increase in offending during adolescence, followed by a reduction in offending when entering adulthood, are gen-

Figure 2.4. Age-Specific Arrest Rate Trends, 1980, 1988, 2010

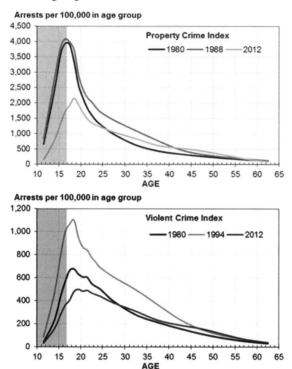

Source: http://ojjdp.gov/ojstatbb/crime/faqs.asp

erally referred to as **adolescence-limited offenders**. The majority of adolescents tend to fall into this category.

There are a number of explanations as to why individuals may increase their offending during adolescence. Adolescents experience a number of biological and social changes associated with adolescence (Agnew & Brezina, 2012; Agnew, 2005). For example, hormonal changes occur during adolescence, such as an increase in *testosterone* for both males and females. Further, the prefrontal cortex still is not fully developed, which is the portion of the brain responsible for rational decision-making and long-term planning. In terms of social changes, adolescents may experience a reduction in their *stake in conformity* (e.g., ties to parents may weaken), they may have trouble achieving goals (e.g., money, autonomy), and they may experience an increase in the *social learning* for crime (e.g., association with delinquent peers) (Agnew, 2005; also see Agnew & Brezina, 2012). These offenders generally stop offending once entering adulthood, as they begin to exercise greater self-control, reduce their irritability, reestablish stakes in conformity, and reduce their association with delinquent peers (Agnew, 2005).

Another broad category of offending is **life-course persistent offenders.** This group only makes up a very small portion of offenders (less than 10%); however, they are an important group as they account for a majority of the delinquency and crime that occurs in the U.S. These individuals tend to start committing delinquency earlier in their lives and offend at higher rates over the majority of their lives. It is thought that they continue to offend across their life-course because traits (e.g., irritability and low self-control) and poor family experiences (e.g., school, peer, work, and family problems) tend to persist across time (Agnew, 2005).

## *Biological Sex and Crime and Delinquency*

According to notable criminologists, "Gender is the strongest and most consistent correlate of crime and delinquency" (Bernard, Snipes, & Gerould, 2010: 287). The relationship between biological sex, or what the others above refer to as *gender*, and offending is apparent when examining the differences in the number of arrests for crime. For example, Table 2.4 shows the number of arrests, by demographic factors, in 2010. Notice in this table that more males than females are arrested in the United States for violent crimes, property crimes, and drug offenses. Self-report and victimization data also confirm that males are more likely to offend than females, but why?

Some argue that differences in socialization reinforces females' dependence on others, as well as their concern for others and submissiveness. At the same time, males are more likely to be socialized to be assertive, independent, and competitive (Chesney-Lind & Shelden, 2013; Messerschmidt, 1993; Steffensmeier & Allan, 1996). In addition, there are biological differences, such as differences in social cognitive skills (Bennett, Farrington & Huesmann, 2005) and testosterone levels (Booth, Granger, Mazur & Kivlighan, 2006). It is argued that a combination of both biological and social factors may account for these differences in offending based on sex.

## *Race, Ethnicity, and Crime and Delinquency*

Other factors associated with crime and delinquency are *race* and *ethnicity*, defined in Chapter 1. In the United States, certain racial and ethnic groups are disproportionately involved in crime and delinquency, at least at the street level (see Hawkins & Kempf-Leonard, 2005). Earlier, Table 2.4 showed that Whites make up the majority of those arrested in the U.S.; yet, people of color are disproportionately likely to be arrested. This disparity emerges during adoles-

Table 2.4. Demographics of Individuals Arrested in the United States, 2010

| Offense | Total | Sex | | Age Group | | Race | | | | |
|---|---|---|---|---|---|---|---|---|---|---|
| | | Male | Female | Juvenile | Adult | White | Black | American Indian | Asian |
| Violent Crime Index | 552,080 | 444,890 | 107,180 | 75,890 | 476,190 | 327,840 | 210,150 | 7,300 | 6,790 |
| Property Crime Index | 1,643,960 | 1,031,870 | 612,1000 | 366,590 | 1,277,370 | 1,125,260 | 474,550 | 21,650 | 22,510 |
| Drug Offenses | 1,638,850 | 1,324,860 | 313,980 | 170,570 | 1,468,270 | 1,093,910 | 519,830 | 11,240 | 13,870 |
| Other Offenses Except Traffic | 3,720,400 | 2,827,140 | 893,260 | 296,790 | 3,423,610 | 2,470,680 | 1,146,150 | 55,580 | 48,000 |

Source: http://www.bjs.gov/content/pub/pdf/aus9010.pdf

**Figure 2.5. Juvenile Arrests Rates, by Race, 1980–2011**

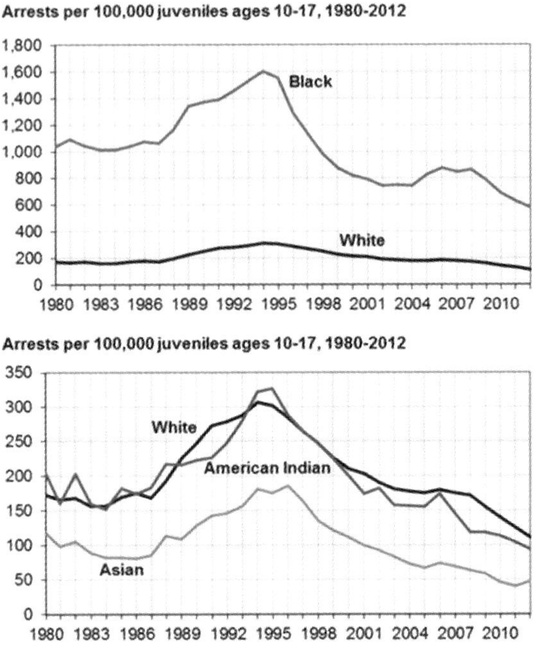

Arrests per 100,000 juveniles ages 10-17, 1980-2012

Arrests per 100,000 juveniles ages 10-17, 1980-2012

Source: http://www.ojjdp.gov/ojstatbb/crime/JAR_Display.asp?ID=qa05261

cence and continues throughout the life-course (Hawkins, Laub, & Lauritsen, 1998). Further, these disparities are apparent when examining any of the measures of delinquency (official, self-report, and victimization data). For example, using the *National Youth Survey*, Elliott (1994) finds that African Americans are almost two times more likely than Whites to persist in violent offending upon entering adulthood. Further, Latinos are more likely than Whites to get into trouble with the law, whereas other groups are less likely to do so (e.g., Asians).

Figure 2.5 shows two images created by the Office of Juvenile Justice and Delinquency (OJJDP) Prevention with regard to race and arrests of juveniles for violent acts between the years of 1980 and 2011. As you can see, African Americans are most likely to be arrested for these acts, whereas Whites and American Indians have nearly identical rates of arrests for violence, followed by Asians. OJJDP does not include data on ethnicity.

There are a number of reasons why these disparities may exist, which will be discussed in great depth in this book. For now, it is important to note that a number of researchers point to other variables, such as economic factors, employment prospects, and community disadvantage, to explain this relationship (Agnew, 2005; Bellair & McNulty, 2005; Haynie, Weiss, & Piquero, 2008; Krivo, Peterson, & Kuhl, 2009). That is, many criminologists assert that it is not race, per se, that explains why some racial minorities—people of color—disproportionately engage in some forms of crime. Indeed, economic and cultural factors unique to individuals living in certain environmental conditions likely contribute to higher rates of delinquency and crime, suggesting the possibility of a criminal *ecotype* that is broader than just race (see Chapter 1).

A final point about demographic factors and crime needs to be made. If we were to examine white-collar and corporate crimes, the majority of offenders would not be young or of color (or poor, for that matter), but instead would be older White men.

Now that we have an understanding of the nature and extent of crime in the United States, we can examine the justice systems that are responsible for governing these behaviors. We begin with a discussion on the criminal justice system and the specific components that makes up this system. This is followed by a discussion on the juvenile justice system, in order to explain the similarities and differences between the two systems.

# How Does the Criminal Justice System Respond to Crime?

The *justice system* in the United States is responsible for maintaining social control, deterring potential offenders, and sanctioning those who violate the law. As noted earlier, there are two intertwined systems that share these responsibilities—the *criminal justice system* and the *juvenile justice system*. Both are made up of a number of individual agencies that are charged with administering justice.

The criminal justice system in Colonial America was founded on the English common law system, which relied mostly on previous judicial decisions instead of statutes or legal codes. The early version of the criminal justice system also lacked a large law enforcement presence, a separate juvenile justice system, and modern punishments such as probation and the use of parole. Today, the criminal justice systems looks much different, and this section provides an overview of the three major components of the system: the police, the courts, and corrections. The final section of this chapter then explains the juvenile justice system, and examines how the two systems differ.

## The Police

The **police** are responsible for upholding and enforcing federal, state, and local laws. There are over 17,000 local and state law enforcement agencies in the United States. In addition, there are 65 federal agencies and 27 offices of inspector general that employ federal law enforcement personnel. The police are usually the first point of contact in the justice system for both juvenile and adult offenders. In 2008, approximately 17% of United States residents aged 16 and over had some form of face-to-face contact with the police (Eith & Durose, 2011). Among those who had contact with the police, about 25% had more than one contact during the year (Eith & Durose, 2011). The most common reason for these interactions is traffic stops, although the police were responsible for upholding much more than traffic laws.

The three principle roles of the police include: *law enforcement, order maintenance*, and *service* (Wilson, 1968). Thus, police attempt to respond to and detect crimes, maintain public order, and provides services to the public. Contrary to what most individuals may believe, the police spend little time combatting serious crime. One study notes that police report spending 78% of their time on routine duties, such as roll call, attending meetings, paperwork, and patrol (Korre, Farioli, Varvarigou, Sato, & Kales, 2014). The issue of policing and race and ethnicity will be addressed fully in Chapter 5 of this book.

## The Courts

The **courts** are the next major component in the criminal justice system. A suspect may enter the court system if formal charges have been filed. The United States has two legal systems—federal and state courts. Each state has its own individual court system, while in the federal system there are 94 federal district courts and 13 U.S. Courts of Appeal, as well as the United States Supreme Court. Minor offenses are handled on the local level, whereas federal courts enforce federal law and handle appeals that meet certain criteria.

In the United States, an **adversarial system** is ideally used to determine guilt. This is a legal system where two advocates represent both parties involved in the case before an impartial person or group (usually the judge or the jury). The defendant is the one being charged with the offense, while the prosecutor is the one who brings charges against an individual or entity. Based on the evidence presented by the defendant and prosecution, the jury or judge determines if an individual is guilty or not guilty.

In court, individuals have a number of **due process rights** created by the US Constitution and *case law* that are in place to ensure they are treated fairly and justly. Examples of certain protections that may be afforded to adults in court include the right to counsel, the right to cross-examine witnesses, and the right to a trial by jury. The purpose of these due process rights are twofold. First, due process is thought to result in more accurate results by using fair procedures. Second, due process helps ensure basic fairness across individuals. When differential treatment of individuals based on race or ethnicity exists, this is often seen as a threat to due process. When examining the juvenile justice system, we will see that juveniles do not have the same due process rights as adults.

In reality, an adversarial system is rarely used (e.g., only about five percent of people charged with felonies actually receive a criminal trial). Instead, a system of **plea bargaining**, where prosecutors and defense attorneys agree to a charge or charges and sentence in exchange for a guilty plea by the defendant without even establishing factual guilt. Thus, the reality of American courts is typically not at all adversarial, but instead is characterized by a presumption of guilt rather than innocence. The issue of courts and race and ethnicity will be addressed fully in Chapters 6 and 7 of this book.

## Corrections

The last major component of the criminal justice system is **corrections**. If a defendant is found guilty of a criminal offense, they may be sentenced and placed under a form of corrections. This could include probation, parole, placement in a halfway house, or confinement in prisons or jails. Thus, the correctional system is in charge of punishing, detaining, supervising, and rehabilitating offenders. Offenders may be placed in jail if they are awaiting trial or transfer, or if they have been convicted of a misdemeanor and are serving a sentence of up to one year. Offenders may be sent to prisons if they have committed a felony and are serving a sentence of one year or more. As an alternative to incarceration, offenders may be placed on **probation**, which supervises the offender in the community, while sometimes providing treatment and services. **Parole** is different from probation, as it supervises offenders who have been released from prison to ensure they do not pose a public safety risk and to help reintegrate them back into the community. Parole also may include treatment or services.

At the end of 2012, there were 6,937,600 offenders supervised under the adult correctional system. This equals out to be about 1 in every 35 adults in the United States were under some form of correctional supervision in 2012. Almost 70% of these offenders were placed on a form of community supervision, like probation or parole (Glaze & Herberman, 2013). The issue of corrections and race and ethnicity will be addressed fully in Chapters 9 and 10 of this book.

But what about juveniles? This last section discusses the juvenile justice system and how the treatment of juveniles differ from adults.

# How Does the Juvenile Justice System Respond to Delinquency?

The **juvenile justice system** differs from the criminal justice system both in its function and history. Unlike the adult criminal justice system, only juvenile offenders are processed through the juvenile justice system. This separate system for juveniles has just developed over the past 100 years. Before the development of the juvenile justice system, juveniles were treated in a very similar manner to adult offenders.

The first juvenile court was established in 1899 in Cook County, Illinois, mostly due to the push from the child-saving movement. "Child-savers" were advocates who expressed their concerns about child welfare and how youth were treated. The juvenile court acted under the doctrine of *parens patriae* ("parent of the nation"), which allows the state the authority to act in the place of the parent, in order to make decisions in the best interest of the child. This doctrine provided the juvenile court with jurisdiction over children who needed a form of legal intervention. Juvenile courts began to emerge in the United States based on the belief that juveniles should not be viewed and treated the same as adults. It was not until 1945 before every state established a juvenile court.

Although each state had its own individual juvenile justice system by 1945, the driving philosophy behind these courts were similar. *Punishment* was a goal of the juvenile court, but the primary purpose was to *rehabilitate* and reform wayward youth. Even today, the juvenile court still operates under a similar philosophy of rehabilitating juveniles and providing necessary services and treatment, while still holding juveniles accountable for their behavior.

In the beginning of juvenile courts, youth were not afforded the same due process rights as adults. In theory, juvenile hearings were supposed to be very informal and non-adversarial, although this atmosphere often led to arbitrary decisions (Bishop, 2000). However, a series of decisions beginning in the 1960s changed the way juveniles were treated in court. Juveniles now have some, but not all, of the same due process rights as adults. For instance, juveniles have the right to an attorney, the right to be informed of their charges and rights, the right to cross-examine witnesses, and the right against self-incrimination (not having to testify against oneself). However, juveniles still do not have a right to a trial by jury like adults.

The juvenile court experienced a heavy shift in focus during the 1990s, when a fear of so-called *super predators* emerged. These juveniles were supposedly "a different breed" of the typical juvenile delinquent. They were thought to be excessively violent and unforgiving, showing no remorse and no signs of halting their violent offending behavior. We now know that these myths were unfounded. Yet, during this time period, the juvenile justice system experienced a punitive shift towards treating juveniles more like adult offenders in terms of punishment. Fortunately, there is some evidence that we are beginning to move away from this punitive focus with the pendulum starting to swing back toward a more rehabilitative ideal.

## How Does the Juvenile Justice System Differ from the Adult Criminal Justice System?

The juvenile justice system differs from the adult criminal justice system in a number of ways. The primary reasons for these differences is based on the belief that juveniles should be treated differently than adult offenders. It is thought that juveniles are more amenable to treatment and rehabilitation compared to hardened adult criminals. Further, they are more immature and, thus, not fully developed adults capable of controlling their impulses and behaviors.

Based on these different views of juveniles, the juvenile justice system places much more emphasis on rehabilitation than the adult system. Because of this focus, the juvenile justice system is still more informal than the adult criminal justice system. For example, juveniles do not have the right to a trial by jury, so the hearings usually are held in front of a juvenile court judge, and the hearings are typically brief. The hearings also are held in private, away from the public and the media.

The differences in the way juveniles are viewed in the two systems also are apparent when examining the different terminology employed. For example, juveniles are not technically "arrested," but are "taken into custody." Further, those who are taken into custody are not "found guilty," but instead may be "adjudicated delinquent." In addition, delinquents are not given a "sentence," but instead a "disposition," which is the sanction imposed upon the juvenile. This difference in terminology is symbolic of how the juvenile justice system views juveniles as more amenable to treatment, and less responsible for their actions.

Opposed to the adult criminal justice system, the focus in the juvenile system is placed on the offender rather than the offense. Instead, the juvenile court system attempts to see the "bigger picture" and focus not only on the juvenile's behavior, but what potential factors are contributing to the behavior.

Thus, the court may consider relevant factors other than the offense, such as the social background of the juvenile. Instead of responding to the juvenile's action, the court seeks to address some of the juvenile's underlying issues. Because the juvenile justice system tends to view juveniles as less responsible for their behavior when compared to an older adult, many juvenile courts allow for juveniles to "seal" or erase their juvenile records, as long as they remain out of trouble while they are still a juvenile. This helps ensure that juveniles are not eternally punished for their young, immature behavior.

The juvenile justice system also seeks to punish juveniles differently than the adult system. Many times, juveniles have distinct detention facilities (the adult equivalent of a jail) or institutions (the adult equivalent of a prison). These facilities focus on treatment and punishment, and keep juveniles away from "sight and sound" of adult offenders, as required by the Juvenile Justice and Delinquent Prevention Act (JJDPA) of 1974.

In addition to differences in detention facilities and institutions, there a number of other alternatives to confinement. First, cases may be placed in **diversion programs** rather than formally processed through the juvenile justice system. These programs differ dramatically depending on the court system, but the overall goal is to divert usually first-time offenders away from the system in hopes that they will avoid being labeled as delinquent. Usually there is a requirement of informal probation, where the juvenile is monitored informally over a period of time, to ensure they are not getting into further trouble. Juveniles also may be required to attend programs, such as counseling, mentoring, or drug treatment. If the juvenile successfully completes the requirements of the diversion program, then his or her case is typically dismissed and the juvenile court takes no further action.

Juveniles also can receive regular probation if they are adjudicated delinquent. This is where the juvenile is formally monitored by the court for a specified period of time to ensure the juvenile is not engaging in further delinquency. In addition, juveniles can be placed into residential treatment facilities, such as mental health or drug treatment facilities, in order to address some of the underlying problems of the juvenile.

The last important difference to note is obvious, but worthy of comment. Juveniles can only be processed in juvenile justice systems. However, juveniles also can be processed in the adult criminal justice system. Depending on the specific state law, juveniles can be **waived** or transferred to the adult system if they meet certain requirements. Usually waivers apply to older juveniles who have typically committed serious, violent offenses. The majority of those who are waived to the adult system are male, aged 16 or older, and have committed violent offenses. These waivers are a lasting consequence of the get tough era from the 1990s when the juvenile justice system shifted toward a more punitive mindset. These waiver laws have been criticized for holding youth to the same standard as adults in terms of accountability, while juveniles lack the same decision-making ability that adults have.

# Conclusion

There are many differences between the adult criminal justice system and the juvenile justice system, and many of these differences stem from the idea that juveniles are not as responsible for their behavior as adult offenders and they should be treated differently than adult offenders.

The purpose of this chapter was to provide an overview of crime and delinquency, an introduction to the nature and extent of crime and delinquency, as well as to explain the similarities and differences among and between the adult criminal justice system and the juvenile justice system. It is important to have this overview and foundation, in order to more fully understand complex issues that plague these systems, such as the role of race and ethnicity within the justice system.

# Discussion Questions

1. Define crime using a normative and legalistic definition.
2. What are the differences between crime and delinquency?
3. Define status offenses. Why do you think we have defined status offenses as illegal? Can you think of any other status offenses not discussed in this chapter?
4. What are some of the advantages and disadvantages of official statistics? What is the most commonly used official statistic when discussing the extent and trends of crime and delinquency?
5. What are some of the advantages and disadvantages of self-report data? What are some examples of self-report data?
6. What are some of the advantages and disadvantages of victimization data? What is the most commonly used victimization survey?
7. Considering the three sources of data discussed in this chapter (i.e., official statistics, self-report, victimization), overall, is crime increasing or decreasing?
8. What is the relationship between age and crime/delinquency?
9. What is the relationship between sex and crime/delinquency?
10. Describe the relationship between race, ethnicity, and crime/delinquency.

11. What are the three components of the criminal justice system?
12. Discuss how the juvenile justice system was developed.
13. What rights do adults have that juveniles do not?
14. How are juveniles viewed and treated differently than adult offenders?

# References

Agnew, R. (2005). *Why do criminals offend? A general theory of crime and delinquency.* Los Angeles: Roxbury Publishing.

Agnew, R., & Brezina, T. (2012). *Juvenile delinquency causes and control* (4th ed.). New York: Oxford.

Bachman, J. G., Johnston, L. D., & O'Malley, P. M. (2014). *Monitoring the Future: Questionnaire responses from the nation's high school seniors, 2012.* Ann Arbor, MI: Institute for Social Research.

Bellair, P. E., & McNulty, T. L. (2005). Beyond the bell curve: Community disadvantage and the explanation of black-white differences in adolescent violence. *Criminology, 43,* 1135–1168.

Bennett, S., Farrington, D. P., & Huesmann, L. R. (2005). Explaining gender differences in crime and violence: The importance of social cognitive skills. *Aggression and Violent Behavior, 10,* 263–288.

Bernard, T., Snipes, J., & Gerould, A. (2010). *Vold's theoretical criminology.* New York: Oxford University Press.

Bishop, D. M. (2000). Juvenile offenders in the adult criminal justice system. *Crime and Justice, 27,* 81–167.

Booth, A., Granger, D. A., Mazur, A., & Kivlighan, K. T. (2006). Testosterone and social behavior. *Social Forces, 85,* 167–191.

Bureau of Justice Statistics. (n.d.). *NCVS Victimization Analysis Tool (NVAT).* Retrieved from: http://www.bjs.gov/index.cfm?ty=nvat.

Chesney-Lind, M., & Shelden, R. G. (2013). *Girls, delinquency, and juvenile justice* (4th ed.). Malden, MA: John Wiley & Sons.

Eith, C., & Durose, M. R. (2011). *Contacts between police and the public, 2008.* Washington, DC: Bureau of Justice Statistics.

Elliott, D. S. (1994). Serious violent offenders: Onset, development course, and termination. *Criminology, 32,* 1–21.

Elliott, D. S., Huizinga, D., & Ageton, S. S. (1985). *Explaining delinquency and drug use.* Beverly Hills: Sage Publications.

Federal Bureau of Investigation (2013a). *2012 crime clock statistics.* Retrieved from http://www.fbi.gov/about-us/cjis/ucr/crime-in-the-u.s/2012/crime-in-the-u.s.-2012/offenses-known-to-law-enforcement/national-data.

Federal Bureau of Investigation (2013b). *Summary of the Uniform Crime Reporting (UCR) program.* Retrieved from http://www.fbi.gov/about-us/ cjis/ucr/crime-in-the-u.s/2012/crime-in-the-u.s.-2012/resource-pages/ about-ucr/aboutucrmain.pdf.

Glaze, L. E., & Herberman, E. J. (2013). *Correctional populations in the United States, 2010.* Washington DC: Bureau of Justice Statistics.

Gove, W. R., Hughes, M., & Geerken, M. (1985). Are Uniform Crime Reports a valid indicator of the index crimes? An affirmative answer with minor qualifications. *Criminology, 23,* 451–502.

Hawkins, D. F., & Kempf-Leonard, K. (2005). *Our children, their children: Confronting racial and ethnic differences in American juvenile justice.* Chicago: University of Chicago Press.

Hawkins, D. F., Laub, J. H., & Lauritsen, J. L. (1998). Race and ethnicity and serious juvenile offending. In D. P. Farrington & R. Loeber (Eds.), Serious and violent juvenile offenders: Risk factors and successful interventions (pp. 30–46). Thousand Oaks, CA: Sage.

Haynie, D. L., Weiss, H. E., Piquero, A. (2008). Race, the economic maturity gap, and criminal offending in young adulthood. *Justice Quarterly, 25,* 595–622.

Johnston, L. D., O'Malley, P. M., Bachman, J. G., Schulenberg, J. E., & Miech, R. A. (2014). *Monitoring the Future national survey results on drug use, 1975–2013: Volume II, college students and adults ages 19–55.* Ann Arbor: Institute for Social Research, The University of Michigan.

Korre, M., Farioli, A., Varvarigou, V., Sato, S., & Kales, S. N. (2014). A survey of stress levels and time spent across law enforcement duties: Police chief and officer agreement. *Policing, 8*(2), 109–122.

Krivo, L. J., Peterson, R. D., & Kuhl, D. C. (2009). Segregation, racial structure, and neighborhood violent crime. *American Journal of Sociology, 114,* 1765–1802.

Messerschmidt, J. W. (1993). *Masculinities and crime: Critique and reconceptualization of* theory. Lanham, MD: Rowman & Littlefield Publishers.

National Center for Juvenile Justice (2014). *Easy access to FBI arrest statistics.* Office of Juvenile Justice and Delinquency Prevention. Retrieved from: http://ojjdp.gov/ojstatbb/ezaucr/.

O'Connor, T. (2011). *Crime theory overview.* Retrieved from http://www.dr-tomoconnor.com/1010/1010lect02.htm.

Reiman, J., & Leighton, P. (2009). *The rich get richer and the poor get prison: Ideology, class, and criminal justice.* Upper Saddle River, NJ: Prentice Hall

Robinson, M. (2013). *Crime prevention: The essentials.* San Diego, CA: Bridgepoint Education.

Robinson, M., & Murphy, D. (2009). *Greed is good: Maximization and elite deviance in America*. Lanham, MD: Rowman & Littlefield.

Schwartz, I. M., Guo, S., & Kerbs, J. J. (1993). The impact of demographic variables on public opinion regarding juvenile justice: Implications for public policy. *Crime & Delinquency, 39*(1), 5–28.

Steffensmeier, D., & Allan, E. (1996). Gender and crime: Toward a gendered theory of female offending. *Annual Review of Sociology, 22*, 459–487.

Weitekamp, E. (1989). Some problems with the use of self-reports in longitudinal research. In M. W. Klein (Ed.), *Cross-national research in self-reported crime and delinquency* (pp. 329–346). Los Angeles: Kluwer Academic Publishers.

Wilson, J. Q. (1968). Dilemmas of police administration. *Public Administration Review, 28*, 407–417.

# Chapter 3

# How Race and Ethnicity Impact the Criminal Law

*by Matthew Robinson, PhD*

## Introduction

When criminologists, sociologists, and other scholars examine criminal justice practice looking for evidence of racial or ethnic biases in criminal justice, they tend to study policing, courts, and corrections. They regularly find evidence that problems remain with regard to disparities in criminal justice outcomes when it comes to these branches of criminal justice. For example, people of color (e.g., African Americans and Latinos) are more likely than Whites to be stopped by the police, and when stopped, to be searched. In some places, they are also more likely to be detained prior to trial than Whites, and, under some circumstances, when they are convicted, they are more likely to sentenced to harsher sentences than Whites. Finally, people of color now make up a majority of people housed in jails and prisons (Gabbidon & Greene, 2008; Walker, Spohn, & DeLone, 2012). Much of this evidence will be reviewed later in this book.

Yet few scholars examine what could be the most significant source of bias in criminal justice—the *criminal law*. As you'll see in this chapter, the criminal law is created by, voted for by, and funded by people who are not demographically representative of all Americans. For these reasons, it is African Americans and Latinos who have the least impact on the criminal law, raising a significant possibility that the law does not represent their interests (Robinson, 2015). In this chapter, the author examines the law, with special attention devoted to who makes the law, who votes for the law, and who funds the law. The goal is to determine whose interests are best (and least) served by it. Finally, the author identifies and discusses disparities and discrimination created by the law.

# What Is the Law?

The **law** is the term we use to describe the body of rules that are *codified* or written down by lawmakers in order to maintain order in society by specifying which behaviors are allowed and which are prohibited or forbidden (Dressler, 2012). Some laws define **torts** or personal harms that are not violations of the criminal law but instead are violations of the civil law. Other laws define **crimes** or behaviors that produce harm which violate the criminal law. An example of a tort is *wrongful death* while an example of a crime is *murder*. The law specifies potential sanctions of consequences for violating the law, as well as explains how the law must be enforced based on Americans' **due process rights** (i.e., the rights you are *due* or owed as a citizen) (Samaha, 2013).

## Types of Law

As you probably could guess, there are numerous types of laws. These include, at minimum, *administrative law, civil law, common law, criminal law, environmental law, international law, military law,* etc. Our focus in this book is on the **criminal law**, which can be defined as a body of rules that prohibit some behaviors (e.g., stealing) and mandates others (e.g., paying taxes), which also specifies potential punishment for violating the rules. The criminal law includes both *substantive law* (i.e., the substance of the law, which includes the crime itself, its definition, and the potential consequences for violating it), as well as *procedural law* (i.e., the procedures of the law, which include the way a person must be processed by the police, courts, and corrections to uphold his or her due process rights) (Robinson, 2009).

The **substantive criminal law** is the type of criminal law that determines which harmful acts are considered crimes and which are not. As you'll see in this chapter, the types of harmful behaviors committed by the powerful (who are most likely to be White) are least likely to be defined as crimes. And, as noted in the last chapter, when racial and ethnic disparities exist in criminal justice, it is considered by many to be a threat to due process or the procedural law, especially when the disparities do not result from differential level of offending across races and ethnicities.

# Who Makes the Law?

Do lawmakers represent Americans? It's a question many citizens have probably asked themselves. One way to answer the question is to consider whether lawmakers share demographic characteristics with the citizens they are elected to represent. The term **sociological representation** refers to "a type of representation in which representatives have the same racial, gender, ethnic, religious, or educational backgrounds as their constituents. It is based on the principle that if two individuals are similar in background, character, interests, and perspectives, then one could correctly represent the other's views" (Ginsberg, Lowi, Weir, & Tolbert, 2013: 472). To the degree that lawmakers are representative of all of society, it is likely that laws will represent all people in society; to the degree it is not, sociological representation is not a reality.

Table 3.1 compares demographic characteristics of state and federal legislators with those of the general US population. Starting with gender, a majority of people in the US in 2011 were women (50.8%) (US Census, 2012). Yet, in the same year, both the US Senate and the US House of Representatives, 83% of lawmakers were men, and only 17% were women. Thus, men are vastly overrepresented among members of Congress. At the state level, only 24% of state legislators were women, whereas 76% were men (National Conference of State Legislatures, 2012e). Thus, at the state level, women again are underrepresented as lawmakers.

Table 3.1. Comparing Lawmakers and Citizens

|  | US population | US Senate | US House | State legislatures |
|---|---|---|---|---|
| Female | 51% | 17% | 17% | 24% |
| Male | 49% | 83% | 83% | 76% |
| White | 78%* | 96% | 82% | 86% |
| Hispanic | 17%* | 2% | 6% | 3% |
| Black | 13%* | 0% | 10% | 9% |
| Average age | 37 years | 62 years | 57 years | 56 years |
| Income | $27,915 per capita $52,762 per household | $174,000 | $174,000 | $7,000–$95,000 (85% are part-time) |
| Net worth | $57,000 | $13 million | $6 million | not available |

* People may report more than one "race" to the US Census.

Source: Robinson, M. (2015). *Criminal injustice: How politics and ideology distort American ideals*. Durham, NC: Carolina Academic Press.

Turning to race and ethnicity, a large majority of Americans were Caucasian, as Whites made up 78% of the population of the United States in 2011; Hispanics or Latinos made up 17% and Blacks made up another 13%. The remaining population was made up of Asians, American Indians, people of two or more races, and other groups (US Census, 2012). Compare this with lawmakers at the federal level, and you see that the US Senate was 96% White, 2% Latino, and 2% Asian (with no African Americans whatsoever). The US House was 82% White, only 10% Black, 6% Hispanic, and 2% other. Thus, Whites are also greatly overrepresented among federal lawmakers. Benjamin Ginsberg and his colleagues (2013: 473) note that "African Americans, women, Latinos, and Asian Americans have increased their congressional representation in the past two decades ... but the representation of minorities in Congress is still not comparable to their proportions in the general population." The same is true at the state level, where state lawmakers were overwhelmingly White; only 9% were African American and 3% were Latino (National Conference of State Legislatures, 2012a, 2012d).

Figure 3.1 depicts members of the 113th Congress only by race and gender. As you can see, US House and Senate members are largely White men.

As for age, the last census showed 26% of Americans were between the ages of 45 and 64 years, and only 13% of the US population was made up of people 65 years of age or older (US Census, 2012). And the average age in the US

Figure 3.1. A White Male Congress

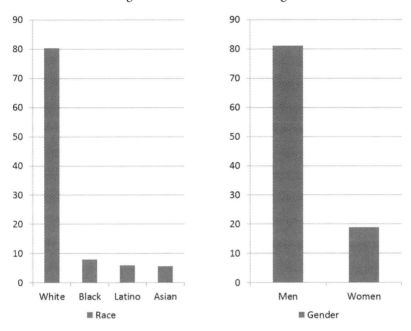

in 2011 was 37.1 years (CIA, 2012). The average age of House members was 57 years and the average age of Senators was 62 years (Manning, 2011). Thus, members of Congress are much older than the average American. The average age of lawmakers at the state level was 56 years, and the largest percentage of legislators (48%) was between the ages of 50 and 64 years. Another 24% were 65 years or older (National Conference of State Legislatures, 2012b). Clearly, lawmakers are older than the general population that they supposedly represent.

Finally, the median per capita income of American citizens from 2007–2011 was $27,915, whereas the median household income during the same time was $52,762 (US Census, 2012). And a recent study found the average net worth of Americans in 2010 was only $57,000, down to its lowest level since 1969 (Wolff, 2012). It is probably not surprising that federal lawmakers are generally far wealthier than the average person in the United States. First, the beginning salary for both Senate and House members in 2012 was $174,000. Party leaders in the House and Senate received salaries of $193,400, and the Speaker of the House earned a salary of $223,500 (Longley, 2012). Meanwhile, the average wealth held by a US Senator was about $13 million and for a House member about $6 million (Open Secrets, 2012). Compare this to the average income of US citizens and households, described above.

Further, as Americans have recently seen their wealth decline (e.g., Americans lost about 40% of their net worth during the latest recession), members of Congress actually got richer by about 5% (while the wealthiest one-third of lawmakers reported increases in wealth of about 14%). Now, between 40% and 50% of members of Congress are millionaires, compared to only 1% of all Americans. Federal lawmakers are clearly much wealthier than citizens.

At the state level, average pay for legislators varies widely, from a low of about $7,000 per year to a high of more than $95,000 per year (Ballotpedia, 2012). Yet, keep in mind that about 85% of state legislators are part-time positions, and legislators tend to already be employed in other profitable businesses or industries as attorneys, business owners, business executives, and so forth (National Conference of State Legislatures, 2012c). Thus, we can be confident that even state lawmakers are significantly wealthier than the citizens they represent.

This review of the demographic characteristics of citizens and lawmakers shows that the latter are in no way representative of the former, making *sociological representation* impossible. Specifically, when compared to the average person in the US, lawmakers at both the federal and state levels tend to be wealthier, older, predominantly White, and disproportionately male.

Since lawmakers are not demographically or sociologically representative of American citizens, it raises the very real possibility that they do not represent the interests of Americans when they make the law. This would be a significant source of bias in the criminal law. Yet keep in mind that it is we, the people, who elect lawmakers into their positions. So it is also important to examine the characteristics of voters.

# Who Votes for the Law?

It is important to first note that most Americans do not *regularly* vote. Data from the US Census show that only about two-thirds of people eligible to vote (18 years or older) are registered to vote in any given year. Thus, about one-third of people who are eligible to vote cannot vote for the simple reason that they are not registered. Specifically, about 60% of eligible voters vote in presidential elections, about one-third vote in mimed-term congressional elections, and turnout is even lower for local elections (Ginsberg et al., 2013: 306). This, at the onset, suggests that lawmakers *cannot* represent the interests of all Americans, since all Americans do not vote.

Of those registered to vote, only 45.5% voted in the 2010 Congressional elections, and 63.6% voted in the 2008 Presidential election (US Census, 2013). About 57.5% voted in 2012. Turns out these voters are also not representative of the US population. For example, data from the US Census show that Whites are more likely to vote than Blacks and Hispanics. There is also a positive relationship between voting and age—as age increases, so too does participation in voting. The same kind of relationship exists between voting and education—as education increases, so too does participation in voting (Robinson, 2015).

This suggests the very real possibility that wealthier people are more likely to vote than poorer citizens. In fact, there is a positive relationship between income and voting behaviors. That is, the highest level of voter registration and reported voting is for people who earn more than $150,000 per year, and the lowest is for those earning less than $10,000 per year.

Voting is generally lowest in the South, where poverty and minority residence are very high. According to John Harrigan (2000), lower rates of voting by the poor should be attributed to the fact that poor people have been systematically shut out of the electoral process, not that they are bad citizens. In essence, economic stress threatens good citizenship.

From all these data, we see that voters tend to share three of the same demographic characteristics of lawmakers—they are White and older and richer than the average person. Only on gender are they different since women are slightly more likely than men to participate in voting. As one example, in the 2012 Presidential and Congressional elections, voting was highest among Whites (followed by Blacks and Hispanics), 45–64-year-olds, and women (Kliff, Mathews & Plumer, 2012). All of this suggests the law will not likely represent all people equally well, again making *sociological representation* impossible.

Voters can still have tremendous power to the degree that politicians fear voters will be antagonized. Yet John Harrigan (2000) shows how very powerful interest groups have their will enacted into law, even when the interests of the voting public are not served. A recent study is consistent with this argument. The study found that American politics is more consistent with an **oligarchy** (a government or entity ruled by a small, powerful group) rather than a **democracy** (a government or entity ruled by the people, for the people) (Gilens & Page, 2014).

According to the authors: "When the preferences of economic elites and the stands of organized interest groups are controlled for, the preferences of the average American appear to have only a minuscule, near-zero, statistically non-significant impact upon public policy" (Gilens & Page, 2014, p. 21). That is, we, the people, have little impact on the law.

The authors further note:

> Nor do organized interest groups substitute for direct citizen influence, by embodying citizens' will and ensuring that their wishes pre-

> vail … Interest groups do have substantial independent impacts on
> policy, and a few groups (particularly labor unions) represent aver-
> age citizens' views reasonably well. But the interest group system as a
> whole does not. Overall, net interest group alignments are not sig-
> nificantly related to the preferences of average citizens. The net align-
> ments of the most influential, business oriented groups are *negatively*
> related to the average citizen's wishes. (p. 22)

The authors thus reject the idea that the law directly serves the people (which
they refer to as *majoritarian electoral democracy*) as well as the notion of pluralism that favors common, everyday Americans (which they call *majoritarian pluralism*).

Instead, their findings indicate support for *biased pluralism* (where "corporations, business associations, and professional groups predominate" [p.3])
and *economic elite domination* (where "policy making is dominated by individuals who have substantial economic resources, i.e., high levels of income and/
or wealth—including, but not limited to, ownership of business firms" [p.
6]). The authors assert that "preferences of economic elites … have far more
independent impact upon policy change than the preferences of average citizens do. To be sure, this does not mean that ordinary citizens always lose out;
they fairly often get the policies they favor, but only because those policies happen also to be preferred by the economically elite citizens who wield the actual
influence" (p. 22).

The conclusion of the authors is that, in America:

> the majority does *not* rule—at least not in the causal sense of actually
> determining policy outcomes. When a majority of citizens disagrees
> with economic elites and/or with organized interests, they generally lose.
> Moreover, because of the strong status quo bias built into the U.S. po-
> litical system, even when fairly large majorities of Americans favor
> policy change, they generally do not get it. (p. 23)

If there is any *one* reason why the law tends to benefit the wealthy and powerful, it is because of who funds the law.

## Who Funds the Law?

So who funds the law? That is, who pays for political campaigns that allow
lawmakers to come to power? Is it regular folks from all races and ethnicities?
Or is it those corporations, business associations, and professional groups, as
well as economic elites, discussed by the authors in the study above?

As you surely know, it is the wealthy and powerful who also tend to fund the law, meaning it is from them that the vast majority of money in politics comes. This is the most significant reason why the law tends to serve the interests of corporations, business associations, and professional groups, as well as those individuals who have substantial economic resources, as identified by the studies above.

Interestingly, money from the powerful is what usually determines the outcomes of most elections. Table 3.2 illustrates just how much money is involved is involved in the federal system. During the 2010–2012 election cycles, Republicans and Democrats received a total of $9.35 billion (Center from Responsive Politics, 2013).

### Table 3.2. Money in Politics

|  | House of Reps. | US Senate | President |
|---|---|---|---|
| Number of candidates: | 1,711 | 251 | 16 |
| Amount raised: | $1,111,628,101 | $699,077,040 | $1,368,861,431 |

Source: http://www.opensecrets.org/overview/

According to the Center for Responsive Politics (2013), in 2012, 1,711 House candidates raised a total of $1.1 billion to run for office, and 251 Senate candidates raised a total of $700 million to run for office. And of the 11 candidates for President, they raised a combined $1.4 billion, including about $732 million raised just by one candidate—incumbent President Barack Obama. Incumbents in the House raised an average of about $1.6 million while incumbents in the Senate raised an average of $11.8 million. If candidates had to raise this money in one year in order to run, House incumbents would have to raise an average of $4,382 every single day, and Senate incumbents would have to raise $32,328 every single day! That gives you an idea of how much money is involved in federal politics.

From where does this money come? Not from average Americans. According to the Center for Responsive Politics (2013): "Only a tiny fraction of Americans actually give campaign contributions to political candidates, parties or PAC [Political Action Committees]. The ones who give contributions large enough to be itemized (over $200) is even smaller. The impact of those donations, however, is huge." Specifically, far less than 1% of the US adult population (0.53% of adults) gave more than $200 to a political candidate, party, or lobbying group in 2012, and even less (0.1% of all adults) gave $2,500 or more.

These donations made up 67.3% of all dollars raised in politics in 2012. Interestingly, consistent with what we already know about lawmaking activities, men were twice more likely than women (0.66% versus 0.31%) to have donated $200 or more.

A study by Americans for Campaign Reform (2014) found that it is less than 1% of Americans who contribute 80% of all the funds for political campaigns! Incredibly, only about 4% of Americans made contributions in any amount in 2008 and less than 0.1 percent of Americans contributed $2,300 or more but yet accounted for 60 percent of the total raised. Further:

> Only four in one million Americans neared or reached the aggregate contribution limit of $117,000 in 2012 — 1,219 people. But one in six billionaires has a spot among these elite donors, including three of the richest five Americans: Larry Ellison, Charles Koch, and David Koch. Other names on the list include Hollywood moguls Steven Spielberg and Jeffrey Katzenberg, K Street power lobbyists Tony Podesta and H. Stewart Van Scoyoc, and Wall Street titan Charles Schwab. (Public Campaign, 2013)

The great bulk of money in federal politics thus comes from wealthy people — either individuals, major corporations, Political Action Committees (PACs), Super PACs, and interest groups, in the form of campaign donations. Although Americans like to think of the law as representing them, in reality, both "voters and individuals making political contributions tend to be more affluent and educated than nonvoters" (Ginsberg et al, 2013: 242). The impact of PACs, SUPER PACs, and interest groups is discussed below.

## PACs

**Political Action Committees (PACs)**, in operation since the 1940s, are groups organized to raise and spend money on political campaigns, and they typically represent corporate, labor, and ideological interests. Federal law allows them to give $5,000 to a candidate committee per election (primary, general or special), up to $15,000 annually to any national party committee, and $5,000 annually to any other PAC. They may also receive up to $5,000 from any one individual, PAC or party committee per calendar year (Center for Responsive Politics, 2013).

Both major parties are well funded by PACs — Democrats by groups of workers and teachers and Republicans by large corporations (Center for Responsive Politics, 2013). In 2012, public-interest and ideological PACs were the most common, followed by corporate PACs, trade PACs, labor PACs, and other

PACs. In 2010, corporate PACs gave the following amounts: finance, insurance and real estate—$63 million; health—$55 million; miscellaneous business—$38 million; energy and natural resources—$29 million; communications and electronics—$28 million; agribusiness—$23 million; transportation—$21 million; lawyers and lobbyists—$16 million; construction—$16 million; defense—$14 million. Ideological groups—conservative and liberal—gave $60 million and labor groups donated $64 million (Ginsberg, 2013: 459). PACs contributed about 15% of all money spent in federal, state, and local elections in 2012, whereas 50% came from other interest groups (including 527s and 501(c)(4)s, discussed later) and Super PACs (Ginsberg et al., 2003: 458).

## Super PACs

**Super PACs** are a new kind of political action committee created in July 2010 following the outcome of a federal court case, *SpeechNow.org v. Federal Election Commission* (No. 08-5223). This case, decided by the DC Circuit Court of Appeals, held that groups of individuals cannot be denied the right to engage in political speech in order to help or harm political candidates or organizations.

While legally referred to as "independent expenditure-only committees," Super PACs are allowed to "raise unlimited sums of money from corporations, unions, associations and individuals" and then can "spend unlimited sums to overtly advocate for or against political candidates." Unlike PACs, Super PACs are not allowed to donate money directly to political candidates. Instead, they "make independent expenditures in federal races—running ads or sending mail or communicating in other ways with messages that specifically advocate the election or defeat of a specific candidate." For such activities, no limits or restrictions are placed "on the sources of funds that may be used for these expenditures" (Center for Responsive Politics, 2013). That is, money can come from anyone and unlimited amounts of money can be spent to help or hurt political candidates.

Then in the case, *Citizens United v. Federal Election Commission*, 558 U.S. 310, parts of two laws—the Federal Elections Campaign Act of 1971 (FECA), and the Bipartisan Campaign Reform Act of 2002 (BCRA)—were struck down. FECA provided campaign finance reform but still allowed corporations and unions to establish political action committees (PACs) to finance campaign contributions. BCRA, according to the Court, prohibited "corporations and unions from using general treasury funds to make direct contributions to candidates or indirect expenditures that expressly advocate the election or defeat of a candidate, through any form of media, in connection with certain qualified federal elections." This includes any publically distributed electioneering

communications such as "broadcast, cable, or satellite communication" referring to a candidate for federal office made within 30 days of a primary election
or 60 days within a general election. Violations of this law amounted to crimes,
punished as felonies in the federal court system.

The case dealt with whether corporations (as well as unions) could spend
limitless amounts of money trying to sway voters through direct expenditures
so close to election day; the Court held that they can. The reason? Any effort
by the government to restrict a "person" (which the Court holds to include a
corporation) from providing information to citizens amounts to "censorship
to control thought," something unlawful according to the majority. The Court
wrote that the "First Amendment confirms the freedom to think for ourselves"
and the more information citizens have in this process the better.

The ruling was based in part on the Court's assertion that "the public begins
to concentrate on elections only in the weeks immediately before they are held"
and because there "are short timeframes in which speech can have influence."
Thus, federally imposed limits of speech during the final two months of elections are particularly harmful to corporations (as well as unions) because it is
only during this time that voters supposedly pay attention to elections.

In the wake of the *Citizens United* decision, powerful individuals and corporations have been empowered to spend endless amounts of money to sway
elections in their favor. As a result, we've witnessed a flood of donations to
political races at both the federal and state levels. This is a direct result of the
US Supreme Court holding that corporations are people and that money is
equivalent to speech.

## Interest Groups

**Interest groups** are collectives of individuals with a common interest or goal
who seek to influence public policy. Most of the lobbying groups in the United
States represent corporations from the United States and abroad but some also
represent average Americans. The latter are funded by their members and thus
have greater difficulty raising funds. Interest groups include *527*s, which are committees that aim to promote particular candidates or ideas within politics. According to the Center for Responsive Politics (2013):

> These groups represent a variety of positions on a variety of issues,
> but they have one thing in common: they influence how you look at
> the candidates. Their activities may not instruct you to vote for or
> against a specific candidate, but often they will try to shape your opin-
> ion of a political candidate or party in the context of a specific issue.

Such "issue advocacy" won't explicitly tell you to elect or defeat a particular candidate, but the advocacy group's view of the candidate's stance on their issue is clear.

527 groups took in about $460 million in 2012 and spent about $416 million, mostly on state and local elections.

Another type of interest group is *501(c)(4)s*, which are non-profit groups and corporations, supposedly set up for the common good, which can not only lobby for legislation but can also participate in the elections process by making donations to political campaigns. As it turns out, wealthy individuals and corporations funnel money into these groups to elect candidates that will be more approachable and legislate in ways favorable to their interests. As noted by Benjamin Ginsberg and colleagues (2013: 458): "One powerful but little-known campaign finance tactic is the formation of strategic alliances between corporate interest groups and ideological or not-for-profit groups." Why? "Politicians are reluctant to accept money directly from what might have seemed to be unsavory sources, and corporate interests may find it useful to hide campaign contributions by laundering them through a not-for-profit." Groups use a tactic called *money swapping*, whereby they make large contributions to seemingly unrelated groups who then lobby for or against legislation in the former groups' interests.

According to the Public Broadcasting System (2012):

> Social welfare nonprofits don't fall under the Federal Election Commission's standard definition of a political committee, which, under FEC guidelines, must disclose its donors. Because 501(c)(4)s say their primary purpose is social welfare, they can keep their donors secret. The only exception is if someone gives them money and specifically states the funds are for a political ad.
>
> And unlike political committees, social welfare nonprofits have a legal right to keep their donors secret. That stems from the landmark 1958 Supreme Court case, *NAACP v. Alabama*, which held the NAACP didn't have to identify its members because disclosure could lead to harassment.
>
> Fast forward to the post-*Citizens United* world of campaign finance where outside groups can now spend unlimited amounts of money to influence elections so long as they are independent of candidates. Seeing the advantages offered by groups that can engage in political activity while keeping their donors secret, both Democrats and Republicans have seized onto this opening in the tax code.
>
> That's why in recent years, many new 501(c)(4)s have popped up right before the election season, focusing heavily on television adver-

tising, usually attacking, though sometimes promoting, candidates running for office.

These nonprofits do have to report some of their activities to the FEC. When they run ads directly advocating for the election or defeat of a candidate, they have to tell regulators how much and what they spend money on—but not where the money comes from.

An investigation of these non-profit groups (which thus pay no taxes) by the media organization called *ProPublica* focused on documents filed with the Internal Revenue Service and the Federal Election Commission, and found "that dozens of these groups do little or nothing to justify the subsidies they receive from taxpayers. Instead, they are pouring much of their resources, directly or indirectly, into political races at the local, state and federal level." According to Barker (2012):

> ProPublica reviewed thousands of pages of filings for 107 nonprofits active during the 2010 election cycle, tracking what portion of their funds went into politics. We watched TV ads bought by these groups, looked at documents from other nonprofits that gave them money, and interviewed dozens of campaign finance experts and political strategists.
>
> We found that some groups said they would not engage in politics when they applied for IRS recognition of their tax-exempt status. But later filings showed they spent millions on just such activities.

The investigation also found that some groups "told the IRS they spent far less on politics than they reported to federal election officials" and others "classified expenditures that clearly praised or criticized candidates for office as 'lobbying,' 'education' or 'issue advocacy'" on their tax returns. Still others donated to other 501(c)(4)s who then spent that money on political activities. Such financial donations to political activities have risen dramatically over the past several years and most of it comes from conservative groups, according to the analysis.

## Summary of Money and the Law

It is fair to say that American politics has essentially become a fund raising contest: whoever raises the most money (and spends it) is almost guaranteed to win. While some may claim that the best candidates are the ones most likely to raise the most money—meaning that money does not really determine the winner but merely reflects citizen perceptions of quality candidates—the fact remains that in order to even be heard by citizens through media coverage, candidates must raise enormous amounts of money in order to have their candidates covered by the mainstream media. For this reason, candidates for federal office must rely on wealthy individuals, PACs, Super PACs, and interest groups in order to be elected. Logically, this should make them less responsive to citizen influence, especially considering that most people don't vote.

The picture is the same at the state level, as well. According to the National Institute on Money in State Politics (2012), candidates for legislative and statewide offices raised $2.3 billion during the 2012 election cycle. Again, most of this money comes not from normal, everyday citizens but instead from wealthy donors, corporations, PACs, Super PACs, and interest groups.

An analysis of the impact of these funds on state-level elections found that money was the second-best predictor of winning elections behind incumbency. According to the study, those candidates for office who raised more money than their opponents won 76% of the time in the 2009 and 2010 primary and general elections: "In other words, fundraising, and the ability to spend large sums of money to persuade voters, helped lead almost eight of 10 candidates to victory. In contested general elections, the fundraising advantage was similar — successful candidates won 77 percent of the time" (Casey, 2012).

Incumbency, or already holding a lawmaking seat, was the best predictor, as 87% of incumbents won re-election in the 2009 and 2010 primary and general elections: "And those incumbents in contested general election races saw a similar success rate of 85 percent" (Casey, 2012). Since incumbents tend to raise more money than challengers, this finding is also not surprising. According to the National Institute on Money in State Politics, between 88% and 94% of incumbents with the most money win elections.

Political scientists assert that incumbency "tends to preserve the status quo in Washington." Further, "incumbency advantage makes it harder for women [and people of color] to increase their numbers in Congress because most incumbents are [White] men" (Ginsberg et al., 2013: 479).

## Race, Ethnicity, and Political Donations

What does all this have to do with race and ethnicity? Take a look at Table 3.3, which examines some key facts of political life in the US. There you see that it is largely men, Whites, and the rich who are large donors to political campaigns.

---

Table 3.3. Demographic Characteristics of Political Donors in the US

- Men contributed 68 percent of all money to federal candidates, compared with 32 percent from women.

- Of campaign contributions in the 2000–2004 elections, 89.4 percent of money came from predominantly non-Hispanic White zip codes and 10.6 percent came from predominantly racial/ethnic minority zip codes.
- Nearly half of the elite donors (47.6 percent) live in the richest one percent of neighborhoods, as measured by per capita income, and more than four out of every five (80.5 percent) are from the richest 10 percent.
- While more than one in six Americans live in a neighborhood that is majority African-American or Hispanic, less than one in fifty superlimit donors do. Women are also underrepresented, making up only one-quarter of the elite donors.

Sources: http://www.acrreform.org/research/money-in-politics-who-gives/; http://www.publicampaign.org/files/CountryClubPolitics.pdf; http://www.google.com/url?sa=t&rct=j&q=&esrc=s&source=web&cd=23&cad=rja&uact=8&ved=0CC4QFjACOBQ&url=http%3A%2F%2Fwww.democracymatters.org%2Fwp-content%2Fuploads%2F2013%2F10%2Fchapter1.doc&ei=1aTKU9r9MoPV8AHVioG4AQ&usg=AFQjCNHUfaVqP3Jczsi6jn-kLmIoIDUq07w&sig2=hx7vEhr228WDsoG4feoNfA

A study by Public Campaign (2013) of top-level donors found that, "no matter how you slice it, these donors don't look like the rest of America. In wealth, occupation, gender, and race, these donors look much more like the traditional elite group of power brokers than a portrait of the diversity found across America." That is, large donors are the most educated, wealthiest, business executives and working professionals in America, who are disproportionately older and White (Francia, Green, Herrnson, Powell, & Wilcox, 2003).

Given the data, it is clear that those who donate to political campaigns, lobbyists, PACs, Super PACs, and interest groups are generally not representative of the US population. As with lawmakers and voters, those who donate to political campaigns through these means are generally White, and are wealthier and older than the average person in the US. Data from the Sunlight Foundation (2014), for example, show that:

> In the 2012 election, 28 percent of all disclosed political contributions came from just 31,385 people. In a nation of 313.85 million, these donors represent the 1% of the 1%, an elite class that increasingly serves as the gatekeepers of public office in the United States.
>
> …
>
> Not a single member of the House or Senate elected last year won without financial assistance from this group. Money from the nation's 31,385 biggest givers found its way into the coffers of every successful congressional candidate. And 84 percent of those elected in 2012 took

more money from these 1% of the 1% donors than they did from all of their small donors (individuals who gave $200 or less) combined.

Finally:

> The nation's biggest campaign donors have little in common with average Americans. They hail predominantly from big cities, such as New York and Washington. They work for blue-chip corporations, such as Goldman Sachs and Microsoft. One in five works in the finance, insurance and real estate sector. One in 10 works in law or lobbying. The median contribution from this group of elite donors? $26,584. That's a little more than half the median family income in the United States. (Sunlight Foundation, 2014, emphasis added)

And, as noted above, these donors tend to be older, White men.

## *Disparities and Discrimination Created by the Law*

Because the law is largely written by, voted for by, and funded by wealthy Whites, it is logical to assume that it is largely written in their interests. In other words, it should logically serve their interests the most. Of most importance for this book is the potential influence that race and ethnicity (as well as social class and gender) have on the *criminal law*. That is, we should expect the criminal law to most serve the interests of older, wealthy Whites. As a result, we should expect definitions of *crime* and even *serious crime* to be in the interests of the ruling classes, consistent with *conflict criminology* (Bernard, Snipes & Gerould, 2009; Quinney, 2001).

Keeping in mind that the acts that are called serious crimes in the US have been called serious crimes since the 1930s, it is important to point out that the law has always been written largely by wealthy, older, White men (and in the past was *exclusively* written by them). The demographic characteristics of Congress from above refer to the most diverse Congress in the history of the US (Diversity, 2014), still largely White and male. So the fundamental question is whether the criminal law as it is currently written, and as it has been written for decades, serves the interests of the ruling classes or the common man? The answer, this author would argue, is both.

For example, most people agree that serious street crimes such as murder and robbery are wrong, so it is in our interests that they be legislated as crimes (Robinson, 2009). Yet these are crimes committed disproportionately by poor men of color, meaning that our focus on them will assure we will continue to arrest, convict, and punish many of them (Shelden, 2007). Of course, there are other ways of killing people and taking their property that are also viewed as wrong (Robinson & Murphy, 2009). Incredibly, many of these acts actually do not tend to violate the criminal law and are thus often called by terms such as *excluded harms* or *crimes by another name* (Reiman & Leighton, 2013). Examples include manufacturing defective products; manufacturing, advertising, and selling legal drugs such as alcohol and tobacco; polluting the environment; prescribing drugs and conducting surgeries unnecessarily; and maintaining hazardous workplaces (Cullen, Cavender, Maakestad & Benson, 2006; Simon, 2006).

Such acts and practices tend to be committed by older, wealthy, White men—the same kind of people who make the law, vote for the law, and fund the law. When the law is used to address their behaviors, it is generally the *civil law* that is used, so rarely is anyone ever arrested or incarcerated for committing these acts. Instead, wealthy individuals and corporations that commit these acts pay large sums of money as fines without admitting any wrong doing.

So perhaps such acts do not violate the criminal law simply because of who commits them. If so, this amounts to a serious bias which operates in the favor of older, wealthy, White men and against younger, poor, minority men who tend to commit the street crimes on which we are so heavily focused. This perhaps explains why serious harmful acts committed by the powerful are generally handled as *torts* or violations of the civil law rather than as *crimes* or violations of the criminal law, meaning those who commit them pay fines when charged and found liable rather than get arrested and incarcerated.

## The Bias of the Criminal Law

Indeed, there is significant research suggesting that the criminal law may be biased against people of color, especially African Americans (Alexander, 2012; Tonry, 2012). According to this work, criminal justice is a tool to maintain the status quo of racial stratification in the United States. Other research suggests the criminal law targets and most harms poor people (Reiman & Leighton, 2013; Shelden, 2007). According to this work, criminal justice is a mechanism used to serve the wealthy by controlling the poor and thus it can be seen as a social class maintenance system. Still other research concludes that, given the very close relationships between race and social class in the US, it is difficult to determine if criminal justice practice is biased against people of color *or* poor people, and that criminal justice is at least sometimes biased against people of color *and* the poor, reflecting the reality of *intersectionality* first introduced in Chapter 1 (Walker, Spohn & DeLone, 2012). What is clear is that it is largely poor people of color—especially young men—who tend to garner the most attention in the criminal justice system.

Consider, for example, the argument of Michelle Alexander (2012), which suggests that criminal justice is a mechanism intended to control African Americans. Specifically, she sees mass imprisonment of especially African American males as an intentional **racial caste system**, which she says denotes "a stigmatized racial group locked into an inferior position by law and custom" (p. 12). Her argument is based on the fact that America has always had racial caste systems—from slavery to the current day—and she says such systems do not end, they are just redesigned or change forms over time.

Alexander examines US history and suggests that when slavery was abolished, a new form of racial caste system eventually emerged called **Jim Crow**, a system named after a minstrel show character. At the heart of the Jim Crow system was the notion of "separate but equal," where Blacks would supposedly have equal access to societal institutions, but this access must remain separate from that of Whites. So there were separate entrances to buildings, separate water fountains, segregated schools, and even separate seating arrangements on city buses, in movie theaters, restaurants, and so much more. Alexander also discusses the intense domestic terrorism Blacks faced at the hands of groups such as the Ku Klux Klan, not to mention the police, in order to maintain this racial caste system.

After the Jim Crow system was finally defeated legally as a result of the Civil Rights Movement—meaning the nation's institutions would finally have to be desegregated so that, among other things, Blacks could attend the same schools as Whites—America's racial caste system would have to change again. This time, according to Alexander, it was the criminal justice system that would step in to take the lead (just as police maintained Jim Crow by enforcing the criminal laws at the time). So today, where it is not legally permissible to discriminate using race in America's "colorblind society," we instead use the "legitimate" or "race neutral" factor of "criminality" to control minorities. To Alexander, Black is synonymous with criminal.

How did this happen, according to Alexander? The "law and order" approach to crime control that started in the 1960s was born in response to the Civil Rights Movement, which was depicted by Southern politicians as a breakdown in law and order. That is, the acts of civil disobedience engaged in by groups such as the National Association for the Advancement of Colored People (NAACP), Student Nonviolent Coordinating Committee (SNCC), Congress on Racial Equality (CORE), and Martin Luther King Jr.'s Southern Christian Leadership Conference (SCLC) were often depicted by national, state, and local politicians as criminal behaviors in need of criminal justice intervention. As noted by Katherine Beckett and Theodore Sasson (2000: 49):

## Figure 3.2. American Imprisonment

U.S. State and Federal Prison Population, 1925-2012

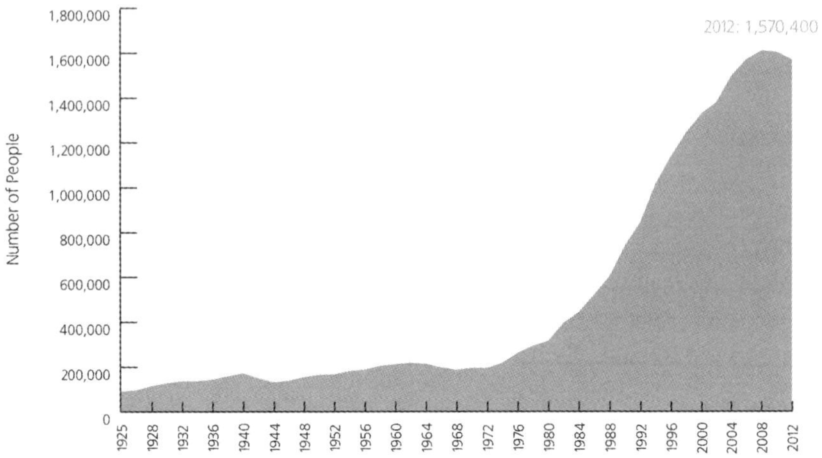

Source: http://www.sentencingproject.org/template/page.cfm?id=107. Used courtesy of The Sentencing Project.

> In an effort to sway public opinion against the civil rights movement, southern governors and law enforcement officials characterized its tactics as 'criminal' and indicative of the breakdown of 'law and order.' Calling for a crackdown on the 'hoodlums,' 'agitators,' 'street mobs,' and 'lawbreakers' who challenged segregation and Black disenfranchisement, these officials made rhetoric about crime a key component of political discourse in race relations.

And of course, participants as well as leaders in the movement were arrested by police, hosed down by firefighters, attacked by police and police dogs, as well as assaulted and murdered.

When Jim Crow laws were overturned, something else had to take the place of Jim Crow; Alexander claims it is America's current system of mass imprisonment, which is shown in Figure 3.2. According to Alexander, such a development does "not require racial hostility or overt bigotry to thrive" (p. 14), only indifference to the suffering of millions of Americans who are seen simply in the eyes of Americans as criminals. As noted by Alexander, "Today, mass incarceration defines the meaning of blackness in America: black people, especially black men, are criminals. That's what it means to be black" (p. 197). So today, to many Americans, *Black* and *crime* are synonymous and thus imprisoning people viewed as dangerous appears perfectly normal.

Alexander acknowledges that lawmakers are wealthy, older, White males, and she points out that it is White men who dominate politics, control the nation's wealth, and write the rules by which we all have to live (p. 255). One specific set of laws that help target young, Black men, according to Alexander, are those pertaining to the drug war. It works like this:

- Phase one—police round up large numbers of young Black men as part of the drug war;
- Phase two—courts deny these people meaningful legal representation and coerce them to plead guilty; and
- Phase three—correctional facilities house them, largely invisibly, until their release dates, after which the stigma of conviction follows and harms them for the rest of their lives (pp. 185–186).

The **drug war** is a term that summarizes America's approach to fighting drug producers, growers, manufacturers, sellers, possessors, and users in order to reduce drug use. Why do we fight a drug war? Because of the criminal law, which first determined that certain drugs are illegal and that second called for strict criminal penalties for producing, growing, manufacturing, selling, possessing, and using drugs. So, according to Alexander's argument, the law really is the problem. Keep in mind that the laws that have produced disparate and discriminatory outcomes were mostly written by older, wealthy, White men at both the state and federal levels of government.

Other scholars acknowledge that race does in fact impact criminal justice and even that discrimination exists, yet they suggest that the major bias of criminal justice is actually one of social class. For example, Jeffrey Reiman and Paul Leighton (2013) suggest that the criminal justice system is biased against the poor at all stages of the process, from policing, to courts, all the way through corrections. Reiman and Leighton argue that criminal justice loses in its fight against crime and its efforts to be fair, but this failure amounts to a victory for those who benefit from these failures. So they suggest that criminal justice is really aimed at failing to reduce crime and achieve fairness because these failures produce enough benefits to powerful people that they amount to a success.

Reiman and Leighton suggest that criminal justice processes are actually aimed at *controlling the population* in order to *serve limited interests*. Their main argument is that interests of those in power are served when we focus almost exclusively on street crimes rather than other types of harmful behaviors, including white-collar crimes, corporate crimes, and even governmental deviance. At the same time, those people whom we fear most (e.g., young, minority males) are routinely rounded up by the police and sent off to some form of government-controlled institution (e.g., jail or prison) or community alternative (e.g., halfway house, boot camp). This amounts to a form of population control, so that the enemies in the war on crime can never win and can never achieve the types of success that can be enjoyed by those with the power to achieve.

Among other things, Reiman and Leighton argue that the label of "crime" (particularly "serious crime") is not used for the most harmful and frequently occurring acts that threaten us. They claim that the criminal law distorts the image of crime so that the most dangerous threats are seen as coming from below us (i.e., from the lower class) when they really come from above us (i.e., from the upper class). They refer to this as a *carnival mirror* (p. 67). Extremely dangerous acts committed by the wealthy and powerful (such as unsafe workplaces, environmental pollution, unnecessary surgery, and unnecessary prescriptions) are either not illegal or are but are not vigorously pursued by criminal justice agencies even though they kill and injure far more people than crime every year (more on this in Chapter 5).

Thus, these authors agree with the argument of this book that the primary source of bias in criminal justice is the law. Reiman and Leighton state this simply when they write, "when crimes are defined in the law, the system concentrates primarily on the predatory acts of the poor and tends to exclude or deemphasize the equally or more dangerous predatory acts of those who are well off" (p. 4). They add that the label of crime "is not used in America to name all or the worst of the actions that cause misery and suffering to Americans. It is reserved primarily for the dangerous actions of the poor" (p. 66).

Reiman and Leighton review studies of white-collar and corporate crime, along with government and non-government estimates of the damages these acts cause. And they demonstrate that behaviors such as occupational disease and injury, unnecessary medical care, misuse of prescription drugs, environmental pollution, and so forth, injure and kill far more Americans than street crime (p. 95). Further, they cause far more property loss than street crime (p. 131).

Reiman and Leighton argue that the criminal justice system is designed to function in a way that "aims its weapons against the poor, while ignoring or treating gently the rich who prey upon their own fellows"—that it is designed to fail "to protect Americans from predatory business practices and to [not] punish those well-off people who cause widespread harm" (p. xvii). So, rather than being aimed at eliminating crime or achieving justice, Reiman and Leighton entertain the idea that the goal of the criminal justice system is "to project to the American public a credible image of the threat of crime as a threat from the poor." In order to do this, we must be presented "with a sizable population of poor criminals" so the system must "fail in the struggle to eliminate the crimes that poor people commit, or even to reduce their number dramatically" (p. 1).

To these authors, criminal justice is not a system specifically designed to harm African Americans — not a racial caste system — but instead is a system that actually targets the poor. Yes, minorities including Blacks are greatly impacted by criminal justice, but that is mostly because they are disproportionately likely to be poor. In America, African Americans have lower incomes than Whites, less overall wealth, and are more likely to suffer from unemployment, poverty, child-poverty, and so on (Walker, Spohn & DeLone, 2012).

So a system that targets poor crime will undoubtedly catch a large number of African Americans, although these authors also acknowledge that racial discrimination does exist in criminal justice. Reiman and Leighton are more specific and describe the "typical criminal" (or who the system pursues) as male, young, urban, poor, and Black: "Poor, young, urban, (disproportionately) black males make up the core of the enemy forces in the crime war" (p. 69).

Figure 3.3 shows the odds or imprisonment by race, ethnicity, and gender. Is it a coincidence that White, old, rich men write the law, while Black (and brown), young, poor men tend to suffer most from it?

Figure 3.3. Odds of Incarceration, by Race, Ethnicity and Gender

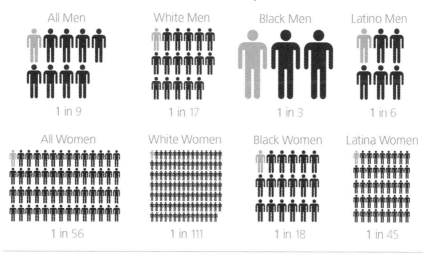

Source: Bonczar, T. (2003). *Prevalence of Imprisonment in the U.S. Population, 1974–2001.* Washington, D.C.: Bureau of Justice Statistics

Source: http://www.sentencingproject.org/template/page.cfm?id=122. Used courtesy of The Sentencing Project.

# Conclusion

The law is meant to be a source of good in our lives. And while it generally serves our interests by prohibiting some very serious harmful behaviors (e.g., murder, robbery), there are other forms of harmful behaviors that the law generally ignores, especially the *criminal law*. When the law is used to address these behaviors, it is generally the *civil law* that is used, so that rarely is anyone ever arrested or incarcerated for committing these acts.

This amounts to a serious potential bias in the criminal justice system that is found in the criminal law. This bias benefits those groups who write the law, vote for the law, and who fund it through political donations. Yet it harms those who do not write it, do not vote for it, and who do not fund it. The importance of race and ethnicity on the law can be seen here—along with other factors such as gender and age—for it is generally wealthy, older, White males who write the law and fund it, and it is generally poorer, younger men of color who suffer most at its hands. The main benefit to wealthy, older, White males and against poorer, younger men of color is that the former rarely suffer from arrest, conviction, and serious punishment whereas the latter are the main target of criminal justice agencies.

Since the criminal law defines what is illegal (and what is not), as well as what is serious (and what is not), this is a significant realization. All other branches of criminal justice—police, courts, and corrections—are merely enforcement mechanisms of this law, meaning that any bias found in the law is likely to be seen within these agencies of criminal justice as well.

# Discussion Questions

1. Define the law.
2. What kinds of laws are there?
3. What is the criminal law?
4. Contrast the substantive criminal law with the procedural criminal law.
5. Describe the typical lawmaker.
6. Describe the typical voter.
7. Explain who funds the law by examining lobbyists, PACs, Super PACs, and interest groups.
8. How does race and ethnicity matter when it comes to funding the law? Which groups are most involved in funding political campaigns, and which are least involved?

9. How does the criminal law create disparities and discrimination in criminal justice?
10. Summarize the argument of Alexander? Do you believe the criminal justice system is a racial caste system? Explain.

# References

Alexander, M. (2012). *The new Jim Crow: Mass incarceration in the age of colorblindness*. New York: The New Press.

Americans for Campaign Reform (2014). Money in politics: Who gives. Downloaded from: http://www.acrreform.org/research/money-in-politics-who-gives/.

Ballotpedia (2012). Comparison of state legislative salaries. Downloaded from: http://ballotpedia.org/Comparison_of_state_legislative_salaries.

Barker, S. (2012). How nonprofits spend millions on elections and call it public welfare. August 18. Downloaded from: http://www.propublica.org/article/how-nonprofits-spend-millions-on-elections-and-call-it-public-welfare.

Beckett, K., & Sasson, T. (2000). *The politics of injustice: Crime and punishment in America*. Belmont, CA: Sage.

Bernard, T., Snipes, J., & Gerould, A. (2009). *Vold's theoretical criminology*. New York: Oxford University Press.

Casey, L. (2012). The role of money & incumbency in 2009–2010 state elections. Downloaded from: http://www.followthemoney.org/press/ReportView.phtml?r=489.

Center for Responsive Politics (2013). Influencing & lobbying. 527 organizations. Downloaded from: http://www.opensecrets.org/527s/index.php.

Center from Responsive Politics (2013). Influence & Lobbying. Lobbying database. Downloaded from: http://www.opensecrets.org/lobby/index.php.

Center from Responsive Politics (2013). Influence & Lobbying. What is a PAC?. Downloaded from: http://www.opensecrets.org/pacs/pacfaq.php.

Center from Responsive Politics (2013). Politicians & elections. Donor demographics. Downloaded from: http://www.opensecrets.org/overview/donordemographics.php.

Center from Responsive Politics (2013). Politicians & elections. Incumbent advantage. Downloaded from: http://www.opensecrets.org/overview/incumbs.php.

Center for Responsive Politics (2013). Politicians & elections. Stats at a glance. Downloaded from: http://www.opensecrets.org/overview/index.php.

CIA (2012). World factbook. Media age. Downloaded from: https://www.cia.gov/library/publications/the-world-factbook/fields/2177.html.

Cullen, F., Cavender, G., Maakestad, W., & Benson, M. (2006). *Corporate crime under attack: The fight to criminalize business violence.* Cincinnati, OH: Anderson.

Diversity Inc. (2014). Most diverse Congress sworn in. Downloaded from: http://www.diversityinc.com/diversity-and-inclusion/most-diverse-congress-sworn-in/.

Dressler, J. (2012). *Understanding criminal law.* Cincinnati, OH: LexisNexis.

Francia, Peter L., Green, John C., Herrnson, Paul S., Powell, Lynda W., & Wilcox, Clyde, (2003). *The financiers of Congressional elections: Investors, ideologues and intimates.* New York: Columbia University Press.

Gabbidon, S., & Greene, H. (2008). *Race and crime.* Thousand Oaks, CA: Sage.

Gilens, M., & Page, P. (2014).Testing theories of American politics: Elites, interest groups, and average citizens. Forthcoming in *Perspectives on Politics.* Downloaded from: http://www.princeton.edu/~mgilens/Gilens%20homepage%20materials/Gilens%20and%20Page/Gilens%20and%20Page%202014-Testing%20Theories%203-7-14.pdf.

Ginsberg, B., Lowi, T., Weir, M., & Tolbert, C. (2013). *We the People: An Introduction to American Politics.* New York: WW Norton.

Harrigan, J. (2000). *Empty dreams, empty pockets: Class and bias in American politics.* New York: Addison-Wesley Longman.

Kliff, D., Mathews, D., & Plumer, B. (2013). The 2012 election in charts. *Washington Post Wonk Blog.* November 7, 2012. Downloaded from: http://www.washingtonpost.com/blogs/wonkblog/wp/2012/11/07/the-2012-election-in-charts/.

Longley, R. (2012). Salaries and benefits of US Congress members. Downloaded from: http://usgovinfo.about.com/od/uscongress/a/congresspay.htm.

Manning, J. (2011). Membership of the 113th Congress: A profile. Downloaded from: http://fas.org/sgp/crs/misc/R42964.pdf.

National Conference of State Legislatures (2012a). 2009 Latino legislators. Downloaded from: http://www.ncsl.org/legislatures-elections/legisdata/latino-legislators-overview.aspx.

National Conference of State Legislatures (2012b). Legislator & legislative staff information. Downloaded from: http://www.ncsl.org/legislatures-elections.aspx?tabs=1116,113,782.

National Conference of State Legislatures (2012c). Legislators' occupations in all states, 1976, 1986, 1993,1995, 2007 (percentages). Downloaded from: http://www.ncsl.org/legislatures-elections/legisdata/legislator-occupations-national-data.aspx.

National Conference of State Legislatures (2012d). Number of African American legislators 2009. Downloaded from: http://www.ncsl.org/legislatures elections/legisdata/african-american-legislators-1992-to-2009.aspx.

National Conference of State Legislatures (2012e). Women in state legislatures: 2011 legislative session. Downloaded from: http://www.ncsl.org/ legislatures-elections/wln/women-in-state-legislatures-2011.aspx.

National Institute on Money in State Politics (2012). Explore. Features. National overview map. Downloaded from: http://www.followthemoney.org/ database/nationalview.phtml.

Open Secrets (2012). Average wealth of members of Congress. Downloaded from: http://www.opensecrets.org/pfds/averages.php.

Public Broadcasting (2012). The rules that govern 501(c)(4)s. Downloaded from: http://www.pbs.org/wgbh/pages/frontline/government-elections-politics/ big-sky-big-money/the-rules-that-govern-501c4s/.

Public Campaign (2013). Country club politics: How McCutcheon v. FEC could tee up elite donors for more influence. Downloaded from: http:// www.publicampaign.org/files/CountryClubPolitics.pdf.

Quinney, R. (2001). *The social reality of crime*. Piscataway, NJ: Transaction.

Reiman, J., & Leighton, P. (2013). *The rich get richer and the poor get prison: Ideology, class, and criminal justice*. Upper Saddle River, NJ: Prentice Hall.

Robinson, M. (2015). *Criminal injustice: How politics and ideology distort American ideals*. Durham, NC: Carolina Academic Press.

Robinson, M. (2009). *Justice blind? Ideals and realities of American criminal justice*. Upper Saddle River, NJ: Prentice Hall.

Samaha, J. (2013). *Criminal law*. Belmont, CA: Cengage.

Shelden, R. (2007). *Controlling the dangerous classes: A history of criminal justice in America*. Boston, MA: Allyn and Bacon.

Simon, D. (2006). *Elite deviance* (8th Ed.). Boston, MA: Allyn & Bacon.

Sunlight Foundation (2014). The political 1% of the 1% in 2012. Downloaded from: http://sunlightfoundation.com/blog/2013/06/24/1pct_of_the_1pct/.

Tonry, M. (2012). *Punishing race: A continuing American dilemma*. New York, NY: Oxford University Press.

US Census (2013). Voting hot report. Downloaded from: http://smpbff1.dsd.census.gov/TheDataWeb_HotReport/servlet/HotReportEngineServlet?reportid=767b1387bea22b8d3e8486924a69adcd&emailname=essb@boc&filename=0328_nata.hrml.

US Census (2012). State & county QuickFacts. Downloaded from: http:// quickfacts.census.gov/qfd/states/00000.html.

Walker, S., Spohn, C., & DeLone, M. (2014). *The color of justice: Race, ethnicity, and crime in America*. Belmont, CA: Wadsworth.

Wolff, E. (2012). The asset price meltdown and the wealth of the middle class. Downloaded from: http://washington.cbslocal.com/2012/11/30/study-american-households-hit-43-year-low-in-net-worth/.

# Chapter 4

# Relationships between Race, Ethnicity, and Crime

*by Catherine D. Marcum, PhD, and Bethany Poff, BS*

## Introduction

The concept of race and ethnicity is at the center of many controversial arguments in the United States, especially surrounding the criminal justice system. Multitudes of studies have indicated that minority racial and ethnic groups are more likely to participate in various forms of criminal offending compared to Whites (Blumstein & Graddy, 1982; Bonzcar & Beck, 1997; Hawkins, Laub, & Lauritsen, 1998; Morenoff, 2005; Reiss & Roth, 1993; Sampson & Lauritsen, 1997). However, there is no common agreement of why this disparity in offending patterns occurs. Is it because these minority groups commit more crime than Whites, or is it because they are unfairly targeted by members of the criminal justice system?

Scholars from a variety of disciplines have provided a variety of explanations over the years about race-ethnicity-crime relationships. Early assertions regarding minorities stated that they were childlike and had weak inhibition, hence their increased criminal involvement (Brearley, 1932). *Cultural theorists* have asserted that historical experiences unique to African Americans, such as slavery and Southern upbringing, influenced values and beliefs regarding the acceptance of violence as an appropriate social behavior (Curtis, 1975; Wolfgang & Ferracuti, 1967). However, no empirical support was found for these theories and they were eventually diffused.

As time progressed, practitioners and academics alike have investigated the race-crime phenomenon utilizing more advanced forms of data collection and analysis. The purpose of this chapter is to examine those different data outlets. First, the official sources of crime data produced by practitioners of criminal justice will be discussed. Next, empirical studies further examining the frequency, as well as the predictors, of criminal behavior will be examined. Lastly, we will consider what all this evidence indicates and if we are any further along in understanding the differences in offending between racial and ethnic groups.

# Race and Ethnicity Revisited

Before further exploring the relationship of race and ethnicity to crime, it is important to define the concepts involved. Recall from Chapter 1 that **race** refers to socially constructed divisions distinguished by skin color, hair color and texture, and other physical features (Walker, Spohn & DeLone, 2007). While early literature regarding race asserted there to be three major groups— Caucasian, Negroid, and Mongoloid—anthropologists and sociologists do not believe this to be true as years of racial intermarriage and evolutionary changes make it difficult to create clear categories of race. Instead, race is now a social construct and individuals define themselves based on their own beliefs, as well as the labels from other groups (Spickard, 1992). Politically and culturally powerful entities define these groups, as well as attitudes by subordinate groups of where they belong.

Historically, Whites embraced the "drop of blood" theory with Black citizens; anyone with the slightest African heritage would be classified as Black. As a result, datasets from that time period classified participants as "White" or "non-White." However, after the civil rights movement in the 1960s, the federal government prohibited the use of the non-White label (U.S. Office of Management and Budget, 1977). As the non-White label expanded into various races, it is still difficult to create labels that are accepted by all members of a racial group. For instance, some individuals prefer the term Black, while others prefer to be called African American.

The United States Census Bureau allows individuals to self-identify racial identity, so respondent demographic data is based on perception (Walker, Spohn & DeLone, 2007). Categories presented by the Census Bureau, as well as multiple other entities, were those developed by the Office of Management and Budget (1997): 1) American Indian/Alaska Native; 2) Asian; 3) Black or African American; 4) Hispanic or Latino; 5) Native Hawaiian or Pacific Islander; and 6) White.

*Ethnicity* is not the same as race, but is often used interchangeably. As noted in Chapter 1, **ethnicity** is the differences between groups based on culture, such as religious beliefs, food preparation, families, and language (Allen & Turner, 1998). Race and ethnicity are often intertwined in a complex way. For example, individuals who identify as Hispanic (ethnicity) may also label themselves White or Black (race) based on their genetic heritage. Further, Hispanics are different based on their own country of origin. Naber (2000) presents an interesting discussion of the presence of the Arab community in America. Arab Americans are a group just as difficult to classify as White or Black, and they are not all Muslims, as is often assumed. Their socially constructed group include individuals from multiple national origins, religious backgrounds, and ethnicities.

The major racial and ethnic groups are disproportionately located in different pockets of the United States. The level of diversity is higher in urban areas, and smaller communities lack racial and ethnic diversity (Frey, 1998). Five states (California, Florida, Illinois, New York and Texas) contain over half of the minority population. A large portion of African Americans live in the Southeast, or large cities in the North and Midwest, while over half of Hispanics live in Texas and California (Walker, Spohn & DeLone, 2007). This diverse makeup has a dramatic effect on the criminal justice system in these areas, as these groups are often responsible for the outcome for elections of sheriffs, prosecutors and other elected officials.

# Sources of Crime Data Revisited

While there is no way of knowing exactly how much crime occurs in the United States, there is no shortage in efforts to get as close as possible to figuring it out. Several government agencies attempt to decrease the **dark figure of crime**, or the amount of crime unknown to us, by regularly collecting information on the crimes that have taken place. The Census Bureau and the Federal Bureau of Investigation, as well as independent surveys, attempt to get as complete of a picture as possible of what really goes on out on the streets, though none are without their flaws.

Figure 4.1. Dark Figure of Crime

**Reported Victimizations**

▨ Known to the police    ▪ Not known to the police

The dark figure of crime can be estimated by comparing those crimes known to the police via the Uniform Crime Reports (UCR) with those reported to researchers who, attempting to discover the true amount of victimization, put together the National Crime Victimization Survey (NCVS). Both these sources of data were first introduced in Chapter 2 and are discussed below. Figure 4.1 illustrates the dark figure of crime, showing that most crimes are not reported to or discovered by the police.

## Uniform Crime Reports

Each year, a statistical summary of crime reported from local agencies to the FBI is compiled into the **Uniform Crime Reports** (UCR). This source was first introduced in Chapter 2. Since 1930, this report has produced a useful but incomplete picture of crime. For starters, only 29 types of crimes, only eight of which are major crimes, are listed in the UCR, and the definitions of these crimes are not the legal definitions, but FBI definitions (Schmalleger, 2011). Since reporting to the Uniform Crime Reports is voluntary, not all departments report and what is reported may not be an accurate representation of what actually occurred. The data from this report are listed in three ways: raw figures, percent change, and rate per 100,000 people.

The crimes measured by the UCR are divided into two categories: Index 1 and Index 2, with Index 1 being more serious. Index 1 offenses include murder and nonnegligent manslaughter, forcible rape, robbery, aggravated assault, burglary, larceny-theft, and motor vehicle theft. Other offenses, labeled Index 2 offenses, are only counted if a person has been arrested and charged with the crime. This precludes the reporting of such crimes as shoplifting, drug sale or use, fraud, prostitution, simple assault, vandalism, receiving stolen property, and all other non-traffic offenses unless someone is arrested in relation to these crimes (Maxfield & Babbie, 2006) Crimes are reported with offender descriptors and arrest rates. Table 4.1 shows the major, or most serious, crimes of the UCR.

---

### Table 4.1. Serious Crimes of the UCR

*Criminal homicide*—a.) Murder and nonnegligent manslaughter: the willful (non-negligent) killing of one human being by another. Deaths caused by negligence, attempts to kill, assaults to kill, suicides, and accidental deaths are excluded. The program classifies justifiable homicides separately and limits the definition to: (1) the killing of a felon by a law enforcement officer in the line of duty; or (2) the killing of a felon, during the commission of a felony, by a private citizen. b.) Manslaughter by negligence: the killing of another person through gross negligence. Deaths of persons due to their own negligence, accidental deaths not resulting from gross negligence, and traffic fatalities are not included in the category Manslaughter by Negligence.

*Forcible rape*—The carnal knowledge of a female forcibly and against her will. Rapes by force and attempts or assaults to rape, regardless of the age of the victim, are included. Statutory offenses (no force used—victim under age of consent) are excluded.

Note: In December 2011, the UCR Program changed its SRS definition of rape: "Penetration, no matter how slight, of the vagina or anus with any body part or object, or oral penetration by a sex organ of another person, without the consent of the victim." The effect of this definition change will not be seen in reported crime data until after January 2013. Data reported from prior years will not be revised.

*Robbery*—The taking or attempting to take anything of value from the care, custody, or control of a person or persons by force or threat of force or violence and/or by putting the victim in fear.

*Aggravated assault*—An unlawful attack by one person upon another for the purpose of inflicting severe or aggravated bodily injury. This type of assault usually is accompanied by the use of a weapon or by means likely to produce death or great bodily harm. Simple assaults are excluded.

*Burglary (breaking or entering)*—The unlawful entry of a structure to commit a felony or a theft. Attempted forcible entry is included.

*Larceny-theft (except motor vehicle theft)*—The unlawful taking, carrying, leading, or riding away of property from the possession or constructive possession of another. Examples are thefts of bicycles, motor vehicle parts and accessories, shoplifting, pocketpicking, or the stealing of any property or article that is not taken by force and violence or by fraud. Attempted larcenies are included. Embezzlement, confidence games, forgery, check fraud, etc., are excluded.

*Motor vehicle theft*—The theft or attempted theft of a motor vehicle. A motor vehicle is self-propelled and runs on land surface and not on rails. Motorboats, construction equipment, airplanes, and farming equipment are specifically excluded from this category.

*Arson*—Any willful or malicious burning or attempt to burn, with or without intent to defraud, a dwelling house, public building, motor vehicle or aircraft, personal property of another, etc. Arson statistics are not included in this table-building tool.

Source: http://www.ucrdatatool.gov/offenses.cfm

As discussed above, the UCR reports the frequency of crimes occurred, and also separates crime occurrence by racial groups (Federal Bureau of Investigation, 2013a). In regard to Index 1 crimes for adults, African Americans committed slightly more homicides than Whites (49.4% versus 48.2%). In addition, African Americans also committed more robberies than Whites (54.9% versus 43.4%). The other racial groups (American Indiana/Alaska Native or Asian/Pacific Islander) included in the analysis committed less than 2% of the reported arrests for all crime categories. However, based on the earlier discussion of the complex nature of race and ethnicity, it is difficult to assert that these figures are completely valid. Identification of races and ethnicities for crime data are performed by a multitude of criminal justice system employees, and are often based on visual perception of a person rather than questioning an offender.

Nevertheless, an important point needs to be made here: African Americans, who comprise only about 12% of the US population, commit roughly half of the murders and robbery in the US. Thus, African Americans are overrepresented among these offenders, meaning they commit more than their fair share of these crimes. Why this is so is the focus of this chapter.

For the remaining Index 1 crimes, more Whites were arrested compared to all other racial groups, contradictory to public belief that minorities always commit more crimes than Whites. There were especially notable differences between Whites and African Americans for forcible rape (65.0% versus 32.5%) and aggravated assault (62.8% versus 34.1%). This trend was the same for Index 1 crimes reported for juveniles as well (Federal Bureau of Investigation, 2013a). Once again, African Americans are overrepresented among offenders for these crimes.

Index 2 crime arrests followed the same pattern for adults and juveniles. All crimes in this category, with the exception of gambling, had more arrests of White offenders compared to all other racial groups.

Other than the reporting issues inherent to the UCR, there are also several problems with the way this information is presented. First, no white-collar or corporate crimes are reported since they often go undiscovered. Second, because it is entirely voluntary, the accuracy of the reports vary to an unknown extent (Schmalleger, 2011) Third, due to the way crimes are defined in this report, multiple acts by a single offender are listed as a single crime, which is known as the hierarchy rule (Maxfield & Babbie, 2006). For instance, if an individual was charged with breaking and entering, burglary, and murder, only the murder charge would be reported to the UCR.

Fourth, UCR data are restricted to the analysis of the reporting departments and their governing policies. Some states, for example, have a zero tolerance policy for particular crimes. In those states, every instance of that crime would result in a criminal charge and would therefore be reported. However, in states that do not have a zero tolerance policy for that crime, discretion for pressing charges is left to the officer, so there would be far fewer instances in that state. Lastly, uncompleted or "attempted" acts such as robbery or murder are reported as completed (Schmalleger, 2011). While this report might be a reliable indicator of longitudinal crime in a given area, it is certainly not a complete picture of overall crime rates. In 1988, the National Incident Based Reporting System was created to revise the UCR.

## National Incident Based Reporting System

In order to fill the gaps left by the Uniform Crime Report, the **National Incident Based Reporting System** (NIBRS) required all agencies to report their crime statistics annually and to give a brief summary of each act or arrest as well as provide information about the victim and the offender. Forty-six different crimes were included and, to date, twenty-two states participate. The data recorded in NIBRS includes: nature/type of event, characteristics of victim and offender, types and value of property stolen/recovered, and characteristics of the arrest (Federal Bureau of Investigation, 2013a).

According to the FBI (2013), a total of 6,115 law enforcement agencies submitted NIBRS data. This represents only 90 million Americans and 33.4% of all law enforcement agencies that participate in the UCR Program. These agencies reported 5,001,060 incidents involving 5,734,653 offenses, 6,050,049 victims, and 4,556,183 known offenders in 2012.

Table 4.2 presents data related to extra-legal or demographic factors such as sex and race. These data should be taken with caution because NIBRS is not representative of the nation, as noted above.

### Table 4.2. NIBRS Crime Data

| | |
|---|---|
| **Victims of crime** | 4,044,275 |
| Gender | |
| Male | 48.3% |
| Female | 50.9% |
| Unknown | 0.8% |
| Race | |
| White | 72.7% |
| Black | 21.0% |
| Asian/Pacific Islander | 1.2% |
| American Indian/AK Native | 0.5% |
| Unknown | 4.7% |
| **Known Criminal Offenders** | 3,971,642 |
| Gender | |
| Male | 63.0% |
| Female | 24.7% |
| Unknown | 12.3% |
| Race | |
| White | 55.4% |
| Black | 28.1% |
| Other | 1.5% |
| Unknown | 15.1% |

Source: FBI (2013). FBI releases annual crime statistics from the National Incident-Based Reporting System. http://www.fbi.gov/news/pressrel/press-releases/fbi-releases-annual-crime-statistics-from-the-national-incident-based-reporting-system

## National Crime Victimization Survey

While the Uniform Crime Report and the National Incident Based Reporting System provide useful summaries of crimes that have occurred and have been reported to the police as well as the victims and offenders of those crimes, there is still a large portion of crime, criminals, and victims that go unaccounted for under those methods. There is no way to know for sure the extent of the number of crimes unknown (dark figure of crime), but the **National Crime Victimization Survey** (NCVS) attempts to come close by bypassing police agencies and going straight to the potential victims. The NCVS was first introduced in Chapter 2.

Started in 1972, redesigned in 1992, and piloted by the Census Bureau, surveys are sent out and interviews are conducted on almost 42,000 households and include individuals within those households that are twelve years of age or older (Schmalleger, 2011). In some cases, these interviews and surveys are conducted twice a year for up to three years and new households are rotated into the sample regularly. Crimes measured include rape, sexual assault, robbery, assault, burglary, personal and household larceny, and motor vehicle theft and are reported with a profile of the victim, relation to offender, context of the crime, and the extent of the injury (Schmalleger, 2011). This report gives a more complete picture of the nature of crime by focusing on the victim's experience, which may have gone unreported to police.

In the year 2013, the NCVS results indicated that Asians were least likely of all racial groups to experience violent victimization (0.4%) (Truman & Langton, 2014). American Indians and Alaska Natives were more likely to report violent victimization (2.8%). In addition, there were over three times the number of White victims of violent victimization (1.9 million) compared to Black victims (430,380) and Hispanic victims (540,130). Overall, the violent victimization rate did decrease from 2012 to 2013 for Whites, African Americans and Asians, but remained stable for Hispanics, American Indians and Alaska Natives (Truman & Langton, 2014).

Table 4.3 shows victimization rates by race and ethnicity. As you can see, victimization rates for violence and serious violence are higher for males than females. When it comes to race and ethnicity, the highest rates of victimization are for American Indians/Alaskan Natives, followed by African Americans, Latinos, and then Whites and Asians/Native Hawaiians/Pacific Islanders.

Importantly, most street crimes are *intra-racial*, meaning that they tend to be committed by people of one race against a person of the same race; this means that it is logical to assume that African Americans and Latinos commit higher rates of street crime than Whites and Asians. In 2013, about 83% of Whites were murdered by other Whites and 90% of Black victims were killed by other Blacks (Ye Hee Lee, 2014).

Table 4.3. Victimization Rates by Race and Ethnicity,
Per 1,000 People Ages 12 Years and Older, 2012

**Violent crime**

Sex

| | |
|---|---|
| Male | 29.1 |
| Female | 23.3 |

Race/Ethnicity

| | |
|---|---|
| White | 25.2 |
| Black | 34.2 |
| Latino | 24.5 |
| American Indian/Alaskan Native | 46.9 |
| Asian/Native Hawaiian/Pacific Islander | 16.4 |

**Serious violent crime**

Sex

| | |
|---|---|
| Male | 9.4 |
| Female | 6.6 |

Race/Ethnicity

| | |
|---|---|
| White | 6.8 |
| Black | 11.3 |
| Latino | 9.3 |
| American Indian/Alaskan Native | 26.2 |
| Asian/Native Hawaiian/Pacific Islander | 9.1 |

Source: http://www.bjs.gov/content/pub/pdf/cv12.pdf

As for Native Americans, the Bureau of Justice Statistics reports that "American Indians" tend to experience "violence at a rate ... more than twice the rate for the Nation" (Perry, 2004). According to Lawrence Greenfeld (2004), who was Director of the Bureau of Justice Statistics: "American Indians are more likely than people of other races to experience violence at the hands of someone of a different race, and the criminal victimizer is more likely to have consumed alcohol preceding the offense." Most alarming may be the fact that Native Americans are four times more likely than non-Natives to be raped or sexually assaulted, and that one in three Native American women reports that she was raped or a victim of attempted rape.

As with any survey, problems exist inherently within the method used by the NCVS. Potential over-reporting occurs due to a misinterpretation of questions or definition of crimes. Likewise, potential under-reporting occurs out of embarrassment, fear of getting in or starting trouble, or failure to remember accurately what happened. The survey does not ask about the perpetration of criminal acts of those being interviewed and thus does not get at potential victimless crimes or crimes the interviewee might have committed that have gone unreported. Sampling errors are probable, including the exclusion of individuals not living in a household, and inadequate question format could hinder getting a complete picture of the victim's experiences (Maxfield & Babbie, 2006; Schmalleger, 2011).

## Self-Report Surveys

Like the National Crime Victimization Surveys, other **self-report surveys** will ask subjects to describe their own victimization as well as offending. As noted in Chapter 2, this is another way of discovering information that went unreported and therefore would not show up in official reports (Maxfield & Babbie, 2006). Often, these surveys will be used to sample specific populations, such as youths or households, regarding alcohol and drug use. Benefits to these surveys include anonymity, focusing on a specific type of crime among a specific demographic, obtaining a cross-section of individuals in the community, and getting an idea of the dark figure of crime in a community (Maxfield & Babbie, 2006). Problems exist when those surveyed exaggerate or forget crimes they have committed or experienced, as well as an overabundance of trivial offenses being reported. Missing data from dropouts, truants, and those who are incarcerated are also attrition issues that must be considered.

A notable self-report survey is the Monitoring the Future survey, discussed in Chapter 2. This project is annually funded by the National Institute of Drug Abuse and surveys 8th, 10th and 12th graders, regarding their drug and alcohol use. Results from 2012 indicated African American students were less likely to smoke compared to White students (10% versus 19%). In addition, African American students (13%) were less likely to participate in heavy drinking compared to White (26%) and Hispanic (22%) students. White students were more likely to use drugs such as marijuana, salvia, Ritalin, and Oxycontin. Yet, Hispanics were more likely to use hard drugs such as crack cocaine and crystal methamphetamine (ice) (Johnson, O'Malley, Bachman, Schulenberg & Miech, 2013). So, race and ethnicity do seem to be related to drug use among young people. More than anything, this is likely due to availability of different drugs to different groups.

## *Evidence of Racial and Ethnic Disparities in Offending*

While official statistics do provide us with a clearer picture of the frequency of occurrence of racial involvement in crime, academic empirical research often produces different results than practitioner-based studies. Multiple research studies have indicated that involvement in the criminal justice system is much higher for some minority groups compared to Whites. For example, African Americans and Latinos have demonstrated higher levels of violent crimes compared to Whites (Hawkins, Laub, Lauritsen, & Cothern, 2000; Martinez, 2002). Kubrin and Weitzer (2003) found that retaliatory killings are much more frequent in neighborhoods of disadvantage, which have higher populations of African Americans and Hispanics. For example, the risk of being arrested and incarcerated is high for Black and Hispanic males (Blumstein & Graddy, 1982; Bonzcar & Beck, 1997). This example reminds us that higher crime rates correlating with race and ethnicity may actually be produced by economic factors such as **poverty** and **income inequality**, two factors found to be associated with higher rates of different kinds of crimes (Bernard, Snipes, & Gerould, 2009).

Yet multiple studies have indicated that African Americans are much more likely to be involved in serious violent acts, as well as personal violence and homicide victimization, compared to Whites (Hawkins, Laub, & Lauristen, 1998; Morenoff, 2005; Reiss & Roth, 1993; Sampson & Lauritsen, 1997). In fact, Sampson, Morenoff, and Raudenbush (2005) found that the odds of violence for African Americans are 85% higher compared to Whites.

---

### Table 4.4. African Americans and Violent Crime

| | |
|---|---|
| Portion of the US population (2013) | 13.2% |
| Portion of all arrests (2011) | |
| Murder | 49.7% |
| Robbery | 55.6% |
| Portion of all convictions (2002) | |
| Murder | 51% |
| Robbery | 59% |

Sources: http://quickfacts.census.gov/qfd/states/00000.html; http://www.albany.edu/sourcebook/pdf/t5452002.pdf; http://www.albany.edu/sourcebook/pdf/t4102011.pdf

---

Recall that crimes of murder and robbery—discussed earlier—are two of the most serious crimes in America. African Americans may not disproportionately commit these crimes, but they actually make up a majority of people arrested and convicted for them. That is, slightly more than half of murders and robberies in any given year are committed by African Americans. This is incredible considering that African Americans make up only about 12% of the US population. Table 4.4 illustrates the disparities in offending for these crimes.

When it comes to Latinos, they are also more likely to participate in violent acts compared to Whites, but less likely than African Americans (Morenoff, 2005). Sampson et al. (2005) examined three waves of data from the Project on Human Development in Chicago Neighborhoods and found that Latino violence was 75% higher compared to Whites, but lower then Black rates of violence.

No matter the data used, it is evident there is a racial and ethnic divide regarding commission of crimes. In other words, racial and ethnic groups are committing criminal acts with greater frequency, and in many cases, the differences are drastic. This makes it evident that there are factors associated and experienced by one group over another; therefore, the need for empirical research to explain these predictive factors of delinquency and crime is imperative. The next section will explore what past research has found and the potential repercussions of these predictive factors.

Before we move on to that, however, it is important to revisit an issue first pointed out in Chapter 2. Remember that the focus of the criminal justice system is squarely focused on street crimes; this is because of the factors identified in Chapter 3, which showed that the law is written by, voted for, and paid for almost universally by Whites. The focus of the people who study crime for a living—criminologists—are also focused almost exclusively on street crime; the studies by criminologists cited above are all focused on acts of delinquency and crime at the street level. Studies of white-collar and corporate offenders would, however, find that the vast majority of offenders of these offenses would be Whites, because it is Whites who largely make up the population of the US workforce, especially at the highest levels of power. Unfortunately, the data sources discussed above do not measure most forms of white-collar and corporate crimes.

## Explanations of Racial and Ethnic Disparities in Offending

Currently, there are two main competing explanations for the racial and ethnic disparities in offending rates when it comes to the street crimes measured by the data sources discussed earlier. The **differential involvement hypothesis** asserts that African Americans commit more crime than other races, which leads to increased involvement in the criminal justice system (Blumstein, 1982; Wilbanks, 1987). Further, this hypothesis explains that Whites age out of crime before African Americans, who are more likely to commit crime into adulthood (Elliott, 1994).

Elijah Anderson's (1999) *street code thesis* supports the differential involvement theory. He stated that life circumstances of individuals who live in the ghetto include poverty and racial residential segregation, both of which are specific to minority communities. The code of the street, or the behavior promoted by individuals in these communities, is that of violence and criminality. With this deviancy comes respect. In other words, Anderson asserted that African Americans receive respect and status by participating in law-breaking behaviors. This code of the streets was more recently identified in Hispanic neighborhoods as well (Bourgois, 2003). Further, individuals who live in these neighborhoods have little faith in formal authorities (i.e., the police) for protection or fair justice administration. In other words, they cannot rely on formal social control as a means of regulating their neighborhoods and take matters into their own hands (Matsueda, Drakulich, & Kubin, 2004).

To the degree that there is a code of the street, this supports the idea of a criminal *ecotype* (defined in Chapter 1) which correlates with race, ethnicity, and social class, as well as street crime. The important point is that it is not race or ethnicity per se that explains higher involvement in street crime; instead it is economic and cultural factors that are to blame. For example, scholars such as Anthony Walsh (2009) posit that negative historical experiences of African Americans led to a **subculture of violence** in largely Black communities that embraces values inconsistent with traditional America, including reckless sexual behavior, the celebration of out-of-wedlock births and single parent families, as well as the devaluation of education—all of which combines with the ecology of the inner city to produce higher crime rates.

Interestingly, other scholars have shown that, ironically, criminal justice practice itself has created this reality. For example, 40 years of targeting the same poor communities of color has resulted in large numbers of African American men being incarcerated—so that today, one in three Black men can expect to be imprisoned at some point in his life—which creates a high female to male ratio in these already dysfunctional neighborhoods (Clear, 2009). In essence, few "good men" who conform to the law and thus do not have substantial criminal records are left, creating an incentive *not* to settle down with just one woman. This produces reckless sexual behavior because there are numerous women for every man in the community, leading to higher rates of out-of-wedlock births, more single parent families (largely led by females), less positive male role models, and this higher rates of poverty and disadvantage in these places.

With regard to the higher rate of violence victimization suffered by Native Americans, three different tribal victimization surveys showed that more than 40% of violence crime victimization were preceded by alcohol use by offenders, especially when it came to domestic violence (Greenfeld, 2004). This suggests drug use and abuse by some groups is associated and thus might help explain higher involvement in crime.

Further, a lack of response by criminal justice agencies might also help us understand higher crime rates on Native American lands. For example, according to Williams (2012), the nation's 310 reservations "have grappled for years with chronic rates of crime higher than all but a handful of the nation's most violent cities. But the Justice Department, which is responsible for prosecuting the most serious crimes on reservations, files charges in only about half of Indian Country murder investigations and turns down nearly two-thirds of sexual assault cases, according to new federal data."

The second position, the **differential criminal justice system selection hypothesis**, insinuates that discrimination in all components of the criminal justice system (i.e., police, courts and corrections) against African Americans explains the disparities in the criminal justice system experiences of African Americans and Whites (Chambliss, 1995; Tonry, 1995; Zimring & Hawkins, 1997). This causes an elevated presence in the amount of African Americans arrested, tried, and convicted (Sorenson, Hope & Stemen, 2003). Further, this hypothesis asserts that as more discretion is available in dealing with "victimless" crimes (e.g., drug crimes, public order crimes, prostitution), there is a definite disparity between races.

*Labeling theorists* support this hypothesis, as they assert that differences in official crime statistics are a result of the biased reactions to labels given to an offender by criminal justice professionals (Paternoster & Iovanni, 1989). As a result, these theorists believe we can assume there are no important differences between races in offending, but rather the prejudices against these groups cause the disparity (Goldkamp, 1976).

Research pertaining to bias in the police, courts, and corrections is offered in subsequent chapters of this book. There has also been some research that has questioned the actuality of racial bias in the criminal justice system. For instance, D'Alessio and Stolzenberg (2003) used data from the National Incident-Based Reporting System to investigate the relationship between offender race and likelihood of arrest for rape, robbery and assault in 17 states in 1999. Results indicated that Whites were more likely to participate in robbery and that other factors, such as age, were better predictors than race for arrest. Further, there was no evidence the Black offenders who victimize Whites were more likely to be arrested, discrediting the *offender-victim race interaction thesis* (which asserts that people who offend against Whites are most likely to be arrested). D'Alessio and Stolzenberg (2003) stated that these findings contradicting the systematic racial bias hypothesis against African Americans "suggest some rethinking of traditional held notions about the underlying causes of the elevated arrest rates for Black" (p. 1392).

Other recent studies have uncovered other predictors for racial differences in adolescent offending. McNulty and Bellair (2003) utilized *Add Health* to look at racial and ethnic differences regarding adolescent violence (e.g., fighting, assault, and weaponry). They found that minorities in the sample (Black, Hispanic and Native American adolescents) did report higher involvement than White youth, and Asian youth were less likely to be involved in violence compared to Whites. However, they found that offending predictors were different for each minority group: *community disadvantage* for Black youth, *lack of social bonds* for Native American youth, *gang involvement* for Hispanic youth, and other *situational variables* for Asian youth. This is important because it shows that race itself is not actually the reason some people of color commit higher rates of some crimes, and is also highly supportive of the concept of criminal ecotypes introduced earlier.

In addition to the differential involvement hypothesis and the differential criminal justice system selection hypothesis, criminological theories have also attempted to explain the race/crime debate. However, this has been a slow and often ambiguous process, as most theories assert their universality in explaining crime despite race, gender, or other demographics (Leiber, Mack & Featherston, 2009). Multiple scholars have asserted the reluctance to investigate the racial context of crime is due to fear of racism accusations (Hawkins, 1995; Sampson & Wilson, 1995; Wilson, 1987). Further, scholars like Chesney-Lind (1989) argue that criminological theories are *androcentric* (designed to explain male offenders); hence, the development of feminist theory. This explanation could also be expanded in regard to race and ethnicity, and only recently have theorists begun to attempt to utilize theories to specifically explain crimes committed by specific races.

A popular application of a criminological theory and the race/crime controversy is Agnew's (1992) **General Strain Theory** (GST). Agnew explained that individuals cope with strains in their lives by committing crime. Stressful events can include failure to achieve positive goals, removal of positive stimuli, and presentation of negative stimuli. These events can in turn cause a range of negative emotions, such as anger, depression, and rage, which can lead to crime, depending on other factors in a person's life (i.e., support from family and friends, level of self-esteem, learned coping mechanisms) (Agnew, 1992). Strain theory as an explanation for crime as a whole has been supported by multiple studies (e.g., Agnew, 2006; Baron, 2004; Mazerolle & Piquero, 1998; Mazerolle, Piquero & Capowich, 2003).

In addition and as a complement to strain theory, empirical research has indicated that factors in a person's life that exist in difference races and ethnicity can affect criminal behavior. African Americans experience *risk factors* at higher levels compared to non-African Americans, such as poverty, stress, and biased behavior, as well as living in urban areas (Massey & Denton, 1993; Smelser, Wilson & Mitchell, 2001; Wilson, 1987); **risk factors** are things that, when exposed to them, increase the odds of criminal behavior. As a result, Agnew (2006) asserted that African Americans have higher rates of offending simply because they are more likely to experience more life strains (broken families, deficient schooling, poverty, unstructured parenting). Further, they are more likely to view this strain as unjust and have negative emotions regarding the strain, hence causing more criminal behavior as a coping mechanism.

Numerous risk factors exist for violence. For example, according to the American Academy of Child and Adolescent Psychiatry (2011): "Numerous research studies have concluded that a complex interaction or combination of factors leads to an increased risk of violent behavior in children and adolescents." Table 4.5 shows known risk factors for violent behavior among children and adolescents. When looking at these risk factors, are these things that certain racial and ethnic groups in society are more or less likely to be influenced by?

---

### Table 4.5. Risk Factors for Violent Behavior

- Previous aggressive or violent behavior
- Being the victim of physical abuse and/or sexual abuse
- Exposure to violence in the home and/or community
- Genetic (family heredity) factors
- Exposure to violence in media (TV, movies, etc.)
- Use of drugs and/or alcohol
- Presence of firearms in home
- Combination of stressful family socioeconomic factors (poverty, severe deprivation, marital breakup, single parenting, unemployment, loss of support from extended family)
- Brain damage from head injury

Source: http://www.aacap.org/AACAP/Families_and_Youth/Facts_for_Families/Facts_for_Families_Pages/Understanding_Violent_Behavior_In_Children_and_Adolescents_55.aspx

---

A stunning study by the Centers for Disease Control and Prevention—referred to as the *Adverse Childhood Experiences Study*—shows that adverse childhood experiences (ACE) are associated with later health problems as well as other bad outcomes in life. In essence, difference forms of *child maltreatment* (including "all types of abuse and neglect of a child under the age of 18 by a parent, caregiver, or another person in a custodial role" [Centers for Disease Control and Prevention, 2015]) are found to lead to negative outcomes. Abuse (physical, sexual, or emotional), neglect (physical or emotional), and even household dysfunction (e.g., the presence of certain conditions in families like mental illness, abuse of one's parent by an intimate partner, early divorce, family substance abuse, and having an incarcerated relative) can produce not only physical and mental health problems (e.g., obesity, diabetes, heart disease, cancer, stroke, broken bones, chronic obstructive pulmonary disease, sexually transmitted diseases, depression, suicide attempts), but also bad behavioral outcomes (e.g., lack of physical activity, missed work, smoking, alcoholism, drug use) (Starecheski, 2015). Thus, this study is highly supportive of the risk factor approach as well as GST.

ACE is thought to lead to social, emotional, and cognitive (i.e., brain) impairment, adapting highly risky behaviors, and then disease, disability, and early death, as well as social problems. Higher ACE scores—meaning a person has experienced *more* negative experiences in childhood—are found to correlate with high offending rates (Reavis, Looman, Franco, & Rojas, 2013). Higher ACE scores are found more often among poor, inner-city minority children than children of middle class, White kids, again verifying the reality of *intersectionality* and revealing the importance of a *criminal ecotype* as first introduced in Chapter 1.

Other studies have indicated that race-related differences in strain experiences, also including exposure to violence and victimization rates, provide explanation of why African Americans commit crime at a higher rate (Eitle & Turner, 2002; Kaufman., Rebellon, Thaxton, & Agnew, 2005). More recently, studies have also looked at the Hispanic experiences and its relationship to criminal activities. Perez, Jennings and Gover (2008), using a school-based sample of 1,700 Mexican adolescents, found the *acculturation process* subjects Hispanics to unique types of discrimination, which can increase crime. Jennings, Piquero, Gover, and Perez (2009) applied GST to a sample of Mexican adolescents to understand gender and ethnic differences in offending, finding that anger led to interpersonal and property offending in both sexes.

Even more recently, Piquero and Sealock (2010) used data from the *Substance Abuse Subtle Screening Inventory* to question youth at juvenile detention facilities. However, their findings were contradictory to Agnew's (2006) past assertions indicating that minorities were more likely to experience strains compared to Whites. Piquero and Sealock (2010) found that White youth reported more forms of strain, anger and depression and non-White youth were more likely to have better coping resources available to them, as well as better family communication.

Sampson and Wilson (1995) took a different approach to explain the race/crime conundrum. They integrated concepts from **social disorganization theory** (Shaw & McKay, 1942), *cultural adaptation theory* (Hannerz, 1969), and Wilson's (1987) *structural transformation theory*. They stressed that the effect of the concentration of public housing in low income neighborhoods and unemployment rates disrupted social organization of the African American communities. The lower levels of structural disadvantage experienced among Whites, along with the segregation of African Americans in specific neighborhoods, equated to lower levels of social disorganization in White neighborhoods (i.e., less crime). These findings were supported by Phillips (2002), who stated the White-Latino homicide gap would be diminished if Latinos had as much structural advantage as non-Latino Whites.

Here, it is important to point out that different levels of social disorganization have their roots in the actions of elites. For example, poverty, unemployment, and racial segregation are actually created by policies such as downsizing and outsourcing by large corporations, as well as loan discrimination by banks (Tonry, 2011). The people carrying out such acts tend to be powerful Whites, a reality that cannot be ignored in a book about race, ethnicity, and crime.

Lastly, it is important to consider the effect of immigration issues on racial minorities, specifically Hispanics/Latinos. Immigration has been attributed to crime for a variety of reasons: 1) it contributes to social disorganization due to communication and cooperation issues; 2) immigrants may choose to commit crime due to blocked legitimate opportunities; and 3) immigrants live in communities where the culture promotes criminality (Butcher & Piehl, 1998; Lee, Martinez, & Rosenfeld, 2001). Studies have supported the assertion that immigration issues have an effect on minority crime, as well as the *racial/ethnic invariance hypothesis* which predicts that disadvantages in life impact people from all race and ethnicity in the same way (Lee & Martinez, 2002; Martinez, 2000, 2002, 2003). However, research performed in California and Texas has indicated that immigration has insignificant effect on violence in cities (Alaniz, Cartmill & Parker, 1998; Hagan & Palloni, 1999).

# Conclusion

This chapter showed that there are indeed relationships between race, ethnicity, and crime. Specifically, even though Whites commit the majority of street crime in the US—because they comprise a large portion of the US population—it is people of color who are overrepresented among criminal offenders. And for some types of crimes, African Americans even commit a majority of some of the most serious offenses (e.g., murder, robbery). Yet this is explained by non-racial factors such as economic and cultural impacts (including even adverse childhood experiences).

Yet, since the criminal justice system is squarely focused on street crimes, the fact that people of color are overrepresented among criminal offenders does not actually mean that people of color are more dangerous than Whites. As mentioned in Chapter 2, white-collar and corporate crimes are more dangerous than street crimes, because they produce more harm than street crimes. Since these crimes tend to be committed by Whites, one could easily argue that it is Whites that are more dangerous, since they cause more harm than people of color. This is a message that has generally been ignored by criminologists because they generally focus their attention on street crime.

The next section of the book will delve into the experiences of how each component of the criminal justice system (i.e., policing, courts and corrections) operates and the realities associated with the racial disparity of offenders processed through the system. As the reader investigates the functioning and ideals of each component, consider the issues presented in this chapter and potential explanations for racial disparity in our system. Is it is a basic matter of choice to commit more crime, or are there other issues influencing the behaviors of different minorities?

# Discussion Questions

1. What are the majors sources of data used by criminologists to assess relationships between race, ethnicity, and crime?
2. What is the dark figure of crime?
3. Outline and discuss relationships between race, ethnicity, and crime.
4. How does this relationship change when you include white-collar and corporate crimes?
5. Why do you think there is a notable difference between official government reports versus academic empirical research in regard to racial disparities in crime?
6. Summarize general strain theory. How can it help explain differences in offending between racial and ethnic groups?
7. Summarize social disorganization theory. How can it help explain differences in offending between racial and ethnic groups?

8. Which criminological theory presented do you think best explains racial disparity in criminal behavior?
9. What types of programs and policies should be implemented in order to address the issues impacting disadvantaged neighborhoods?

# References

Agnew, R. (1992). Foundation for a general strain theory of crime and delinquency. *Criminology, 30*, 47–87.

Agnew, R. (2006). *Pressured into crime: An overview of general strain theory.* Los Angeles, CA: Roxbury.

Alaniz, M., Cartmill, R., & Parker, R. (1998). Immigrants and violence: The importance of neighborhood context. *Hispanic Journal of Behavioral Science, 20*, 155–174.

Allen, J. & Turner, E. (1988). *We the people: An atlas of America's ethnic diversity.* New York: Macmillan.

American Academy of Child & Adolescent Psychiatry (2011). Understanding violent behavior in children and adolescents. Downloaded from: http://www.aacap.org/AACAP/Families_and_Youth/Facts_for_Families/Facts_for_Families_Pages/Understanding_Violent_Behavior_In_Children_and_Adolescents_55.aspx.

Anderson, E. (1999). *Code of the street: Decency, violence and the moral life of the inner city.* New York: Norton.

Baron, S. (2004). General strain, street youth, and crime: A test of Agnew's revised theory. *Criminology, 42*, 457–483.

Bernard, T., Snipes, J., & Gerould, A. (2009). *Vold's theoretical criminology.* New York: Oxford University Press.

Blumstein, A. (1993). Racial disproportionality of U.S. prison populations revisited. *University of Colorado Law Review, 64(3)*, 743–760.

Blumstein, A. & Graddy, E. (1982). Prevalence and recidivism in index arrests: A feedback model. *Law and Society Review, 16(2)*, 265–290.

Bonzcar, T. & Beck, A. (1997). *Lifetime likelihood of going to state or federal prison.* Washington, DC: Bureau of Justice Statistics.

Bourgois, P. (2003). *In search of respect: Selling crack in el barrio* (2nd ed.). New York: Cambridge University Press.

Brearley, H. (1932). *Homicide in the United States.* Chapel Hill: University of North Carolina Press.

Butcher, K. & Piehl, A. (1998). Cross-city evidence on the relationship between immigration and crime. *Journal of Policy Analysis Management, 17*, 457–493.

Centers for Disease Control and Prevention (2015). Injury prevention & control: Division of violence prevention. Child maltreatment prevention. Downloaded from: http://www.cdc.gov/violenceprevention/childmaltreatment/index.html.

Chambliss, W. (1995). The institutionalization of racism through law. In Darnell Hawkins (Ed.), *Race, ethnicity, and crime* (pp. 235–258). Albany: State University of New York Press.

Chesney-Lind., M. (1989). Girls' crime and woman's place: Toward a Feminist model of female delinquency. *Crime and Delinquency, 35,* 5–29.

Clear, T. (2009). *Imprisoning communities: How mass incarceration makes disadvantaged neighborhoods worse.* New York: Oxford University Press.

Curtis, L. (1975). *Violence, race and culture.* Lexington, MA: Lexington Books.

D'Alessio, S. & Stolzenberg, L. (2003). Race and the probability of arrest. *Social Forces, 81(4),* 1381–1397.

Eitle, D. & Turner, R. (2003). Exposure to community violence and young adult crime: The effects of witnessing violence, traumatic victimization, and other stressful live events. *Journal of Research in Crime and Delinquency, 39,* 214–237.

Elliott, D. (1994). Serious violent offenders: Onset, developmental course and termination. *Criminology, 32(1),* 1–22.

Federal Bureau of Investigation. (2013a). *Crime in the United States.* Retrieved from http://www.fbi.gov/about-us/cjis/ucr/crime-in-the-u.s/2012/crime-in-the-u.s.-2012/tables/43tabledatadecoverviewpdf.

Federal Bureau of Investigation. (2013b). *2012 National Incident Based Reporting System.* Retrieved from http://www.fbi.gov/about-us/cjis/ucr/nibrs/2012.

Frey, W. (1998). The diversity myth. *American Demographics, 20,* 41.

Goldkamp, J. (1976). Minorities as victims of police shootings: Interpretations of racial disproportionality and police use of deadly force. *Justice System Journal, 2,* 169–183.

Greenfeld, L. (2004). Foreword. In Perry, S. American Indians and crime. Washington, DC: Bureau of Justice Statistics.

Hagan, J. & Palloni, A. (1999). Sociological criminology and the mythology of Hispanic immigration and crime. *Social Problems, 46,* 617–632.

Hannerz, U. (1969). *Soulside: Inquiries into ghetto culture and community.* New York: Columbia University Press.

Hawkins, D. (Ed.). (1995). *Ethnicity, race, and crime: Perspectives across time and place.* Albany: State University of New York Press.

Hawkins, D., Laub, J., & Lauritsen, J. (1998). Race, ethnicity, and serious juvenile offending. In R. Loeber & D.P. Farrington (Eds.), *Serious and vio-*

*lent juvenile offenders: Risk factors and successful interventions* (pp. 30–46). Thousand Oaks, CA: Sage.

Hawkins, D., Laub, J., Lauritsen, J., & Cothern, L. (2000). *Race, ethnicity, and serious and violent juvenile offending.* Washington, DC: US DOJ, OJJDP, NCJ: 181202.

Jennings, W., Piquero, N., Gover, A., & Perez, D. (2009). Gender and general strain theory: A replication and extension of Broidy and Agnew's gender/ strain hypothesis among a sample of southwestern Mexican American adolescents. *Journal of Criminal Justice, 37,* 404–417.

Johnson, L., O'Malley, P., Bachman, J., Schulenberg, J., & Miech, R. (2013). *College students and adults, ages 19–55.* Monitoring the Future National. Survey Results on Drug Use 1975–2013. Retrieved from http:// www.monitoringthefuture.org/pubs/monographs/mtf-vol2_2013.pdf.

Kaufman, J., Rebellon, C., Thaxton, S., & Agnew, R. (2005). A general strain theory of the race-crime relationship. In Mazerolle Paul & Robert Agnew (Eds.), *General strain theory: Essential readings.* Los Angeles: Wadsworth.

Lee, M. & Martinez, R. (2002). Social disorganization revisited: Mapping the recent immigration and black homicide relationship in northern Miami. *Sociological Focus, 35,* 363–380.

Lee, M., Martinez, R., & Rosenfeld, R. (2001). Does immigration increase homicide? Negative evidence from three border cities. *Sociological Quarterly, 42,* 559–580.

Leiber, M., Mack, K., & Featherston, R. (2009). Family structure, family processes, economic factors and delinquency. *Youth Violence and Juvenile Justice, 7,* 79–99.

Martinez, R. (2000). Immigration and urban violence: The link between immigrant Latinos and types of homicide. *Social Science Quarterly, 81,* 363–374.

Martinez, R. (2002). *Latino homicide: Immigration, violence and community.* New York: Routledge.

Massey, D. & Denton, N. (1993). *American apartheid: Segregation and the making of the underclass.* Cambridge, MA: Harvard University Press.

Matsueda, R., Drakulich, K., & Kubrin, C. (2004). *Neighborhood codes of violence.* Presented at Workshop to Set a National Agenda for the Study of Race, Ethnicity, Crime and Criminal Justice, Columbus, OH.

Mazerolle, P. & Piquero, A. (1998). Linking exposure to strain with anger: An investigation of deviant adaptations. *Journal of Criminal Justice, 26,* 195–211.

Mazerolle, P., Piquero, A., & Capowich, G. (2003). Examining the links between strain, situation and dispositional anger, and crime. *Youth and Society, 35,* 131–157.

Maxfield, M., & Babbie, E. (2006). Concepts, Operationalization, and Measurement. In *Basics of research methods for criminal justice and criminology* (pp. 110–116). Belmont, CA: Thomson/Wadsworth.

McNulty, T. & Bellair, P. (2003). Explaining racial and ethnic differences in serious adolescent violent behavior. *Criminology, 41(3)*, 709–748.

Morenoff, J. (2005). Racial and ethnic disparities in crime and delinquency in the United States. In M. Rutter & M. Tienda (Eds.), *Ethnicity and causal mechanisms* (pp. 139–173). Cambridge, UK: Cambridge University Press.

Naber, N. (2000). Ambiguous insiders: An investigation of Arab American Invisibility. *Ethnic and Racial Studies, 23,* 37–61.

National Crime Victimization Survey (NCVS). (n.d.). Retrieved September 30, 2014, from http://www.bjs.gov/index.cfm?ty=dcdetail&iid=245.

National Incident-Based Reporting System (NIBRS). (n.d.). Retrieved September 30, 2014, from http://www2.fbi.gov/Uniform Crime Report/faqs.htm.

Paternoster, R. & Iovanni, L. (1989). The labeling perspective and delinquency: An elaboration of the theory and assessment of the evidence. *Justice Quarterly, 6(3)*, 359–394.

Perez, D., Jennings, W., & Gover, A. (2008). Specifying general strain theory: An ethnically relevant approach. *Deviant Behavior, 29,* 544–578.

Perry, S. (2004). American Indians and crime. Downloaded from: http://www.justice.gov/sites/default/files/otj/docs/american_indians_and_crime.pdf

Piquero, N. & Sealock, M. (2010). Race, crime and General Strain Theory. *Youth Violence and Juvenile Justice, 8(3)*, 170–186.

Reavis, J., Looman, J., Franco, K., & Rojas, B. (2013). Adverse childhood experiences and adult criminality: How long must we live before we possess our own lives? *Perm J. 17*(2), 44–48.

Reiss, A. & Roth, J. (Eds.). (1993). *Understanding and preventing violence.* Washington, DC: National Academy Press.

Sampson, R. & Lauritsen, J. (1997). Racial and ethnic disparities in crime and criminal justice in the United States. In M. Tonry (Ed.), *Ethnicity, crime and immigration: Comparative and cross-national perspectives, crime and justice. An Annual Review of Research* (Vol. 21, pp. 311–374). Chicago: University of Chicago Press.

Sampson, R., Morenoff, J., & Raudenbush, S. (2005). Social anatomy of racial and ethnic disparities in violence. *American Journal of Public Health, 95(2)*, 224–232.

Sampson, R., & Wilson, W. (1995). Toward a theory of race, crime and urban inequality. In J. Hagan and R. Peterson (Eds.), *Crime and inequality* (pp. 37–54). Stanford, CA: Stanford University Press.

Schmalleger, F. (2011). The Crime Picture. In *Criminal justice today: An introductory text for the 21st century* (11th ed., pp. 38–59). Upper Saddle River, N.Y.: Pearson Prentice Hall.

Shaw, C., & McKay, H. (1942). *Juvenile delinquency and urban areas.* Chicago: University of Chicago Press.

Smelser, M., Wilson, W., & Mitchell, F. (Eds.). (2001). *America becoming: Racial trends and their consequences* (Vol.1). Washington, DC: National Research Council.

Sorenson, J., Hope, R., & Stemen, R. (2003). Racial disproportionality in state prison admissions: Can regional variation be explained by differential arrest rates? *Journal of Criminal Justice, 31(1),* 73–84.

Spickard, P. (1992). The Illogic of American Racial Categories. In M. Root (Ed.), *Racially mixed people in America* (pp. 18). Newbury Park, CA: Sage.

Starecheski, L. (2015). Take the ACE quiz—and lear what it does and doesn't mean. *NPR*, March 2. Downloaded from: http://www.npr.org/blogs/health/2015/03/02/387007941/take-the-ace-quiz-and-learn-what-it-does-and-doesnt-mean.

Tonry, M. (2011). *Punishing race.* New York: Oxford University Press.

Tonry, M. (1995). *Malign neglect: Race, crime and punishment in America.* New York: Oxford University Press.

Truman, J. & Langton, L. (2014). *Criminal Victimization, 2013.* United States Department of Justice, Office of Justice Programs, Bureau of Justice Statistics. NCJ 247648. Retrieved from http://www.bjs.gov/content/pub/pdf/cv13.pdf.

U.S. Office of Management and Budget (1977). *Race and ethnic standards for federal statistics and administrative reporting,* OMB Circular No. A-46 (1974, rev. 1977). Washington, DC: U.S. Government Printing Office, 1977.

U.S. Office of Management and Budget (1997). *Revisions to the Standards for Classification of Federal Data on Race and Ethnicity.* Retrieved from www.whitehouse.gov/omb/fedreg/ombdir15.html.

Walker, S., Spohn, C., & DeLone, M. (2007). *The color of justice: Race, ethnicity and crime in America* (4th ed.). Belmont, CA: Wadsworth/Cengage Learning.

Walsh, A. (2009). Race and crime: A biosocial analysis. New York: Nova Science Publishers.

Wilbanks, W. (1987). *The myth of a racist criminal justice system.* Monterey, CA: Brooks/Cole.

Williams, T. (2012). High crime, fewer charges on Indian land. *New York Times*, Feb. 20. Downloaded from: http://www.nytimes.com/2012/02/21/us/on-indian-reservations-higher-crime-and-fewer-prosecutions.html?_r=0.

Wilson, W. (1987). *The truly disadvantaged.* University of Chicago Press.

Wolfgang, M. & Ferracuti, F. (1967). *The subculture of violence towards an integrated theory in criminology.* London: Tavistock.

Ye Hee Lee, M. (2014). Fact checker. Guiliani's claim that 93 percent of black murder victims are killed by other blacks. *Washington Post,* Nov. 25. Downloaded from: http://www.washingtonpost.com/blogs/fact-checker/wp/2014/11/25/giulianis-claim-that-93-percent-of-blacks-are-killed-by-other-blacks/.

Zimring, F. & Hawkins, G. (1997). *Crime is not the problem: Lethal violence in America.* New York: Oxford University Press.

# Chapter 5

# Policing in a Multicultural Society

*by Tammatha Clodfelter, PhD, and Matthew Robinson, PhD*

## Introduction

As the gatekeepers to the criminal justice system, the **police** are often under a microscope in terms of how they perform their duties. Unlike the correctional or judicial systems, which are largely conducted behind closed doors, law enforcement officers are routinely in the public's eye as they interact with citizens, patrol neighborhoods, respond to calls for service, conduct traffic stops and investigations, and conduct other standard duties. Because of this degree of intimacy, the behaviors and responses of officers are subject to criticism by those directly involved with law enforcement (e.g., offenders or victims) or by community members.

Withstanding policy and procedural mandates, law enforcement officers utilize a spectrum of *discretion* in the determination of their responses and behaviors. **Discretion** is usually understood to mean the ability of officials to act according to their own professional judgment; officers have wide discretion in some cases to give tickets or warnings, for example. Some agencies grant officers a wide amount of latitude for situations such as handling a minor offense committed by a juvenile, while other circumstances require certain responses and thus their scope of discretion is narrow. Because prescribed responses for every variation of a potential situation are impossible, officers are provided a framework and then left to make decisions that should be rooted in training and experience, and which balances respecting the rights of the individual while protecting the community and upholding the law; this discretion obviously can produce abuse, and often abuse or discretion relates to issues of race and ethnicity.

In this chapter, the authors examine the ideal of American policing (which stresses *equality* in treatment of all citizens) and contrast it with the reality of contemporary policing (which is at times characterized by *unequal treatment*). While an assessment of the history of policing is beyond the scope of this chapter, it is important to keep in mind that throughout US history, police officers have been used in many ways to maintain status quo arrangements in society, including racial and social class inequalities—as in when police have been used to maintain slavery, uphold *Jim Crow laws*, bust strikes, infiltrate peace groups, and so forth. Keep in mind as you read this chapter that, to some degree or another, policing has always been used to uphold inequality rather than to assure equality (Robinson, 2010).

# Policing: The Ideals

The ideals of policing can be nearly fully understood by the popular phrasing of the purpose of police officers: "to protect and serve." In the ideal world, the police are us and they exist and work to serve us, especially by protecting us from crime, but also by carrying out a wide variety of service functions for us. Yet, according to policing scholars, officers can be expected to carry out five different functions. These are discussed below.

## Roles of Policing

While we often think of police officers as *law enforcement* officers, the police often do so much more than this. The five basic functions of police are shown in Table 5.1.

---

### Table 5.1. Functions of Police Officers

- *Enforcing laws*: This includes investigating reported crimes, collecting and protecting evidence from crime scenes, apprehending suspects, and assisting the prosecution in obtaining convictions.
- *Preserving the peace*: This includes intervening in noncriminal conduct in public places that could escalate into criminal activity if left unchecked.
- *Preventing crime*: This includes activities designed to stop crime before it occurs, such as education campaigns, preventive patrols, and community policing.
- *Providing services*: This includes performing functions normally served by other social service agencies, such as counseling, referring citizens for social services, assisting people with various needs, and keeping traffic moving.
- *Upholding rights*: This includes respecting all persons' rights regardless of race, ethnicity, class, gender, and other factors, and respecting individual Constitutional protections.

Source: Robinson, M. (2009). *Justice blind? Ideals of American criminal justice.* Upper Saddle River, NK: Prentice Hall.

---

Of these five roles, the *typical police officer* in the US spends most of his or her time each day *not* fighting crime. The majority of a police officer's time is spent providing social services (Hess, Orthmann, & Cho, 2013). Services provided by police include checking buildings for security violations, regulating traffic, investigating accidents, providing information to citizens, finding lost children, providing first aid, handling animal calls, mediating disputes, and negotiating settlements between citizens (Cox & Wade, 1998). As noted by Manning (1997, p. 93), "Of the police functions or activities most central to accumulated police obligations, none is more salient than supplying the range of public services required in complex, pluralistic, urban societies." So, although *law enforcer* or *crime fighter* is the stereotypical image of the police officer, the typical city patrol officer or county sheriff in the United States spends the smallest amount of his or her day dealing with crime.

Some would argue that police should spend the majority of their time and effort fighting crime and enforcing the law; these people are more likely politically conservative and favor maintaining status quo arrangements in society. Others — especially political liberals — would like to see the police devote the majority of their time and effort to serving the people (Robinson, 2015). What is clear from even recent policing incidents in the mainstream news is that the more police lose sight of their historic role of serving the people in the communities where they work, the more problems we seem to have with regard to race and ethnicity (e.g., shooting of unarmed civilians, who are often young, urban men of color).

## Law Enforcement Code of Ethics

The International Association of Chiefs of Police issued a code of ethics for police officers that they expect officers across the country will follow. This code is found in Table 5.2. As you see in the table, officers are expected *not* to abuse their discretion and *not* to use excessive force, among many very high expectations for their profession. But of most relevance for issues of race and ethnicity is this statement: "A police officer shall perform all duties impartially, without favor or affection or ill will and without regard to status, sex, race, religion, political belief or aspiration. All citizens will be treated equally with courtesy, consideration and dignity." Thus, we clearly expect police to be "blind" to extra-legal factors like those listed above and treat everyone equally, to the degree possible. Compare this statement with your own experiences with officers as well as major recent stories in the news of officers engaged in allegedly inappropriate and/or biased behaviors and consider whether the realities of policing actually match the ideals.

---

### Table 5.2. Law Enforcement Code of Ethics

All law enforcement officers must be fully aware of the ethical responsibilities of their position and must strive constantly to live up to the highest possible standards of professional policing.

The International Association of Chiefs of Police believes it important that police officers have clear advice and counsel available to assist them in performing their duties consistent with these standards, and has adopted the following ethical mandates as guidelines to meet these ends.

*Primary Responsibilities of a Police Officer*

A police officer acts as an official representative of government who is required and trusted to work within the law. The officer's powers and duties are conferred by statute. The fundamental duties of a police officer include serving the community, safeguarding lives and property, protecting the innocent, keeping the peace and ensuring the rights of all to liberty, equality and justice.

### Performance of the Duties of a Police Officer

A police officer shall perform all duties impartially, without favor or affection or ill will and without regard to status, sex, race, religion, political belief or aspiration. All citizens will be treated equally with courtesy, consideration and dignity.

Officers will never allow personal feelings, animosities or friendships to influence official conduct. Laws will be enforced appropriately and courteously and, in carrying out their responsibilities, officers will strive to obtain maximum cooperation from the public. They will conduct themselves in appearance and deportment in such a manner as to inspire confidence and respect for the position of public trust they hold.

### Discretion

A police officer will use responsibly the discretion vested in his position and exercise it within the law. The principle of reasonableness will guide the officer's determinations, and the officer will consider all surrounding circumstances in determining whether any legal action shall be taken.

Consistent and wise use of discretion, based on professional policing competence, will do much to preserve good relationships and retain the confidence of the public. There can be difficulty in choosing between conflicting courses of action. It is important to remember that a timely word of advice rather than arrest—which may be correct in appropriate circumstances—can be a more effective means of achieving a desired end.

### Use of Force

A police officer will never employ unnecessary force or violence and will use only such force in the discharge of duty as is reasonable in all circumstances.

The use of force should be used only with the greatest restraint and only after discussion, negotiation and persuasion have been found to be inappropriate or ineffective. While the use of force is occasionally unavoidable, every police officer will refrain from unnecessary infliction of pain or suffering and will never engage in cruel, degrading or inhuman treatment of any person.

### Confidentiality

Whatever a police officer sees, hears or learns of that is of a confidential nature will be kept secret unless the performance of duty or legal provision requires otherwise.

Members of the public have a right to security and privacy, and information obtained about them must not be improperly divulged.

*Integrity*

A police officer will not engage in acts of corruption or bribery, nor will an officer condone such acts by other police officers. The public demands that the integrity of police officers be above reproach. Police officers must, therefore, avoid any conduct that might compromise integrity and thus undercut the public confidence in a law enforcement agency. Officers will refuse to accept any gifts, presents, subscriptions, favors, gratuities or promises that could be interpreted as seeking to cause the officer to refrain from performing official responsibilities honestly and within the law. Police officers must not receive private or special advantage from their official status. Respect from the public cannot be bought; it can only be earned and cultivated.

*Cooperation with Other Police Officers and Agencies*

Police officers will cooperate with all legally authorized agencies and their representatives in the pursuit of justice.

An officer or agency may be one among many organizations that may provide law enforcement services to a jurisdiction. It is imperative that a police officer assist colleagues fully and completely with respect and consideration at all times.

*Personal-Professional Capabilities*

Police officers will be responsible for their own standard of professional performance and will take every reasonable opportunity to enhance and improve their level of knowledge and competence.

Through study and experience, a police officer can acquire the high level of knowledge and competence that is essential for the efficient and effective performance of duty. The acquisition of knowledge is a never-ending process of personal and professional development that should be pursued constantly.

*Private Life*

Police officers will behave in a manner that does not bring discredit to their agencies or themselves.

A police officer's character and conduct while off duty must always be exemplary, thus maintaining a position of respect in the community in which he or she lives and serves. The officer's personal behavior must be beyond reproach.

Source: International Association of Chiefs of Police. As printed in Robinson, M. (2009). *Justice blind? Ideals and realities of American criminal justice.* Upper Saddle River, NJ: Prentice Hall.

---

# The Realities of Policing

As with other branches of criminal justice, examined in later chapters of this book, the realities of policing are often not consistent with the ideals. Policing can be viewed as a continuous overlapping of social interactions that are influenced by the behaviors of both the citizens and the officers. In some situations, it is expected that citizens may be acting in a questionable manner due to being the focus of traffic stops, calls for service, or criminal investigations. Officers may also know from experience that certain citizens or particular areas in their communities may have a higher prevalence of mental illness or substance abuse, which clearly affects their ability to interact with others.

However, officers are not privy to much if any leniency, and the behavioral expectations are set forth by agency and professional standards and largely by society. For example, when interacting with the public, officers are expected to maintain professionalism, even when under extreme personal stress due to factors such as caring for a sick child or battling fatigue related to shift work. Simply put, officers are not permitted to have a bad day. Their actions must be rational and calculated, even when encountering significant situational or personal strain, or serious or even fatal consequences can result.

Officer behavior is a vital and complex component of policing and has prompted intense public discourse and investigation. Behaviors, good or bad, can be viewed from the perspectives of the institution or individual. A prominent policing expert paints the picture of *rotten apples* (i.e., a bad or racist individual officers) and *rotten barrels* (i.e., flawed police policies or institutionalized bias in policing) (Walker, 2005). Both can cause direct and significant harm to the community and the agency. In turn, as evidence of poor behaviors accumulates—as in the case or racial and ethnic disparities in police outcomes such as arrest—the trust of the public is damaged. This results in the inability of the police to work in partnership with the community and hinders the ability to reduce crime and disorder.

Before returning to such issues and demonstrating how race and ethnicity actually impact policing, it is important to understand some basic facts about American policing. Below, the authors show that most policing in the US is local in nature, and that most police focus on street crimes.

## Most Policing Is Local

In 2011, there were about 570,000 police officers working in cities the United States (Sourcebook of Criminal Justice Statistics, 2011). As of 2008, there were about 120,000 full-time sworn police officers working for federal agencies, another 60,000 working for state law enforcement agencies, about 57,000 working for special jurisdiction agencies, and almost 3,500 working as constables and marshals. The largest share of these officers (almost 90%) work for local governments, either cities or counties. And city or county agencies employ about 75% of all police officers in the US.

Given these data, it is clear that policing is very much a local level phenomenon. This is consistent with the idea that police should come from the communities which they serve, and have a good relationship with the citizens of the communities they serve. Perhaps of most importance is that when people talk of the *typical cop* in the US, they are talking about a local police officer.

## *Most Police Are Focused on Street Crime*

Given that the large majority of police officers work for local governments, there is little question that the major focus of the typical cop is on street crimes like the Index offenses of the Uniform Crime Reports identified in Chapter 4 of this book. That is, most police officers in the US are on the lookout for murders, robbers, rapists, assaulters, thieves, car thieves, burglars, and arsonists, as well as drug offenders and so forth. And although many local level agencies have *fraud* investigative units—and even though state and federal agencies routinely investigate higher level crimes—Robinson (2009) estimates that less than five percent of all police officers in the US are focused on acts of white-collar and corporate crimes.

This reality has major importance for understanding how race and ethnicity impacts policing in the US: since police are focused almost exclusively on street crime, we should expect them to investigate and then ultimately apprehend the types of people who are most likely to commit those crimes. Whites, who make up a large portion of the US population, tend to make up the majority of offenders for most types of crimes. Yet, as shown in Chapter 4 of this book, people of color (and especially African Americans) are often overrepresented among offenders. Thus, we should expect people of color (and especially African Americans) to be subjected to more police investigations as well as arrests. Later in the chapter we will show that this is true.

Yet, if police officers were focused on white-collar and corporate crimes, there is little question that a huge majority of offenders would be White rather than of color. As suggested in Chapter 3 of this book, that the police do not focus on these types of offenses is largely because of the criminal law, which tends to diminish the severity of these offenses, in spite of the serious harms they impose on society.

If individual police officers are biased against certain groups of people, we may conclude that they are involved in unjust activity; this is an example of *individual discrimination*, first defined in Chapter 1. Yet bias in policing does not require "bad cops." Biased law enforcement only requires bad law. In Chapter 3, it was shown that the criminal law is biased in favor of the interests of the powerful and thus logically against poor people and people of color. Given this fact, enforcement of this law (through policing) will logically reinforce the bias within the law.

This means that even if every individual police officer was not biased, prejudiced, or bigoted, American law enforcement would still be biased because it simply reflects the biases of the law. This is what Robinson (2009) calls *innocent bias*—a bias arising from the law that is not intended by individual actors of criminal justice. According to Robinson (2009), innocent bias can arise from the following factors:

- the particular focus of police on certain types of crimes;
- the location of police on the streets of the United States;
- the use of police discretion;
- the use of *racial profiling*; and
- policing the *war on drugs*.

In a nutshell, it is clear that police are focused on street crime, that they are largely located in the inner cities of America, and that the use of discretion and racial profiling especially in conjunction with the war on drugs produces significant racial and ethnic disparities in criminal justice. Some of these issues are addressed below.

# Persistent Problems with Policing

In spite of the best efforts to reduce serious problems of race and ethnic disparities in policing, some problems persist. Below, the authors examine racial profiling, disproportionate minority contact with police, and excessive use of force by police.

## *Racial Profiling*

*Race* is commonly used in law enforcement in a manner similar to gender, height, or physical build; it is a reasonable way to describe a person or narrow a viable suspect pool. However, when a person is targeted for no other reason than race or ethnicity, a question of *racial profiling* may be raised. **Racial profiling** occurs when police use race or ethnicity (especially skin color) as a sign of risk or dangerousness in people which then impacts the behaviors of officers (e.g., who they pull over and/or question and search people because of their skin color).

Consistent with *contextual discrimination*, police in some jurisdiction are found to use race and ethnicity to profile people, and that African Americans and Hispanics are generally more likely to be stopped, questioned, searched, and arrested by the police than Whites; they are also more likely to have force used against them, including excessive force and lethal force (Walker, Spohn, & DeLone, 2014). Part of this is owed to higher involvement in serious street crime by people of color and part of it is due to *racial profiling* by the police.

Studies routinely find that police most commonly stop, question, search, and arrest people of color, especially African Americans (Britton, 2000). In fact, a meta-analysis of more than two dozen data sets that produced 40 research reports found "with strong consistency that minority suspects are more likely to be arrested than White suspects" (Kochel, Wilson, & Mastrofski, 2011, p. 473). This is probably mostly because police are looking for the types of crimes that people of color are most likely to be involved with (as shown in Chapter 3 of this book), and because there are more police in the places where they live, both of which relate in part to race.

Even for relatively minor offenses such as marijuana possession, it is young, poor African American males who are most likely to be arrested. This is especially true since the early 1990s when the drug war continued to pick up steam as part of the conservative wars on crime and drugs (Nguyen & Reuter, 2012). In fact, national evidence now exists to show that arrests for drug crimes among people of color went up while arrests for Whites did not increase, even as rates of drug use for people of color did not go up; scholars suggest that as economic conditions worsened, police were utilized to step up enforcement of drug offenses (Parker & Maggard, 2005).

A study of drug enforcement in the city of Seattle is particularly revealing. The authors examined drug arrests and police enforcement practices there and found that African Americans were vastly overrepresented among arrests for drug crimes in the city. Specifically, 64% of the people arrested for selling methamphetamine, ecstasy, powder cocaine, crack cocaine, and heroin were African Americans even though the majority of people who sell these drugs are White (Beckett, Nyrop & Pfingst, & Bowen, 2006).

According to the authors, there were three reasons that explained the fact that Blacks made up a majority of those arrested even though most drug dealers are White: 1) the police focused heavily on crack cocaine (the one drug where African Americans were most involved in selling); 2) the police put more emphasis on outdoor drug venues (where African Americans were more likely to be selling); and 3) the police devoted more resources to racially heterogeneous areas (meaning far less attention to predominantly White drug dealing areas) (Beckett et al., 2006).

The authors suggest that race plays either an implicit or explicit role in each of these disparity-producing factors. That is, race helps account for why police targeted certain drugs, places, or people (Beckett et al., 2006). Yet it is not *just* race that explains the greater crack or outdoor markets. First, crack cocaine is perceived as a dangerous drug, even though it is no more dangerous than powder cocaine. It is perceived to be more associated with street-level violence associated with the marketplace than powder; hence, police will devote more resources to it. Second, outdoor markets are more visible and thus are more likely to generate citizen complaints; hence, police will devote more resources to them. Finally, that police devote more resources to racially heterogeneous areas may be explained by the fact that they are more likely to be found in lower-class areas whereas predominantly White outdoor markets are more likely to be found in middle-class areas.

So even though race is *not* the exclusive reason racial disparities exist in Seattle drug arrests (as well as in other large cities and for other crimes), it remains a fact that race has a good deal to do with it. Recall the arguments from Chapter 3 that race and racial stereotypes are so clearly intertwined with perceptions of dangerousness and criminality. That is, "blackness" is now strongly correlated with criminal and it is people of color—especially poor young men of color—whom we fear.

When New York City recently released data on the people it stops and questions using its controversial **stop and frisk policy** meant to reduce crime by identifying people with guns *before* they commit crimes, the data merely served to continue if not intensify a controversy associated with racial disparity. According to the police data, all from 2011, almost 90% of those targeted by the police department through its stop and frisk policy were either African American or Hispanic; together, African Americans and Hispanics make up less than 53% of the city's population (Velez, 2013). Precinct by precinct data showed similar results, including:

- The precinct with the most stops was Brooklyn's 75th (including East New York and Cypress Hills). There, more than 31,000 people were stopped and frisked, and 97% were either African American or Hispanic.
- The precinct with the second highest number of stops was Brooklyn's 73rd Precinct (including Brownsville). There, 25,167 people were stopped and frisked, and about 98% were either African American or Hispanic.
- The precinct with the third highest number of stops was the 115th precinct (including East Elmhurst, Corona and Jackson Heights in Queens). There, 18,156 were stopped and frisked, and about 93% were either African American or Hispanic.

- The precinct with the fourth highest number of stops was the 40th Precinct in the Bronx (covering Mott Haven and Melrose). There, 17,690 were stopped and frisked, and almost 99% were either African American or Hispanic.
- The precinct with the fifth highest number of stops was the 90th precinct in Williamsburg, Brooklyn. There, 17,566 people were stopped and frisked, and about 89% were either African American or Hispanic (Velez, 2013).

A large majority of people stopped and frisked did not have a weapon and were not arrested. Thus, an official with the New York Civil Liberties Union suggested the data proved racial profiling by the police, saying: "While it appears at first blush to be a slick, fact-filled response, nothing in the report can dispute the reality that stop and frisk NYPD-style is targeted overwhelmingly at people of color, so innocent of any criminal wrongdoing, that all but 12% walk away without so much as a ticket" (Velez, 2013). Of course, the police denied they were profiling people based on race and instead insisted they were targeting the people and places were crime risks were highest. Yet, just as with the example of drug arrests in Seattle, race has much to do with why police target certain people and places.

As long as police have discretion, we will find racial disparities in police statistics (Jones, 2012), especially when the stereotypical image of the offender produced by the criminal law and media coverage of crime is a Black man, as discussed in Chapter 3; it is young, poor, minority men who are perceived to be the most threatening to society, and so as the police (including lawmakers, city and county officials, and so forth) perceive a greater social threat—often referred to as the **minority threat** or **racial threat** or **social threat** hypothesis— we can expect arrests and other negative outcomes including police brutality to rise (Smith & Holmes, 2003). According to this hypothesis, police direct more resources to areas where larger portions of the population are made up of people perceived to be dangerous (e.g., people of color).

Numerous studies have investigated racial disparities of traffic stops across numerous American cities (Alpert, Dunham, & Smith, 2007; Rojek, Rosenfeld, & Decker, 2012; Scheb, Lyons, & Wagers, 2009; Tyler & Wakslak, 2004). Some of these studies find evidence of racial profiling, consistent with the idea of *contextual discrimination*. For example, one recent study of a large, Midwestern municipal jurisdiction over an 8-month period found that young, Black males were most likely to be searched by the police for discretionary reasons—i.e., in cases where a search was not required (Tillyer, Charles, & Robin, 2012).

Another way to look for racial profiling is to examine all face-to-face contacts with police. Data from the Bureau of Justice Statistics showed, for example, that in 2005 about 19% of residents aged 16 years or older had some face-to-face contact with a police officer. This is down slightly from 21% in 2002. About nine out of ten people said the police acted properly, although Blacks (82.2%) were less likely than Whites (91.6%) to feel the police acted properly during a contact. At the same time, there were no differences found in the percentages of Whites and Blacks who felt the police behaved improperly when helping with a traffic accident or providing assistance (Robinson, 2009).

Blacks tended to believe the police acted improperly during traffic stops and during criminal investigations (Robinson, 2009). The percentage of drivers who felt their stop was legitimate also varied by race. Nearly nine in ten of White drivers felt the stop was legitimate (87.6%), versus 85.1% of Hispanic drivers and only 76.8% of Black drivers. Pronounced differences by race were found in stops for vehicle checks, as 66.5% of Blacks felt it was appropriate, versus 72.2% of Whites.

According to the data, the most common reason for contact with police in 2005 involved a traffic stop (41% of all contacts), and speeding was the most common reason for being pulled over in 2005. The vast majority of drivers (86%) said they were pulled over for a legitimate reason. Although White, Black, and Hispanic drivers were stopped by police at similar rates, Blacks and Hispanics were more likely than Whites to be searched by the police. This either suggests a higher rate of suspicious behavior on the part of people of color or racial profiling by the police.

Police only found evidence of some form of wrongdoing (e.g., drugs, illegal weapons) in 11.6% of searches, suggesting that the vast majority of people being searched were not involved in any criminal activity (at the time). Those drivers most likely to be arrested were males (three times more likely than female drivers to be arrested), and Blacks (twice as likely as White drivers to be arrested). Black drivers were more likely than White drivers to be arrested (4.5% versus 2.1%, respectively). Hispanics were more likely than Blacks or Whites to receive a ticket (65% versus 56.2% and 55.8%, respectively). Whites were more likely to receive a warning than Hispanics (9.7% versus 5.9%) and also more likely than Blacks to receive a verbal warning (18.6% versus 13.7%, respectively). A higher arrest rate is suggestive of higher rates of wrongdoing by those stopped. The differential in warnings is consistent with possible differential favors by the police. Updated data from 2013 are shown in Table 5.3.

### Table 5.3. Face-to-Face Contacts with the Police, 2013

Black drivers (13%) were more likely than White (10%) and Hispanic (10%) drivers to be pulled over by police in a traffic stop; however, Blacks, Whites and Hispanics were equally likely to be stopped in a street stop (less than 1% each). Among those involved in street or traffic stops, Blacks were less likely than Whites and Hispanics to believe the police behaved properly during the encounter.

About eight in ten drivers involved in traffic stops and six in ten persons involved in street stops believed they were stopped for a legitimate reason. Regardless of the reason for the traffic stop, a smaller percentage of Black drivers (67%) than Hispanic (74%) and White (84%) drivers believed the reason for the stop was legitimate.

When the street or traffic stops involved residents and officers of the same race or Hispanic origin, the individuals were more likely to believe the reason for the stop was legitimate and that police behaved properly than when the stops involved residents and officers of a different race or Hispanic origin.

About 3% of drivers in traffic stops and 19% of persons involved in street stops were searched or frisked by police. White drivers involved in traffic stops were searched at lower rates than Black and Hispanic drivers. During both traffic and street stops, the majority of persons who were searched or frisked did not believe the police had a legitimate reason for the search.

An estimated 31.4 million persons, or one in eight U.S. residents, requested assistance from police at least once in 2011, most commonly to report a crime, suspicious activity or neighborhood disturbance. The majority of persons who requested police assistance in 2011 thought the officers spent an appropriate amount of time with them during the contact (93%) and were helpful (86%). About nine in 10 reported that they were just as likely or more likely to contact the police again for a similar problem.

A larger percentage of persons reporting noncrime emergencies (91%) than persons reporting crimes or neighborhood disturbances (82%) were satisfied with the police response. Similar percentages of Whites, Blacks and Hispanics who reported a crime or neighborhood disturbance thought the police were helpful. Among persons who reported a noncrime emergency, Blacks (83%) were less likely than Hispanics (96%) or Whites (94%) to think the police were helpful.

Other findings include

- In 2011, there were small racial differences in the percentage of drivers who were ticketed. A greater percentage of Black (7%) and Hispanic (6%) drivers were ticketed than White drivers (5%).

- About 1% of drivers pulled over in traffic stops had physical force used against them by police. Of these drivers, 55% believed the police behaved properly during the stop.
- About six in 10 requests for police assistance involved face-to-face contact with an officer.

Source: http://www.bjs.gov/content/pub/press/pbtss11rpa11pr.cfm

---

The complexity and ambiguity of racial profiling incites considerable distrust and confusion among minority citizens. This can lead to a breakdown of cooperation between law enforcement and community members, which further deepens suspicions that law enforcement illegitimately targets certain communities and/or individuals. As the relationship continues to dissipate or remains in a state of disrepair, belief systems are solidified and passed on to younger generations. In communities where profiling and other abuses are currently or historically prevalent, residents may ultimately disregard law enforcement altogether and police themselves. The belief that police unjustly pursue individuals or communities due to race or ethnicity hinders their ability to protect the communities. Residents are often hesitant or unwilling to assist in criminal investigations. If known criminals are actively committing crime or residing in a neighborhood, law abiding residents may turn a blind eye in fear of retaliation or because they do not want any involvement. These are characteristics of communities that lack collective efficacy and social organization. Communities, particularly urban areas, suffering from social disorganization are at an increased risk of crime and victimization (Braga & Clarke, 2014). As shown by years of research, such communities are often urban, disadvantaged, and comprised predominantly of minority residents.

From a crime prevention and enforcement perspective, when determining the most efficient and effective allocation of resources, a common practice is to concentrate efforts that will produce the greatest gains. For example, agencies may focus on **hot spots**, which are locations associated with the highest density of crime and disorder. Another approach is to target volume drivers, whether they are crime types that contribute most to the overall crime rate or known offenders that are prolifically active in the jurisdiction. For communities with significant violent crime rates, the goal may be gang eradication or reduction to alleviate the rates of homicide and other offenses associated with gang activity such as robbery, weapons, or drugs. Due to distrust or a history of discriminatory practices, these efforts may be misconstrued as racially biased rather than sensible responses to crime problems that are grounded in data and logic. However, one would be remiss to overlook the history of abuse endured by minority citizens. Therefore, the question posed is how to discern whether law enforcement behavior is the result of discriminatory beliefs and practices or if appropriate actions are being taken in response to relevant crime problems that are shown to occur in minority communities.

Systematic long-term data for types of police contact (e.g., traffic stops, field interviews, citizen contacts) and officer behavior are not readily available for a considerable proportion of law enforcement agencies. While is it common to maintain records regarding use of lethal or less than lethal force, citizen complaints, and internal affairs investigations, how such information is maintained and its depth of detail widely varies across the approximately 18,000 law enforcement agencies. Therefore, allegations of discriminatory patterns of behavior are more difficult to prove than other types of encounters, such as excessive use of force or illegitimate use of lethal force (which we discuss later in this chapter).

The good news is that, when law enforcement agencies are alleged to practice systematic racial or ethnic discrimination, they may be subject to federal investigation and potential litigation of whether the *Violent Crime Control and Law Enforcement Act of 1994*, 42 U.S.C. §14141 was violated (The United States Department of Justice, n.d.). This authority is delegated to the Special Litigation section of the Civil Rights Division of the United States Department of Justice (DOJ). Agencies of various sizes and notoriety have been investigated and held accountable by employing external mechanisms such as *consent decrees* and *court monitors*. These cases often garner national attention and serve as explicit examples that such behaviors are still an ever-present part of the debate on police professionalism and unlawful treatment of minorities.

Federal litigation is not the only means of corrective action available to some communities. Lawsuits can be initiated by private attorneys as well on behalf of the state legislation that enables them to do so (Walker, 2005). Walker argues that the DOJ is limited in their resources to investigate and bring suit against local law enforcement agencies. Therefore, if equipped with the legal authorization, issues of racial profiling and other abuses can be addressed on a local level.

## *Disproportionate Minority Contact*

A widely respected finding regarding race is that minorities are disproportionately represented in the juvenile justice system and criminal justice system compared to the general population. **Disproportionality** in this context means that the proportion of minorities in the general population is not equal to those in the criminal justice system. In layman's terms, race proportionality is

### Table 5.4. Arrests by Race and Ethnicity, 2011

| | White | Black | Amer. Indian | Asian/Pacific Islander |
|---|---|---|---|---|
| Murder | 48% | 49.7% | 1.3% | 1% |
| Rape | 65% | 32.9% | 1.2% | 0.9% |
| Robbery | 43% | 55.6% | 0.8% | 0.7% |
| Aggravated Assault | 63.9% | 13.6% | 1.5% | 1% |
| Burglary | 66.7% | 31.7% | 0.9% | 0.7% |
| Theft | 68.6% | 28.8% | 1.5% | 1.1% |
| Motor Vehicle Theft | 64% | 33.9% | 1.3% | 0.8% |
| Arson | 72.3% | 25.7% | 1.2% | 0.9% |
| Forgery/Counterfeit | 65.5% | 32.9% | 0.5% | 1% |
| Fraud | 66.5% | 31.8% | 0.9% | 0.8% |
| Embezzlement | 65.5% | 32.4% | 0.5% | 1.6% |
| Weapons | 58.1% | 40.3% | 0.7% | 0.8% |
| Drugs | 66.9% | 31.7% | 0.7% | 0.7% |

Source: http://www.albany.edu/sourcebook/pdf/t4102011.pdf

calculated by the number of individuals from a particular racial category involved with justice systems relative to the number of individuals of the racial category in the general population.

Particularly within law enforcement, minorities represent a greater proportion of arrestees compared to the general population. According to the most recently published Uniform Crime Report statistics, 28.3% of the arrestees in 2013 were Black and 2.9% were other races (U.S. Department of Justice, 2015). Yet an estimator of the general population that utilizes the U.S. Census data shows that, in 2013, 13% of the general population was Black and 7.2% was from other races (Puzzanchera, Sladky, and Kang, 2014).

Among juveniles—defined as younger than 18 years of age regardless of state statutes—minorities made up 37% of the arrestee population with 34.4% being Black and 2.7% from other races (U.S. Department of Justice, 2015). However, minorities only constitute 24.4% of the general juvenile population with 16.6% being Black (Puzzanchera et al., 2014). Clearly, people of color are overrepresented among those arrested. Table 5.4 shows arrests in the US by race and ethnicity.

Arrests serve as the most widely available quantitative measure of contact reported by law enforcement agencies. The UCR counts one arrest for each separate time a person is "arrested, cited or summoned" for one of the 28 monitored offenses in the UCR (U.S. Department of Justice, 2014, para.1). This is an indicator of the number of formal interactions between law enforcement and citizens. However, several factors should be discussed to illustrate that this is a somewhat limited perspective. First, arrests are only one type of interaction. Officers spend a considerable amount of time on other efforts that fall within the five responsibilities of officers identified earlier law enforcement (Walker & Katz, 2012). Second, UCR arrest statistics for juveniles may not accurately reflect delinquent activity. For example, if an adult is arrested with a juvenile for a specific offense, the arrest is considered an adult arrest (Puzzanchera, 2013). Third, an historical limitation of the UCR is that it embraces the hierarchy method of reporting crime, which means only the most serious offense committed in the incident is reported. This means that if multiple crimes were committed in a single criminal event, only one is reported and the other less serious offenses are not counted. These latter two factors together must create hesitation in discerning just how much crime is committed and by whom.

If one were to only rely on crime statistics to discern if minority juveniles commit more delinquent acts than White juveniles, the numbers would suggest that race is a primary determinate factor of delinquent activity. However, other types of research and data collection efforts demonstrate that is too simplistic of an explanation. Studies, such as those reviewed within this discussion, range from longitudinal studies that track juveniles from youth until the end of adolescence (Fite, Wynn, & Pardini, 2009; McAra & McVie, 2007), assessments of juvenile court referrals which originate from arrest (Huizinga et al., 2007), policy and practice guides (National Conference of State Legislatures, n.d.), and theoretical discussions from researchers well-invested in this realm of investigation (Piquero, 2008). This collective body of research illustrates patterns or consistent findings to explain that other factors more prevalent among minority communities and families may have a greater influence on the likelihood of police contact.

To begin, Piquero (2008) discusses two contemporary theories of disproportionate minority contact: *differential involvement* and *differential selection and processing* hypotheses. As shown in Chapter 4, **differential involvement theory** asserts that the disparity between minorities and non-minorities is due to greater levels of criminal activity that are persistent for longer periods of time and that are more serious types of crimes, which leads to greater involvement with the criminal justice system (Piquero, 2008, p. 64). On the surface this explanation is consistent with official statistics. However, Piquero (2008) warns that this proposition is not well researched due to numerous constraints.

**Differential selection and processing theory** is more widely examined and supported (Piquero, 2008). The foundation of this explanation is centered on how minorities are treated differently across the various stages of the juvenile and criminal justice processes. For the purposes of this discussion that is focused on law enforcement, this means that minority juveniles are more likely to garner the attention of law enforcement. One rationalization for the increased attention is that police often purposefully have a greater presence in more criminogenic neighborhoods as a tool for crime prevention. These neighborhoods are often composed of minority residents from a lower socioeconomic status (SES) with higher unemployment or underemployment rates. Further, minority juveniles attend and graduate high school at lower rates (Heckman & LaFontaine, 2011) and therefore may be more visible to law enforcement in their communities because they are not in school. In sum, being a juvenile living in a neighborhood characterized by poverty, higher dropout rates, and more crime may increase the likelihood of being subject to police interaction.

The focus on neighborhood dynamics and its potential influence on the likelihood of police presence and subsequent police contact is prevalent across other research as well (Fite et al., 2009; Huizinga et al., 2007; McAra & McVie, 2007; National Conference of State Legislatures, n.d.). For example, in a longitudinal study of youth, Fite et al. (2009) found that neighborhood problems are a significant factor for young Black males for violent crime, particularly when these problems exist in combination with other individual risk factors such as poor educational attainment and conduct problems. Further, a guide composed with legislators as the target audience strongly emphasizes that race is less of an explanation for the disparities between minority and White juveniles when viewed in the context that it is common police practice to target low-income urban neighborhoods, which increases the likelihood that minorities will be involved with the police (National Conference of State Legislators, n.d.). Both works lend support for differential selection and processing theory.

Another aspect of differential selection and processing theory is the degree of discretion an officer has when responding to a situation regarding a juvenile and how such discretion can be influenced. Piquero (2008) emphasizes this point when reviewing research that demonstrates that a juvenile's demeanor and prior history may persuade an officer's decision. In other words, if a juvenile displays a negative attitude towards the officer or has already been involved with the police, the police may treat him more harshly than a juvenile that is compliant or without prior complaints, even though the offense may be the same. Minority attitudes have been the subject of other research and one specific study finds that how juveniles perceive police treatment of them impacts their attitudes towards the police (Lurigio, Greenleaf, & Flexon, 2009). Other research supports the impact of a juvenile's criminal history as McAra and McVie (2007) found that having a lengthier history with police is a primary indicator of being charged by law enforcement, although other factors also matter such as neighborhood dynamics.

In conclusion, various explanations are readily available to demonstrate why minority youth have disproportionate contact with law enforcement compared to White youth. Statistics alone could paint a picture that youth of color are simply more delinquent and statistics, such as the UCR, are frequently used to make that point. But such an assertion is wildly problematic because any assumption of criminal behavior solely based on the percentage of arrests or criminal activity of a given population relative to their percentage of the overall population ignores too many fundamental contributing factors. These include environmental factors, particularly neighborhood dynamics, individual factors such as poor educational attainment and conduct, and most often a combination of numerous underlying conditions. As suggested by Huizinga et al. (2007), more research is needed that does not examine this incredibly important topic in a vacuum.

## Excessive Use of Force

Using lethal force or a greater degree of less than lethal force than what is necessary by law enforcement is a consistent concern reported by minority communities. Prior to the widespread access to devices that can instantly capture and disseminate images, it was difficult and rare to view visual evidence of police brutality. Thus, it was known about, but difficult to hold an officer accountable without sufficient proof beyond a reasonable doubt. Not until the beating of Rodney King in 1991 by multiple officers was video recorded and provided to the mainstream media did the issue of excessive use of force garner such national attention and demand corrective action. Much of the responses implemented since 1991 involve formalizing policies regarding use of force, increased officer training, more selective recruitment practices, and implementing various types of oversight. While each of these areas of progress will be discussed in the next following section, a few key issues regarding use of force warrants discussion.

Foremost, a universal definition of **use of force** is not available, but it is generally understood as when a police officer has to resort to some level of aggression in order to subdue a suspect. It is widely accepted that two factors must be established to assess the appropriateness of an officer's level of force

(Walker, 2005). The fundamental question is whether the need to utilize force is legitimate. Simply stated, an officer cannot use any type of active force unless it is warranted. **Active force** refers to actions directed towards an individual, whereas **passive force** is indirect such as officer presence which only requires an officer to be within a reasonable distance from an individual.

The second criterion is if the level of force used is reasonable. The purpose of using force is to gain compliance. If the first criterion is not met, no degree of force is reasonable. For example, if an individual cooperates with an officer's request to provide identification, compliance is gained and therefore no amount of force is justified. If the individual refuses to comply and attempts to flee, the officer is authorized to use the amount of force necessary to subdue the subject, but how much force is realistically necessary must be carefully considered. As an extreme point, it is not reasonable to shoot fleeing subjects unless officers perceive there to be imminent danger to themselves or others.

Historically, police were able to shoot **fleeing felons**, a rule that was struck down by the US Supreme Court in the case, *Tennessee v. Garner*, 417 US 1 (1985). The Court ruled by a 6–3 margin that using deadly force against a suspected felon to prevent escape is a violation of the Fourth Amendment; the only time an officer can use lethal force against a suspected felon is when an officer has probable cause to believe the suspect poses a significant threat of violence against the community of officers.

The *Garner* case was based on the case of 15-year-old Edward Eugene Garner, who was shot dead in the back of the head with a police hollow point bullet after allegedly burglarizing a house. Officer Elton Hymon said he saw no evidence that Garner was armed and "figured" that he was unarmed; yet, he shot him dead anyway. In part because of this ruling, police agencies created and/or revised their use of force policies.

Most agencies recognize some variation of the **Use of Force Continuum**. The continuum categorizes the types of force at the officer's disposal and ranks them incrementally according to the severity of force (National Institute of Justice, 2009). The continuum takes into consideration the behaviors of the subject. A simplistic visual presentation is a pyramid, shown in figure 5.1, in which the base signifies the least severe type of force, but as the layers built towards the peak level of force becomes more critical. Because the base is the broadest layer, it represents the type of force that is used most frequently and then narrows to demonstrate that more serious types of force are utilized at lower rates. Officer presence is the most prevalent and least invasive as most citizens comply due to simply being in the presence of an officer and therefore this category serves as the base of the pyramid. For example, many driv-

## Figure 5.1. Use of Force Continuum

ers will push their breaks and check their speed upon seeing an officer as they do not want to receive a citation for speeding, even if they are not currently speeding.

At the other end of the spectrum is lethal force, which is used the least often and has the most detrimental impact. A clear distinction of intent must be made between lethal force and less than lethal force. If an officer determines that the situation warrants lethal force, the goal is to terminate the subject's life or more simplistically to kill. A person can also be fatally wounded by less than lethal force, as demonstrated by cases when officers use weapons such as conducted energy devices (e.g., Tasers). However, the purpose of engaging in that type of force would be to gain control of the situation.

The continuum of force is an administrative and training tool and numerous conceptual and visual models are easily accessible. Therefore, it is important to emphasize there is variation in the depth and flexibility of the models. Also, the models do not confine officers to move across the continuum in a predetermined order. For example, if officers respond to calls for service that demand less than lethal force to obtain compliance, they are authorized to use that level of force. Further, officers are encouraged to deescalate a situation when possible, which broadly means to use techniques (e.g., verbal judo) to reduce the potential need for physical force (Walker & Archbold, 2014). Walker and Archbold (2014) support de-escalation or disengagement as one of the best practices to reduce force by officers. Because policies or standard operating procedures cannot forecast the endless array of potential situations encountered by officers, they are expected to respond within reason given a set of parameters set forth by the officer's training and agency protocols.

Allegations of excessive force assert that lethal force was unwarranted or that the degree or severity of force was unnecessary given the parameters of the particular situation. One approach for determining the reasonableness of force is referred to as the **force factor** which attempts to quantify the level of resistance by the individual in relation to the level of force used by the officer to gain control over the individual (see Terrill, Alpert, Dunham, & Smith, 2003). Using the same scale to measure the degree of resistance and force, the amount of resistance is deducted from the amount of force (i.e., force – resistance = force factor: Terrill et al., 2003, p. 155). The authors emphasize that in order to evaluate the levels of force by both parties, agencies must collect data for both parties rather than just reports for officer behavior. This is crucial to evaluate whether an officer was justified and reasonable.

Data from the Bureau of Justice Statistics show that, in 2005 males, as well as Blacks and Hispanics, suffered from the highest rates of serious police actions following a stop. For example, male drivers were more likely than female drivers to be ticketed and/or arrested. Additionally, while less than 2% (1.6%) of the most recent contacts resulted in the use of force or a threat of force by the police, Blacks and Hispanics were more likely than Whites to have force used against them. Of those who had force used against them, a sizable majority (83%) said they thought the force was excessive. Whites (84.3%) involved in force incidents were only slightly more likely than Blacks (81.5%) to feel the force was excessive (versus 85.6% for Hispanics), although the differences are likely due to random error.

Blacks (4.4%) and Hispanics (2.3%) were more likely than Whites (1.2%) to have force used against them by police in 2005. Although Blacks made up only one out of every ten police contacts, they made up roughly one out of every four contacts where force was used. This is suggestive of either differential suspect behavior by police or a greater willingness by police to use force against Blacks.

National data for police use of force are collected from English-speaking US residents that are 16 years or older as part of the *National Crime Victimization Survey* (NCVS) as a supplement titled **Police-Public Contact Survey** (PPCS) (Langton & Durose, 2013). Findings from the most recent PPCS are shown in Table 5.5. As you can see in table, use of force by the police is actually quite rare. When force is used, it is more often used against males, as well as against Blacks more than Whites or Latinos. Nearly three in four (74%) of citizens felt the use of force was excessive, although less than 20% were injured during the incident.

## Table 5.5. Police Use of Force

- Among persons who had contact with police in 2008, an estimated 1.4% had force used or threatened against them during their most recent contact, which was not statistically different from the percentages in 2002 (1.5%) and 2005 (1.6%).
- Males were more likely than females to have force used or threatened against them during their most recent contact with police during 2008, and Blacks were more likely than Whites or Hispanics to experience use or threat of force.
- Of persons who had force used or threatened against them by police in 2008, an estimated 74% felt those actions were excessive.
- Of those individuals who had force used or threatened against them in 2008, about half were pushed or grabbed by police. About 19% of persons who experienced the use or threat of force by the police reported being injured during the incident.
- Among persons experiencing police use or threat of force in 2008, an estimated 22% reported that they argued with, cursed at, insulted, or verbally threatened the police.
- About 12% of those involved in a force incident reported disobeying or interfering with the police.
- Among individuals who had force used or threatened against them in 2008, an estimated 40% were arrested during the incident.
- An estimated 84% of individuals who experienced force or the threat of force felt that the police acted improperly. Of those who experienced the use or threat of force in 2008 and felt the police acted improperly, 14% filed a complaint against the police.

Source: http://www.bjs.gov/index.cfm?ty=tp&tid=703

Research by an investigative media organization called Propublica shows that "young black males are 21 times more likely to be shot by police than their white counterparts." The data show that: "The 1,217 deadly police shootings from 2010 to 2012 captured in the federal data show that blacks, age 15 to 19, were killed at a rate of 31.17 per million, while just 1.47 per million White males in that age range died at the hands of police" (Harvard School, 2015). Yet it is not only race that predicts stops, searches, arrest, and use of force (including lethal force): research shows the relationship between race and such outcomes are mediated by neighborhood level factors as well as other extra-legal statuses held by citizens and suspects, consistent with the notion of *intersectionality* identified in Chapter 1. Of course, recent cases of fatal shootings as well as other fatal interactions with the police have come to our attention repeatedly in the past couple of years. Most infamous among these are the shooting of unarmed Michael Brown in Ferguson, Missouri (who was shot dead after being warned about walking in the middle of a street), unarmed Jonathan Ferrell in Mecklenberg County, North Carolina (who was shot dead after surviving a car accident and trying to seek help), unarmed 12-year-old Tamir Rice (who was shot dead by two officers seconds after they arrived on the scene of a call from who caller who told the police a male was pointing a pistol at people but that was it was "probably fake" [it was]), unarmed John Crawford in Beavercreek, Ohio (who was shot dead in Walmart while holding a toy gun), and of course Eric Garner (who was strangled to death on camera with an illegal chokehold maneuver in New York City).

The Ferguson case has likely received the most media attention, in part because the officer who shot Brown dead was not even charged in the case, and also because the US Department of Justice subsequently released a damning report about the police department in Ferguson. Although the officer who shot Michael Brown was not charged with any crime by the state of federal government, the report about the Ferguson Police Department (US Department of Justice, 2015) found that officers routinely violated citizens' First Amendment rights, as well as engaged in unconstitutional stops and arrests and used excessive force in violation of the Fourth Amendment. The DOJ held that it was the African American residents that were most harmed by these practices, and that policing there erodes community trust, produced resentment, and endangered public safety. The DOJ also found that the court system in Ferguson imposed substantial and unnecessary barriers to resolving city code violations as well as unduly harsh penalties for missing payments.

The policing numbers are alarming: African Americans make up 67% of the population of Ferguson, but from 2012 to 2014, 85% of vehicle stops were of African American drivers, 90% of citations were given to African Americans, and 93% of arrests were of African Americans. Blacks were more than twice as likely to be searched after a vehicle stop even though they were 26% less likely than Whites to be found in possession of contraband. Finally, about 90% of documented use of force incidents were committed against Blacks.

These findings, according to the DOJ, are attributable partially to racial bias: "Our investigation indicates that this disproportionate burden on African Americans cannot be explained by any difference in the rate at which people of different races violate the law. Rather, our investigation has revealed that these disparities occur, at least in part, because of unlawful bias against and stereotypes about African Americans. We have found substantial evidence of racial bias among police and court staff in Ferguson" (p. 5).

Although these biases can be considered *systematic discrimination*, at least in the city of Ferguson, they count as evidence of *contextual discrimination*, because they amount to biases found in some places and contexts but not others (see Chapter 1). Clearly policing is not like this everywhere; life for African Americans in Ferguson—even in the 21st century—is yet plagued by systematic racial bias at the hands of the police and courts.

## Differences in Perceptions of Police

Although it is difficult to discern patterns of racial profiling across many types of police encounters, traffic stops have provided more ample opportunities to study this complex problem. Unlike the *Uniform Crime Reports* (UCR), a national effort to collect traffic stop data is not currently operating. However, PPCS data are useful here, as well (Langton & Durose, 2013).

Racial profiling is not directly investigated, but a wealth of information regarding drivers' perceptions of their interactions with law enforcement has been generated (Langton & Durose, 2013). Among the many findings, it is demonstrated that minorities are more likely to be ticketed and searched at higher rates than Whites and less likely to believe the reason for the stop was legitimate. Also, Blacks are more likely to believe that the police do not conduct themselves appropriately. When stopped, Hispanics are least likely to believe that being subjected to a record check is justifiable. Further, it indicates that drivers are more likely to view the traffic stop as legitimate when the officer is the same race or ethnicity as the driver. To reiterate, this does not prove racial profiling and it is not the intent of the questionnaire, but it does illuminate how race or ethnicity may correlate with perceptions of legitimate police behavior.

The influence of officer's race or ethnicity is the subject of several additional studies utilizing the PPCS data (Cochran & Warran, 2012; Huggins, 2012). In support of Langton and Durose's (2013) finding that citizens are more positive about their involuntary contact when the officer's race or ethnicity is the same as the driver, both Huggins (2012) and Cochran and Warren (2012) highlight that intra-racial dynamics correlate with greater perceptions of officer legitimacy. When the dynamic is inter-racial, the strongest discord is between Black drivers and White officers as the overall perspective of Hispanic drivers does not differ significantly from other drivers (Cochran & Warren, 2012; Huggins, 2012). Cochran and Warren further suggest that when the officer is a minority, drivers are more likely to report the actions of the officer are legitimate. An obvious conclusion is that increasing officer diversity may reduce negative perceptions among minority drivers. With findings from studies such as the aforementioned one are coupled with the statistic that in 2007 only approximately 25% of local law enforcement officers were identified as a minority and that Hispanics made up about 10% of the local law enforcement community (Bureau of Justice Statistics, 2015), it would seem that the law enforcement community only hires and ethically serves citizens similarly situated to them in race or ethnicity. However, extreme caution must be used before making such conclusions. In the previous studies (i.e., Cochran & Warren, 2012; Huggins, 2012; Langton & Durose, 2013), the proportions of minority drivers and minority officers across the different years of data used are not easily comparable.[1] Also, the PPCS data are collected as part of the NCVS that randomly selects households across the nation to participate and only ascertains accounts from those first willing to participate in the NCVS. Also, there are further methodological limitations discussed by Langton and Durose (2013) that warrant hesitation such as only English-speaking respondents were included and the samples are statistically weighted to reflect the general population.

The exclusion of non-English respondents and weighting samples is common practice in survey research, but it should not be overlooked. However, the critical objection to solely relying on this type of data is that the PPCS and other surveys of perceptions cannot fundamentally inquire whether a particular agency operates with the malicious intent of targeting members of a certain race or ethnicity. Patterns of racial disparity should be investigated within the confines of a particular agency or geographic area and should include data (e.g., years of data, frequency of citizen contacts) that can produce reliable patterns across a variety of demographics, contexts, and outcomes as well as spatial and temporal aspects of the interactions.

# Conclusion

Policing in America is ideally aimed at protecting and serving members of the community where officers work, as well assuring equality in society. Yet, the reality of police practice often conflicts with these ideals. First, most policing is focused on street crime, meaning that the most harmful criminal acts committed in America (i.e., white-collar and corporate crime) are the least likely to produce arrests and subsequent punishment. This also assure racial disparities in policing, since these offenders tend to be White.

---

1. Cochran and Warren used PPCS 2005 data; Huggins utilized data from 1999 survey named "Contacts between Police and the Public"; Langton & Durose utilized PPCS 2011 data.

Second, there are persistent problems in policing that pertain specifically to race and ethnicity. Police continue in some places to engage in racial profiling, which leads not only to disproportionate minority juvenile confinement, but also higher rates of stops, searches, arrests, and excessive force incidents against people of color. Finally, people of color tend to have different perceptions of police as a result of their differential treatment at the hands of police. This not only harms citizens but also policing, making it harder to solve crimes, for example,

# Discussion Questions

1. Outline the ideals of policing in the US.
2. List and define the five major roles of police. Give examples of each.
3. Summarize the law enforcement code of ethics. How does this relate to the ideals of policing?
4. What is meant by the term "the *typical cop*"?
5. Describe where the typical cop works and on what type of crime he or she focuses attention.
6. Define racial profiling? Does it still exist? What is your evidence?
7. Read the US Department of Justice report on Ferguson and then summarize it. Do you think this behavior exists elsewhere? If so, what are the implications for justice? http://www.justice.gov/usao/moe/news/2015/march/Ferguson%20Police%20Department%20Report.pdf.
8. Define *disproportionate minority juvenile contact* and provide evidence for its existence.
9. Summarize use of force and explain why you think minorities are more likely to be exposed to excessive use of force.
10. Do all citizens have positive views of police? Explain.
11. How can readily available statistics, such as the Uniform Crime Report, contribute to a general misperception about the disparity of minorities involved in criminal offenses?

# References

Alpert, G. P., Dunham, R. G., & Smith, M. R. (2007). Investigating racial profiling by the Miami-Dade Police Department: A multimethod approach. *Criminology & Public Policy, 6*(1), 25–55. doi: 10.1111/j.1745-9133.2007.00420.x

Beckett, K., Nyrop, K., Pfingst, L., & Bowen, M. (2006). Drug use, drug possession arrests, and the question of race: Lessons from Seattle. *Social Problems, 52*(3), 419–441.

Braga, A. A., & Clarke, R. V. (2014). Explaining high-risk concentrations of crime in the city: Social disorganization, crime opportunities, and important next steps. *Journal of Research in Crime and Delinquency* published online 30 January 2014. doi:10.1177/0022427814521217.

Britton, N. (2000). Race and policing. *The British Journal of Criminology, 40*(4), 639–658.

Bureau of Justice Statistics. (2015). Local police. Retrieved from http://www.bjs.gov/index.cfm?ty=tp&tid=71.

Cochran, J. C., & Warren, P. Y. (2012). Racial, ethnic, and gender differences in the perceptions of the police: The salience of officer race within the context of racial profiling. *Journal of Contemporary Criminal Justice, 28*(2), 206–227. doi:10.1177/1043986211425726.

Cox, S., & Wade. J. (1998). *The criminal justice network: An introduction.* New York: McGraw-Hill.

Fite, P. J., Wynn, P., & Pardini, D. A. (2009). Explaining discrepancies in arrest rates between black and white juveniles. *Journal of Consulting and Clinical Psychology, 77*(5), 916–927. doi:10.1037/a0016626.

Harvard School (2015). Journalist's resource. Excessive or reasonable force by police? Research on law enforcement and racial conflict in the wake of Ferguson. Retrieved from http://journalistsresource.org/studies/government/criminal-justice/police-reasonable-force-brutality-race-research-review-statistics#sthash.xUFDzbw4.dpuf.

Heckman, J. J., & LaFontaine, P. A. (2010). The American high school graduation rate: Trends and levels. *The Review of Economics and Statistics, 92*(2), 244–262. doi:10.1162/rest.201012366.

Huggins, C. M. (2012). Traffic stop encounters: Officer and citizen race and perceptions of police propriety. *American Journal of Criminal Justice, 37*(1), 92–110. doi:10.1007/s12103-010-9097-8.

Huizinga, D., Thornberry, T. P., Knight, K. E., Lovegrove, P. J., Loeber, R., Hill, K., & Farrington, D. P. (2007). Disproportionate minority contact in the juvenile justice system: A study of differential minority arrest/referral to court in three cities. A report to the Office of Juvenile Justice and Delinquency Prevention (NCJ Report Number 219743). Retrieved from the National Criminal Justice Reference System at http://www.ncjrs.gov/pdffiles1/ojjdp/grants/219743.pdf.

Jones, C. (2012). Confronting race in the criminal justice system. *Criminal Justice, 27*(2), 10–15.

Kochel, T., Wilson, D., & Mastrofski, S. (2011). Effect of suspect race on officers' arrest decisions. *Criminology, 49*(2), 473–512. doi:10.1111/j.1745-9125.2011.00230.x

Langton, L., & Durose, M. (2013, September). *Police behavior during traffic and street stops, 2011.* (Special Report NCJ 242937). U.S. Department of Justice, Office of Justice Programs, Bureau of Justice Statistics.

Lurigio, A. J., Greenleaf, R. G., & Flexon, J. L. (2009). The effects of race on relationships with police: A survey of African American and Latino youths in Chicago. *Western Criminology Review, 10*(1), 29–41.

Manning, P. (1997). *Police work: The social organization of policing* (2nd Ed.). Prospect Heights, IL: Waveland Press.

McAra, L., & McVie, S. (2007). Youth justice?: The impact of system contact on patterns of desistance from offending. *European Journal of Criminology, 4*(3), 315–345. doi:10.1177/1477370807077186.

National Conference of State Legislatures (n.d.). Disproportionate minority contact: Juvenile justice guide book for legislators. Retrieved from http://www.ncsl.org/documents/cj/jjguidebook-dmc.pdf.

National Institute of Justice (2009). The use-of-force continuum. Retrieved from http://www.nij.gov/topics/law-enforcement/officer-safety/use-of-force/Pages/continuum.aspx.

Parker, K., & Maggard, S. (2005). Structural theories and race-specific drug arrests: What structural factors account for the rise in race-specific drug arrests over time? *Crime and Delinquency, 51*(4), 521–547.

Piquero, A. R. (2008). Disproportionate minority contact. *Juvenile Justice, 18*(2), 59–79.

Puzzanchera, C. (December, 2013). *Juvenile arrests 2010.* (Juvenile offenders and victims: National Report Series). U.S. Department of Justice, Office of Justice Programs, Office of Juvenile Justice and Delinquency Prevention.

Puzzanchera, C., Sladky, A., & Kang, W. (2014). Easy access to juvenile populations: 1990–2013. Retrieved from http://www.ojjdp.gov/ojstatbb/ezapop/

Robinson, M. (2009). *Justice blind? Ideals and realities of American criminal justice.* Upper Saddle River, NJ: Prentice Hall.

Robinson, M. (2010). Assessing criminal justice practice using social justice theory. *Social Justice Research 23*, 77–97.

Robinson, M. (2015). *Criminal injustice: How politics and ideology distort American ideals.* Durham, NC: Carolina Academic Press.

Rojek, J., Rosenfeld, R., & Decker, S. (2012). Policing race: The racial stratification of searches in police traffic stops. *Criminology, 50*(4), 993–1024. doi:10.1111/j.1745-9125.2012.00285.x

Scheb, J. M., Lyons, W., & Wagers, K. A. (2009). Race, gender, and age discrepancies in police motor vehicle stops in Knoxville, Tennessee: Evidence of racially biased policing? *Police Practice and Research, 10*(1), 75–87. doi:10.1080/15614260802674081.

Smith, B., & Holmes, M. (2003). Community accountability, minority threat, and police brutality: An examination of civil rights criminal complaints. *Criminology, 41*(4), 1035–1063.

Sourcebook of Criminal Justice Statistics (2011). Table 1.66.2011. Number and rate (per 1,000 inhabitants) of full-time law enforcement employees. Downloaded from: http://www.albany.edu/sourcebook/pdf/t1662011.pdf.

*Tennessee v. Garner*, 417 US 1 (1985).

Terrill, W., Alpert, G. P., Dunham, R. G., & Smith, M. R. (2003). A management took for evaluating police use of force: An application of the force factor. *Police Quarterly, 6*(2), 150–171. doi:10.1177/1098611102250491.

Tillyer, R., Charles, F., & Robin, S. (2012). The discretion to search: A multilevel examination of driver demographics and officer characteristics. *Journal of Contemporary Criminal Justice, 28*(2), 184.

U.S. Department of Justice (2015). Crime in the United States 2013. Retrieved http://www.fbi.gov/about-us/cjis/ucr/crime-in-the-u.s/2013/crime-in-the-u.s.-2013/tables/table-43.

U.S. Department of Justice (2015). Investigation of the Ferguson Police Department. Retrieved from http://www.justice.gov/usao/moe/news/2015/march/Ferguson%20Police%20Department%20Report.pdf.

U.S. Department of Justice (2014). Crime in the United States, 2013. Retrieved from http://www.fbi.gov/about-us/cjis/ucr/crime-in-the-u.s/2013/crime-in-the-u.s.-2013/persons-arrested/arrestmain_final.pdf.

U.S. Department of Justice (n.d.). Conduct of law enforcement agencies. Retrieved from http://www.justice.gov/crt/about/spl/police.php.

Velez, N. (2013). NYPD releases stop-and-frisk data for first time. *New York Post*, February 5. Retrieved from http://www.nypost.com/p/news/local/nypd_releases_stop_frisk_data_whf644ouNc8P7dP8u7NPcJ.

Walker, S. (2005). *The new world of police accountability.* Thousand Oaks, CA: Sage Publication.

Walker, S. & Archbold, C. A. (2014). *The new world of police accountability* (2nd ed.). Thousand Oaks, CA: Sage Publication.

Walker, S. & Katz, C. M. (2012) *The Police in America: An Introduction* (8th ed). Boston, MA: McGraw-Hill College.

# Chapter 6

# The Courts in a Color-Blind Society

*by Marian Williams, PhD*

## Introduction

The United States has a **dual court system**, which is characterized by 50 different state court systems and a federal court system. All states and the federal government organize their court systems as they see fit; as a result, no two court systems are alike. Despite this, each court system in the United States is supposed to follow a process that balances the prosecutor's desire to prosecute and hold offenders accountable with the alleged offender's right to defend himself.

At each stage of the criminal court process, offenders have rights that allow them to fight the charges against them. These rights were first laid out in the Bill of Rights to the US Constitution, shown in Table 6.1.

**Table 6.1. US Bill of Rights**

*Amendment I*

Congress shall make no law respecting an establishment of religion, or prohibiting the free exercise thereof; or abridging the freedom of speech, or of the press; or the right of the people peaceably to assemble, and to petition the Government for a redress of grievances.

*Amendment II*

A well regulated Militia, being necessary to the security of a free State, the right of the people to keep and bear Arms, shall not be infringed.

*Amendment III*

No Soldier shall, in time of peace be quartered in any house, without the consent of the Owner, nor in time of war, but in a manner to be prescribed by law.

*Amendment IV*

The right of the people to be secure in their persons, houses, papers, and effects, against unreasonable searches and seizures, shall not be violated, and no Warrants shall issue, but upon probable cause, supported by Oath or affirmation, and particularly describing the place to be searched, and the persons or things to be seized.

*Amendment V*

No person shall be held to answer for a capital, or otherwise infamous crime, unless on a presentment or indictment of a Grand Jury, except in cases arising in the land or naval forces, or in the Militia, when in actual service in time of War or public danger; nor shall any person be subject for the same offence to be twice put in jeopardy of life or limb; nor shall be compelled in any criminal case to be a witness against himself, nor be deprived of life, liberty, or property, without due process of law; nor shall private property be taken for public use, without just compensation.

*Amendment VI*

In all criminal prosecutions, the accused shall enjoy the right to a speedy and public trial, by an impartial jury of the State and district wherein the crime shall have been committed, which district shall have been previously ascertained by law, and to be informed of the nature and cause of the accusation; to be confronted with the witnesses against him; to have compulsory process for obtaining witnesses in his favor, and to have the Assistance of Counsel for his defence.

*Amendment VII*

In Suits at common law, where the value in controversy shall exceed twenty dollars, the right of trial by jury shall be preserved, and no fact tried by a jury, shall be otherwise re-examined in any Court of the United States, than according to the rules of the common law.

*Amendment VIII*
Excessive bail shall not be required, nor excessive fines imposed, nor cruel and unusual punishments inflicted.

*Amendment IX*
The enumeration in the Constitution, of certain rights, shall not be construed to deny or disparage others retained by the people.

*Amendment X*
The powers not delegated to the United States by the Constitution, nor prohibited by it to the States, are reserved to the States respectively, or to the people.

Source: http://www.archives.gov/exhibits/charters/bill_of_rights_transcript.html

---

Over the course of American history, the rights granted Americans by the US Constitution were expanded and clarified, both by state constitutions as well as through *case law* created by court decisions. Whereas alleged offenders have long enjoyed rights such as the right to a speedy, public, and local trial, the right to be informed of the charges against them, the right to an attorney, and the right to *due process* generally, other rights have been granted more recently. For example, an offender's *initial appearance* before a judge after an arrest must be "without unnecessary delay"; the purpose of this is to reduce the likelihood that police will engage in misconduct between arrest and initial appearance. With regard to this right, every state has its own understanding and definition of what "without unnecessary delay" means, and the Supreme Court of each state ultimately decides by hearing cases appealed to it by defendants accused and/or convicted of crimes.

Despite these protections, many defendants waive their constitutional rights and/or are not given these rights to begin with. For example, about 95% of convictions in state and federal courts are obtained by guilty pleas, with defendants waiving their right to a jury trial (Covey, 2008). Also, in *Baldwin v. New York* (1970), the U.S. Supreme Court ruled that defendants charged with "petty offenses," or those for which less than six months incarceration is authorized, are not entitled to a jury trial. Thus, the ideals of the American courts are quite different from the reality.

In this chapter, the author compares and contrasts the ideals of American courts with its realities. A special focus is placed on the role that race and ethnicity continue to play in the US court system, in spite of efforts to eliminate the effects of extra-legal factors on the judicial process.

# What Are the Courts?

The **courts** are the institutions in the US which interpret broadly written laws to tell us what they mean, which settle disputes when there are disagreements over what the law means and/or how to apply it, and which determine the legal guilt of people accused of delinquency or crime as well as sentence those that are adjudicated delinquent in juvenile courts or convicted in adult courts. When it comes to the criminal justice system, the courts simply take over where the police leave off, so that after a person is arrested and booked, the courts determine what to do with the alleged offender. Figure 6.1 shows the organization of the US court system.

# Functions of the Courts

As noted above, the courts serve numerous functions in American society. At a minimum, these functions include:

- *Making law*—by interpreting broadly written statutes created by state and federal legislative bodies (i.e., state legislatures and Congress), courts actually create law by ultimately determining what laws mean and which parts are constitutional;
- *Solving disputes*—**civil courts** allow individuals to sue for damages— both compensatory and punitive—for violations of civil law (i.e., *torts*). **Criminal courts** allow the government to seek "justice" against those who have allegedly harmed others by committing *crimes*, which are violations of state and federal criminal laws;
- *Specifying due process rights*—since the meaning of the Constitution changes over time as contemporary standards of justice evolve, protections afforded to civilians as well as criminal defendants often change over time, and generally tend to get expanded to include more and more protections (but sometimes lead to erosions of rights, such as in the case of the Fourth Amendment protection against unreasonable search and seizures by the police). The court system is responsible for ensuring that all aspects of the criminal justice system (specifically, police and the correctional system) are performing their roles in a fair and equitable manner; and
- *Maintaining a balance between due process and crime control*—even as they seek to protect due process rights of individuals, courts also are charged with assuring social order by assisting criminal justice agencies

Figure 6.1. US Court System

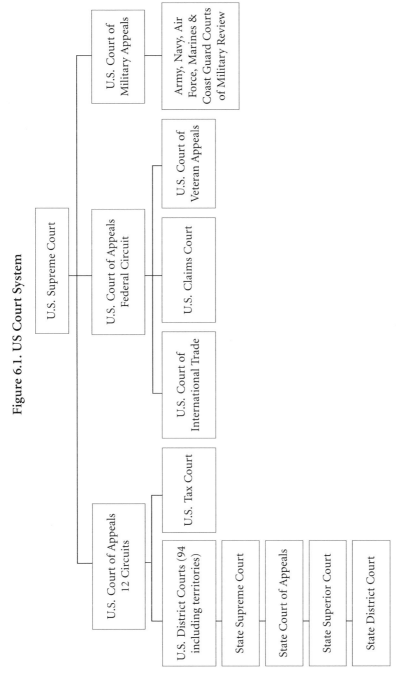

Source: http://www.aoc.state.nc.us/www/copyright/resource/3trans3.gif

with their legitimate fight against crime; thus, courts often allow agencies such as the police the right to seek and gather evidence even in cases where it appears to be inconsistent with individual civil liberties. With regard to the adjudication of offenders, the court system follows a process of adjudication which allows prosecutors to investigate and file charges against offenders, but also allows offenders the right to defend themselves in open court. As such, prosecutors are bound by provisions in the U.S. Constitution and the Bill of Rights when seeking to prosecute offenders. These provisions, such as the right against self-incrimination and the right against double jeopardy, serve to protect offenders from an overreaching government.

## Ideals of American Courts

As noted in Chapter 2, the American court system ideally operates as an **adversarial system**, where the prosecution represents the interests of the people as they seek to obtain "justice" for crime victims and the defense tries to assure "justice" for the person(s) charged with the crimes. In the ideal, the criminal courts operate as a battle for the truth between one side which seeks to make sure guilty offenders are punished for their wrongdoings, and the other side which seeks to assure that the due process rights of the accused are protected so that innocent people are not wrongly convicted and to assure fairness in judicial processes. The best representation of this adversarial system would be the **criminal trial** where individual defendants enjoy the *presumption of innocence* and the government has the burden to prove guilt *beyond a reasonable doubt*.

Figure 6.2 illustrates the typical phases of a criminal trial. These stages occur in each trial, the goal of which is to determine the legal guilt of the defendant, as well as the criminal sentence for those convicted of crimes.

## Realities of American Courts

As mentioned earlier, the reality of American courts is vastly different from the ideals of the American courts. Instead of an adversarial system, American courts generally utilize an administrative approach where the prosecution, defense, and judges all seek the same outcome—to dispose of cases as quickly as possible. Under this approach, guilt of the accused is assumed, explaining why about 95% of convictions in state and federal courts are obtained by guilty pleas, as noted above. Table 6.2 shows the number of plea bargains in state and federal courts.

## Figure 6.2. Stages of the Criminal Trial

| Voir dire | • Jury selection by both sides<br>• Goal to obtain a fair jury |
|---|---|
| Opening statements | • A promise of what is to come by both sides<br>• Cannot be argumentative and is not evidence |
| Prosecution case | • State goes first because it has burden of proof<br>• Must prove case beyond reasonable doubt |
| Defense case | • Defense is not required to put on case if prosecution case is not proven |
| Rebuttal witnesses | • Both sides can call additional witnesses to refute claims made during trial |
| Jury instructions | • Both sides influence these written instructions with guidance from the judge |
| Verdict | • Jury delivers verdict of guilty or not guilty to court |

## Table 6.2. Plea Bargaining in American Courts

State Courts(2006)
        Total convictions                    1,132,290
        Convictions via plea bargaining   1,064,353 (94%)
Federal Courts (2010)
        Total convictions                    89,741
        Convictions via plea bargaining   87,418 (97%)

Sources: http://www.albany.edu/sourcebook/pdf/t5442006.pdf; http://www.albany.edu/sourcebook/pdf/t5462006.pdf

Under **plea bargaining**, the accused agrees to plead guilty without trial, in exchange for a reduction in charges and/or a less severe sentence; pleading guilty requires that defendants agree to waive their rights to a trial, to offer a defense, to confront their accuser(s), to appeal their conviction and sentence, and so forth. None of the stages of the criminal trial occur in plea bargaining, because plea bargaining does not involve a jury or any proving of facts against a defendant. Instead, guilt is assumed and the only issues are which charges will the defendant agree to plead guilty to, and what will be the criminal sentence?

In spite of this reality, courts continue to be seen as arbiters of "justice" and "fairness," but they are not immune from allegations of discrimination and disparity. It is well known that the court system (or, rather, the actors within the court system) has issued discriminatory rulings. One such instance was the U.S. Supreme Court case *Plessy v. Ferguson* (1896), in which the Court ruled that "separate but equal" public facilities for Blacks and Whites were constitutional. Although overruled in 1954 by *Brown v. Board of Education*, the *Plessy* decision is evidence that the court system—in this case, the U.S. Supreme Court—is not necessarily an arbiter of "justice" or "fairness." Nor was it designed to assure equality across races and ethnicities. There remains questionable treatment of certain individuals in the court system and these are discussed below.

# Disparities in American Courts

In spite of the tremendous progress America has made in terms of achieving fairness and equality within government institutions and across criminal justice processes, disparities remain within criminal justice agencies. In the sections that follow, the author examines disparities in pre-trial outcomes and trial outcomes. Disparities in sentencing are discussed in Chapter 7.

## *Disparities in Pre-Trial Outcomes*

**Pre-trial processes** in the court system encompass a wide range of procedures; these include first appearance, appointment of counsel, preliminary hearings, and plea agreements. However, three issues—bail hearings, the right to counsel, and jury selection—are fraught with racial issues that have yet to be remedied.

**Bail hearings.** The Eighth Amendment to the U.S. Constitution prohibits the use of excessive bail by the government; it does not give defendants the right to bail. However, many states grant the right to bail through statute. As such, defendants are subject to bail hearings to determine if they will be released pending the outcome of their case. Research on bail hearings is not extensive, but it has enjoyed an increase in attention in the past ten years. This research has largely focuses on racial disparities in both the granting of bail by judges and the ability of defendants to secure their release.

Regarding the granting of bail by judges, Reaves (2103) stated that less than 5% of defendants are actually denied bail and, of these, 45% are charged with murder. Therefore, most defendants are given the opportunity to make bail. Thus, it would appear as if race is not a significant factor in determining pre-trial release. A number of studies have found that there are no race effects in pretrial release decisions (see Albonetti, 1989; Holmes et al., 1987); however, other studies have indicated that race effects exist, consistent with the notion of *contextual discrimination* defined in Chapter 1 (see Demuth & Steffensmeier, 2004; Wooldredge, 2012). Therefore, are judges taking into account a defendant's race when making a bail decision? Studies have indicated that the seriousness of the charge is the primary determinant of bail decisions by judges (Gottfredson & Gottfredson, 1986; Walker, 2006), but **extra-legal factors** (i.e., factors outside of the law which are not supposed to impact cases) have also been implicated. For example, the gender of the defendant has affected bail decisions, in that female defendants are treated more leniently than male defendants (Daly, 1989; Demuth & Steffensmeier, 2004; Williams 2013).

With regard to race, Wooldredge (2012) states that some studies have found race effects, but that they are not as direct as the gender effects. One of the reasons for this is perhaps due to the strong relationship between race and economic disadvantage. Since bail decisions are economic in nature, poor defendants are less able to secure their release, even when given the opportunity for release. Black defendants are overrepresented among poor defendants; thus, they are less likely to be released (Richey-Mann, 1993). This is also true for Hispanic defendants (Demuth & Steffensmeier, 2004; Holmes et al., 1996). Another reason could be that Black and Hispanic defendants are charged with more serious crimes; therefore, another indirect effect of seriousness of the crime affects the ability of Black and Hispanic defendants to be released.

Finally, some researchers dismiss the indirect effects of economic disadvantage and crime seriousness and posit that direct effects do exist with regard to race and pretrial release decisions. These researchers argue that judges take into account certain stereotypes about offenders and this influences their decisions directly. For example, Steffensmeier et al. (1998) argue that judges rely on stereotypes when assessing whether defendants would be threats to public safety if released. In these stereotypes, Black defendants, particularly those who are young and male, are seen as more dangerous to the community and, thus, more likely to receive an unfavorable bail decision. Hispanics may also be subject to these stereotypes, as Steffensmeier and Demuth (2004) indicate that Black *and* Hispanic defendants are less likely to be released, even when controlling for legal factors such as seriousness of the crime. It is important to note that stereotypes of race and ethnicity do not require overt racism to exist.

Regardless of the reason for the inability of a defendant to obtain pretrial release, the fact that many defendants are not released leads to repercussions as the case moves along. Defendants who are not able to secure their release are more likely to be convicted, to receive more severe sentences, and to suffer economic and personal losses during the time they are incarcerated (Wooldredge, 2012).

**Right to counsel.** The Sixth Amendment states that a defendant has the right to the assistance of counsel. Initially, this was interpreted to mean that a defendant could have an attorney present if he/she could afford one. Today, this right extends to defendants who are deemed too poor to afford an attorney. This equates to approximately 80% of defendants in state courts (Office of Justice Programs, 2011; Wolf Harlow, 2000).

Since a large majority of defendants in the court system need appointed counsel, many attorneys who provide such counsel are inundated with cases to defend. This, coupled with a lack of adequate funding, has caused a crisis in indigent defense. According to Majd and Puritz (2009), funding for indigent defense usually comes from state and local sources. State-funded systems generally provide better defense services than local or county-funded systems. Local systems vary in terms of the revenue that is generated for indigent defense. Affluent communities are able to provide enough revenue for a number of services, but low-income areas typically cannot. This clearly harms people of color, who tend to be disproportionately poor. Majd and Puritz (2009) argue that low-income areas have higher crime rates and are disproportionately comprised of minorities and, as a result, "the counties most in need of indigent defense services are often the ones that least can afford to pay for it" (p. 550).

Also, according to Marcus (1994), the underfunding of indigent defense leads to inadequate representation of poor defendants, such that case outcomes for defendants with appointed counsel could be markedly different than case outcomes for defendants with retained counsel. Some studies have supported this contention; these studies indicate that defendants with appointed counsel are more likely to be detained pending the outcome of their cases (Farrell & Swigert, 1978; Williams, 2013), to be convicted (Nagel, 1973; Silverstein, 1965; Williams, 2013), to plead guilty (Anderson & Heaton, 2012; Champion, 1989), and to be incarcerated (Gitelman, 1971; National Center for State Courts, 1992). Marcus (1994) argues that disparate case outcomes due to the type of defense attorney used are an assault on the poor and, by extension, minorities and are, therefore, a violation of due process.

**Charging decisions.** The importance of the right to counsel becomes even more evident when the power of the prosecutor is highlighted. Prosecutors have the most discretion of any actor in the court system and this discretion is on display during the charging decision. According to Davis (2007), the decisions of prosecutors, " ... control ... the direction and outcome of criminal cases and have greater impact and more serious consequences than those of any other criminal justice official" (p. 5). In the charging decision, prosecutors decide if they want to charge defendants and, if so, what those charges will be.

This decision is based on a number of factors—lack of evidence, victim apprehension, considerations of fairness, etc.

Yet extra-legal factors also play a role in a prosecutor's decision to charge. For example, Spohn, Gruhl, and Welch (1987) state that Black and Hispanic defendants are more likely to be prosecuted, controlling for seriousness of the charge. The authors stated that this was more prominent in "marginal" cases, or those that could go either way with regard to charges. This was supported by Crutchfield et al. (1995), who state that prosecutors are more likely to file charges against Black and Hispanic defendants than White defendants, controlling for the seriousness of the charge. Differential charges were more pronounced in violent and drug offenses. Relatedly, Bernstein et al. (1977) found that Black defendants were less likely to receive charge reductions compared to White defendants. This is supported in later research by Farnsworth and Teske (1995).

That race and ethnicity seem to matter in marginal cases that could go either way—charges or no charges—makes sense when you consider that it is here where race and ethnicity *can* impact decision-making. That is, in contemporary America, it would be extremely hard for court actors to treat people differently across races and ethnicities when it comes to serious crimes such as murders; in these cases, the most important determinants of charging decisions by prosecutors are the quantity and quality of evidence against the accused (Walker, 2006). In borderline cases, where the evidence is not as clear, prosecutors have *discretion* to press charges or not, as well as which charges to press; this allow racial and ethnic biases to creep into the judicial process (Walker, Spohn, & DeLone, 2004).

In the study conducted by Crutchfield et al. (1995), differences in charging decisions were more pronounced in violent and drug offenses. Other studies have indicated that differences also occur in sexual assault cases, especially if the defendant is a minority and the victim is White. Some researchers have indicated that sexual assault cases involving Black defendants and White victims may be more likely to result in charges than other defendant-victim race dyads (Chandler and Torney, 1981; Spohn, 1994). Other research, however, refutes these results (Alderden & Ullman, 2012; Spohn & Spears, 1996). Kingsnorth et al. (1998) speculate that the seriousness of the offense drives charging decisions in these cases, regardless of the race of the defendant and victim. Yet, once a defendant has been charged with sexual assault, the likelihood of conviction and the punishment may involve racial considerations (Kingsnorth et al., 1998).

**Guilty pleas.** Although the right to a trial by jury is embedded within the U.S. Constitution, the vast majority of defendants to not have such a trial. Instead, approximately 90% of convictions in state and federal courts are the result of guilty pleas (Covey, 2008). Johnson (2003) differentiates between two types of guilty pleas and indicates that race plays more of a role in one than the other. In non-negotiated guilty pleas, prosecutors and judges exercise the least amount of discretion because there is nothing to negotiate; defendants are treated according to the "going rate" for their offenses. As such, extra-legal factors, such as race, rarely come into play. For negotiated pleas, however, discretion is increased and prosecutors are able to use their own judgment with regard to what charges to file and what sentences to recommend. This allows extra-legal factors to enter into negotiations (Johnson, 2003).

Relatedly, the strength of the evidence and the seriousness of the charge tend to predict guilty pleas for many defendants; that is, stronger evidence and more serious charges entice a defendant to plead guilty in order to receive a less severe sentence (Mather, 1979). However, Johnson (2003) noted that Black and Hispanic defendants who pleaded guilty through negotiated pleas were more likely to receive upward departures in their sentences compared to White defendants. In other words, they were given a sentence above the recommended range for the crime committed. This could partially explain why, in general, Black and Hispanic defendants are less likely to plead guilty than go to trial, even when controlling for evidence and offense seriousness (Albonetti, 1990; Johnson, 2003; LaFree, 1980). In effect, even if a negotiated plea gives them a lesser sentence than they would have gotten at trial, Black and Hispanic defendants are still treated more punitively than White defendants.

Other reasons for Black and Hispanics not engaging in guilty pleas are speculative. For example, Albonetti (1990) states that Black defendants may have less confidence in the court system to abide by the provisions of the plea agreement. Also, Black defendants may feel that, by pleading guilty, they are not given their full panoply of rights (Albonetti, 1990). Finally, LaFree (1980) and Albonetti (1990) state that, perhaps, prosecutors may be unwilling to offer guilty pleas to Black defendants or that the attorneys for Black defendants are unable to negotiate a favorable settlement.

**Jury selection.** One of the most controversial issues in the court system is the relationship between race and jury selection. A number of U.S. Supreme Court cases have addressed the issue; with the Court ultimately stating that jury selection practices based on race are unconstitutional (see *Batson v. Kentucky*, 1986). The journey to the *Batson* decision was fraught with controversy, however, and, even today, this decision has critics.

The right to a jury trial is found in three places within the Constitution. First, Article III states that, "[t]he trial of all crimes, except in cases of impeachment, shall be by jury." Second, the Sixth Amendment to the Constitution states that, "[i]n all criminal prosecutions, the accused shall enjoy the right to a speedy and public trial, by an impartial jury ..." Finally, the Seventh

Amendment to the Constitution states that, "[i]n suits at common law, where the value in controversy shall exceed twenty dollars, the right of trial by jury shall be preserved …." Thus, it has been argued that the right to a jury trial was deemed exceedingly important by the Framers, both for potential jurors and defendants. For potential jurors, the opportunity to participate in a democratic process was deemed essential to " … safeguard … a person accused of crime against the arbitrary exercise of power by prosecutor or judge" (see Duncan v. Louisiana, 1968).

Additionally, the rights of potential jurors must be protected so that the public has faith in the system of justice and that potential jurors are not excluded due to stereotypes about their fitness to serve. This, in turn, denies the defendant the right to a fair and impartial jury of his peers. In *Strauder v. West Virginia* (1880), the U.S. Supreme Court overturned a West Virginia statute that only allowed White men to serve on juries. Strauder was a Black defendant who claimed that an all-White jury violated his constitutional rights. The Court agreed, stating that,

> [t]he statute of West Virginia which, in effect, singles out and denies to colored citizens the right and privilege of participating in the administration of the law as jurors because of their color, though qualified in all other respects, is, practically, a brand upon them, and a discrimination against them which is forbidden by the amendment. It denies to such citizens the equal protection of the laws, since the constitution of juries is a very essential part of the protection which the trial by jury is intended to secure. The very idea of a jury is that it is a body of men composed of the peers or equals of the person whose rights it is selected or summoned to determine; that is, of persons having the same legal status in society as that which he holds. (p. 304)

Despite this ruling, Fukurai, Butler, and Krooth (1993) state that the future of race and jury selection was far from over. The idea that juries should be composed of the "peers or equals" of defendants was difficult to fully put into place. This was later defined as a "cross-section of the community," but this proved problematic as well. The issue is that states have certain requirements for members of the public to serve as jurors, such as voter registration. The problem with this was illustrated in *Patton v. Mississippi* (1947), in which an all-White jury convicted a Black defendant of murder. During jury selection, it was noted that, of the adult Black population of 12,511, only 25 Blacks were deemed as "qualified electors." Although the U.S. Supreme Court reversed the conviction, it illustrated the problem of finding Black citizens who were qualified to serve.

Another U.S. Supreme Court case addressed the standard of "cross-section of the community." In *Swain v. Alabama* (1965), the Court upheld the conviction of a Black defendant who was convicted by an all-White jury. Even though eight of the potential jurors were Black, they were all dismissed. When Swain claimed that an all-White jury was a violation of his constitutional rights, the U.S. Supreme Court disagreed. Justice White stated that proportionate representation was not required on every jury and, unless purposeful discrimination was shown, then a disproportionate jury based on race was acceptable. One of the issues highlighted in this case was the use of *peremptory challenges*. "Challenges" allow prosecutors and defense attorneys to remove potential jurors from the jury pool. **Challenges for cause** are utilized when attorneys wish to remove jurors for specified legal reasons. These reasons are outlined in state statutes and include such things as not being a citizen of the state in which the trial is taking place, being related to someone involved in the trial, and not being charged with a crime. These challenges must be specified to the court and are unlimited in number. **Peremptory challenges** enable attorneys to remove jurors for no specified reason. The reason can be anything from a juror smiling too much to a juror being a woman. Thus, an attorney can use his peremptory challenges to remove only women, only Blacks, or only Catholics and, as such, these have been used in the past to stack the jury in favor of or against a defendant. Due to this, there are a limited number of peremptory challenges allowed for each side.

In the *Swain* case, two of the original eight potential jurors were excused due to legal reasons, but the remaining six were removed by prosecutors using their peremptory challenges. Though Fukurai, Butler, and Krooth (1993) argue that this was obvious racial exclusion, the Court disagreed, stating that the removal of Blacks through peremptory challenges is permissible, "on the assumption that the prosecutor is acting on acceptable considerations related to the case he is trying, the particular defendant involved, and the particular crime charged" (p. 224) and, in this case, Swain could not prove that the prosecutor was "bent on striking Negroes" (p. 227).

Peremptory challenges have long been the subject of intense scrutiny due to attorneys' ability to remove potential jurors for discriminatory reasons. In *Batson v. Kentucky* (1986), the U.S. Supreme Court addressed the use of race in peremptory challenges. The Court affirmed its ruling in *Swain*, stating that the use of race in peremptory challenges is prohibited. The Court stated that "purposeful discrimination" not only violates the juror's right to serve, but also the defendant's right to equal protection of the laws, "because it denies him the protection that a trial by jury is intended to secure" (p. 87). That is, the jury trial is to, "safeguard … a person accused of crime against the arbitrary exercise of power by prosecutor or judge"(Duncan v. Louisiana,1968, p.156). As a result, "those on the venire must be 'indifferently chosen,' to secure the defendant's right under the Fourteenth Amendment to 'protection of life and liberty against race or color prejudice'" (Strauder v. West Virginia, 1880, p. 309).

The U.S. Supreme Court has recognized that race discrimination has occurred in jury selection procedures; however, has race discrimination been eliminated in such procedures? According to the Equal Justice Institute (2010), there is still widespread racial discrimination in jury selection. One of the reasons for this is the low standard of proof promulgated by the U.S. Supreme Court in *Batson v. Kentucky* (1986). If a defendant feels that race is a factor in jury selection, he must make a prima facie showing that a prosecutor utilized race as a basis for the challenge. According to Weddell (2013), "[t]his includes proving that the defendant is a member of a cognizable racial group and that there is a pattern of excluding members of this racial group through the use of peremptory challenges" (p. 473). After this, the prosecutor must provide a race-neutral reason for dismissing certain jurors. This is problematic for the defendant, because, according to the Justice Marshall's concurring opinion in *Batson*,

> [a]ny prosecutor can easily assert facially neutral reasons for striking a juror, and trial courts are ill-equipped to second-guess those reasons. How is the court to treat a prosecutor's statement that he struck a juror because the juror had a son about the same age as defendant ... seemed 'uncommunicative' ...'never cracked a smile' and, therefore 'did not possess the sensitivities necessary to realistically look at the issues and decide the facts in this case' (p. 106).

Indeed, according to the Equal Justice Initiative's (2013) research in eight states, "[p]rosecutors have struck African Americans from jury service because they appeared to have 'low intelligence,' wore eyeglasses, walked in a certain way, dyed their hair, and countless other reasons that the courts have rubber-stamped as 'race-neutral'" (p. 18, 24). In *Batson*, Justice Marshall also contends that prosecutors could lie about their reasons for dismissing a juror and there really is no way of knowing whether it is true or false. Due to this, the legacy of *Batson* suggests that racial discrimination is alive and well during jury selection (Weddell, 2013). The consequences not only include racially biased juries involving cases especially with Black defendants, but at times even the difference between life and death in capital cases (Walker et al, 2004).

## Disparities in Trial Outcomes

As noted earlier, Black and Hispanic defendants are less likely to plead guilty and will instead go to trial (Albonetti, 1990). A number of studies have indicated that race plays a role in jury decision-making (see Sommers & Ellsworth, 2001; Sweeney & Haney, 1992). As indicated in *Batson v. Kentucky* (1986), Black defendants facing all-White juries are at an extreme disadvantage and this has played out in the research. Walker, Spohn, and DeLone (2004) argue that Black defendants who are tried by all-White juries are disproportionately convicted. In earlier research, Kalven and Zeisel (1966) noted that judges in their study felt that juries were prejudiced against Black defendants.

Many current studies on the effect of race on jury decision-making utilize mock juries. Mock juries tend to utilize college students or do not do a very good job at simulating an actual jury trial (e.g., not giving jury instructions, not giving the jury enough time to deliberate, etc.) (King, 1993). Nonetheless, these studies do provide some insight into jury decision-making.In a meta-analysis of 34 studies, Mitchell et al. (2005) indicated that race plays a role in conviction, in that jurors are more likely to find a defendant guilty if the defendant is of a different race than the juror. This was particularly true if the defendant was Black and the juror was White.

Specific studies measured in the meta-analysis by Mitchell et al. (2005) provide some detail. Klein and Creech (1982) showed a video summary of a trial to mock White jurors. One group of White jurors saw a video featuring a Black defendant, while a second group of White jurors saw the same video as the first group, but the defendant was now White. Results indicated that the White jurors who watched the video featuring the Black defendant were more likely to conclude the defendant was guilty than the White jurors who watched the video featuring the White defendant.

Johnson et al. (1995) also provided summaries to mock jurors to gauge the relationship between race and decision-making. In this study, Johnson et al. (1995) provided White mock jurors with two summaries of a bank robbery trial; in one summary, the defendant was Black, and in the second summary, the defendant was White. The authors also introduced incriminating evidence of a confession that was ruled inadmissible. The White jurors who heard the summary with the White defendant tended to ignore the inadmissible evidence, but this was not the case with the White jurors who heard the summary with the Black defendant. In effect, the inadmissible evidence was held against the Black defendant, but not the White defendant (1995).

In another instance of mock jury research, Perez et al. (1993) showed a videotaped trial to White and Hispanic jurors. One video featured a White defendant, while a second video featured a Hispanic defendant. The authors stated that White-majority juries were more likely to convict when the defendant was Hispanic, but there was no difference in conviction rates for the defendants when the jury was majority Hispanic.

Figure 6.3. Race/Ethnicity and Exonerations from
Death Row in the US since 1973

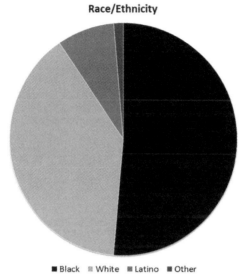

Source of data: http://deathpenaltyinfo.org/innocence-and-death-penalty#race

Mock and real jury research also indicates that the type of crime plays a role in whether Black or Hispanic defendants are more likely to be convicted compared to Whites. For example, research has shown that in cases where the death penalty is a possible punishment, there are increased odds that a Black defendant will be convicted by a jury, with that same jury then recommending death (see Baldus et al., 1998). Similarly, Black defendants accused of rape or sexual assault are more likely to be convicted, especially if the victim is White (see Johnson, Griffith, & Barnaby, 2013; LaFree, Reskin, & Visher, 1985).

One of the consequences of juries utilizing race when convicting defendants is **wrongful convictions**, meaning the wrong person is convicted of a crime he or she did not commit. According to Smith and Hattery (2011), data from the Innocence Project reveal that Black males represent approximately 70% of exonerees and this increases to 84% when taking into account rape cases in which Black males were convicted of raping and/or murdering White females. According to the authors, "... [Black] men are four times more likely to be exonerated for raping White women compared to the number of times they actually commit this crime" (p. 83). Figure 6.3 shows the racial and ethnic breakdown of people exonerated from death row in the US since 1973. As you can see, African Americans make up more than half of those freed from death row.

# Explanations for Disparities

According to some researchers, the reasons for the differential treatment of Black defendants can be traced to a long, cultural history of racism in this country. According to Gaertner and Dovidio (1986), although overt racism is not a prevalent as in the past, it still occurs in more subtle forms. Whites may harbor racist ideas even though their overt actions do not reflect this. Sommers and Ellsworth (2003) contend that Whites, " … who sincerely believe themselves to be non-prejudiced often harbor anti-Black sentiment that influences their behavior" (p. 1012). An example of this, according to Kinder and Sears (1981), is opposition to affirmative action policies. Johnson (1998) attributes this to what she calls "unconscious racism." In effect, racist attitudes may not be conscious, but racist behavior may still occur.

In the courtroom, this may play a role in prosecutors' decisions. As evidenced in *Batson v. Kentucky* (1986) and other U.S. Supreme Court cases, race has played a role in prosecutors' decisions during jury selection. Whether this was due to racist attitudes and behaviors or to trial strategy has been debated. However, there is no doubt that the result of such behavior was differential treatment of Black jurors and defendants.

From a victim standpoint, Hernandez (1989) implies that prosecutors are less likely to vigorously investigate and prosecute hate-motivated crimes and that prosecutors may not see Black victims as credible as White victims. Hernandez (1989) and Johnson (1988) wonder from where these particular attitudes are coming. It is argued that prosecutors and others may not see their behaviors as racist, but as merely a reality of the system. However, Gaertner and Dovidio (1986) argue that the history of racism in this country plants the seed in everyone's mind and that racist attitudes and behaviors will come to the surface eventually. Gibbs (1988) argues that mass media play a role in showing Black males as dangerous and dysfunctional, which may allow racist behaviors to surface.

Relatedly, Steffensmeier, Ulmer, and Kramer (1998) posited a **focal concerns theory** of sentencing that has since been applied to other decision-making points. The theory explains that there are three factors that judges take into account when sentencing. First, the blameworthiness of the offender is considered, which factors in the offender's culpability and the degree of harm suffered by the victim. Second, the protection of the community is considered, reflecting the desire to incarcerate the offender so that public safety is preserved. Finally, practical constraints and consequences are featured, which focus on the effects of the sentencing decision not only on the court itself, but also on the offender. Since judges do not have complete information at their disposal when making a sentencing decision, they rely on "perceptual short-hand" or stereotypes about certain offenders and behaviors.

Steffensmeier, Ulmer, and Kramer (1998) argue that judges and other court actors are not immune to the cultural history and mass media effects with regard to race. In their research, they found that young, Black males are seen as more dangerous and more of a threat to the community than other defendants. Also, judges did not feel that Black defendants would be harmed as much as White defendants by going to prison. The authors also found that Black defendants were seen as less "reformable" than White defendants.

Relying on this focal concerns perspective, a number of researchers examined other decision-making points in the court process and found that the focal concerns theory is supported. Steffensmeier, Ulmer, and Kramer (1998) stated that blameworthiness and protection of the community were the primary determinants of many decisions in the criminal justice process. Demuth (2003) focused on the bail decision, stating that perceptual shorthand would be even more pronounced during this stage because judges have even less information before them than at the sentencing stage. Along with the perceptual shorthand about Black defendants, Demuth (2003) argued that Hispanic defendants may also be subject to stereotyping due to their immigration status and risk of flight. The results of Demuth's (2003) research support this, claiming that Hispanics were treated more harshly during the bail process and this was attributed to stereotypes about Hispanics and drug use/trafficking. Spohn, Gruhl, and Welch (1987) found similar results in their analysis of charging decisions—Hispanic and Black males were less likely to received reduced charges or charge dismissals. Shermer and Johnson (2010) attribute this to the focal concerns perspective—" … prosecutorial decision-making is guided by a set of focal concerns that include offender dangerousness and culpability as well as practical considerations focusing on case convictability, political consequences, social justice, and organizational efficiency concerns" (p. 404).

## Differences in Perceptions of Courts

In general, research has shown that minorities tend to have less favorable attitudes than Whites regarding the criminal justice system (Albonetti & Hagan, 1982). This occurs both for the criminal justice system as a whole as well as for the court system in particular. Whitaker (1995) highlights the O.J. Simpson trial in 1995 as reflective of minority and White attitudes toward the system. This trial was heavily racialized, with a Black defendant accused of murdering two White victims. Whitaker (1995) documents public opinion polls, which indicated that a majority of White respondents felt Simpson was guilty, while

a majority of Black respondents felt Simpson was innocent. Further, Black respondents were more likely to believe that Simpson was framed by the criminal justice system. Other research has confirmed these findings. Hagan and
Albonetti (1982) found that Blacks were more likely to perceive injustice in
the criminal justice system.

Some of this research involves perceptions of the police, first illustrated in
Chapter 5. Wortley, Hagan, and Macmillan (1997) state that Blacks are more
likely to have negative perceptions of the police, while Alpert and Dunham
(1988) state that Blacks (and Mariel Cubans in Miami) had more negative suspicions of police than Whites. With regard to the court system in particular, a
number of researchers have found negative perceptions as well. Regarding the
court system, Curran (1977) states that Blacks are less likely than Whites to
believe that defendants will receive a fair trial, while Meislin (1988) states that
Blacks feel that the court system shows favoritism towards White defendants.
This is supported by more recent research from Sun and Wu (2006), who indicated that both Blacks and Hispanics have more negative attitudes than
Whites about the court system. Sun and Wu (2006) speculate that the reason
for this is that Blacks and Hispanics have different experiences with the court
system than Whites. Blacks are more likely than Whites to be arrested, convicted, and incarcerated. Blacks also more likely to be victims of crime (Maguire
& Pastore, 2004). This leads to the assumption by Sun and Wu (2006) that
Blacks, "develop … resentful attitudes toward agencies of social control including the criminal courts" (p. 458).

More recently, research has indicated that Blacks are not of the same opinion when it comes to their views of the criminal justice system. Gabbidon et al.
(2014) state that younger, male, less educated, and lower income Blacks tend
to have more favorable views of the system than other Blacks. The authors speculate that older Blacks lived through periods of more overt criminal justice system discrimination, especially by police, and that has shaped their views of the
system. Additionally, today, there more Blacks in positions of authority in the
criminal justice system and this has created fewer negative impressions of the
system by young Blacks. This is supported in research by Sun and Wu (2006),
who found that higher-income Blacks had less favorable views of the system.

# Conclusion

The court system is expected to provide equal justice to all; however, it has
been documented and supported by numerous studies of the pre-trial and trial
process that this simply is not the case. Disparate treatment of minorities, in-

cluding Blacks and Hispanics, has been seen at various stages of the court process. As shown in this chapter, race and ethnicity continues to play a role in bail decisions, the right to counsel, charging decisions, guilty pleas, jury selection, and even conviction. Race also plays a role in how the court system is perceived by the public.

Nonetheless, strides have been made to reduce disparate treatment of some offenders in the court system, although these strides have not been enough. Cultural stereotyping and views about minorities are difficult to change, so disparate treatment will likely be present in the court system for the foreseeable future. One challenge for contemporary Americans is to continue to strive for equal treatment for all people in the courts, regardless of race and ethnicity.

## Discussion Questions

1. What are the courts?
2. What is the dual court system?
3. Identify and define the major functions of the courts in the US.
4. Contrast the ideal of America's adversarial system with the reality of America's administrative system in the courts.
5. Contrast the criminal trial with plea bargaining.
6. Identify and discuss the major types of disparities present in pre-trial processes in the United States.
7. Identify and discuss the major types of disparities present in trial processes in the United States.
8. What explanations of disparities in court processes do you find more convincing? Explain.
9. What explains different perceptions of American courts across racial and ethnic groups?

## References

Albonetti, C. (1989). Bail and judicial discretion in the District of Columbia. *Sociology and Social Research, 74,* 40–47.

Albonetti, C. (1990). Race and the probability of pleading guilty. *Journal of Quantitative Criminology, 6,* 315–334.

Alderden, M., & Ullman, S. (2012). Creating a more complete and current picture: Examining police and prosecutor decision-making when processing sexual assault cases. *Violence Against Women, 18,* 525–551.

Alpert, G., & Dunham, R. (1988).*Policing multi-ethnic neighborhoods: The Miami study and findings for law enforcement in the United States.* New York: Greenwood Press.

Anderson, J., & Heaton, P. (2012). How much difference does a lawyer make? The effect of defense counsel on murder case outcomes.*Yale Law Journal, 122,* 154–187.

Baldus, D. C., Woodworth, G., Zuckerman, D., Weiner, N. A., & Broffitt, B. (1998). Racial discrimination and the death penalty and the death penalty in the post-Furman era: An empirical and legal overview, with recent findings from Philadelphia. *Cornell Law Review, 83,* 1638–1770.

Bernstein, I., Kick, E., Leung, J., & Schulz, B. (1977). Charge reduction: An intermediary stage in the process of labeling criminal defendants. *Social Forces, 56,* 362–384.

Champion, D. (1989). Private counsels and public defenders: A look at weak cases, prior records, and leniency in plea bargaining. *Journal of Criminal Justice, 17,* 253–263.

Chandler, S., & Torney, M. (1981). The decisions and the processing of rape victims through the criminal justice system. *California Sociologist, 4,* 155–168.

Covey, R. (2008). Fixed justice: Reforming plea bargaining with plea-based ceilings. *Tulane Law Review, 82,* 1237–1290.

Crutchfield, R., Weis, J., Engen, R., & Gainey, R. (1995). *Racial and ethnic disparities in the prosecution of felony cases in King County: Final report to the Washington State Minority and Justice Commission.* Retrieved from: http://www.courts.wa.gov/committee/pdf/November%201995%20Report.pdf.

Curran, B. (1977).*The legal needs of the public: The final report of a national survey.* Chicago: American Bar Foundation.

Daly, K. (1989). Rethinking judicial paternalism: Gender, work-family relations, and sentencing. *Gender and Society, 3,* 9–36.

Davis, A. (2007). *Arbitrary justice: The power of the American prosecutor.* New York: Oxford University Press.

Demuth, S. (2003). Racial and ethnic differences in pretrial release decisions and outcomes: A comparison of Hispanic, Black, and White felony arrestees.*Criminology, 41,* 873–908.

Demuth, S. & Steffensmeier, D. (2004). The impact of gender and race/ethnicity in the pretrial release process. *Social Problems, 51,* 222–242.

Equal Justice Initiative. (2010). *Illegal racial discrimination in jury selection: A continuing legacy.* Retrieved from www.eji.ortg/files/EJIRaceandJuryReport.pdf

Farnsworth, M., & Teske, R. (1995). Gender differences in felony court processing: Three hypotheses of disparity. *Women & Criminal Justice, 6,* 23–44.

Farrell, R., & Swigert, V. (1978). Prior offense record as a self-fulfilling prophecy. *Law and Society Review, 12*, 437–453.

Fukurai, H., Butler, E., & Krooth, R. (1993). *Race and the jury: Racial disenfranchisement and the search for justice.* New York: Plenum Press.

Gabbidon, S., Jordan, K., Penn, E., & Higgins, G. (2014). Black supporters of the no-discrimination thesis in criminal justice: A portrait of an understudied segment of the community. *Criminal Justice Policy Review, 25,* 637–652.

Gaertner, S. L., & Dovidio, J. F. (1986). The aversive form of racism. In J. F. Dovidio & S. L. Gaertner (Eds.), *Prejudice, discrimination, and racism*(pp. 61–89). San Diego, CA: Academic Press.

Gibbs, J.W. (Ed.). (1988). *Young, black, and male in America: An endangered species.* Dover: Auburn Publishing Company.

Gitelman, M. (1971). The relative performance of appointed and retained counsel in Arkansas felony cases: An empirical study. *Arkansas Law Review, 24,* 442–452.

Gottfredson, S., & Gottfredson, D. (1986). Accuracy of prediction models. In A. Blumstein, J. Cohen, J. Roth, & C. Visher (Eds.), *Criminal careers and career criminals* (pp. 212–290). Washington, DC: National Academy Press.

Hagan, J., & Albonetti, C. (1982). Race, class, and the perception of criminal justice in America. *American Journal of Sociology, 88,* 329–355.

Hernandez, T. K. (1990). Bias crimes: Unconscious racism in prosecution of racially motivated violence. *Yale Law Review, 99,* 845–864.

Holmes, M., Daudistel, H., & Farrell, R. (1987). Determinants of charge reductions and final dispositions in cases of burglary and robbery. *Journal of Research in Crime and Delinquency, 24,* 233–254.

Holmes, M., Hosch, H., Daudistel, H., Perez, D., & Graves, J. (1996). Ethnicity, legal resources, and felony dispositions in two southwestern jurisdictions.*Justice Quarterly, 13,* 11–30.

Johnson, J. D., Whitestone, E., Jackson, L. A., & Gatto, L. (1995). Justice is still not colorblind: Differential racial effects of exposure to inadmissible evidence.*Personality and Social Psychology Bulletin, 21,* 893–898.

Johnson, S. (1998). Unconscious racism and the criminal law. Retrieved from http://scholarship.law.cornell.edu/cgi/viewcontent.cgi?article=1717&context=facpub.

Johnson, B. (2003). Racial and ethnic disparities in sentencing departures across modes of conviction. *Criminology, 41,* 449–489.

Johnson, M., Griffith, S., & Barnaby, C. (2013). African-Americans wrongly convicted of sexual assault against Whites: Eyewitness error and other case features. *Journal of Ethnicity in Criminal Justice, 11,* 277–294.

Kalven, H., & Zeisel, H. (1966). *The American jury.* Boston: Little Brown.

Kinder, D., & Sears, D. (1981). Prejudice and politics: Symbolic racism versus racial threats to the good life. *Journal of Personality and Social Psychology, 40,* 414–431.

King, N. (1993). Postconviction review of jury discrimination: Measuring the effects of juror race on jury decisions.*Michigan Law Review, 92,* 63–130.

Kingsnorth, R., Lopez, J., Wentworth, J., & Cummings, D. (1998). Adult sexual assault: The role of race/ethnic composition in prosecution and sentencing.*Journal of Criminal Justice, 26,* 359–371.

Klein, K., & Creech, B. (1982). Race, rape, and bias: Distortion of prior odds and meanings changes. *Basic and Applied Social Psychology, 3,* 21–33.

LaFree, G. (1980). The effect of sexual stratification by race on official reactions to rape. *American Sociological Review, 45,* 842–854.

LaFree, G., Reskin, B., & Visher, C. (1985). Jurors' responses to victims' behavior and legal issues in sexual assault trials. *Social Problems, 32,* 389–407.

Maguire, K., & Pastore, A. (Eds.). (2004). *Sourcebook of criminal justice statistics.* Retrieved from www.albany.edu/sourcebook.

Majd, K., & Puritz, P. (2009). Cost of justice: How low-income youth continue to pay the price of failing indigent defense systems. *Georgetown Journal of Poverty Law and Policy, 16,* 543–583.

Marcus, R. (1994). Racism in our courts: The underfunding of public defenders and its disproportionate impact upon racial minorities. *Hastings Constitutional Law Quarterly, 22,* 219–268.

Mather, L. (1979).Review: Plea bargaining reexamined: Plea bargaining: The experiences of prosecutors, judges, and defense attorneys. *Michigan Law Review, 77,* 884–891.

Meislin, J. (1988, Jan. 19). New Yorkers say race relations have worsened in the last year. *New York Times,* A1.

Mitchell, T. L., Haw, R. M., Pfeifer, J. E., & Meissner, C. A. (2005). Racial bias in mock juror decision-making: A meta-analytic review of defendant treatment. *Law and Human Behavior, 29,* 621–637.

Nagel, S. (1973). Effects of alternative types of counsel on criminal procedural treatment. *Indiana Law Journal, 48,* 404–426.

National Center for State Courts. (1992). *Indigent defenders: Get the job done and done well.* Washington, DC: National Center for State Courts.

Office of Justice Programs. (2011). *Fact sheet: Indigent defense.* Retrieved from www.ojp.usdoj.gov/newsroom/factsheets/ojpfs_indigentdefense.html.

Perez, D. A., Hosch, H. M., Ponder, B., & Trejo, G. C. (1993). Ethnicity of defendants and jurors as influences on jury decisions. *Journal of Applied Social Psychology, 23,* 1249–1262.

Reaves, B. (2013). *Felony defendants in large urban counties, 2009 — Statistical tables.* Retrieved from http://www.bjs.gov/content/pub/pdf/fdluc09.pdf.

Richey-Mann, C. (1993). *Unequal justice: A question of color.* Bloomington, IN: Indiana University Press.

Shermer, L & Johnson, B (2010). Criminal prosecutions: Examining prosecutorial discretion and charging decisions in U.S. Federal District Courts. *Justice Quarterly, 27,* 394–430.

Silverstein, L. (1965). *Defense of the poor in criminal cases in American state courts: A field study and report.* Chicago: American Bar Association.

Smith, E., & Hattery, A. (2011). "Race, wrongful conviction and exoneration." *Journal of African American Studies, 15,* 74–94.

Sommers, S. R., & Ellsworth, P. C. (2001). White juror bias: An investigation of racial prejudice against black defendants in the American courtroom. *Psychology, Public Policy, and Law, 7,* 201–229.

Sommers, S. R., & Ellsworth, P. C. (2003). How much do we really know about race and juries? A review of social science theory and research. *Chicago-Kent Law Review, 78,* 997–1031.

Spohn, C., Gruhl, J., & Welch, S. (1987). The impact of ethnicity and gender of defendants on the decision to reject or dismiss felony charges. *Criminology, 25,* 175–191.

Spohn, C. (1994). A comparison of sexual assault cases with child and adult victims. *Journal of Child Sexual Abuse, 3,* 125–148.

Spohn, C., & Spears, J. (1996). The effect of offender and victim characteristics on sexual assault case processing decisions. *Justice Quarterly, 13,* 649–679.

Steffensmeier, D., Ulmer, J., & Kramer, J. (1998). The interaction of race, gender, and age in criminal sentencing: The punishment cost of being young, black, and male. *Criminology, 36,* 763–797.

Sun, I., & Wu, Y. (2006). Citizen perceptions of criminal courts: The impact of gender, race, and recent experience. *Journal of Criminal Justice, 34,* 457–467.

Sweeney, L. T., & Haney, C. (1992). The influence of race on sentencing: A meta-analytic review of experimental studies. *Behavioral Sciences and the Law, 10,* 179–195.

Walker, S. (2006). *Sense and nonsense about crime and drugs.* Belmont, CA: Thomson.

Walker, S., Spohn, C., & DeLone, M. (2004). The color of justice: Race, ethnicity, and crime in America. Belmont, CA: Wadsworth.

Weddell, H. (2013). A jury of whose peers? Eliminating racial discrimination in jury selection procedures. *Boston College Journal of Law & Social Justice, 33,* 453–486.

Whitaker, M. (1995, October 16). The reaction: Whites v. Blacks. *Newsweek, 126,* 28–35.

Williams, M. (2013). The effectiveness of public defenders in four Florida counties. *Journal of Criminal Justice, 41,* 205–212.

Wolf-Harlow, C. (2000). *Defense counsel in criminal cases.* Retrieved from www.bjs.ojp.usdoj.gov/content/pub/pdf/dccc.pdf.

Wooldredge, J. (2012). Distinguishing race effects on pretrial release and sentencing decisions. *Justice Quarterly, 29,* 41–75.

Wortley, S., Hagan, J., & Macmillan, R. (1997). Just des(s)erts? The racial polarization of perceptions of criminal injustice. *Law and Society Review, 31,* 637–676.

# Chapter 7

# How Race and Ethnicity Impact Criminal Sentencing

*by Rhys Hester, JD, PhD*

## Introduction

This chapter examines how race and ethnicity impact criminal sentencing. States and the federal system have undertaken significant changes in their sentencing schemes in the past few decades and much of this change relates to concerns over racial disparities in sentencing. This chapter begins with an overview of the criminal sentencing process. The chapter then discusses the purposes of punishment before proceeding to a brief sketch of state sentencing systems and a review of the dramatic reforms that have occurred in many jurisdictions since the 1970s. The final sections address the realities of sentencing in the United States and the social science literature on the extent of racial and ethnic disparities and discrimination in American sentencing systems.

The evidence to date suggests that disparities are often present in sentencing, but the overall magnitude of direct race effects is relatively small and does not account for many of the substantial differences in disparate incarceration rates. However, this broad-sweeping conclusion must be qualified in important ways.

First, while direct race effects appear minimal in criminal sentencing (though nevertheless a public policy concern), racial disparities are more pronounced when *indirect effects* and *interactive effects* are examined (where, for example, race works through factors like criminal history or in conjunction with characteristics like gender and age so that Blacks are sentenced more punitively because they tend to have longer criminal histories, or young Black men tend to be singled out for the harshest treatment of any age-race-gender combination).

To say that interactive effects occur simply reaffirms the reality that all extralegal factors (i.e., race, class, and gender) impact one another and become relevant for criminal justice practice. As noted in Chapter 1, Walker, Spohn, and DeLone (2000) define **institutionalized discrimination** as disparities that arise because of seemingly legitimate factors such as seriousness of offense and prior record, which impact criminal justice outcomes. For instance, poor minorities are more likely to be arrested, convicted, and sentenced to correctional punishment for some crimes, especially those crimes that are more likely to happen in the neighborhoods in which they tend to live; this occurs in part because of selective enforcement by the police.

Second, location matters. General patterns and sentencing disparities appear to vary by jurisdiction (from state to state) and even within jurisdictions (e.g., from county to county within one state). Accordingly, we should be cautious not to rely on conclusions that mask substantial disparate impacts in some locations and contexts. Finally, although many sentencing studies exist, they tend to be examinations of the same locations over and over. We still do not have sentencing research in most U.S. jurisdictions and we also lack data on other important sentencing-related stages of the process.

The final takeaway is that sentencing does not appear to be a leading reason why one in nine Blacks is under correctional supervision or why Blacks make up about 40% of the prison population but only around 13% of the general population. Nevertheless, racial disparities are present at some sentencing stages and this should cause practitioners and policymakers to take a close look at the impact laws and decisions make on the presence and extent of disparities in the judicial process.

## Overview of the Sentencing Process

**Criminal sentencing** is the process that assigns a penalty to an individual who has been declared guilty of a crime. Sentences can range from fines, orders to pay restitution to victims, and probation to jail, prison, and even death. The concept of discretion is a key feature of American sentencing systems. **Discretion** refers to the ability to choose from among an array of lawful options. Traditionally, trial judges have exercised considerable discretion over the sentence imposed on an offender. This chapter discusses some major sentencing reforms (like *sentencing guidelines*) that have curtailed judicial discretion in some U.S. jurisdictions, but these have not been universally adopted; some states still allow judges wide discretion—for example, to impose anything from probation up to 15 years in prison for certain offenses. Considering the tremendous potential discretion and the substantial liberty interests involved with imprisonment, it should come as no surprise that sentencing and judicial decision-making is a topic of active discussion among criminal justice practitioners and policymakers.[1]

One positive aspect of *discretion* is that it allows a judge to individualize a criminal sentence to the particular circumstances of the crime and offender. As Tonry (1996) has elucidated:

> A suburban stockbroker who sells cocaine elicits different judgments of moral culpability than does a disadvantaged ghetto youth who sells the same amount. A mentally retarded, easily led boy who participates in a street mugging may elicit different culpability judgments than does the gang member who persuaded him to participate. A formerly abused wife who attacks her drunken husband with a knife elicits different culpability judgments than when the knife is in the husband's hand. And so on; circumstances matter in attributions of blameworthiness. (p.18–19)

Yet the same discretion that allows a judge to individualize sentences also opens the door for the judge to impose different sentences on two offenders whose circumstances and contexts are very nearly the same. To illustrate, assume two offenders commit identical crimes of breaking and entering and are alike on all meaningful characteristics—both broke into houses during the daytime and stole around $500 in electronic equipment; both are married, White, males; both have steady but menial employment; both take responsibility for their crime; and both are sentenced by the same trial judge. Assume the judge, lawfully exercising discretion, sentenced one offender to three years in prison and sentenced the other to community service. Imagine the sense of injustice the imprisoned offender might feel if he learned his criminal doppelganger merely had to spend a few weekends washing fire trucks while he (Offender #2) loses 3 years of his life to prison.

This potential for differential treatment raises concerns, since one aspect of justice is that like cases be treated alike—that punishment be fairly distributed, not haphazard, arbitrary, or discriminatory. It shouldn't matter, for example, that the judge is in a bad mood when he sentences Offender #1 but feels jolly when he sentences Offender #2. Neither should it matter if Offender #1 is Black and Offender #2 is White. But because of discretion, it is possible that illegitimate factors like the judge's mood or the offender's race could impact sanctions imposed. Race *could* matter, but does it? And if race does matter, is this evidence of outright racism, unconscious bias, correlations with legitimate factors like differential offending rates, or some other cause? Before proceeding to these issues of whether and why disparities exist, it will be helpful to review the purposes of punishment and how and why sentencing policy has changed in recent decades.

# Purposes of Sentencing

Broadly speaking, there are two primary reasons put forth to justify punishment: (1) because the offender deserves punishment in some moral sense (known as *retributivism* or just deserts), and (2) because punishing the offender will bring about some benefit to society (known as *utilitarianism* and including several well-known punishment theories such as *deterrence, incapacitation*, and *rehabilitation*). According to **retributivism**, society punishes offenders because they deserve it based on some breech of law; retributive theory is often described by the ancient adage "an eye for an eye, a tooth for a tooth, a life for a life." Retribution-based theorists see a criminal act as a moral wrong which must be made right by the infliction of punishment on the wrongdoer. Once the wrongdoer has been made to suffer the appropriate amount to account for the severity of the offense, the situation is equalized and justice has been served.

A key characteristic of retributivism is *proportionality*: the severity of punishment should fit the seriousness of the crime, typically measured by the nature of the offense and the level of harm inflicted and the offender's level of culpability or blameworthiness (Frase, 2005). Murder, rape, and robbery are very serious in nature and inflict significant harm. By contrast, recreational drug use is less serious in nature and inflicts less harm. Laws that embody retributive punishment philosophy should reflect these differences. Punishment would not conform to retributive ideals if Offender X, who committed a less serious crime, received a more severe penalty than Offender Y, who committed a more serious crime.

A second key characteristic of retributivism is the *equity principle*: like cases should be treated alike, and different cases should be treated differently (Tonry, 2013). Recall the example raised in the introduction of the two individuals who commit identical crimes but are given two very different punishments—

one community service and the other several years in prison. Such a lack of uniformity raises concerns that punishment is *arbitrary* and possibly *discriminatory*. Notice too how judicial discretion (discussed in the introduction to this chapter) is required for the second tenet of treating different cases differently. One way to ensure uniform sentences would be to entirely remove judicial discretion by fixing immutable sentences for an offense—e.g., everyone who commits burglary must serve five years in prison. But if uniformity were elevated as the paramount principle of sentencing, offenders who were qualitatively different in their levels of *culpability* (i.e., responsibility) would be sentenced the same, thereby creating new proportionality concerns.

Thus, sentencing policy necessarily involves a search for the best of an imperfect balance between allowing judicial discretion to tailor a sentence that most fairly fits an offender's blameworthiness on the one hand while avoiding sentencing outcomes that are arbitrary or discriminatory on the other. The very discretion that provides for individualization of sentences means that the following concerns may arise: (1) the same judge may sentence similar offenders differently, (2) different judges may sentence similar offenders differently, (3) sentencing practices may vary substantially in different geographical locations within a jurisdiction (*i.e.*, from county to county or in the city versus rural areas), and (4) patterns based on illegitimate factors such as race may be introduced.

The second major school of punishment thought is **utilitarianism**, which focuses on the consequences of the punishment inflicted and seeks a penalty with the maximum utility to benefit the most people. Rehabilitation, deterrence (both specific and general), and incapacitation are all influential examples of utilitarian punishment theory and will be discussed below. They are also summarized briefly in Table 7.1.

---

### Table 7.1. Purposes of Punishment

- **Retribution**—imposing a proportional punishment ("an eye for an eye, a tooth for a tooth") based on a moral perception that the offender deserves to suffer because they perpetrated the crime.
- **Rehabilitation**—treating an offender to prevent the reoccurrence of crime.
- **Deterrence**—preventing future offending by causing fear in an offender so that, after punishment, he does not commit another crime (*specific deterrence*) and by causing fear in other would-be offenders so that they do not commit crime (*general deterrence*).
- **Incapacitation**—preventing an offender from future offending by removing them from society.

---

**Rehabilitation** refers to a sanction that involves some form of treatment for the offender—for example, requiring a drug offender to attend a drug treatment program, or a criminal domestic violence perpetrator to undergo an anger management program. **Deterrence** theory seeks to impose a sanction calculated to prevent future offending. Deterrence takes two forms: **specific deterrence** which seeks to punish an offender enough to "teach him a lesson" and prevent him from reoffending, and **general deterrence** which seeks to punish an offender enough to set an example for other would-be offenders. Deterrence theory assumes individuals are rational and think about the costs and benefits of potential criminal activity. Thus, by structuring the costs of offending to be greater than the benefits, offenders will choose not to offend. For deterrence to be effective, the punishment should be certain, appropriately severe, and swiftly imposed. If any of these is missing, deterrence is compromised.

For example, if punishment is certain and swiftly imposed but not severe enough, offenders will not be deterred. As another example, even if the potential penalty is appropriately severe, but the certainty of getting punished is slight, offenders will not be deterred from criminal activity. The evidence generally suggests that, of these elements of punishment, certainty of punishment matters the most.

Finally, **incapacitation** refers to removing offenders (usually serious or habitual offenders) from society in order to prevent future offending. Mechanisms for incapacitation include long prison sentences, life without parole, and even the death penalty. The death penalty, or capital punishment, is the ultimate form of incapacitation because an offender's freedom is taken away forever.

One key utilitarian characteristic asserted by many punishment theorists is what Norvall Morris called the principle of *parsimony* (see Frase, 2005, 2013). In this context, punishment parsimony requires imposition of the least intrusive punishment that will achieve the desired result. If six months in a drug treatment program is as effective a preventative punishment as a two-year prison sentence, the sanction should be drug treatment since it inflicts less suffering and is less costly to society.

In contrast to retributivism which looks back to the crime committed and seeks to equalize the past wrong, these utilitarian theories look forward; they ask: which punishment inflicted today will bring the best results tomorrow? If giving an offender a special form of treatment would likely cause him to stop offending and would also be cost-effective (and by contrast a term in prison would be less likely to rehabilitate and would cost more) the offender should be given the treatment. It is irrelevant whether the treatment program causes the offender to suffer an equivalent amount of pain that he inflicted on his victim, as retributivism would prescribe.

Retributivism and the various utilitarian theories are all present to some degree in current U.S. sentencing policy, but the emphasis policymakers place on one theory tends to shift over time and specific policy initiatives. Examples include the rehabilitative emphasis that generally prevailed in the early 1900s through the 1960s, the incapacitation emphasis behind policy initiatives like "three-strikes" laws, and the retributive emphasis behind reforms such as some sentencing guidelines, all to be discussed in further detail in the next section below.

# U.S. Sentencing Systems: A Brief History of Reform

As of the 2010s there are substantial jurisdictional differences in sentencing laws and policy. However, for most of the 1900s through the early 1970s every state and the federal government operated under similar sentencing policies (Rothman, 1980; Tonry, 1996). Under this scheme called **indeterminate sentencing**, judges enjoyed wide discretion in making "front-end" sentencing decisions (what sentence to pronounce) and parole boards likewise had extensive discretion over the "back-end" decision of when to release an offender (*i.e.*, whenever the board deemed it appropriate, regardless of what sentence had been pronounced by the judge).

The operation of indeterminate sentencing was predicated on utilitarian, rehabilitative punishment philosophy and often called the **medical model** as the system confronted crime as a disease and criminals as treatable individuals (Rothman, 1980). Given the emphasis on treatment and rehabilitation, judges were vested with an array of sanctioning options from which to choose the most appropriate for the benefit of a particular offender. Parole boards were seen as best suited to determine when the offender had been cured and was ready for release back into the community (Feeley & Simon, 1992; Savelsburg, 1992). The process, from start to finish, was highly individualized. Not only were the states universal in their use of the indeterminate model, but the use of this model had been remarkably stable, characterizing sentencing and punishment in the United States for decades (Rothman, 1980; Tonry, 1996, 1999; Zalman, 1977).

Beginning in the 1970s things began to change. The attack on the medical model came from several different fronts; indeed, one of the intriguing aspects of the reform movement is that reform was supported by just about everyone, from liberals to conservatives (Bushway & Paternoster, 2009; Stith

& Cabranes, 1998). There were two primary attacks against the rehabilitative status quo of indeterminate sentencing. The first involved progressive concerns over discretion, fairness, equity, and disparities based on race (Davis, 1969; Feeley, 1983; Frankel, 1972; Singer, 1978; von Hirsch, 1976). The second was connected to *crime control*, the conclusion that with rehabilitative programs "nothing works," and a growing get-tough mentality by those who felt that judges were too lenient and that offenders were not getting adequate punishment for their crimes (see Feeley & Simon, 1992; Marvell & Moodey, 1996; Wilson, 1975).

Federal Judge Marvin Frankel's (1973) influential book *Criminal Sentences: Law Without Order* offered a scathing critique of the indeterminate model. According to Judge Frankel, "the almost wholly unchecked and sweeping powers we give to judges in the fashioning of sentences are terrifying and intolerable for a society that professes devotion to the rule of law" (1973: 5). Frankel quoted real life examples from the former director of the Federal Bureau of Prisons which are similar to the hypothetical posed earlier in this chapter:

> Take, for instance, the cases of two men we received last spring. The first man had been convicted of cashing a check for $58.40. He was out of work at the time of his offense, and when his wife became ill and he needed money for rent, food and doctor bills, he became the victim of temptation. He had no prior criminal record. The other man cashed a check for $35.20. He was also out of work and his wife had left him for another man. His prior record consisted of a drunk charge and a nonsupport charge. Our examination of these two cases indicated no significant differences for sentencing purposes. But they appeared before different judges and the first man received 15 years in prison and the second man 30 days [in jail]. (Frankel, 1973:22–23)

Frankel also provided several additional examples of the tremendous discretion afforded federal trial judges in sentencing offenses at the time: 0 to 10 years for assault on an officer; 0 years to any term of years, a life sentence, or the death penalty for rape; and 0 to 25 years for bank robbery.

Ultimately, reformers mounted an attack on the rehabilitative model using arguments based on proportionality and equity as well as utilitarian themes of crime control, deterrence, and incapacitation. For certain reforms, these two general points of view worked in concert to bring about change; for some they worked against each other; but all told, the reemphasis on proportionality, deterrence, and incapacitation in the punishment policy arena meant certain change for much of the indeterminate structure.

Table 7.2. Key Sentencing Reforms, 1970s–2000s

| Type of Reform | Definition |
| --- | --- |
| Determinate Sentencing | The abolition of discretionary parole board release. |
| Sentencing Guidelines | Sentencing systems, usually designed by sentencing commissions, which prescribe a sentence based on a narrow range of factors, typically the severity of the offense and the offender's prior criminal record. Guidelines can be merely advisory or presumptively binding on judges. |
| Truth-in-Sentencing | Statutory requirements that offenders serve a predetermined amount of their sentence (usually 85%) before being eligible for parole. |
| Three Strikes Laws | Statutes that provide for long prison terms or life in prison for offenders upon conviction of a third offense; generally only very serious offenses qualify for three strike laws. |
| Mandatory Minimums | Laws that totally remove a judge's sentencing discretion by prescribing a mandatory minimum penalty which the judge cannot sentence below. |
| War on Drugs | A policy era beginning in the 1970s during which U.S. jurisdictions adopted aggressively punitive laws targeted at drug offending. |

## Six Key Sentencing Reforms

Although numerous laws contributed to the changing legal landscape, Table 7.2 lists six of the most substantial, including: determinate sentencing; sentencing guidelines; truth in sentencing legislation; drug laws; three strikes laws; and mandatory minimums. Of those, the two most significant sentencing structure characteristics are whether a jurisdiction still maintains parole and whether a jurisdiction uses sentencing guidelines.

First, **determinate sentencing** refers to the abolition of discretionary parole board release (Lowenthal, 1993; Miethe, 1987). Parole abolition was favored by policymakers who believed that criminals were not being punished severely enough because they were being released well before their imposed sentence was served. Some progressives were also in favor of abolishing parole since parole boards might be exercising their discretion in discriminatory ways—e.g., granting parole for White offenders more often than similarly situated Black offenders.[2]

Second, a number of states have adopted **sentencing guidelines** which are designed to restrict, if not remove, the front-end judicial discretion and make sentences more uniform and less likely to result in disparities based on extralegal characteristics such as race. Guidelines frequently operate according to a two-way matrix grid where the rows demarcate offense severity and the columns identify categories of prior criminal record status. (The North Carolina sentencing guidelines grid is provided in Figure 7.1 for illustration purposes.) Guidelines provide judges with a window from within which to choose a sentence. Thus, referring to the grid provided in Figure 7.1, if an offender were being sentenced for a Class D felony and that offender's criminal history classified them as a Prior Record Level III offender, the presumptive range within which the judge could sentence would be 67 to 84 months, a much narrower range than what would be permissible in many non-guidelines jurisdictions.

Not all guidelines are created alike: they vary along a continuum of being merely advisory to presumptive. In *advisory guidelines states*, judges are not legally bound by the recommended sentence, and sentences outside the guideline recommendations are not reviewable on appeal (Tonry, 1996). Thus advisory guidelines are effectively unenforceable, but may constitute some degree of moral authority or persuasive appeal for general uniformity among the state's bench. In *presumptive guidelines states*, the guidelines have more import, though in most jurisdictions a judge is still able to depart from guidelines by justifying his or her decision, subject to appeal. Figure 7.2 provides a map of jurisdictions operating under a guidelines scheme as of 2015.[3] (See the Robina Institute's Sentencing Guidelines Resource Center website for an exhaustive comparison of guidelines jurisdictions: http://robinainstitute.org/projects/.)

Along with changes in the use of parole and the implementation of sentencing guidelines, four additional types of laws and policy reforms have significantly shaped jurisdictional sentencing policies since the 1970s. First, a majority of states have adopted *truth-in-sentencing* or similar time served laws (Stemen et al., 2006). These efforts offer an alternative to determinate sentencing as a way to limit discretionary parole release (see Sabol et al., 2002). **Truth-in-sentencing laws** generally require offenders to serve at least 85% of their sentences, although states have varying practices (Sabol et al., 2002). Depending on the state, the 85-percent requirement may apply to all felonies, or only specific types of felonies, such as violent or drug offenses (Stemen et al., 2006).

Second, *three strikes laws* gained popularity in many states beginning in the 1990s. Although states have had various forms of habitual offenders laws for decades, most of which focused on offense-specific repeat offending (i.e., increased penalties for a burglar who continues to burglarize), the three strikes movement was different because these new laws typically count many types of offenses as a strike (Clark, Austin, & Henry, 1997; Harris & Jeslow, 2000).

## Figure 7.1. The North Carolina Felony Sentencing Guidelines Grid

### *** Effective for Offenses Committed on or after 10/1/13 ***

**FELONY PUNISHMENT CHART**
**PRIOR RECORD LEVEL**

| Offense Class | Range | I 0-1 Pt | II 2-5 Pts | III 6-9 Pts | IV 10-13 Pts | V 14-17 Pts | VI 18+ Pts |
|---|---|---|---|---|---|---|---|
| A | | Death or Life Without Parole — Defendant Under 18 at Time of Offense: Life With or Without Parole | | | | | |
| B1 | Aggravated | A / 240 - 300 | A / 276 - 345 | A / 317 -397 | A / 365 - 456 | A / Life Without Parole | A / Life Without Parole |
| B1 | Presumptive | 192 - 240 | 221 - 276 | 254 - 317 | 292 - 365 | 336 - 420 | 386 - 483 |
| B1 | Mitigated | 144 - 192 | 166 - 221 | 190 - 254 | 219 - 292 | 252 - 336 | 290 - 386 |
| B2 | Aggravated | A / 157 - 196 | A / 180 - 225 | A / 207 - 258 | A / 238 - 297 | A / 273 - 342 | A / 314 - 393 |
| B2 | Presumptive | 125 - 157 | 144 - 180 | 165 - 207 | 190 - 238 | 219 - 273 | 251 - 314 |
| B2 | Mitigated | 94 - 125 | 108 - 144 | 124 - 165 | 143 - 190 | 164 - 219 | 189 - 251 |
| C | Aggravated | A / 73 – 92 | A / 83 - 104 | A / 96 - 120 | A / 110 - 138 | A / 127 - 159 | A / 146 - 182 |
| C | Presumptive | 58 - 73 | 67 - 83 | 77 - 96 | 88 - 110 | 101 - 127 | 117 - 146 |
| C | Mitigated | 44 - 58 | 50 - 67 | 58 - 77 | 66 - 88 | 76 - 101 | 87 - 117 |
| D | Aggravated | A / 64 - 80 | A / 73 - 92 | A / 84 - 105 | A / 97 - 121 | A / 111 - 139 | A / 128 - 160 |
| D | Presumptive | 51 - 64 | 59 - 73 | 67 - 84 | 78 - 97 | 89 - 111 | 103 - 128 |
| D | Mitigated | 38 - 51 | 44 - 59 | 51 - 67 | 58 - 78 | 67 - 89 | 77 - 103 |
| E | Aggravated | I/A / 25 - 31 | I/A / 29 - 36 | A / 33 - 41 | A / 38 - 48 | A / 44 - 55 | A / 50 - 63 |
| E | Presumptive | 20 - 25 | 23 - 29 | 26 - 33 | 30 - 38 | 35 - 44 | 40 - 50 |
| E | Mitigated | 15 - 20 | 17 - 23 | 20 - 26 | 23 - 30 | 26 - 35 | 30 - 40 |
| F | Aggravated | I/A / 16 - 20 | I/A / 19 - 23 | I/A / 21 - 27 | A / 25 - 31 | A / 28 - 36 | A / 33 - 41 |
| F | Presumptive | 13 - 16 | 15 - 19 | 17 - 21 | 20 - 25 | 23 - 28 | 26 - 33 |
| F | Mitigated | 10 - 13 | 11 - 15 | 13 - 17 | 15 - 20 | 17 - 23 | 20 - 26 |
| G | Aggravated | I/A / 13 - 16 | I/A / 14 - 18 | I/A / 17 - 21 | I/A / 19 - 24 | A / 22 - 27 | A / 25 - 31 |
| G | Presumptive | 10 - 13 | 12 - 14 | 13 - 17 | 15 - 19 | 17 - 22 | 20 - 25 |
| G | Mitigated | 8 - 10 | 9 - 12 | 10 - 13 | 11 - 15 | 13 - 17 | 15 - 20 |
| H | Aggravated | C/I/A / 6 - 8 | I/A / 8 - 10 | I/A / 10 - 12 | I/A / 11 - 14 | I/A / 15 - 19 | A / 20 - 25 |
| H | Presumptive | 5 - 6 | 6 - 8 | 8 - 10 | 9 - 11 | 12 - 15 | 16 - 20 |
| H | Mitigated | 4 - 5 | 4 - 6 | 6 - 8 | 7 - 9 | 9 - 12 | 12 - 16 |
| I | Aggravated | C / 6 - 8 | C/I / 6 - 8 | I / 6 - 8 | I/A / 8 - 10 | I/A / 9 - 11 | I/A / 10 - 12 |
| I | Presumptive | 4 - 6 | 4 - 6 | 5 - 6 | 6 - 8 | 7 - 9 | 8 - 10 |
| I | Mitigated | 3 - 4 | 3 - 4 | 4 - 5 | 4 - 6 | 5 - 7 | 6 - 8 |

**DISPOSITION**
*Aggravated Range*
**PRESUMPTIVE RANGE**
*Mitigated Range*

A – Active Punishment    I – Intermediate Punishment    C – Community Punishment
Numbers shown are in months and represent the range of <u>minimum</u> sentences

Revised: 09-09-13

Source: http://www.nccourts.org/Courts/CRS/Councils/spac/Documents/FelonyChart_
1013MaxChart.pdf

**Three strikes laws,** as the metaphor implies, require that once an offender has collected the requisite number of prior felony offenses, serious consequences are invoked—i.e., "you're out," usually meaning life in prison.

Several studies of the implementation of three strikes laws in states like California find evidence of major disparities in how the law has been applied.

Figure 7.2. Map of Sentencing Guidelines Jurisdictions

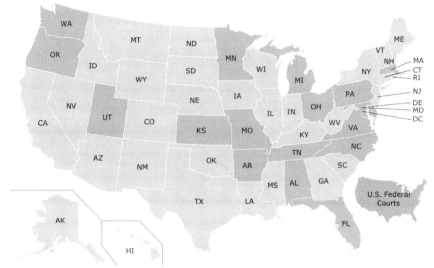

Note: Dark shading denotes sentencing guidelines jurisdiction.

Source: The Robina Institute of Criminal Law and Criminal Justice, Sentencing Guidelines Repository (http://www.robinainstitute.org/projects/). Used with permission.

(Ehlers, Schiraldi, & Lotke, 2004; Chen, 2008) For example, Chen (2008) found that Blacks were more likely than Whites or Latinos to receive third strike sentences, controlling for other legally relevant variables. Figure 7.3 shows that Blacks and Latinos have been more likely to be prosecuted under the California three strikes law, but using second- and third-strike provisions.

Third, virtually every state and the federal government have expanded **mandatory minimum penalties** (Tonry, 1992, 2009). These laws remove discretion from the judge by mandating a minimum specified prison term. Examples of mandatory penalties can be found well before the 1970s, though in much smaller numbers than they currently exist (Stith & Cabranes, 1998; Tonry, 1992). In the 1970s the federal government repealed almost all mandatory minimums for drug offenses because the penalties were seen as too harsh and prosecutors were not charging cases to avoid the injustice (Tonry, 1992). But between 1985 and 1991, the federal congress enacted numerous new mandatory penalties, as did state legislatures. Many of the modern mandatory penalties apply to drug violations and firearms offenses (Tonry, 1999), and their notable reach is illustrated by a number of media reports about mandatory minimums, including on occasions when several celebrities such as rap icon Lil' Wayne and the New York Giants Super Bowl–winning receiver Plaxico Bur-

Figure 7.3. Race, Ethnicity, and California's Three Strikes Laws

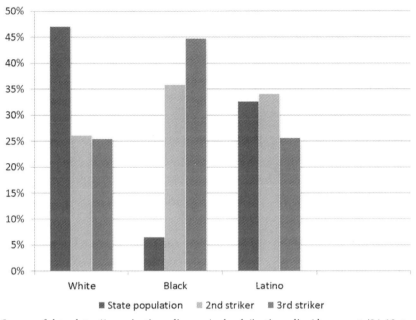

Source of data: http://www.justicepolicy.org/uploads/justicepolicy/documents/04-10_tac_caracialdivide_ac-rd.pdf

ress faced mandatory penalties for firearms violations in New York (Chan & Moynihan, 2009; Eligon, 2009).

Finally, since the 1970s most states and the federal government have increased penalties for drug laws as part of the **war on drugs** (see Chapter 3 of this book). The war on drugs has had a significant toll on prison growth altogether (Blumstein, 1998; Tonry, 1995) and for minorities in particular (Tonry, 1995, 2004; Walker et al., 2000). Between 1980 and 2003, the number of drug offenders sent to jail or prison increased by over one thousand percent (King, 2008). More than half of all federal prisoners are incarcerated for a drug offense (Carson, 2014), and currently around 25% of state prison admissions are for drug offenses (Carson & Golinelli, 2013). Clearly, the war on drugs has been a defining feature of the last quarter century of sentencing policy in the U.S.

## *Racial Impacts of Sentencing Reforms*

These six types of reforms may have different and potentially countervailing impacts on race disparities in prison populations. Supporters touted guidelines as a way to promote proportionality and uniformity, to help jurisdictions manage correctional resources, and to reduce racial disparities. Some sentencing scholars argue that, indeed, states that have implemented guidelines—particularly presumptive guidelines in conjunction with determinate sentencing—have been successful on these marks (Tonry, 2013; but see Koons-Witt, 2002; Stolzenberg & D'Alessio, 1994; Wooldredge, 2009). However, more recently, scholars have also recognized that guidelines may themselves introduce disparities. Frase (2009), for instance, found that around two-thirds of the Black-White disparities in presumptive prison recommendations in Minnesota were attributable to higher criminal history scores of Blacks. Bushway and Piehl (2011) have noted that the way certain factors such as possession of a gun enter sentencing guidelines formulations can have disparate impacts on minorities despite their facially neutral appearance.

While guidelines were at least partially motivated by the belief that such reforms would lead to less discretion and therefore less opportunity for disparities, scholars have fiercely attacked policies like mandatory minimums and the war on drugs for the race disparities they interject. Tonry (2011: 5–6), for instance, states that

> If policy makers' aim in setting drug and crime control policies had been to reduce poor black men's chances of earning a decent living, or becoming a good husband and father, or being socialized into positive social values, it is hard to see how they could have done it more effectively.

The abolition of parole (which was at least partially motivated by concerns over disparities in the minority of states that have adopted determinate sentencing) and truth-in-sentencing laws have the net effect of increasing time served and imprisonment rates (since inmates will occupy beds for longer and a steady stream of new inmates persists). These time-served laws likely exacerbate racial disparities indirectly where Blacks are more likely to commit more serious offenses subject to longer sentences and drug offenses with long or mandatory sentences.

Recall from Chapter 3 Michelle Alexander's argument that modern criminal justice policies have created a "New Jim Crow"—a caste system that politicians either knew or should have known would detrimentally and systematically oppress non-Whites. While some lawmakers may have had nefarious racial motivations, it is also likely that many policymakers—including some Black policymakers—were swept up in the get-tough spirit of the times and reactions to moral panics over misperceived threats of drugs and high-profile criminal incidents. Garland (2000) argues that the many get-tough reforms that have come to characterize recent American criminal justice policy are not just a matter of politicians imposing punitive policies from the top down. Rather, the punitive initiatives are a reflection of public sentiment and particularly a shift in the views of the professional middle class as they adapted to the rising crime experienced throughout the 1960, 70s, and 80s. While by the 2000s very few Americans considered crime to be one of the country's leading problems, during the 1980s Americans listed crime as one of the top three problems facing the country (Tonry, 2004). And public concern over violent crime reached its highest level in 1994 (Robinson, 2009).

Whatever the motivations of sentencing-related criminal justice policies of the last half-century, there is evidence that as of the early 2000s, policymakers are ready to revisit sentencing laws. Since 2001, and especially following the 2008 financial collapse, some states have begun to scale back mandatory minimum laws, increase alternatives to incarceration, expand prison release options, and minimize the impact of technical probation and parole violations (A. Austin, 2010; J. Austin, 2010). It is yet unclear whether or not these measured reforms will reverse the trend of the past decades of punitiveness or what their impact might be on racial disparities in the justice system.

This section has focused on sentencing laws and policies, how they have changed, and their impact—positive and negative—on race disparities in the criminal justice system. This analysis has been at the system-level: what the formal laws are and their likely impact on race in the aggregate. The next section shifts the focus of analysis from lawmakers to law implementers—a return to the issue of discretion by policymakers—and examines disparities in sentencing decisions at the level of the offender and his or her case. Stated differently, once we focus on a particular jurisdiction and the set of formal laws and policies that make up the sentencing structure of that place, is a Black offender likely to be treated differently than a White offender, and if so, why? As the final section explains, disparities do not appear pervasive in the individual sentencing process, but there are contexts that merit careful scrutiny and raise concerns over equal treatment under the law.

# Realities of American Sentencing

## Disparities in Sentencing

Hundreds of studies have examined sentencing outcomes in American jurisdictions; with the vast majority of these, at least one of the motivations for the research was to investigate whether racial disparities or discrimination existed in the sentencing process (Baumer, 2013). Recall from Chapter 1 of this book the difference between disparity and discrimination with disparity referring to a difference between groups and discrimination referring to differential treatment on the basis of an illegitimate factor such as race (see also Spohn, 2000).

As noted in Chapter 2, substantial racial disparities exist in U.S. incarceration rates. Nationwide Blacks make up around 13% of the general population but almost half of the prison population. This is highly suggestive of disparity or differential effects according to race. And while Blacks do appear more likely to be involved in criminal activity (or at least the types of crimes that people typically go to prison for), this differential involvement does not fully explain their differential incarceration rates. Moreover, in recent years violent offending by Blacks has fallen while the disparate incarceration rate between Blacks and Whites has not (Tonry, 2011).

This chapter thus concludes with an examination of the level of race disparities in the criminal justice system attributable to the sentencing process. The general consensus from several systematic reviews of the research is that only a modest level of direct disparity comes from imposition of the sentence. For instance, Baumer (2013:242) concluded, "There are often relatively small but statistically significant direct race differences in the probability of imprisonment to the disadvantage of Blacks (compared to Whites), and comparatively smaller and statistically nonsignificant direct race differences in prison sentence lengths between these groups." Mitchell (2005), Spohn (2000), Pratt (1998), and Chiricos and Crawford (1995) have all drawn similar conclusions in their respective reviews of the research.

To illustrate what scholars mean by these general conclusions that the direct effects of race are small or modest, consider a few examples:

- Freiburger and Hilinski (2013) examined offenders sentenced in an urban Michigan county and found that Whites had a 65% probability of receiving probation (rather than jail) versus just 57% for Blacks. However, Blacks were not more likely than Whites to receive prison rather than jail.
- Wooldredge and colleagues (2005:853), examining a sample of felony offenders in Ohio, found the probability of imprisonment was eight percentage points higher for African Americans relative to Whites (61% versus 53%).
- Holleran and Spohn (2004) found that among the most severe property offenders in Pennsylvania, the predicted probabilities of incarceration were 19% for Blacks compared to 8% for Whites and 43% for Hispanics. However, the race differences for mid-level offenders were less pronounced: 2–4% of Blacks were incarcerated versus 1–2% of Whites and 7–15% of Hispanics.

- Koons-Witt (2002) found that in Minnesota the predicted probability of incarceration was only one percentage point higher for non-White males versus White males. (But notably, non-White males had predicted probabilities of incarceration that were around six percentage points *less* than White males before the guidelines.)
- Johnson (2006:283) studied felony offending in Pennsylvania and found that while Blacks and Hispanics were more likely to be incarcerated than Whites, there were no statistically significant differences in the sentence lengths between Blacks and Whites, while Hispanics received roughly 7% longer sentences than Whites on average.
- Spohn and Holleran (2000) studied felony offending in three cities—Chicago, Miami, and Kansas City. They found the predicted probability of incarceration was 12% greater for Blacks than Whites in Chicago, but found no statistically significant differences in Miami or Kansas City. Hispanics had 15% higher predicted probabilities of incarceration than Whites in Chicago and 10% higher in Miami (results were not available for Kansas City).
- Souryal and Welford (1997) found that Whites had a 56% predicted probability of imprisonment under the Maryland advisory guidelines, compared to 65% for Blacks, and 77% for Hispanics.
- Hester and Hartman (forthcoming) found that Blacks had a 6% greater probability of incarceration than Whites in South Carolina's non-guidelines system. Among incarcerated offenders, Blacks were not given longer sentences.

The foregoing are not exhaustive or representative of all of sentencing research—they are merely examples chosen to give some more concrete meaning to the general conclusions typically found in larger reviews of the research such as the general conclusions that the race effect is typically "minimal" or "modest." These examples are of what criminologists call **direct effects**—they represent the effect of race while controlling for other appropriate variables like the seriousness of the offense, prior record, age, gender, and so forth. However, there are sound reasons to look even more closely at race and the criminal sentencing process because the best current evidence suggests that while *overall* race (i.e., direct effects) has a minimal or modest impact on the sentencing process, in certain contexts and in certain places the significance of race may be much more pronounced; this is consistent with *contextual discrimination*. The following discussion highlights three reasons why sentencing disparities may be of greater concern than the "overall consensus" would suggest: indirect and interactive effects, jurisdictional variation, and pre-sentencing processes.

## 1)  The impact of race on sentencing may be indirect or interactive

Racial impacts on sentencing outcomes may manifest through indirect and interaction effects, such as when Blacks end up with more punitive sentences because of more extensive criminal histories, or when the interaction of age, race, and gender results in young minority males being sentenced more severely than other demographic combinations. As Spohn (2000:434–35) explains:

> An indirect effect occurs when an independent variable influences a dependent variable *through* some other factor, rather than directly. If, for example, pretrial detention significantly increases the odds of incarceration, and if black offenders are more likely than white offenders to be detained prior to trial, then one could conclude that race indirectly affects sentencing severity through its effect on pretrial detention.

Thus an **indirect racial effect** occurs when a nonracial factor influences sentencing decisions and when that factor varies by race. Another example is prior criminal history. Blacks generally have more extensive criminal histories than Whites (Frase, 2009). And while prior record is a nonracial factor, the net effect likely increases racial disparities: Blacks are more likely to be incarcerated and for longer because they have more extensive criminal histories.

Other indirect effect examples to consider include differences across race in use of a weapon, drug offenses, mandatory minimums, and type of attorney. With each of these the analysis is the same: if people of color are more likely to be in possession of a gun, arrested for a drug crime, subject to a mandatory minimum, and be represented by a public defender, and if those indirect factors are correlated with a greater likelihood of imprisonment and longer sentences, then indirect racial effects will appear.

Policymakers and practitioners should examine whether a given indirect effect is (1) an unfortunate but necessary collateral consequence of a compelling sentencing justification or (2) an unjustifiable result given the moral or utilitarian benefits relative to the racially disparate burden imposed. If it were found that Blacks were more likely to commit homicide in a jurisdiction or that White men were more likely to commit child rape, the lone fact of indirect racial disparities for such an offense may not be a compelling reason for adjusting penalties because of the overarching significance and impact of those offenses, not to mention the rarity with which they occur and the small number of offenders affected. However, the punitive justifications for some indirect factors might be less compelling than the moral and constitutional imperatives to minimize differences based on race—and in particular differences that disadvantage racial and ethnic minorities.

Frase (2009) makes this point with respect to criminal history. In Minnesota, where Black-to-White inequality ratios are among the highest in the nation, Frase found that approximately two-thirds of the disparity in prison recommendations was attributable to criminal history: non-serious offenders who otherwise would have been recommended for non-prison sentences were it not for their prior records were much likely to be Black. Even if prior record should play some role in sentencing determinations for some offenses, that role is not self-evident or self-justifying. Moreover, Frase notes that as criminal history increases, so too does the offender's age, and one of the most consistent findings of criminological research is that offenders generally "age out" of crime. Longer criminal histories are correlated with older age and the punitive influence of prior record should be offset by the mitigating influence of old age and desistance from crime. Accordingly, policymakers might well conclude that the indirect race effects of prior record are not compelling enough to maintain the status quo of sentencing policies and practices.

Related to indirect effects are **interaction effects**. As Spohn (2000:435) again explains:

> An interaction effect occurs when either the effect of race varies depending on some other factor or the effects of other variables are conditioned by offender race. If the effect of race is confined to certain types of cases (e.g., less serious crimes where judges have greater discretion at sentencing) or to certain types of offenders (e.g., young males), we would conclude that race interacts with crime seriousness and offender age/gender to affect sentence outcomes.

A convincing line of research now shows that the three-way interaction of being a young, minority, male subjects one to more significant punishment disadvantage than just race alone (Spohn & Holleran, 2000; Steffensemier, Ulmer, & Kramer, 1998). Other scholars have found similar interaction effects for being Black and unemployed (Chiricos & Bales, 1991).

The importance of considering interaction effects should be clear. There may be competing reasons why young minority men are singled out for the harshest punishment—it could be because of some *implicit bias* among courtroom actors, it could be because the nature of their offenses and harms to their victims is more substantial and unaccounted for by researchers (who often lack details about the particulars of the offense and harm done to the victim), or for some other reason. The point for now is that ignoring interactions results in a distorted picture of race and sentencing.

*2) The importance of race in sentencing may vary across and within jurisdictions*

The old adage "location matters" is also true in sentencing in at least two respects. First, even just considering the U.S., one is faced with a large and diverse location with an incredibly complex overlay of separate state sentencing systems in addition to the federal system. Important differences exist regionally in terms of culture, politics, racial makeup, migration patterns, attitudes toward punishment and the criminal justice system, and so on. Consequently even if research were able to convincingly explain sentencing patterns and the role of race in, say, the Northwest, researchers would be reticent to assume those same patterns and explanations held true in other locations given these important regional differences.

A separate but related issue is the difference in state laws. For example, the Pennsylvania system has been studied extensively over the past few decades. But—setting aside the potential regional context just alluded to—Pennsylvania has its own particular sentencing structure makeup of advisory sentencing guidelines and the retention of parole (to name just a few of its features). Accordingly, conclusions about sentencing in Pennsylvania may not generalize to states without guidelines or to states with presumptive rather than advisory guidelines or to states that have abolished parole. (Of course, it is also possible that findings from one jurisdiction would generalize to others despite these differences—the point is that we do not know whether conclusions are generalizable or not, so we should be cautious not to assume they are without good reason.)

While there have been dozens and dozens of sentencing studies conducted over the past decades, these studies represent a very small number of U.S. states. Studies have frequently examined the federal system and systems in Florida, Minnesota, Ohio, Pennsylvania, Washington, and a few others states, but these fall far short of even half of all jurisdictions (see Hester & Sevigny, 2014). In addition, a number of studies have used the *State Court Processing Statistics* data collected by the Bureau of Justice Statistics. These data include sentencing decisions from a non-representative sample of around 40 of the 75 largest counties in the U.S. So, at best, we have sentencing results from a small handful of states and some of the largest counties in America. We have no results from most states. Moreover, there is a clear selection bias in the studies: almost all of the state studies are from states that have sentencing guidelines because the state sentencing commissions that typically create the guidelines also collect the statewide data needed to examine the impact of those guidelines. These data then become available for researchers; without this archival data, researchers are faced with the much more difficult task of obtaining data from various courtrooms, court administrative agencies, corrections and parole departments, and the like. As a result, well over half of states currently do not have sentencing guidelines (which, recall, were targeted at reducing racial disparities), while almost all of the research comes from places with sentencing guidelines. If, as proponents claimed, guidelines reduce disparities, we might expect to find even greater disparities in the majority of states that continue to operate without them.

A final point related to jurisdictional variation highlights one of the most active areas of sentencing research since 2000—that of intra-jurisdictional variation (e.g., how sentencing patterns may differ among counties within one state). This could be important for racial impacts if, for instance, Blacks were punished much more severely in a few counties, about the same as Whites in a number of counties, and perhaps even more leniently than Whites in some counties. If we pooled the data together, the overall conclusion might be that race doesn't matter much in our hypothetical state. But if we account for inter-county differences, we might find that race matters much in some places. The studies that have examined county-level patterns have been widely mixed, underscoring the importance of controlling for jurisdictional variation and examining sentencing in as many jurisdictional contexts as possible. All told, the available evidence from sentencing studies suggests the existence of *contextual discrimination*: Discrimination that occurs in some places and at some times but not in all places or at all times (Walker, Spohn, and DeLone, 2000).

### 3) *Race effects may be present at other sentencing-related stages of the criminal justice process*

Finally, it is important to keep in mind that while imposition of the criminal sentence is the ultimate step in the process leading to incarceration, there are critical stages prior to sentencing that could have substantial race implications. Consider the following decision points occurring after arrest[4] and leading up to sentencing, which are also illustrated in Figure 7.4: (1) the prosecutor's initial screening decision; (2) pretrial release or bail procedures; (3) post-screening dismissal decisions; (4) charge reductions (see also Frase, 2009; Kutateladze, Lynn, & Liang, 2012). Assume that in the actual sentence imposition phase (which has been the subject of the preceding discussion) Blacks and Whites are treated very similarly, but assume that Whites are much more likely to have their charges dismissed, or to have serious charges dropped to less serious ones. If true, there would be troubling disparities in the judicial process, even if there appeared to be little disparity present in the sentencing phase due to censoring. Courtroom professionals may well be favoring Whites over Blacks at these other stages where data is generally not available. Thus, conclusions that little disparity exists in the sentencing process could be wrong, a product

**Figure 7.4. Discretionary Steps of Court Actors Leading up to Sentencing**

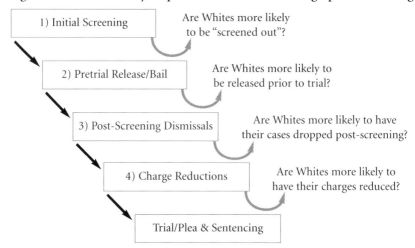

of looking for evidence in the wrong place and ignoring other stages. Though data availability is a problem, scholars are increasingly turning their attention to these pretrial stages involving prosecutorial decision-making, making this area one of the promising forefronts of contemporary sentencing research.

## Explaining Disparities in Sentencing

To recapitulate, racial disparities in sentencing outcomes appear in many jurisdictions, though they tend to be modest and cannot account for the considerable racial disparity in U.S. incarceration rates. Nevertheless, policymakers and the public should be attentive to any level disparity, and, moreover, there are certain contexts in which race disparities are especially pronounced.

In attempting to explain racial disparities in sentencing, social science researchers have generally relied on theoretical explanations rooted in **symbolic interactionism**, a sociological theory which holds that an actor's words and actions toward another entity are based on meanings the actor ascribes to the other person, event, situation, or thing (Blumer, 1969; Wooldredge, 2007). In the court context, symbolic interactionism suggests that the decisions of judges and attorneys are based on meanings the court actors ascribe to the offender's characteristics, actions, and past behavior—e.g., the meaning a judge gives to a "young person," a "Black man," a "violent offender," or a "repeat offender." More specifically, courtroom actors develop patterned responses to certain cues, such as the seriousness of the offense, whether it was violent, and the defendant's criminal record, as well as extralegal characteristics like race, gender, and socioeconomic status (Albonetti, 1991; Steffensmeier et al., 1998). Focal concerns theory is explained beginning on the next page and is presented as an application of sumbolic interactionism to the sentencing realm.

With respect to extralegal characteristics, Albonetti (1991) argued that patterned responses are derived from **causal attributions,** or the views that court actors hold about the differing causes of crime among segments of the population, and whether causation is attributable to internal/personal or external/environmental factors (see also Bridges & Steen, 1998; Kautt & Spohn, 2007). *Internal factors* include one's personal disposition and attitudes while *external factors* include one's family, substance abuse, or association with other criminals (Bridges & Steen, 1998). Thus, for example, a judge or court actor will view a criminal outcome as being premised upon internal factors for some offenders or groups of offenders (i.e., they commit crime because being a criminal is simply "who they are" internally), but premised upon external factors for others (i.e., they commit crime because of external pressures) (Baumer, Messner, & Felson, 2000).

The links between attributions and extralegal characteristics are informed by media reports and stereotypes that associate minorities with certain types of crime (Demuth, 2003; Farrell & Holmes, 1991; Steen, Engen, & Gainey, 2005), as well as by views that minorities are responsible for more street crime than Whites (Lizotte & Bordua, 1980). For example, disparities will be introduced when court actors develop a stereotype associating young minorities with particular types of violent crimes or drug crimes based on past experience processing these types of offenders for these types of crimes (Albonetti, 1991; Sudnow, 1965). This may be especially true when members of the courtroom workgroup are disproportionately White.

These patterned responses also facilitate the organizational goal of avoiding the uncertainty associated with sentencing and the concomitant concerns of punishing the guilty and predicting which defendants are likely to reoffend (Albonetti, 1987, 1991; Eisenstein & Jacob, 1977). Avoiding uncertainty, according to organizational theory, is a paramount concern for decision-makers charged with exercising large amounts of discretion—especially in a context like a criminal court where the available information about the defendant is limited, time and resources do not permit more than a cursory inquiry into the defendant's character and background, and the stakes of allowing a dangerous offender to remain in the community are high (Albonetti, 1987, 1991; Kautt & Spohn, 2007). Thus, courtroom actors develop stereotypes based on the overrepresentation of the perceived "dangerous class" in prison (Albonetti, 1991; Bridges

& Steen, 1998; Farrell & Holmes, 1991; Wooldredge et al., 2005) and sentence those offenders more severely.

The *focal concerns theory* discussed in Chapter 6 adds to the causal attribution concept by proposing that judges and other courtroom actors are guided by three focal concerns when sentencing offenders (Steffensmeier et al., 1995, 1998). First, criminal justice actors are concerned with the offender's blameworthiness, and will doll out more severe sanctions on offenders who are more blameworthy. Blameworthiness is most readily measured by the severity of the offense, the offender's prior criminal history, and the offender's role in the offense (Steffensmeier et al., 1998).

Second, court personnel are concerned with community safety and will use punishment as a means to protect the community from dangerous offenders. Here, decision-makers consider the nature of the offense (e.g., whether it was violent) and prior criminal involvement, as well as personal factors such as family ties, employment status, and substance abuse history (Steffensmeier et al., 1998; Ulmer, 1997).

Third, decision-makers are mindful of a variety of practical constraints connected to their punishment decisions. Examples of this last concern include local jail overcrowding and the desire to avoid case backlogs. These practical constraints impact punishment decisions because court actors wish to ensure appropriate punishment for the most blameworthy and most dangerous offenders. Therefore, if jail space is limited, judges will identify which offenders are most deserving of incarceration pursuant to the first two focal concerns (Steffensmeier, Kramer, & Streifel, 1993; Ulmer & Kramer, 1996). Judgments made about blameworthiness and threat to the community are informed by both attributions and perceptual shorthands, and the three focal concerns essentially provide the frame within which these mechanisms operate.

Sentencing scholars have also given a lot of recent attention to the application of psychological theories revolving around implicit color bias in the sentencing arena. Studies show that "[e]very population group except blacks unconsciously associates blacks with crime" (Tonry, 2011:8). Researchers use *Implicit Association Tests* (IAT) to measure how quickly a respondent classifies a picture or word into a particular category. IATs measure how quickly research subjects associate positive or negative words to pictures or other indictors of White or Black individuals. Rachlinksi and colleagues (2009) found these unconscious biases among a population of trail judges, and similar studies have also shown unconscious color bias among prosecutors, criminal defense attorneys, and other criminal justice professionals (see Ghandnoosh, 2014). (Interested readers can take the Harvard Implicit Association Test at http://www.implicit.harvard.edu/implicit/).

# Conclusion

There exists a wide range of sentencing policies and practices among U.S. jurisdictions. Sentencing laws have continued to be an area of fluid change in many jurisdictions since the 1970s, and concerns over racial disparities have played a primary role in many of these sentencing reforms. If we take the staggering racial disparity present in U.S. prisons as the starting point, it does not appear that criminal sentencing is a primary cause of the level of disparity in prisons. However, most research finds some disparity in the decision to incarcerate. This is especially true in some places and with regard to certain types of crime, consistent with *contextual discrimination*. Current sentencing research appears to be moving away from general statements about overall disparity in entire populations of offenders to more contextualized assessments of the particular circumstances, locations, and situations in which race matter most.

The overall conclusion of the chapter is that race, ethnicity, and other extralegal factors continue to impact criminal sentencing. Although the situation has improved significantly across US history—as America has concerned itself more and more with equality and fairness—problems remain in some places and circumstances within the criminal courts. More work is needed to alleviate these biases.

# Discussion Questions

1. Define criminal sentencing.
2. Explain discretion in the context of the criminal sentencing process (who exercises discretion and how have allocations of discretion changed over time?).
3. Identify and contrast the primary purposes of sentencing.
4. Describe three types of utilitarian punishment theories.
5. Explain how the landscape of sentencing laws has changed since the 1970s.
6. How has sentencing become more about punishment than rehabilitation?
7. Describe what indirect and interaction effects are in sentencing and how those impact racial disparities.
8. What are the main differences between determinate and indeterminate sentences? Which, in your opinion, are more likely to result in disparities in criminal justice processing? Explain.
9. Define truth-in-sentencing laws, three strikes laws, mandatory minimum penalties, and sentencing guidelines.

10. Why is it important to consider prosecutorial charging and bargaining decisions when discussing race disparities in sentencing?
11. Discuss a leading theory that attempts to explain why some courtroom actors might make racial disparate decisions.

# References

Albonetti, C. A. (1987). Prosecutorial discretion: The effects of uncertainty. *Law & Society Review, 21*(2), 291–313.

Albonetti, C. A. (1991). An integration of theories to explain judicial discretion. *Social Problems* 38:247–66.

Alexander, M. (2012). *The new Jim Crow: Mass incarceration in the age of colorblindness.* The New Press.

Austin, A. (2010). *Criminal Justice Trends—Key Legislative Changes in Sentencing Policy, 2000–2010.* New York: Vera Institute of Justice.

Austin, J. (2010). Reducing America's correctional populations: A strategic plan. *Justice Research and Policy, 12*(1), 9–40.

Baumer, E. P. (2013). Reassessing and redirecting research on race and sentencing. *Justice Quarterly, 30*(2), 231–261.

Baumer, E., Messner, S., & Felson, R. (2000). The role of victim characteristics in the disposition of murder cases. *Justice Quarterly, 17*(2), 281–307.

Blumer (1969). *Symbolic interactionism: Perspective and method.* Prentice-Hall: Englewood Cliffs, N.J.

Blumstein, A. (1982). On the racial disproportionality of United States' prison populations. *J. Crim. l. & Criminology, 73*, 1259.

Blumstein, A. (1998). U.S. Criminal Justice Conundrum: Rising Prison Populations and Stable Crime Rates. *Crime and Delinquency, 44*(1), 127–135.

Bridges, G.S. & S. Steen (1998). Racial disparities in official assessments of juvenile offenders: Attributional stereotypes as mediating mechanisms. *American Sociological Review* 63:554–570.

Bushway, S.D. & Paternoster, R. (2009). The impact of prison on crime. In Steven Raphael and Michael Stoll (ed.) *Do Prisons Make Us Safer? The Benefits and Costs of the Prison Boom.* New York: Russell Sage Foundation.

Bushway, S. D., & Piehl, A. M. (2011). Location, location, location: The impact of guideline grid location on the value of sentencing enhancements. *Journal of Empirical Legal Studies, 8*(1), 222–238.

Carson, E. A. (2014). Prisoners in 2013. *Bureau of Justice Statistics,* September.

Carson, E. A., & Golinelli, D. (2013). Prisoners in 2012. *Bureau of Justice Statistics, December.*

Chan, S. and Moynihan, C. (2009, October 22). Lil Wayne changes plea to guilty on felony gun charge. *New York Times*. Retrieved from http://www.nytimes.com/2009/10/23/nyregion/23lilwayne.html?_r=0.

Chiricos, T. G., & W. D. Bales. (1991). Unemployment and punishment: An empirical assessment. *Criminology* 29:701–24.

Chiricos, T. G., & C. Crawford. (1995). Race and imprisonment: A contextual Assessment of the evidence. In *Ethnicity, Race, and Crime: Perspectives Across Time and Space*, edited by D. F. Hawkins. Albany: State University of New York Press.

Clark, J., Austin, J., & Henry, D. A. (1997). Three strikes and you're out: A review of state legislation. NIJ, research in brief.

Davis, K. C. (1969). *Discretionary Justice: A Preliminary Inquiry*. Baton Rouge: Louisiana State University Press.

Demuth, S. (2003). Racial and ethnic differences in pretrial release decisions and outcomes: A comparison of Hispanic, black, and white felony arrestees. *Criminology, 41*(3), 873–907.

Eisenstein, J., & Jacob, H. (1977). *Felony Justice: An Organizational Analysis of Criminal Courts*. Boston, MA: Little, Brown & Company.

Eligon, J. (2009, August 20). Burress will receive 2-year prison sentence. *New York Times*. Retrieved from http://www.nytimes.com/2009/08/21/nyregion/21burress.html.

Farrell, R., & Holmes, M. (1991). The social and cognitive structure of legal decision-making. *Sociological Quarterly, 32*(4), 529–542.

Feeley, M. M. (1983). *Court Reform on Trial: Why Simple Solutions Fail*. New York: Basic Books.

Feeley, M. M., & Simon, J. (1992). The new penology: Notes on the emerging strategy of corrections and its implications. *Criminology, 30*(4), 449–474.

Frase, R. S. (2005). State sentencing guidelines: Diversity, consensus, and unresolved policy issues. *Columbia Law Review, 105*, 1190–1232.

Frase, R. S. (2013). *Just Sentencing: Principles and Procedures for a Workable System*. Oxford University Press.

Frankel, M. (1973). *Criminal Sentences: Law Without Order*. New York: Hall & Wang.

Freiburger, T. L., & Hilinski, C. M. (2013). An examination of the interactions of race and gender on sentencing decisions using a trichotomous dependent variable. *Crime & Delinquency, 59*(1), 59–86.

Garland, D. (2000). The culture of high crime societies. *British journal of criminology, 40*(3), 347–375.

Ghandnoosh, N. (2014). Race and Punishment: Racial Perceptions of Crime and Support for Punitive Policies. The Sentencing Project, Washington

DC. (http://sentencingproject.org/doc/publications/rd_Race_and_Pun-ishment.pdf) [Oct. 7, 2014].

Harris, J. C. & Jeslow, P. (2000). It's not the old ball game: Three strikes and the courtroom workgroup. *Justice Quarterly* 17:185–203.

Harvard Implicit Association Test, https://implicit.harvard.edu/implicit/user/ncsc/ca/. [Oct. 7, 2014].

Hester, R. and Hartman, T. (forthcoming). Conditional disparities in criminal sentencing: A test of the liberation hypothesis from a non-guidelines state.

Hester, R., & Sevigny, E. L. (2014). Court communities in local context: a multilevel analysis of felony sentencing in South Carolina. *Journal of Crime and Justice*, (ahead-of-print), 1–20.

Holleran, D. & C. Spohn. (2004). On the use of the total incarceration variable in sentencing research. *Criminology* 42:211–40.

Johnson, B. D. (2006). The multilevel context of criminal sentencing: Integrating judge-and county-level influences. *Criminology* 44(2): 259–98.

Kautt P. M. & Spohn C. (2007). Assessing blameworthiness and assigning punishment: Theoretical perspectives on judicial decision making in *Criminal Justice Theory: Explaining the Nature and Behavior of Criminal Justice* (David E. Duffee and Edward R. Maguire, Eds). 155–80. New York: Taylor & Francis Group.

King, R. (2008). Disparity by geography: The war on drugs in America's cities. The Sentencing Project. Retrieved from http://sentencingproject.org/doc/publications/dp_drugarrestreport.pdf.

Koons-Witt, B. (2002). The effect of gender on the decision to incarcerate before and after the introduction of sentencing guidelines. *Criminology, 40*(2), 297–327.

Kutateladze, B., Lynn, V., & Liang, E. (2012). Do race and ethnicity matter in prosecution. *Vera Institute of Justice.*

Lizotte, A. J. (1978). Extra-legal factors in Chicago's criminal courts: Testing the conflict model of criminal justice. *Social Problems, 25*(5), 564–580.

Lowenthal, G. T. (1993). Mandatory sentencing laws: Undermining the effectiveness of determinate sentencing reform. California Law Review 81:61–124.

Marvell, T., & Moody, C. (1996). Determinate sentencing and abolishing parole: The long-term impact on prisons and crime. *Criminology, 34*(1), 107–128.

Miethe, T. D. (1987). Charging and plea bargaining practices under determinate sentencing: An investigation of the hydraulic displacement of discretion. *Journal of Criminal Law and Criminology, 78*(1), 155–176.

Mitchell, O. (2005). A meta-analysis of race and sentencing research: Explaining the inconsistencies. *Journal of Quantitative Criminology* 21 (4):439–66.

Pratt, T. C. (1998). Race and sentencing: A meta-analysis of conflicting empirical research results. *Journal of Criminal Justice*, 26(6), 513–523.

Rachlinski, J. J., Johnson, S. L., Wistrich, A. J., & Guthrie, C. (2008). Does unconscious racial bias affect trial judges. *Notre Dame L. Rev.*, 84, 1195.

The Robina Institute of Criminal Law and Criminal Justice, (http://robinainstitute.org/projects/) [October 7, 2014].

Robinson, M. (2009). *Justice blind? Ideals and realities of American criminal justice.* Upper Saddle River, NJ: Prentice Hall.

Rothman, D. J. (1980). *Conscience and Convenience: The Asylum and Its Alternatives in Progressive America.* Boston: Little, Brown.

Sabol, W. J., Rosich, K., Mallik-Kane, K., Kirk, D. P., & Dubin, G. (2002). *The Influence of Truth in Sentencing Reforms on Change in States' Sentencing Practices and Prison Populations*, (Urban Institute Research Report), Washington, DC: The Urban Institute.

Savelsberg, J. J. (1992). Law that does not fit society: Sentencing guidelines as a neoclassical reaction to the dilemmas of substantivized law. *The American Journal of Sociology* 97(5):1346–81.

Singer, R. (1978). In favor of "presumptive sentences" set by a sentencing commission. *Crime & Delinquency* 24: 401–27.

Souryal, C. and Welford, C. (1997). An examination of unwarranted disparity under Maryland's voluntary sentencing guidelines. A report to the Maryland Commission on Criminal Sentencing. (http://www.msccsp.org/Files/Reports/Souryal_Wellford_97_UnwarrantedDisparity.pdf) [October 7, 2014]

Spohn, C. (2000). Thirty years of sentencing reform: The quest for a racially neutral sentencing process. In *Criminal justice 2000: Politics, Processes, and Decisions of the criminal justice system (pp. 427–501).* Washington, DC: National Institute of Justice/National Criminal Justice Reference Service.

Spohn, C. & Holleran, D. (2000). The imprisonment penalty paid by younger, unemployed black and Hispanic male offenders. *Criminology, 38*(1), 281–306.

Steen, S., Engen, R. L., & Gainey, R. R. (2005). Images of danger and culpability: Racial stereotyping, case processing, and criminal sentencing. *Criminology, 43*(2), 435–468.

Steffensmeier, D., Kramer, J., & Streifel, C. (1993). Gender and imprisonment decisions. *Criminology, 31*(3), 411–446.

Steffensmeier, D., Ulmer, J., & Kramer, J. (1998). The interaction of race, gender and age in criminal sentencing: The punishment cost of being young, black and male. *Criminology, 36*(4), 763–797.

Stemen, D., Rengifo, A., & Wilson, J. (2006). *Of Fragmentation and Ferment: The Impact of State Sentencing Policies on Incarceration Rates, 1975–2002.* Final Report to the National Institute of Justice. Washington, DC: National Institute of Justice.

Stith, K., & J. A. Cabranes. (1998). *Fear of judging: Sentencing guidelines in the federal courts.* Chicago: University of Chicago Press.

Stolzenberg, L. & D'Allessio, S. J. (1994). Sentencing and unwarranted disparity: An empirical assessment of the long-term impact of sentencing guidelines in Minnesota. *Criminology* 32(2):301–09.

Sudnow, D. (1965). Normal crimes: Sociological features of the penal code in a public defender office. *Social Problems, 12*(3), 255–276.

Tonry, M. (1992). Mandatory penalties. In M. Tonry (ed.), *Crime and Justice: A Review of Research*, Volume 16. Chicago: University of Chicago Press.

Tonry, M. (1995). *Malign Neglect—Race, Crime, and Punishment in America.* New York: Oxford University Press.

Tonry, M. (1996). *Sentencing Matters.* New York: Oxford University Press.

Tonry, M. (1999). Reconsidering indeterminate and structured sentencing. Sentencing and Corrections: Issues for the 21st Century. NIJ.

Tonry, M. (2004). *Thinking about Crime Sense and Sensibility in American Penal Culture.* New York: Oxford University Press.

Tonry, M. (2009). Mandatory penalties. In M. Tonry (ed.), *Crime and Justice: A Review of Research*, Volume 38. Chicago: University of Chicago Press.

Tonry, M. (2011). *Punishing race: A continuing American dilemma.* Oxford University Press.

Tonry, M. (2013). Sentencing in America, 1975–2025. *Crime and Justice, 42*(1), 141–198.

Tonry, M., & Melewski, M. (2008). The malign effects of drug and crime control policies on black Americans. *Crime and justice, 37*(1), 1–44.

Ulmer, J. T. (1997). *Social Worlds of Sentencing: Court Communities Under Sentencing Guidelines.* Albany, NY: State University of New York Press.

Ulmer, J. T. & Kramer, J. H. (1996). Court communities under sentencing guidelines: Dilemmas of formal rationality and sentencing disparity. *Criminology* 34:383–408.

von Hirsch, A. (1976). *Doing Justice: The Choice of Punishments.* New York: Hill and Wang.

Walker, S., Spohn, C. & DeLone, M. (2000). *The Color of Injustice: Race, Ethnicity, and Crime in America.* Stamford, CT: Wadsworth.

Wilson, J. Q. (1975). *Thinking About Crime*. New York: Vintage Books.

Wooldredge, J. (2007). Neighborhood effects on felony sentencing. *Journal of Research in Crime and Delinquency*, 44(2), 238–263.

Wooldredge, J. (2009). Short- versus long-term effects of Ohio's switch to more structured sentencing on extra-legal disparities in prison sentences in an urban court. *Criminology and Public Policy* 8:285:312.

Wooldredge, J., Griffin, T., & Rauschenberg, F. (2005). Sentencing reform and reductions in the disparate treatment of felony defendants. *Law & Society Review* 39:835–74.

Zalman, M. (1977). Rise and fall of the indeterminate sentence. *Wayne Law Review* 24(1): 45–94.

# Endnotes

1. It should be noted that while it is technically correct to attribute the discretionary sentencing decision to the judge, there is an important strand of courts literature that suggests such decisions are, to varying degrees, actually attributable to a group of courtroom actors known as the "courtroom workgroup." The courtroom workgroup refers to the trial judge, prosecutor, and defense attorney assigned to handle an offender's case. While the formal adversarial model depicts the prosecutor and defense battling over the truth with a jury as the decider of facts and the judge as the impartial referee, we know that in practice very few cases actually go to trial. In fact, around 95% of all charged criminal cases result in a guilty plea, and in some jurisdictions the number is over 98% (see Hester & Sevigny, 2014). Consequently, the typical case involves a prosecutor and defense attorney who appear before a judge having reached a plea agreement. The plea agreement may include an agreed-upon sentence, a sentence recommendation from the prosecutor, or no mention of the sentence. In any case, the trial judge retains the ultimate authority to accept or reject the plea and to ascribe a sentence, but the reality of the dominance of guilty pleas highlights the substantial roles that other members of the workgroup have in sentencing.

2. About a third of the states have changed from indeterminate to determinate sentencing structures since the early 1970s. Note, however, that offenders may still be eligible for early release in some states, but the release time is predetermined or based on modest potential good time credits, with inmates typically serving at least 85% of their sentences (Blumstein et al., 1983). While only a minority of jurisdictions has adopted determinate structures, their numbers are not insignificant and include California, Florida, Minnesota, Washington, and the federal system (Stemen et al., 2006).

3. Furthermore, while much of the preceding discussion refers to guidelines grids, some jurisdictions implement guidelines through worksheets or other methods besides a grid. For example, the Virginia guidelines require the completion of scoring sheets that include a number of different factors besides just severity and criminal history that are found in grid jurisdictions.

4. Several scholars have investigated the portions of racial disproportionality accounted for at each (or at least some) of the decision points outlined above. Blumstein (1982) undertook

the earliest attempt and found that around 80% of the incarceration disparity in the 1970s was attributable to differences in arrest rates which led him to conclude that differential offending was the primary cause of imprisonment disparities. Tonry and Melewski (2008) replicated Blumstein's study using 2004 data and found that the realities had changed. During the time of the Blumstein analysis around 20% of the disparity could have come from a decision point after offending and arrest; by 2004 that number was over 57%, meaning over half of the incarceration disparity is attributable to a decision point after arrest (Tonry 2010). Moreover, Tonry (2010) found that Blacks were becoming less involved in violent crimes between 1984 and 2008. In other words, disproportionate Black offending is becoming less and less the cause of imprisonment disparities, while the level of imprisonment disparities has held relatively constant: accordingly, it appears that over the past few decades disparate treatment of Black offenders has actually been increasing at one or more of the following levels: prosecutorial screening, pretrial procedures, trial/plea, and sentencing.

# Chapter 8

# Race, Ethnicity, and Corrections

*by Barbara H. Zaitzow, PhD*

## Introduction

Notwithstanding a steady reduction in violent crime rates, the United States continues to hold the dubious distinction of having the world's largest proportion of its population behind bars (International Centre for Prison Studies, 2014). Unprecedented prison growth resulted primarily from "get tough" legislation that decreased judicial and parole authority by using sentencing guidelines, mandatory minimums, and three strikes laws.

The explosion of the United States prison population has had a profound effect on young men of color and the legacy of their imprisonment continues to play out in the lives of their families and communities long after their release. Western (2006) estimates that one in three Black men who never completed high school were incarcerated in 2004 and more recent figures suggest that one in every three Black males born today can expect to go to prison at some point in their life, compared with one in every six Latino males, and one in every 17 White males, if current incarceration trends continue (Sentencing Project, 2013). Rose and Clear (1998) argue that mass incarcerations increase disorganization within disadvantaged communities, reduce social cohesion, remove financial resources, and increase single parent households.

Some scholars have argued that mass incarceration is merely an extension of institutions of control that have existed in our society since slavery (Wacquant, 2002). Specifically, these institutions—slavery, Jim Crow, the ghetto, and prison—have controlled African-American men for centuries. Moreover, people of color are viewed as "dangerous classes" that must be managed by way of the criminal justice system (Feeley & Simon, 1992). Society has chosen to manage these dangerous classes by warehousing them in prisons across the country (Irwin, 2005). In the warehouse prison, prisoners experience few rehabilitative programs and their movement throughout the facility is controlled by strict regulations and state-of-the-art surveillance technology. Managing risk has become the sole function of prisons.

The purpose of this chapter is to highlight some of what we know about racial disparity and discrimination within American corrections. Addressing the problem of racial disparity in the corrections system is complex: hence, what is offered here is an effort to spark continued discussion about what can and should be done within our communities, states, and nation. As you read this chapter, keep in mind that corrections is the end result of American criminal justice practice, meaning that any disparities that exist here typically result from the actions of actors earlier in the system (e.g., police, courts).

# What Is Corrections?

As noted in previous chapters, the criminal justice system is composed of the agencies of police, courts, and corrections. How the criminal justice system works in each area depends on the jurisdiction that is in charge: city, county, state, federal or tribal government or military installation or private.

Different jurisdictions have different laws, agencies, and ways of managing criminal justice processes. The corrections system, presumably representing the community's response to suspected and convicted juvenile and adult offenders, is a significant component of criminal justice. This third component within the criminal justice system is charged with carrying out the sentences of our courts. **Corrections** consists of the programs, services, agencies, and institutions responsible for supervising persons who have been caught, arrested, charged with or convicted of some type of criminal conduct.

The correctional components commonly include probation, jails, prisons, parole, and a variety of intermediate sanctions also referred to as community corrections. A brief description of each is provided in Table 8.1.

---

### Table 8.1. American Correctional Populations

**Probation**—a sentence allowing the offender to serve the sanctions imposed by the court while (s)he lives in the community under supervision (Cole, Clear & Reisig. 2013:76). There may be conditions that are imposed on the person during the length of the sentence (e.g., drug testing, enroll in educational programs, seek employment, etc.) which, if not met, could result in the person having to serve the remainder of the sentence in an institutional setting. There are also variations of this sanction such as **intensive probation** or **shock probation** that are an attempt to address at-risk needs of individuals. Between year-end 2012 and 2013, the adult probation population declined by about 32,200 offenders, falling to an estimated 3,910,647 offenders at year-end 2013. Probationers accounted for most (82%) of the adults under community supervision. Males continued to make up about 75% of the adult probation population. Approximately 54% of parolees were non-Hispanic White, 30% were non-Hispanic Black, 14% were Hispanic or Latino, 1% were American Indian/Alaska Native, and 1% were Asian/Native Hawaiian/other Pacific Islander (Bonczar & Herberman, 2015).

**Jails**—an institution that is administered by the local jurisdiction, such as counties and cities, government wherein the offender is required to remain in the care and custody of the local jurisdiction where (s)he is confined for short periods of time (up to one year) though some variations may occur. Jails are used as a (1) holding facility to maintain custody of people who are unable to pay bail if it is required and/or who have been denied bail and are awaiting or are in the midst of his or her trial; (2) detention facility for those who have been convicted of misdemeanors and were sentenced to a period of time in jail; (3) holding facility for those who have been convicted of state or federal crimes and who are awaiting transfer to a state or federal prison. Currently, approximately 731,208 adults are in jails throughout the United States. Males continued to make up about 86% of the adult jail population. Approximately 47% of the jail population were non-Hispanic White, 36% were non-Hispanic Black, 15% were Hispanic or Latino, 1% were American Indian/Alaska Native, less than 1% were Asian/Native Hawaiian/other Pacific Islander, and less than 1% identified as "2 or more" races (Golinelli & Minton, 2014).

Prisons—a state or federal institution that has the responsibility for the care and custody of those persons convicted of serious crimes, usually felonies, and sentenced for long periods of time (over 1 year) to an institutional setting though some variations may occur in different jurisdictions. As of December 31, 2013, 1,574,741 adults were incarcerated in state and federal prisons, which was an increase of 4,300 prisoners from year-end 2012. Of this number, 1,358,875 were in state prisons and 215,866 were in federal prisons. Private prisons held 8% of the total U.S. prison population at year-end 2013 (Carson, 2014). While more males (1,463,454) were incarcerated in prison than females (111,287), the growth in the female prison population (up 1.9% on average annually) was slightly faster than the growth in the male prison population (up 1.4%) during the period. Approximately 37% of imprisoned males were Black, 32% were White, and 22% were Hispanic. Among females in state or federal prison at year-end 2013, 49% were White, compared to 22% who were Black and 17% who were Hispanic (Carson, 2014).

Parole—is actually a reward for good institutional behavior. It provides for the early release of an inmate from a prison so that they can complete their sentence in the community. Strict rules/guidelines are created such that if the person violates his or her parole, (s)he may be required to serve the remainder of his or her sentence back in the prison setting. The adult parole population increased by about 2,100 offenders between year-end 2012 and 2013, to about 853,200 offenders at year-end 2013. Both the state (up about 1,600 offenders) and federal (up 500 offenders) parole populations grew slightly during this period. Males continued to make up about 88% of the adult parole population. Approximately 43% of parolees were non-Hispanic White, 38% were non-Hispanic Black, 17% were Hispanic or Latino, 1% were American Indian/Alaska Native, and 1% were Asian/Native Hawaiian/other Pacific Islander (Bonczar & Herberman, 2015).

Community Corrections—this is more of a "movement" than an actual sanction but deserves comment. **Intermediate sanctions** are a range of punishments that can be varied by the intensity of supervision and combination(s) of sanctions that allows the offender to remain in the com-

munity and receive the programmatic attention necessary to decrease risk
of recidivism. With creative sentencing practices, this sanction has the flexibility to be used as a "front-door" sanction (e.g., a person might be sentenced to probation, completion of a drug treatment program, and home
confinement) or as a "back-door" early release mechanism with added supervision provisions (e.g., a person might be released from prison sooner
than the original sentence called for but along with being on parole they might
be required to live in a halfway house and attend a treatment program(s)
during the parole period). Because of the variations in sentencing options,
one need simply examine the numeric, gender, and racial figures for probation and parole (above) to determine that most people in the correctional system are living in communities throughout our nation.

Source: http://www.bjs.gov/content/pub/pdf/cpus13.pdf

---

While the vast majority of correctional "clients" are currently under some
form of community supervision, mass incarceration within the last 40 years in
the United States has resulted in high incarceration rates and the number of people under correctional supervision today. Further, **mass incarceration** has dis-
proportionally impacted people of color.

As a result of the *war on drugs* and new sentencing policies, the United States
currently has 6.9 million persons under the supervision of the criminal justice
system. Of this number, more than two million people are incarcerated in various local, state, and federal institutional settings. The vast majority of offenders—approximately eight in ten offenders—were under community
supervision at year-end 2013 (3,910,600 on probation compared with 853,200
on parole). Additionally, over half a million ex-prisoners reenter communities each year (Glaze & Kaeble, 2014). The crisis in American prisons, the
record numbers of prisoners returning home, and escalating costs, have profound implications for corrections and communities.

Comparatively, while the U.S. has the highest incarceration rate of any in-
dustrialized nation in the world, America's incarcerated—unlike those in many
other societies—are disproportionately minorities. This growth in incarceration has had a significant impact on young men residing in impoverished inner
cities and rural communities. The existence of race-related differences in the
juvenile and adult criminal justice systems are most commonly described by the
terms: *over-representation*; and *racial disparity*. **Over-representation** is a term
used to compare the percentage of racial and ethnic minorities in a particular
population (e.g., the juvenile justice system) with the percentage of racial and
ethnic minorities in the general population (e.g., county or state); if there is a
larger percentage of racial and ethnic minorities in the particular population

than in the general population, we say minorities are *over-represented* in the particular population or the minority population is disproportionately large (Governor's Summit, 2008).

As noted in earlier chapters, **racial disparity** is a pattern of outcomes in which some racial groups are treated differently from others; specifically, when the proportion of a racial or ethnic group within the system is greater than the portion of such a group in the general population (Sentencing Project, 2008). For example, if minority youth are more likely to receive detention than nonminority youth for the same offense, then racial disparity in sentencing exists. Although illegitimate or unwarranted racial disparity in the criminal justice system is the result of dissimilar treatment of individuals in similar situations based on race, the causes of such disparity will vary and can occur at different points in the criminal justice system. **Discrimination** occurs if and when decisionmakers treat one group of individuals differently from another group of individuals based wholly, or in part, on their gender, racial, and/or ethnic status.

Discrepancies in treatment throughout the system may be due to overt racial bias as well as indirect influences associated with race (Sentencing Project, 2008). The criminal justice system is supposed to be based on the principle that it is making our society a just and safe place; where the punishment fits the crime and all people, as with any institution in America, are treated equally. However, in light of the disproportionate numbers of minority members represented in our punishment system, this assumption or ideology about the American criminal justice system has been questioned.

Despite America's long standing battle for equality, disparity and discrimination have yet to be eliminated. The recent protests in Missouri, New York, and other states have captured the attention of the nation, focusing on injustice and racial disparities in the justice system. The issues raised by the protests are complex, but the frustrations with the disparities in our justice system have been well documented. A new report from the National Academy of Sciences (2014), points to the profound racial disparities in our nation's prison system and calls for an end to the mass incarceration of minorities especially for low-level offenses. While formidable, these challenges provide an opportunity to think more broadly about (1) the purpose of punishment in American society, (2) how the enactment of specific laws and punishments along with extra-legal factors impact who is more likely to become a client of the American correctional system, and (3) consideration of the far-reaching impact of the correctional system on the individuals who live and work in the system, their families, communities, and society as a whole.

Even with the modest reduction of the prison population in the past three years, much of the downsizing occurred in California in response to a Supreme

Court order to relieve prison overcrowding (*Brown v. Plata*, 2011) though, after several appeals, the court extended the deadline for compliance to February 2016. For other states reporting some drop in the number of prisoners, tightened state budgets, plummeting crime rates, changes in sentencing laws, and shifts in public opinion have combined to reverse the trend. Evidence-based changes in state and federal sentencing laws for lower-level offenses like those involving drugs have played a central role in the shift with many states setting up diversion programs for offenders as an alternative to prison. And some states have softened their policies on parole, no longer automatically sending people back to prison for parole violations. Yet, even with the modest imprisonment declines, the corrections system, as a whole, continues to touch the lives of all Americans and especially those in minority communities.

# Functions of Corrections

As a general overview, the primary *philosophical* purposes or goals of corrections are *retribution, deterrence, incapacitation, rehabilitation,* and *restoration.* Many of these terms were first mentioned in Chapter 7 and they are defined in Table 8.2.

---

### Table 8.2. Purposes of Punishment

Retribution—This is based on the concept of *lex talionis,* the law of retaliation, which is similar to the idea of an "eye for an eye" (Seiter 2005). The *just deserts* model demands that punishment match the degree of harm criminals have inflicted on their victims; hence those being processed for less serious crimes should receive less harsh punishment. It assumes that the offender knew what (s)he was doing at the time of crime commission therefore offender responsibility and accountability are at the core of this punishment philosophy. But, there are differences of opinion regarding what punishment should be considered appropriate for particular actions (e.g., what behavior is deemed bad enough to receive imprisonment or a death sentence). Variations in sentencing are based on diverse factors and do not always get uniformly applied throughout the nation.

Deterrence—the principle that people are deterred from involvement in crime by the threat of punishment. While the purpose of the correctional system is to deter everyone in society (*general deterrence*), there are situations and crimes in which the punishment is meant to address the particular individual's behavior (*specific/special deterrence*). The goal of this philosophy is to reduce recidivism and to promote law-abiding behavior through preventive measures. Deterrence has been used for a long time, often in the form of police presence as well as punishment of someone in order to make an example out of them so others see what will happen if they commit that same type of crime. This is crime prevention through fear of punishment.

Incapacitation—punishment that removes the offender from the ability to victimize or harm people outside of the prison setting. There is no concern with deterrence or rehabilitation as much as the sole purpose being to defend society from criminal predation. It is accepted that some criminals will never change and need to be put away, out of society's way, and kept contained in a controlled environment, such as a prison, for others' protection. Incapacitation rarely shows commonalities with the other goals; usually it just means that the criminal is isolated from society in a jail/prison to serve out his/her time. The criminal is restrained from committing other crimes. According to the Sentencing Project, this has "resulted in prison overcrowding and state governments being overwhelmed by the burden of funding a rapidly expanding penal system, despite increasing evidence that large-scale incarceration is not the most effective means of achieving public safety."

Rehabilitation—to restore or return the offender to constructive and/or law-abiding activity through help or treatment. Based on the medical model, the criminal's behavior is thought to result from some moral or social sickness that can be cured or controlled through treatment. Today, such treatment usually involves some form of programming and the goal is to change the criminal to be law abiding, providing them with resources to lead a non-criminal lifestyle. The goal takes the approach of "reintegrating the offender with the community ... making the offender a productive member of society—one who contributes to the general well-being of the whole" (Schmalleger & Smykla, 2009:77).

Restoration—this goal is founded on the premise that the crime is not just breaking the law with the state laws, but it brings harm against the victim and the community as well. Therefore, its goal is to repair the damage done to not only the community but the victim as well. Because of that, restorative justice is based on the idea that both the victim and the community should be involved with the punishment through various programs, mediations, and reconciliations. "A key feature of restorative justice is equity, where all parties not only agree on the proposed solution, but offender accountability is also heightened" (Champion, 2008:189).

While there may be overlap between each, these functions are meant for the purposes of reducing crime and facilitating public safety. In America, people who are caught and formally processed through the criminal justice system are punished in accordance with these philosophical ideals that are reflected in the lawful sanctions allowed depending on the sentencing structure in use at the time (*indeterminate* versus *determinate*). For example, first degree murder convictions typically draw the harshest sentences of any crime. Practically speaking, there is less concern with the rehabilitation of the offender as compared to retribution, deterrence, and incapacitation for the criminal act(s). As with the elements of the crime (e.g., actus reus, mens rea, and concurrence) and defenses available (e.g., insanity, self-defense, etc.), sentencing can vary from state to state (e.g., life without parole, death penalty) but the possible sentences typically depend on whether the prosecution can prove any of a host of *aggravating factors* as outlined in state statutes (FindLaw, 2013). The law, however, like most aspects of social life is subject to change; hence, the popularity of each of the correctional philosophies—and the sanctions that are supposed to embody that philosophy—tend to be created, utilized, and discarded after a period of time, and then resurrected, re-utilized, and eventually again dropped from the repertoire of programs, functions, and attitudes.

# Ideals of American Corrections

The correctional system is presumed to assist with maintaining the integrity of the law and the ability of law to protect society by punishing those convicted of law-violating behavior and deterring the rest of the population from involvement in criminal behavior. The punishment system "helps society to enforce its behavioral norms, since the mere existence of a prison system is supposed to reinforce the belief that there is a place where people can be put who exceed our tolerance for deviant behavior. In this sense, prisons serve to protect society, help define the limits of behavior, and help everyone know and understand what is permissible and what is not permissible. Simultaneously, almost all contemporary correctional systems claim to seek fair punishment as required by *procedural justice*. Public protection (or public safety) is maintained by having a well-regulated set of procedures, facilities, and philosophies that are consistent with what court officials want and what society needs. Fair punishment is accomplished by applying some *corrective* yet still *punitive* action to convicted offenders that most often takes the form of humane security, custody, and control along a range of program opportunities all administered in a just and equitable manner within the least restrictive environment consistent with public safety" (O'Connor, 2012:1).

This ideal, however, has been questioned in recent years in light of the disproportionate number of minority group members subject to the punishment system along with the numerous abuses of those in the care and custody of local, state, and federal governments that have been brought to the attention of the legal system. Here, one of the many examples of abuse of women prisoners is noted in a U.S. Department of Justice report (January 2014) detailing an initial investigation of Julia Tutwiler Prison for Women in Alabama. While the list of abuses is too lengthy to include here, the overarching finding was that Tutwiler had a toxic, sexualized environment that permitted staff, sexual abuse, and harassment. The facts of the case are that such treatment of women prisoners who were in the care and custody of the government had gone on for over two decades in America with no official response. The Equal Justice Initiative (EJI), a private, nonprofit organization that is committed to alleviating as many of the problems that they can that are caused by unfair criminal justice policies, championed the interests of the women prisoners who endured decades of sexual abuse at the hands of their captors.

And, in a different but recent legal action, the case of George Stinney intersects some long-running disputes in the American legal system—the death penalty and race. At 14, he was the youngest person executed in the United States in the past 100 years for the alleged killing of two young White girls in 1944. Because of the lynch mob hysteria that was rampant at the time, Stinney was kept at a jail 50 miles away from his home where he had no family visits and had to endure the trial and death alone. The sheriff at the time said Stinney admitted to the killings, but there is only his word—no written record of the confession has been found. Today, Stinney's conviction is being challenged by a lawsuit filed by supporters asking for a new trial, a move unprecedented in South Carolina for someone already put to death (Death Penalty Information Center, 2014). These cases provide evidence of the often hushed examples of the divide that exists between the ideals and realities of the American justice system. There are countless other cases available for consideration.

The next section will address what we know about the realities of racial disparity in the realm of the correctional system(s). However, the reader should not blindly accept official criminal justice statistics as unbiased representations of "truth" and/or "fairness" as there are many extra-legal factors that can and do impact the justice process. We know, for example, that demographic variables like race, gender, age, and socio-economic status impact the likelihood not only of involvement in certain crime categories but also who is most vulnerable to detection and apprehension, processing by agents of the system as well as the ultimate outcomes for those subject to the punishment system. As shown in Chapter 5, *racial profiling* does occur and while there may be debates on whether it is due to real crime-related issue(s) or personal biases of officers, it does impact who is arrested (Heath, 2014). And, as shown in this book, racial disparity has been empirically documented in various domains including post-arrest decision-making to charge the accused person (Sommers & Marotta, 2015), the plea bargain "deals" offered to minority group members (Kutateladze et al., 2014), and the legal outcomes in cases when the accused is financially able to be represented by a privately retained attorney versus a public defender who is assigned to the case (Hewlett, 2011). So, do prison populations mirror what is just and fair (e.g., people actually committed crimes and were caught, their due process rights were honestly protected at all phases of criminal justice processing, and the punishments fit the crime as per the law) or the numeric representations of resource-challenged individuals who are at the mercy of those in positions of power to render life-changing decisions and punishment outcomes (e.g., the person is willing to accept a plea bargain of "life" imprisonment as compared to risking a death sentence)? The interpretation of the statistical picture of corrections populations requires an on-going and critical assessment of the individuals and processes that comprise the entire criminal justice system.

# Realities of American Corrections

Some consider the American prison system to be a means of punishment that serves no positive purpose and places the economy in financial hardship. Others believe the prison system is justified as it guarantees society protection from those who pose a serious threat to individuals who abide by the laws that govern. No matter what one may believe, America outstrips every other nation in the world in the number of people it puts in its prisons. According to the Bureau of Justice Statistics (2013), one out of every 35 adults in the United States is under some form of correctional supervision in prison or jail (Glaze & Kaeble, 2014). Not only are American prisons among the most populated in the world, they are disproportionately populated by minorities. Different explanations as to why this is the case will be presented in a later section of this chapter. Most will agree, however, that many institutionalized policies and laws of the justice system in America target the poor and people of color who are often in both categories due to other, larger social inequities (e.g., sentencing practices). In particular, due to mandatory imprisonment policies for non-violent drug-related crimes, the population across racial groups remain high.

## Racial Disparity

*Racial disparity* in the correctional population refers to the difference in the number of minorities versus Whites represented inside institutions and/ or on probation or parole. The American Correctional Association acknowledges that "racial disparity exists within adult and juvenile detention and correctional systems. This contributes to the perception of unfairness and injustice in the justice system" (ACA Policies, 2004:68). This difference in proportionality does not necessarily involve *individual discrimination*; it can be explained by a number of combined factors. Correctional agencies do not control the number of minorities who enter their facilities or are placed on their probation/parole caseloads. Therefore, the disparity must come from decisions made earlier in the criminal justice process. Law enforcement, court pre-sentencing policies and procedures, and sentencing all have a direct effect on the over-representation of minorities in the correctional population.

Although the disparate impact of the criminal justice system on minorities is often presented as a "new" issue, it is not. Our history is marred by a long relationship with mistreating other humans, using things like indentured servitude, slavery, Jim Crow and what we now see as *institutional discrimination* or **coded racism.** Criminologists have long debated the presence of racial disparity at various stages in the criminal justice system, from initial on-the-street encounters between citizens and police officers to the sentencing behavior of judges. What is new is the use of statistics designed to persuade the public, and not just other academicians and researchers, that racial disparities exist in the system, and that these disparities necessitate significant policy changes. While the extent of disproportionate minority representation varies at different stages of the criminal justice system, it is consistently present, particularly for Blacks, who make up more than 30 percent of all adult correctional populations but account for only 13 percent of the general population (Carson, 2014; Sentencing Project, 2014).

Because a racially discriminatory process violates the ideals of equal treatment under law under which our criminal justice system is premised (Kansal, 2005) along with events made public in the media during the past year—in particular the number of deaths of Blacks by law enforcement—the topic of institutional racism has resurfaced. Evidence of racial disparity within the community and institutional correctional systems will be presented next.

## Disparities in Probation and Other Community Sanctions

Of the 3,910,647 adults on probation at year-end 2013, 75% were male and 25% were female. Also, 54% of probationers were non-Hispanic Whites, 30% were non-Hispanic Blacks, 14% were Hispanic/Latino, 1% were American Indian/Alaska Native, and 1% were Asian/Native Hawaiian/other Pacific Islander. Property offenses (29%) and drug offenses (25%) were the most serious offenses for all probationers in 2013. Of the 853,215 adults on parole during this time frame, 88% were male and 12% were female. Also, 43% were non-Hispanic Whites, 38% were non-Hispanic Blacks, 17% were Hispanic/Latino, 1% were American Indian/Alaska Native, and 1% were Asian/Native Hawaiian/other Pacific Islander. Again, drug offenses were the most serious offenses for 33% of all parolees in 2013 (Bonczar & Herberman, 2015).

Blacks, who despite constituting just 13% of the US population, account for 30% of adult probationers (versus Whites at 54% of probationers). The explanation for the larger percentage of White probationers is typically couched in terms of the preferential treatment and sentencing that White defendants receive when compared with people of color especially as it relates to drug-related offenses; specifically, that Black defendants are less likely to receive a sentence that keeps them in their communities and instead are sentenced to imprisonment more so than White defendants.

There are more probationers than parolees, prisoners, and jail inmates combined. Probation practice and outcomes thus affect the lives of more adults than any other criminal justice sanction (Glaze & Kaeble, 2014). Further, probation supervision represents an important fork in the road for justice-involved individuals, with failure on probation setting a path for more severe sanctioning, particularly incarceration. Disparities in *probation revocations*, for example, could then contribute to disparities in incarceration. While few studies examine racial and ethnic disparities at this decision point, Janetta et al (2014) investigated this idea and discovered that front-end disparity or bias ("who" receives probation as a sanction) can, indeed, impact revocation decisions. The most striking finding in the study was the consistent presence of disparity in probationer revocation outcomes to the disadvantage of Black probationers. Revocation rates for Black probationers were higher than for White and Hispanic probationers in every study site. This is an emerging line of criticism of actuarial risk assessment, namely that relying on risk assessment for purposes such as setting the intensity of probation supervision and determining appropriate responses to violations exacerbates racial disparities in the justice system.

## Disparities in Jail and Prison

At midyear 2013, US jails were estimated to have held a total of 731,208 inmates. Of these, 624,700 (85.4%) were male and 101,900 (13.9%) were female. The racial and ethnic demographic breakdown was estimated as follows: 344,900 were White (47.2%), 261,500 were Black/African American (35.8%), 107,900 were Hispanic/Latino (14.8%), 10,200 were American Indian/Alaska Native (1.4%), 5,100 were Asian/Native Hawaiian/other Pacific Islander (.7%), and 1600 were reported as two or more races (0.2%) (Minton & Golinell, 2014).

## Male Inmates

With respect to state and federal prison populations, "On December 31, 2013, about 37% of imprisoned males were Black, 32% were White, and 22% were Hispanic. This translates into almost 3% of Black male U.S. residents of all ages being imprisoned during this time frame (2,805 inmates per 100,000 Black male U.S. residents), compared to 1% of Hispanic males (1,134 per 100,000) and 0.5% of White males (466 per 100,000) (Carson, 2014:1).

Approximately 58% of male inmates were age 39 or younger. Among males, White prisoners were generally older than Black or Hispanic prisoners. An estimated 17,300 inmates age 65 or older (54%) were White males. However, Black males had higher imprisonment rates across all age groups than all other races and Hispanic males. In the age range with the highest imprisonment rates for males (ages 25 to 39), Black males were imprisoned at rates at least 2.5 times greater than Hispanic males and 6 times greater than White males. For males ages 18 to 19—the age range with the greatest difference in imprisonment rates between Whites and Blacks—Black males (1,092 inmates per 100,000 Black males) were more than nine times more likely to be imprisoned than White males (115 inmates per 100,000 White males) (Carson, 2014:8).

A recent report on racial disparities that permeate the American criminal justice system noted that if current incarceration trends continue, one in every three Black males born today can expect to go to prison at some point in their life, compared with one in every six Latino males, and one in every 17 White males (Sentencing Project, 2013). Not only are racial minorities more likely than White Americans to be arrested but once arrested, they are more likely to be convicted and are more likely to receive harsh sentences. Based on current figures, the crimes that landed Black men in prison, however, are not too different from their White and Hispanic counterparts. Eighteen percent of Blacks in state prisons were convicted of drug crimes, compared to 15 percent of Whites and 17 percent of Hispanics. And, while White and Blacks may use drugs at similar rates, Blacks are more likely to be arrested for it.

Blacks are also more likely to be arrested for other crimes. For example, both Blacks and Hispanics are slightly more likely than Whites to be convicted of violent crimes, while Whites are slightly more likely to be convicted of property crimes like burglary, larceny, and car theft. But the leading violent crime that lands Blacks in prison is robbery, while the leading violent crime for Whites is rape or sexual assault. More than twice as many Blacks are in state prison for robbery as for rape, while for Whites the proportions are reversed (Waldman, 2013). As a reminder, most inmates are in state prisons and each state has its own crime and sentencing laws—along with variations in levels of economic development and different cultures that might or might not produce more violence—which might contribute to the variance between states.

## Female Inmates

Among females in state or federal prison at year-end 2013, 49% were White, compared to 22% who were Black and 17% who were Hispanic. While there were fewer Black females in state or federal prison at year-end 2013 than in 2012, Black females were imprisoned at more than twice the rate of White females (Carson, 2014). Not unlike male inmates, most female inmates (61%) in state or federal prison were age 39 or younger. Black females ages 18 to 19 (33 inmates per 100,000) were almost five times more likely to be imprisoned than White females (7 inmates per 100,000) (Carson, 2014:1, 8).

A recent report released by the Sentencing Project finds that there has been a dramatic shift in racial disparities among women inmates over the past decade (Mauer, 2013). While Black women were incarcerated in state and federal prisons at six times the rate of White women in 2000, this ratio declined by 53 percent, or about 2.8-to-1, by 2009. While there are likely many factors at play in this laudable shift in racial disparities among incarcerated women—including changes in law enforcement practices, sentencing practices, or the involvement of women in crime—the same report suggests that the reduced number of drug incarcerations is the likely explanation for a significant portion of the trend. Though African-American women were disproportionately affected by drug offense incarceration, any policies that result in a substantial reduction in these types of offenses would also disproportionately benefit them, the disparities still exist implying that more is still needed.

Further, despite these notable improvements, the rising rate of incarcerated women is still a substantial problem. For starters, the narrowing in disparities has not been felt equally among all women of color. While Black women experienced a decline of 30.7 percent in their rate of incarceration between 2000 and 2009, Latino women experienced a 23.3 percent rise over the same time period (Mauer, 2013). Likewise, White women experienced an incarceration rate increase of 47.1 percent. These disparate trends could be explained by the combination of increased methamphetamine enforcement — a drug disproportionately used by Whites and Latinos — and the continued use of harsh sentencing policies.

## Juveniles and "Life" Sentences

Racial disparity has also affected juvenile offenders, as shown in chapter 10. In the last ten years, the Supreme Court has made some monumental decisions about the punishment of young offenders. In *Roper v. Simmons*, decided in 2005, the court held that it was cruel and unusual punishment to impose the death penalty for killings committed by juveniles. As in other areas of criminal punishment, America is an outlier in its imposition of life sentences without the possibility of parole not only for adults (LWOP) but for juveniles (JLWOP) who are adjudicated as adults. The U.S. Supreme Court recently ruled (*Graham v. Florida*, 2010) that life without parole sentences are unconstitutional for those who were under 18 years of age at the time of committing a crime other than homicide. As the Sentencing Project report points out: "While the ruling is limited to juveniles, it raises anew the question of whether it is ever appropriate to sentence individuals to life with no possibility of release when their crime was not a homicide" (Nellis, 2013:8). In a subsequent ruling (*Miller v. Alabama*, 2012), the Supreme Court held that even juveniles found guilty of homicide could not be subject to mandatory life without parole sentences. Judges may still choose to impose life without parole sentences in specific juvenile homicide cases, and many states are still considering whether the ruling applies retroactively, meaning the United States remains the only country in the world to impose LWOP punishment on youth.

In spite of the fact that the prison population in the U.S. has declined modestly in recent years, a report by The Sentencing Project (Nellis, 2013) finds that one in every nine prisoners is serving a life sentence, and that the number of such prisoners has more than quadrupled since 1984 and continues to grow at a startling pace. More prisoners today are serving life terms than ever before — over 159,000 people were serving life sentences in 2012, with nearly 50,000 serving life without parole — under tough mandatory minimumsentencing laws and the declining use of parole for eligible convicts (Nellis, 2013). This accounting does not include the countless others who have effective life sentences, either because they are sentenced to very long terms such as

120 years, or because they are sentenced later in life to terms that effectively mean death in prison. The report includes a series of interesting facts about those serving life sentences and highlights the stark racial disparity for this population, as shown in Table 8.3.

### Table 8.3. Life Without Parole

- The population of prisoners serving life without parole (LWOP) has risen more sharply than those with the possibility of parole: there has been a 22.2% increase in LWOP since 2008, an increase from 40,174 individuals to 49,081.
- Approximately 10,000 lifers have been convicted of nonviolent offenses, including more than 2,500 for a drug offense and 5,400 for a property crime.
- Nearly half of lifers are African-American and 1 in 6 are Latino.
- More than 5,300 (3.4%) of the life-sentenced inmates are female.
- More than 10,000 life-sentenced inmates have been convicted of crimes that occurred before they turned 18 and nearly 1 in 4 of them were sentenced to LWOP.

Source: http://sentencingproject.org/doc/publications/inc_Life%20Goes%20On%202013.pdf

The racial disparities among those persons subject to these penalties make their use even more problematic. Nationally, while almost half (47.2%) of life-sentenced inmates are African-American, the Black population of lifers reaches much higher in states such as Maryland (77.4%), Georgia (72.0%), and Mississippi (71.5%). In the federal system, 62.3% of the life-sentenced population is African-American. With respect to the JLWOP population, of the 2,500 individuals currently serving JLWOP sentences, 61% are African-American, 27% are White, and 12% are "other."

As noted in the study, the proportion of African-Americans serving JLWOP sentences for the killing of a White person (43.4%) is nearly twice the rate at which African-American juveniles overall have taken a White person's life (23.2%). Yet the odds of a JLWOP sentence for a White offender who killed a Black victim are only about half as likely (3.6%) as the proportion of White juveniles arrested for killing Blacks (6.4%) (Nellis, 2013). While there may be factors that could account for this large-scale disparity (e.g., prior record, nature of the victim-assailant relationship), detailed information about these possible variables influencing sentencing decisions is lacking. These data are depicted in Table 8.4.

### Table 8.4. Race of Homicide Victims and Offenders

*White Homicide Victims*

|  | Total | JLWOP Sentences |
|---|---|---|
| Black Offenders | 23.2% (6,488) | 43.4% (319) |
| White Offenders | 76.8% (21,510) | 56.6% (416) |

*Black Homicide Victims*

|  | Total | JLWOP Sentences |
|---|---|---|
| Black Offenders | 93.6% (24,118) | 96.4% (567) |
| White Offenders | 6.4% (1,651) | 3.6% (21) |

Source: http://sentencingproject.org/doc/publications/jj_The_Lives_of_Juvenile_Lifers.pdf

When there is no real and tangible prospect of release for life inmates, many believe the punishment to be cruel and unusual. Replacing the death sentence with another form of penalty in which a prisoner inevitably will die in prison is only a partial success for those interested in reform. As abolition of the death penalty gathers momentum, working on what happens instead arguably becomes a more important issue.

## *Death Penalty*

As further explored in Chapter 9, many studies have shown that there is significant racial bias in the administration of the death penalty (Baldus et al., 1998, 1983; Death Penalty Information Center, 2014). This disparity manifests itself in two forms. First, those convicted of killing Whites are more likely to be sentenced to death than those convicted of killing Blacks even when controlling for crime-specific variables. Second, Black defendants are more likely to be sentenced to death regardless of the race of their victims. When these two factors are taken together, the impact of race on capital sentencing is staggering (Baumgartner et al., forthcoming 2015). This became all too evident on September 21, 2011, when the state of Georgia executed Troy Davis, a Black man, for the murder of a White, off-duty police officer. Mr. Davis was executed despite the fact that evidence of witness coercion, intimidation and fabrication of testimony by police had raised serious doubt as to his guilt. Just as in the Jim Crow era, a Black person can still be executed in America even when his guilt is in question. Statistical disparities in capital punishment have led many of the most respected American jurists to call for the abolition of the death penalty because of its racially disparate impact, among other factors.

At year-end 2013, 35 states and the Federal Bureau of Prisons held 2,979 inmates under sentence of death, which was 32 fewer inmates than at year-end 2012. This represents the thirteenth consecutive year in which the number of inmates under sentence of death decreased. Of prisoners under sentence of death at year-end 2013, 56% were White and 42% were Black. The 389 Hispanic inmates under sentence of death accounted for 14% of inmates with a known ethnicity. Ninety-eight percent of inmates under sentence of death were male, and 2% were female. The race and sex of inmates under sentence of death has remained relatively stable since 2000 (Snell, 2014:1).

Table 8.5 illustrates the racial and ethnic breakdown of America's death row inmates. As you can see, African-Americans are overrepresented among death row inmates in nearly every state that has the death penalty. The other populations are generally underrepresented among death row inmates in the US.

However, the criminal history patterns of death row inmates differed by race and Hispanic origin. More Black inmates had a prior felony conviction (73%), compared to Hispanic (65%) or White (64%) inmates. Similar percentages of White (9%), Black (10%), and Hispanic (7%) inmates had a prior homicide conviction. A slightly higher percentage of Hispanic (32%) and Black (31%) inmates were on probation or parole at the time of their capital offense, compared to 24% of White inmates.

The issue of racial disparity in the administration of the death penalty has been a part of modern law. Starting with *Furman v. Georgia* and continuing on to *McCleskey v. Kemp* (both cases are discussed in Chapter 9) courts have struggled to come to grips with this issue. Every state that has taken a careful look at the application of their death penalty system has found grave racial bias in sentencing, risk of executing an innocent person, and other fundamental flaws such as the systematic exclusion of jurors based on race or religious practice. For example, one study examined jury selection decisions in 173 cases between 1990 and 2010, involving 7,421 potential jurors (82% were White, 16% were Black). In 166 cases, where there was at least one Black potential juror, prosecutors dismissed more than twice as many Blacks from the jury (56%) as others (25%). With Black defendants, the disparity was even greater. Even accounting for "alternative explanations" besides race—for instance, excluding those who expressed ambivalence about the death penalty—the study found Blacks were still more than twice as likely to be dismissed (Grosso & O'Brien, 2012). And a sentencing study by Eberhardt et al (2006) found the impact of race to be even more nuanced: stereotypically Black-looking defendants (broad nose, big lips, darker skin) were twice as likely to be sentenced to death by judges and juries.

These potential jurors are eliminated using **peremptory challenges**, where people sitting in jury pools can be dismissed without cause. Dismissing peo-

Table 8.5. Racial and Ethnic Breakdown of Death Rows Current Death Row Populations by Race as of January 1, 2015

| State | Total | Black | White | Latino | Native Amer. | Asian |
|---|---|---|---|---|---|---|
| Alabama | 198 | 104 | 90 | 3 | 0 | 1 |
| Arizona | 124 | 16 | 76 | 27 | 3 | 2 |
| Arkansas | 34 | 20 | 14 | 0 | 0 | 0 |
| California | 743 | 269 | 254 | 182 | 12 | 26 |
| Colorado | 3 | 3 | 0 | 0 | 0 | 0 |
| Connecticut | 12 | 6 | 5 | 1 | 0 | 0 |
| Delaware | 17 | 10 | 4 | 3 | 0 | 0 |
| Florida | 403 | 152 | 217 | 31 | 1 | 2 |
| Georgia | 87 | 42 | 42 | 3 | 0 | 0 |
| Idaho | 11 | 0 | 11 | 0 | 0 | 0 |
| Indiana | 14 | 3 | 11 | 0 | 0 | 0 |
| Kansas | 10 | 4 | 6 | 0 | 0 | 0 |
| Kentucky | 35 | 6 | 29 | 0 | 0 | 0 |
| Louisiana | 85 | 56 | 25 | 3 | 0 | 1 |
| Maryland | 4 | 3 | 1 | 0 | 0 | 0 |
| Mississippi | 48 | 25 | 22 | 0 | 0 | 1 |
| Missouri | 35 | 13 | 22 | 0 | 0 | 0 |
| Montana | 2 | 0 | 2 | 0 | 0 | 0 |
| Nebraska | 11 | 2 | 4 | 5 | 0 | 0 |
| Nevada | 77 | 29 | 39 | 8 | 0 | 1 |
| New Hampshire | 1 | 1 | 0 | 0 | 0 | 0 |
| New Mexico | 2 | 0 | 2 | 0 | 0 | 0 |
| North Carolina | 158 | 80 | 64 | 5 | 8 | 1 |
| Ohio | 145 | 77 | 63 | 3 | 0 | 2 |
| Oklahoma | 49 | 21 | 23 | 2 | 3 | 0 |
| Oregon* | 36 | 3 | 28 | 3 | 1 | 0 |
| Pennsylvania | 188 | 102 | 67 | 17 | 0 | 2 |

Table 8.5. Racial and Ethnic Breakdown of Death Rows Current Death Row Populations by Race as of January 1, 2015 (cont.)

| State | Total | Black | White | Latino | Native Amer. | Asian |
|---|---|---|---|---|---|---|
| South Carolina | 45 | 24 | 20 | 1 | 0 | 0 |
| South Dakota | 3 | 0 | 3 | 0 | 0 | 0 |
| Tennessee | 73 | 33 | 36 | 1 | 1 | 2 |
| Texas | 276 | 115 | 77 | 79 | 0 | 5 |
| Utah | 9 | 1 | 5 | 2 | 1 | 0 |
| Virginia | 8 | 3 | 4 | 1 | 0 | 0 |
| Washington | 9 | 4 | 5 | 0 | 0 | 0 |
| Wyoming | 1 | 0 | 1 | 0 | 0 | 0 |
| US Gov't | 62 | 28 | 25 | 7 | 1 | 1 |
| US Military | 6 | 3 | 3 | 0 | 0 | 0 |

* One member of Death Row's race is not currently identified.
(In this table, the total of inmates on death row will be slightly higher than the national total of 3,035 because some inmates were sentenced to death in more than one state and hence will be counted twice.)

Figures from NAACP-LDF "Death Row USA (January 1, 2015)." Courtesy of Death Penalty Information Center.

ple based on their race is strictly forbidden by law, yet prosecutors have been shown to disproportionately strike African-Americans from jury pools in several states (Robinson, 2008); in this way, discrimination has been legalized in practice when it comes to the criminal courts (Alexander, 2010).

Legal scholars named *McCleskey* one of the worst decisions since World War II. Law professor Anthony Anderson called it "the Dred Scott of our time," referencing the 1857 decision that upheld slavery while Professor Michelle Alexander (2010) referred to it as the *Plessy v. Ferguson* of our time, referencing the 1896 decision to justify racial segregation. Since *McCleskey*, defense attorneys had a virtually impossible legal task of convincing judges to allow jury studies to be presented in order to prove racial bias not only in death sentencing but also in challenging bias at any stage of the judicial process. But two challenges have arisen from the South. **Racial Justice Acts** were passed in Kentucky in 1998 and in North Carolina in 2009, stipulating that if race is found to be a significant factor in the imposition of the death penalty, then death will be commuted to life without parole. North Carolina's Act allowed (before it was later repealed!) three areas in which to argue significant racial bias: that a death sentence is more likely because of the race of the defendant; that a death sentence is more likely because of the race of the victim; or that jury selection was racially biased. Even with these efforts, however, proving racial bias has been challenging.

The tide is turning and more Americans recognize the death penalty is a failed public policy that does not serve to keep our communities safe. But, the arguments about the death penalty should not be divorced from the considerations of the entire American justice system. After all, capital punishment is just the extreme end of a system riddled with unfairness in our incarceration-hungry country. It is imperative to broaden the discussion to address the larger issue of who we lock up and what we really expect to gain from mass incarceration.

## *Wrongful Conviction*

The United States criminal justice system, proclaimed as "the best in the world," has been rocked in recent years by numerous cases of wrongly convicted individuals being saved from life and death sentences or being freed from institutional settings after unjust convictions were brought to light; oftentimes meeting staunch resistance from state prosecutors until the shackles were ordered removed. African-American defendants are more likely to be wrongfully convicted of crimes punishable by death. In North Carolina, six of the seven most recently exonerated death row inmates were people of color (all of whom were convicted of killing Whites) and the majority of nationwide death row exonerations have also been disproportionately people of color (Stubbs, 2012; National Registry of Exonerations, 2015).

Routinely, innocent people find themselves caught in the turmoil of an overtaxed criminal justice system because of mistaken eyewitness identifications, police misconduct, prosecutorial misconduct, bad lawyering by defense counsel, false testimony of jailhouse snitches and informants, false confessions, and bad science (Innocence Project, 2015). A recent comprehensive study of all exonerations—DNA and non-DNA, death row and non-death row—has found that there have been more than 1,535 people wrongfully convicted and subsequently exonerated in the United States from 1989 through 2012 (Gross & Shaffer, 2012). Table 8.6 breaks down 873 exonerations from 1989–2012.

**Table 8.6. Death Row Exonerations, 1989–2012**

- 93% were men (816/873) and 7% were women (57/873).
- The race of the defendants in 92% of the cases (802/873):
  - 50% were Black (399/802),
  - 38% were White (303/802),
  - 11% were Hispanic (86/802), and
  - 2% were Native American or Asian (14/802)
- 8% pleaded guilty (71/873) and the rest were convicted at trial—87% by juries and 8% by judges.
- 37% were cleared at least in part with the help of DNA evidence (325/873), and 63% were cleared without DNA evidence (548/873).
- Almost all had been in prison for years; half for at least 10 years; more than 75% for at least 5 years.
- As a group, the defendants had spent more than 10,000 years in prison for crimes for which they should not have been convicted—an average of more than 11 years each.

Source: http://www.law.umich.edu/special/exoneration/Documents/exonerations_us_1989_2012_full_report.pdf

As noted by the authors of the report: "It's no surprise that black defendants are heavily over-represented among exonerees: they are heavily over-represented among those arrested and imprisoned for violent crimes and drug crimes. But the disproportions we see are greater than what one would expect" (Gross & Shaffer, 2012:31). Henry Lee McCollum, 50, and Leon Brown, 46, are prime examples of the problem here. The half-brothers, both intellectually disabled, confessed to the rape and murder of an 11-year-old girl in North Carolina in 1984. McCollum spent 30 years on death row, and Brown was serving life after his conviction was thrown out. The North Carolina Innocence Inquiry Commission found that DNA at the crime scene belonged to another man, Roscoe Artis, who was sentenced to death for a similar crime. In half of cases involving DNA exonerations, the real perpetrator is identified. Moreover, in half of cases, the real perpetrator went on to commit other crimes after the exoneree was arrested and convicted. McCollum and Brown became free men in 2014.

Explanations for the disproportionate number of people of color who have been wrongfully convicted could be attributed to deliberate racial stereotyping by law enforcement and jurors or, at the other extreme of the explanation continuum, may be due to unconscious racism by witnesses who are far more likely to misidentify perpetrators of different races from their own even if they hold no conscious racial prejudices. Clearly, more inquiry is needed. While our methods of investigation, rules of criminal procedure, and appellate processes are designed to ensure that the guilty are apprehended, convicted, held accountable, and afforded rehabilitation—and that the innocent are shielded from erroneous legal maneuvers—the ideals of justice are far from the reality of its application.

## Differences in Perceptions of Corrections

The corrections system was created to protect society from criminals, to punish those who commit crimes, and to make criminals better able to return to society once they finished their sentences. Not surprisingly, different people rank these goals differently. And, no matter which goals they emphasize, Americans seem more angry and frustrated with the corrections system than ever before though they should focus that frustration on the laws, police, and the courts that spill into the correctional system. Expressions like "Lock 'em up and throw away the key" and "Don't raise my taxes to build more prisons" have grown increasingly familiar. Some politicians, judges, and criminal justice professionals regularly accuse each other of "mollycoddling" criminals. Others say public officials are using these issues to try to "look tough." None of this rhetoric seems to be leading to productive, lasting solutions. No matter what solutions to the corrections problem we support, one thing is clear: Americans need to consider their priorities for the corrections system, and what they can do to help the system meet those priorities.

Most prison officials state that their primary purpose is *rehabilitation* suggesting that the incarcerated are being given a chance at redemption. The reality, however, does not always square with this stated mission. Many prisons are overcrowded, poorly supervised bureaucracies, where inmates are in danger and suffer abuse at the hands of guards and other prisoners. Popular support for harsh prison conditions is associated with the desire for *retributive* punishment rather than corrective punishment. Yet if prisons are colleges for crime where harsh punishment may actually lead to greater degrees of criminality, in the long term, society will bear a greater cost for retributive punishment because, when convicted criminals are released—as many will be—they will return to a life of crime, often escalating the severity of their offenses. In fact, research that has been conducted on the *Scared Straight* program, where young people are exposed to prisons and prisoners with the assumption that the program will deter crime, has not proven true. Several researchers have demonstrated that exposure to prison and prisoners corresponds to a higher rate of criminal offense (Lilienfeld et al, 2010; Marion & Oliver, 2006).

When law and policy makers talk about reforming the prison system, they are typically talking about the public's safety, or how expensive the incarceration business has become, and on occasion, there might be discussions about how incarceration impacts the people residing in such settings. Less often, the conversation is about those who lose a parent or loved one to a prison sentence. Imprisonment itself brings a multitude of challenges for families who already face systematic impoverishment and disadvantage in the wake of a prison sentence. A recent report (Smith et al., 2007) found several disadvantages associated with imprisonment, including: housing disruption; high rates of depression and physical illness among adults and children; and permanent loss of a parent through deportation of foreign national prisoners. Additionally, the study noted that the pressures borne by families throughout a term of imprisonment had a destabilizing or fragmentary impact on relationships, with negative implications for reunion after release (Smith et al., 2007). Families were vulnerable to financial instability, poverty and debt: household incomes fell as the prisoners' income was lost; those who cared for prisoners' children left paid work; and damaging financial transitions caused further disruption (Smith et al., 2007). Criminal justice and social welfare policy combine to impoverish, disadvantage, and exclude the relatives of people in prison—in particular, prisoners' children.

Most Americans never even see, let alone become ensnared in, the nation's vast correctional system. But the unprecedented prison boom is incurring unprecedented costs—economic, social, and ethical—that are being paid, one way or another, by everyone in this country. Prisons are an enormously costly failure for controlling and reducing crime, expensive beyond belief, debilitating, demeaning, counterproductive (Austin & Irwin, 2001; Ross & Richards, 2003), dangerous to prison staff and the non-violent majority who are imprisoned, and efficient breeders of even more serious future offenses against society. They only work to remove from the streets the relatively small percentage of persistently and irrationally violent, dangerous, and repeat offenders who happen to be apprehended by the agents of social control.

And no matter what the length of the term, doing time in prison is a long, hard ride. Surviving imprisonment requires patience and humility. The imprisoned battle with time, the months and years that pass as one ages behind the wall. The differential effects of incarceration are well known. Sutherland et al., (1992:524) noted that "Some prisoners apparently become 'reformed' or 'rehabilitated,' while others become 'confirmed' or 'hardened' criminals." Similarly, we know that hundreds of thousands of prisoners who, although they were convicted of a crime, are not violent felons and pose little threat to the community. Many times, these individuals are sentenced to prison, for too long a time period (Austin & Irwin, 2001).

A prisoner's greatest challenge lies in their (in)ability to change others' perceptions of them while incarcerated. Society's understanding of comfort, no matter how uninformed or naive, is only getting more insistent on viewing prisons as a place to efficiently house people we are equally afraid to identify with and exist among. And so, those we deem morally corrupt are locked up and fenced in; stuck in a place where no matter whether they strive for dignity, education, or an opportunity to return to a lawful lifestyle, it will always be easier to group them as a threat to people more deserving of the freedoms that come with time and space (Willis & Zaitzow, 2013).

Incarcerating a young Black man seriously impedes his chances of making a successful life. Spending time in jail or prison disrupts schooling, which makes it hard to get a decent job. The unemployment that often follows release from incarceration has rippling effects, contributing to high rates of single parenthood (unemployed men are less likely to marry) and family instability in the Black community (divorce rates are higher in families with unemployed fathers), increasing the likelihood that one generation's difficulties will be passed on to the next. It's a vicious cycle that needs to be broken. One way of breaking it is to stop locking people up who have broken the law but who do not present a genuine danger to the community.

The gauge of success for any undertaking is the achievement of its prime objectives at acceptable cost over a reasonable span of time. The measure of a prison system's success would be the ultimate reduction of crime and the restoration of much of the prison population to law-abiding citizenry. By that standard, United States prisons have failed dismally. U.S. prisons today are dangerously overcrowded because of the myopia of too many judges, prosecutors, legislators, community leaders, editors, and well-meaning, but frightened citizens who wrongly see prisons as the panacea for escalating crime. The clamor for more and stronger prisons and stiffer sentences makes no sense. We cannot build our way out of the crime problem.

As the prison population continues to grow, so too will the number of individuals released back to the community. This is a compelling reason—and there are many other reasons—for doing all we can for civilizing corrections, reducing the number of men and women in prison, and lowering the rate of recidivism. The real problem is a societal one. As long as we have an indifferent and uneducated public with respect to crime issues, the deplorable state of American criminal justice policies and practices will continue.

But the pervasiveness and scale of the racial disparities in America's prisons have led some legal scholars to take a more radical view. They charge that the problems in the administration of justice in America run much deeper than the bias of a few bigoted law enforcement officers and court officials, and that the system itself is founded upon a deliberately discriminatory intent. Recall the argument of Michelle Alexander (2010) from Chapter 3, that the explosive growth in the size of America's prison population over the last 30 years is an extension of the Jim Crow system that deprived African-Americans of their rights for much of the 20th century. In her words:

> In the era of colorblindness, it is no longer socially permissible to use race, explicitly, as a justification for discrimination, exclusion and social contempt. So we don't. Rather than rely on race, we use our criminal justice system to label people of color 'criminals' and then engage in all the practices we supposedly left behind. Today it is perfectly legal to discriminate against criminals in nearly all the ways that it was once legal to discriminate against African-Americans. Once you're labeled a felon, the old forms of discrimination—employment discrimination, housing discrimination, denial of the right to vote, denial of educational opportunity, denial of food stamps and other public benefits, and exclusion from jury service—are suddenly legal (p. 1).

Over time, the damage done breaks down trust between neighbors, destroys whole communities, and weakens public trust and confidence in our system. The total cost and damage to society is difficult to measure in terms of dollars. But it takes its toll in broken spirits and lost dreams. Understanding the ramifications of racial disparity in the U.S. criminal justice system and, specifically, the correctional system, requires synthetic thinking and synthetic data that cross disciplinary boundaries. The entire system of economic well-being, family life, crime, enforcement, and punishment is a set of tightly-interconnected feedback loops, and it is extremely difficult to pull apart the different effects with cross-sectional data or a time series on a limited number of cases or time periods and an inadequately specified model.

Do people of color buy this argument that the criminal justice system intentionally targets people of color and that correctional punishment is fundamentally unfair? Table 8.7 shows some of what we know in terms of public perception of corrections, broken down by race and ethnicity. As you can see, people of color are more likely to favor reducing crime by attacking social problems to reduce crime, and are less likely to favor more law enforcement to reduce crime. They are also more likely to perceive unfairness in criminal justice; yet level of confidence in criminal justice is actually higher for people of color than for Whites.

### Table 8.7. Public Perceptions of Criminal Justice

*Portion that favor attacking social problems to reduce crime (2010)*

| | |
|---|---|
| White | 60% |
| Non-White | 73% |
| Black | 85% |

*Portion that favor more law enforcement to reduce crime (2010)*

| | |
|---|---|
| White | 35% |
| Non-White | 23% |
| Black | 12% |

*Portion that believe criminal justice system is very unfair (2003)*

| | |
|---|---|
| White | 9% |
| Non-White | 15% |
| Black | 19% |

*Portion that have great deal/quite a lot of confidence in criminal justice (2012)*

| | |
|---|---|
| White | 26% |
| Non-White | 39% |
| Black | 24% |
| Hispanic | 51% |

Sources: http://www.albany.edu/sourcebook/pdf/t200132010.pdf; http://www.albany.edu/sourcebook/pdf/t2112012.pdf; http://www.albany.edu/sourcebook/pdf/t245.pdf

# Explanations

There are debates about the forces driving imprisonment rates and racial disparities within the correctional system arenas. Although national-level political decisions are clearly at the center of the process, the extent and speed of adoption of these trends at a local level varies and can shed light on the forces at work. Are racial disparities in arrest and imprisonment fundamentally a response to crime? Are they fundamentally a form of repression, a response to the urban insurrections of the late 1960s and a way of maintaining Black dominance over the Black population? A consequence of migration and age structure patterns? Or perhaps essentially an accident, an unintended effect of policies enacted for other reasons, or the result of diffusion processes?

It is well documented that African-American and Hispanic men are arrested, convicted and imprisoned at far higher rates than Whites, and that once they enter the prison system they usually serve longer terms as well. In fact, such differential outcomes for Blacks and Whites appear at every level of the system, from the officer on the beat's initial decision to make an arrest, to the bail commissioner's determination whether to grant bail and its amount, to prosecutors' choice of what charges to bring and judges' sentencing decisions. At every step along the way, minorities are treated more harshly, face a greater presumption of guilt, have fewer resources to defend themselves and suffer more severe penalties.

One possible explanation for racial disparity and over-representation is, of course, discrimination. This line of reasoning suggests that because of discrimination on the part of criminal justice system decision-makers, minority members face higher probabilities of being arrested by the police, held in short-term detention, adjudicated by the courts, and confined in a secure facility. Thus, differential actions throughout the justice system may account for minority over-representation (Walker et al., 2014).

As shown in Chapter 1, disparity and over-representation, however, can result from factors other than discrimination. Factors relating to the nature and volume of crime committed by minority members may explain disproportionate minority confinement. This line of reasoning suggests that if minority offenders commit proportionately more crime than White offenders, are involved in more serious incidents, and have more extensive criminal histories, they will be over-represented in secure facilities, even if no discrimination by system decision-makers occurred. Thus, the disproportionate numbers of minority members within the criminal justice system may be due to behavioral and legal factors (Walker et al., 2014).

For many years, experts have debated the reasons for racial disparities in the U.S. prison population. The explanations have included systemic bias in the criminal justice system that punishes Blacks more harshly than Whites for similar crimes; poverty; unemployment; and aggressive policing tactics that disproportionately affect minority communities (Alexander, 2010). It is likely that all those factors played some role in creating the disparity in incarceration rates, but the most important may have been changes in drug laws and sentencing guidelines for drug offenses.

Beginning in the 1980s, states began adopting harsh mandatory sentencing guidelines for drug possession that resulted in the imprisonment of thousands of African-Americans for low-level, nonviolent drug offenses. The violence associated with crack cocaine markets, in particular, led lawmakers to make the penalties for possession of even small amounts of crack equivalent to those for much larger quantities of powder cocaine, which was more often used by Whites. The net effect was an explosion in the Black prison population that exacerbated the racial disparities already in the system (Crayton & Zaitzow, 2007).

But revisions in federal and state sentencing laws in recent years have narrowed the sentencing gap between crack and powder cocaine. At the same time, the violence associated with crack cocaine has become less of an issue as use of the drug has declined. That, combined with the fact that many inmates given long sentences for drug offenses are now emerging from prison, has produced a disproportionate exodus of Black inmates that is reflected in lower rates of incarceration for African-Americans as a whole (Sentencing Project, 2015) while adding to the challenges faced by those returning to economically-challenged communities. Meanwhile, the increasing rates of incarceration among Whites suggest that rising numbers of them are being arrested and prosecuted under tough mandatory sentencing laws for methamphetamines that are still in effect. Over the long run, such laws could turn out to be as destructive to Whites as overly harsh crack laws were for Blacks. Thus, while progress toward reducing racial disparities in prison populations and community programs is a topic of national discussion and limited action, much work remains to be done to eliminate the continuing racial disparities in all spheres of social life.

Civil rights advocates have also fought to overturn specific laws that clearly have a racially discriminatory effect. An example would be statutes that impose more severe penalties for possession of crack cocaine, which is more prevalent in Black communities, than powder cocaine, which more often is used by Whites. Or consider the racial profiling inherent in so-called *stop and frisk* laws that allow police to detain and search people without any evidence of wrongdoing. In New York City, more than 80 percent of the 600,000 people stopped and frisked by police last year were African-American or Hispanic.

When we perpetuate a system that incarcerates such a large number of the Black male population, sentences them disproportionately compared to other racial/ethnic groups and prevents them from going straight after they have served their time, we create instability and chaos within the Black community. The history of slavery and racism remains with us today. Until we acknowledge the reality of how it perpetuates itself, it will never cease and our country will continue its downward spiral of economic disparity and debilitating racial/ethnic tension.

# Conclusion

Racial disparity within our justice system concerns both the perception and the reality of justice for a large, and growing, portion of our citizens. We must act now to assure that we have the information needed to make informed decisions and develop effective solutions. We can do more to learn about what is happening within our criminal justice system. More collection of data—on actual crime rates, as well as data at all points within the criminal justice system—will shed additional light on the causes underlying the disparity problem, as well as provide a means for determining whether new strategies are making a difference.

We can also do more to develop an understanding of the reasons for the disparity. Certainly the causes of racial disparity are complex and cannot be oversimplified. But, complexity is no justification for failing to identify the causes and implement solutions. Do issues of disparity arise differently in rural communities than in the metropolitan area? What do those within the criminal justice system—law enforcement, prosecutors, public defenders, judges, probation officers—think about the causes for the disparity? What perspective do victims and families have? What do members of the minority and White communities believe?

Exploring these questions promotes the kind of honest and informed dialogue that is beginning to occur in some communities among those within the criminal justice system and the community as a whole. Such dialogue can help to strengthen communication and build mutual trust and respect. Perhaps most importantly, however, it lays the foundation for action which results in constructive solutions to the problem. Racial disparity in the criminal justice system is not only a problem for minority communities or for those who work within the system. It is a problem we all share and one that we can, and must, work together to address.

Because the problem of racial disparity is systemic, any attempt to eradicate this from the criminal justice system will require a focus on the institutions and structures that generate such disparity. Here, structural reform of the entry and sentencing of offenders is required. Also, the fair administration of such reforms will require diligent and on-going assessment if true reform of racial disparities and "justice for all" is the goal.

# Discussion Questions

1. Describe the racial disparities that exist in the various components of corrections.
2. Do you believe the figures/percentages reflect racism/discrimination or the "truth" about people's involvement in crime? Explain.
3. What do you think accounts for these disparities? Explain.
4. Why should people care about racial disparities in the correctional system?
5. Do our laws, policies and practices reflect public consensus on these priorities? If not, what needs to change?

6.  Do such disparities become part of the prison environment? Describe from the inmate experience as well as the staff member experience.

7.  How would you attempt to empirically establish that racial disparity in the correctional system exists?

8.  Should statistical evaluations of racial disparities be influential in determining whether or not a criminal defendant has been discriminated against? How are discrimination claims evaluated in employment or other discrimination cases?

9.  What safeguards could be put into place, either by statute or by court decisions, to address any racial inequities and disparities with regard to the death penalty, wrongful conviction, or even imprisonment for a crime committed but due process violations occurred?

# References

Alexander, M. (2010). *The new Jim Crow: Mass incarceration in the age of colorblindness.* New York, NY: The New Press.

American Correctional Association (2004). Policies and resolutions. *Corrections Today, 66*(6), 68.

Austin, J. & Irwin, J. (2001). *It's about time.* Belmont, CA: Wadsworth.

Baumgartner, F.R., Grigg, A., & Mastro, A. (forthcoming 2015). #Black lives don't matter: Race-of-victim effects in US executions, 1976–2013. *Politics, Groups, and Identities.* Retrieved from: http://www.tandfonline.com/action/journalInformation?show=aimsScope&journalCode=rpgi20&#.UipqT9LoHsY%5D.

Baldus, D.C., Woodworth, G., Zuckerman, D. Weiner, N.A., & Broffitt, B. (1998). Racial discrimination and the death penalty in the post-Furman era: An empirical and legal overview, with recent findings from Philadelphia. *Cornell Law Review 83* (1997–1998), 1638–1770.

Baldus, D.C., Pulaski, C. & Woodworth, G. (1983). Comparative review of death sentences: An empirical study of the Georgia experience. *Journal of Criminal Law and Criminology 74*(3), 661–753.

Bonczar, T. & Herberman, E. (2014). *Probation and parole in the United States, 2013* (Revised). Bureau of Justice Statistics. October 28, 2014, NCJ 248029. Retrieved from: Retrieved from: http://www.bjs.gov/content/pub/pdf/ppus13.pdf.

*Brown v. Plata*, 131 S. Ct. 1910 (2011).

Carson, E.A. (2014). *Prisoners in 2013.* Bureau of Justice Statistics. September 16, 2014, NCJ 247282. Retrieved from: http://www.bjs.gov/content/pub/pdf/p13.pdf.

Champion, D. (2008). *Probation, parole, and community corrections.* Boston, MA: Pearson Education.

Clear, T.R., Cole G.F., & Reisig, M.D. (2013). *American corrections* (10th. ed). Belmont, CA: Wadsworth/Thomson.

Crayton, A. & Zaitzow, B.H. (2007). The historical evolution of American reentry efforts: How we went from a belief in the perfectability of people to a "what reentry?" debate. Paper presented at the American Society of Criminology Meeting, November 2007, Atlanta, Georgia.

Death Penalty Information Center (2014*). Efforts underway to exonerate 14-year-old executed in South Carolina in 1944.* Retrieved from: http://www.deathpenaltyinfo.org/node/5712.

Eberhardt, J.L., Davies, P.G., Purdie-Vaughns, V., & Johnson, S.L. (2006). Looking deathworthy: Perceived stereotypicality of black defendants predicts capital sentencing outcomes. Research Report. *Psychological Science 17*(5), 383–386.

Feeley, M.M. & Simon, J.S. (1992). The new penology: Notes on the emerging strategy of corrections and its implications. *Criminology, 30*(4), 449–474.

FindLaw (2013). Retrieved from: http://criminal.findlaw.com/criminal-charges/first-degree-murder-penalties-and-sentencing.html.

*Furman v. Georgia,* 408 U.S. 238 (1972).

Glaze, L.E. & Kaeble, D. (2014). *Correctional populations in the United States, 2013.* Bureau of Justice Statistics. December 2014, NCJ 248479. Retrieved from: http://www.bjs.gov/content/pub/pdf/cpus13.pdf.

Governor's Summit: Eliminating disproportionate minority contact in the juvenile system. (2008). Downloaded from: http://www.oregon.gov/OYA/dmcsummit/2008/minovrep.

*Gregg v. Georgia,* 428 U.S. 153 (1976).

Gross, S.R. & Shaffer, M. (2012). Exonerations in the United States, 1989–2012. Report by the National Registry of Exonerations (June). Downloaded from: http://www.law.umich.edu/special/exoneration/Documents/exonerations_us_1989_2012_full_report.pdf.

Grosso, C.M. & O'Brien, B. (2012). A stubborn legacy: The overwhelming importance of race in jury selection in 173 post-*Batson* North Carolina capital trials. *Iowa Law Review 97,* 1531.

Heath, B. (2014). Racial gap in U.S. arrest rates: 'Staggering disparity.' *USA Today* (November 19).

Hewlett, M. (2011). Forsyth defense attorneys off court appointed lists. Winston Salem Journal (May 6). Retrieved from: http://www.journalnow.com/news/local/forsyth-defense-attorneys-off-court-appointed-lists/article_17d3bf50-696a-53f5-a9bd-9d03125b04e2.html.

Innocence Project. (2015). The causes of wrongful conviction: Downloaded from: http://www.innocenceproject.org/causes-wrongful-conviction.

International Centre for Prison Studies (2014). World prison population list. Downloaded from: http://www.prisonstudies.org/sites/prisonstudies.org/files/resources/downloads/wppl_10.pdf.

Jannetta, J., Breaux, J., & Ho, H. (2014). Examining racial and ethnic disparities in probation revocation: Summary findings and implications from a multisite study. New York, NY: The Urban Institute, Jeremy Porter, University of New York (April).

Kansal, T. (2005). Racial disparity in sentencing: A review of the literature. Downloaded from: http://www.prisonpolicy.org/scans/sp/disparity.pdf.

Kutateladze, B., Tymas, W., & Crowley, M. (2014). Race and prosecution in manhattan. Vera Institute of Justice, Research Summary (July). Downloaded from: http://www.vera.org/sites/default/files/resources/downloads/race-and-prosecution-manhattan-summary.pdf.

Lilienfeld, S.O., Lynn, S.J., Ruscio, J., & Beyerstein, B.L. (2010). *50 great myths of popular* psychology: Shattering widespread misconceptions about human behavior. Malden, MA: Wiley- Blackwell.

Marion, N.E., & Oliver, W.M. (2006). *The public policy of crime and criminal justice.* Upper Saddle River, NJ: Pearson.

Mauer, M. (2013). *The changing racial dynamics of women's incarceration.* Downloaded from: http://sentencingproject.org/doc/publications/rd_Changing%20Racial%20Dynamics%202013.pdf.

*McCleskey v. Kemp*, 481 U.S. 279 (1987).

Minton, T.D. & Golinelli, D. (2014). *Jail inmates at midyear 2013—Statistical tables* (Revised). Bureau of Justice Statistics. May 8, 2014, NCJ 245350. Retrieved from: http://www.bjs.gov/content/pub/pdf/jim13st.pdf.

National Academy of Sciences (2014). *The growth of incarceration in the United States: Exploring causes and consequences.* National Research Council of the National Academies.

National Registry of Exonerations (2015). *Exonerations in 2014.* Downloaded from: http://www.law.umich.edu/special/exoneration/Documents/Exonerations_in_2014_report.pdf.

Nellis, A. (2013). *Life goes on: The historic rise in life sentences in america.* Downloaded from: http://sentencingproject.org/doc/publications/inc_Life%20Goes%20On%202013.pdf.

O'Connor, (2012). *The early history of corrections.* Retrieved from: http://www.drtomoconnor.com/1050/1050lect01.htm.

*Plessy v. Ferguson,* 163 U.S. 537 (1896).

Robinson, M. (2008). *Justice blind?: Ideals and realities of American criminal justice* (3rd edition). Upper Saddle, NJ: Prentice Hall.

Rose, D.R. & Clear, T.R. (1998). Incarceration, social capital, and crime: Implications for social disorganization theory. *Criminology, 36*(3), 441–480.

Ross, J.I. & Richards, S.C. (2003). *Convict criminology.* Belmont, CA: Wadsworth.

Schmalleger, F. & Smykla, J. (2009). *Corrections: in the 21st century.* New York, NY: McGraw Hill.

*Scott v. Sandford,* 60 U.S. 393 (1857).

Seiter, R.P. (2005). *Corrections: An introduction.* Upper Saddle River, NY: Prentice Hall.

Sentencing Project (2014). *Addressing racial disparities in incarceration.* Downloaded from: http://sentencingproject.org/doc/publications/Prison%20Journal%20-%20racial%20disparity.pdf.

Sentencing Project (2014). *Shadow report of the sentencing project to the committee on the elimination of racial discrimination regarding racial disparities in the United States criminal justice system* (July). Retrieved from: http://sentencingproject.org/doc/publications/rd_CERD_Shadow_Report_2014.pdf.

Sentencing Project (2013). *Report of the sentencing project to the united nations human rights committee* (August). Downloaded from: http://sentencingproject.org/doc/publications/rd_ICCPR%20Race%20and%20Justice%20Shadow%20Report.pdf.

Smith, R., Grimshaw, R., Romeo, R., and Knapp, M. (2007). Poverty and disadvantage among prisoners' families. Joseph Rowntree Foundation: York, England. Downloaded from: http://www.jrf.org.uk/sites/files/jrf/2003-poverty-prisoners-families.pdf.

Snell, T.L. (2014). *Capital punishment, 2013—Statistical tables* (Revised). Bureau of Justice Statistics. December 19, 2014, NCJ 248448. Retrieved from: http://www.bjs.gov/content/pub/pdf/cp13st.pdf.

Sommers, S.R. & Marotta, S.A. (2015). Racial disparities in legal outcomes: On policing, charging decisions, and criminal trial proceedings. *The Jury Expert.* Retrieved from: http://www.thejuryexpert.com/2015/02/racial-disparities-in-legal-outcomes-on-policing-charging-decisions-and-criminal-trial-proceedings/

Stubbs, C. (2012). Wrongful convictions, wrongful bias. Retrieved from: https://www.aclu.org/blog/capital-punishment/wrongful-convictions-wrongful-bias.

Sutherland, E.H., Cressey, D.R. & Luckenbill, D.F. (1992). *Principles of criminology.* Dix Hills, NY: General Hall.

United States Department of Justice (2014). Investigation of the julia tutwiler prison for women and notice of expanded investigation. Retrieved from: http://www.justice.gov/crt/about/spl/documents/tutwiler_findings_1-17-14.pdf.

Wacquant, Loic. (2002). From slavery to mass incarceration: Rethinking the race question in the U.S. *New Left Review*, 13.

Waldman, P. (2013). Six charts that explain why our prison system is so insane. Downloaded from: http://prospect.org/article/six-charts-explain-why-our-prison-system-so-insane.

Walker, S., Spohn, C., & DeLone, M. (2014). *The color of justice: Race, ethnicity, and crime in America*. Belmont, CA: Wadsworth.

Western, Bruce (2006). *Punishment and inequality*. New York, NY: Russell Sage Foundation.

Willis, A.K. & Zaitzow, B.H. (2013). How do you do it?: The double-edged nature of balancing hope with "life." Paper presented at the American Society of Criminology Meeting, November, 2013, Atlanta, Georgia.

# Chapter 9

# Race, Ethnicity, and the Death Penalty in America

*by Jefferson Holcomb, PhD*

# Introduction

The use of the **death penalty** has varied across cultures and across time within those cultures (Garland, 2011). These variations have included how extensively the death penalty was used, against whom, and the manner in which the condemned was killed. Frequently, changes in the use of the death penalty have occurred within the context of changes in the social, religious, political, or economic domains of a community or culture. As Garland (2011) noted, however, there has remained one important constant in the nature of the death penalty: "The imposition of the death penalty is, first and foremost, an exercise of power—wherever, whenever, and however it occurs" (Garland, 2011, p.37). It should not be a surprise then that the death penalty, since recorded history, has been disproportionately applied to marginalized members of a community.

There are, of course, numerous historical examples of elite members of a society being put to death. These persons, however, were frequently executed for being labeled as traitors or religious or secular threats to those in power. Otherwise, the history of the death penalty, whether legally sanctioned or illegal executions carried out via **lynching** or **mob violence**, is largely the history of a dominant group killing religious, ethnic, and racial minorities or other low-status members of society. Critics note that this feature of the death penalty remains in place today (e.g., Bright, 1995).

This chapter examines the relationship between race and ethnicity and the death penalty in America. This is not to suggest that racial disparity is the only feature of capital punishment in America. For example, there is little doubt of the close ties between economic status and punishment. In the American context, as in other countries of the world, however, many racial and ethnic minority groups are also disproportionately members of a society's underclass. Therefore, it is difficult to discuss economic disparities without addressing racial and ethnic inequality as well, as noted in Chapter 1.

This chapter will use the term *race* in a general manner to refer to both racial and ethnic minorities. As discussed in Chapter 1, there are obvious problems with using the term "race" to refer to differences based on ethnicity and skin-color. The terms *Black* or *African Americans* clearly do not reflect a different race of the human species. The term *ethnicity*, however, seems insufficient to distinguish the unique history and experience of Blacks in America. Unfortunately, the history of legal and illegal executions in America, especially in the South, is closely associated with slavery and discrimination towards Blacks (Bright, 1995; Freidman, 1993; Marquart, Ekland-Olson, & Sorensen, 1994). While other groups, especially Hispanics and Native Americans, have experienced considerable mistreatment by American communities and governments (e.g., Urbina, 2012; also Friedman, 1993), the story of discrimination and disparity in the application of the death penalty in America is predominantly about African Americans (Bright, 1995; see also Allen & Clubb, 2008). In fact, those of African descent represent almost one-half of all persons executed in the United States since 1608 (Death Penalty Information Center, 2015a). Combined, Blacks, Hispanics/Latinos, and Native Americans account for approximately 55% of those executed in the United States since 1608 (DPIC, 2015a).

The chapter begins with a discussion of the use of the death penalty in colonial and early American history. This is followed by a discussion of post-Civil War experiences. Major legal issues and court rulings on race and the death penalty are discussed. This is followed by a discussion on the social science evidence of racial disparities in capital cases. Finally, the chapter ends with a discussion possible developments and the continuing significance of race and ethnicity for the death penalty in America.

# What Is Capital Punishment?

First, it is important to define the term **capital punishment**, which is also known as the *death penalty*—the lawful killing of a citizen of a government by that government for the commission of a *capital crime* (e.g., aggravated murder). Capital punishment is currently legal in 34 U.S. jurisdictions, as shown in Table 9.1.

---

Table 9.1 U.S. Jurisdictions With and Without the Death Penalty

**With the death penalty**

| | | |
|---|---|---|
| Alabama | Louisiana | South Carolina |
| Arizona | Mississippi | South Dakota |
| Arkansas | Missouri | Tennessee |
| California | Montana | Texas |
| Colorado | Nebraska | Utah |
| Delaware | Nevada | Virginia |
| Florida | New Hampshire | Washington |
| Georgia | North Carolina | Wyoming |
| Idaho | Ohio | **ALSO** |
| Indiana | Oklahoma | - Federal Gov't |
| Kansas | Oregon | - U.S. Military |
| Kentucky | Pennsylvania | |

**Without the death penalty** *(year of abolition in parenthesis)*

| | | |
|---|---|---|
| Alaska (1957) | Michigan (1846) | West Virginia (1965) |
| Connecticut (2012) | Minnesota (1911) | Wisconsin (1853) |
| Hawaii (1957) | New Jersey (2007) | **ALSO** |
| Illinois (2011) | New Mexico (2009) | Dist. of Columbia (1981) |
| Iowa (1965) | New York (2007) | |
| Maine (1887) | North Dakota (1973) | |
| Maryland (2013) | Rhode Island (1984) | |
| Massachusetts (1984) | Vermont (1964) | |

Source: http://deathpenaltyinfo.org/states-and-without-death-penalty

---

Of those 34 jurisdictions with the death penalty, only ten (all states) have carried out at least one execution per year since capital punishment was reinstated by the US Supreme Court in 1976 after being abolished in 1972. Thus, capital punishment, even in places where it is legal, is actually quite rare when compared to the number of murders that occur in the US each year. Only about 1% of killers receive death sentences nationally, and about 2% of killers in death penalty states, receive the death penalty (Robinson, 2008).

## *Functions of Capital Punishment*

Although the goals of capital punishment are not defined in the criminal law, it is often assumed that the major functions policy-makers want to achieve through capital punishment include *crime prevention* and *justice*. Specifically, legislators aim to reduce murder both through **incapacitation** (i.e., permanently removing the freedom of killers to kill again by taking their lives) and **deterrence** (i.e., scaring would-be murderers with the threat of execution, thereby reducing murder); they also want to achieve **retribution** for family members of murder victims and society at large; these terms were first defined in Chapters 7 and 8. The rarity and seemingly arbitrary application of capital punishment, however, has led many to question the efficacy of capital punishment (Robinson, 2008).

## *Ideals of American Capital Punishment*

Ideally, capital punishment will be justified by *legal factors* and thus not be influenced by *extra-legal factors*. The US Supreme Court has ruled that only **aggravated murderers** can be sentenced to death and executed, meaning that legally established factors that make murder worse (called *aggravating factors*) must outweigh *mitigating factors* (which tend to lessen culpability of offenders) in the minds of capital jurors. **Extra-legal factors** (factors outside the law such as demographic characteristics of offenders and victims) should not influence the imposition of a death sentences or executions, or capital punishment could be held to be unconstitutional (Robinson, 2008; Baldus et al, 1998).

## Realities of American Capital Punishment

Of course, the reality of capital punishment is in some ways different than the ideal. As noted earlier, the first way that capital punishment does not match the ideal is in its rare nature; the fact that executions are actually very uncommon in the US means that we do not often meet our goals of crime prevention and justice. Another way that capital punishment does not match the ideal is that extra-legal factors do impact the capital punishment. Thus, factors such as race, ethnicity, social class, and gender influence which killers get the death penalty and which do not.

# The Role of Race in America's History with Capital Punishment

Although this book focuses on race and criminal justice, the historical evidence is quite clear that throughout American history, like most cultures, punishment was meted out most severely for those from underprivileged classes or minority groups. As Friedman (1993) notes, "the lash of the law, in all of the colonies, fell overwhelmingly on servants, apprentices, slaves, small holders, and laborers" (p. 51). The earliest colony settlements were made up of rather homogenous ethnic groups, though colonies brought with them indentured servants and slavery began in limited form soon after (see P.B.S., n.d.). While executions in the earliest colonies were somewhat rare, the small number of colonialists resulted in an execution rate much higher than in later America (Allen & Clubb, 2008).

Not surprisingly, the majority of executed persons in the early colonies were of European descent, though it appears that these persons frequently came from the laboring classes (Allen & Clubb, 2008). There were, however, executions of racial minorities. In particular, Native Americans were executed during periods of conflict with colonists such as during the King Phillip's War (Allen & Clubb, 2008). For Native Americans, recurring conflicts with White settlers and Whites' efforts to expand onto tribal lands would frequently result in severe penalties for native people (see also DPIC, 2015d). For exam-

ple, 32 Dakota tribesmen were hanged in a single day in Minnesota in 1862 as
the result of the Dakota War (aka Sioux Uprising) (Friedman, 1993). Friedman
(1993) noted that there were few laws specifically designed to repress Native Americans. Nevertheless, "the history of the Native Americans in this country is a
history of suffering, defeat, banishment, retreat, and all too often, outright
slaughter" (Friedman, 1993, p.97).

As the number of ethnic and racial minorities increased in the colonies,
their representation among those executed increased. While there were considerable regional differences in the use of capital punishment in early America, minority populations, and especially those of African descent, became
increasingly overrepresented among those executed (Allen & Clubb, 2008;
Bowers, 1974).

The particular legal and extra-legal tools used to further marginalize minority groups often depended upon the specific context (Friedman, 1993;
Garland, 2011). In the case of the Chinese and other immigrant groups, the
threat was often of an economic nature. As a result, barriers to legal and business opportunities and deportation were often used against Chinese populations in Western states (Friedman, 1993; Wei, n.d.). Mistreatment by the
criminal justice system and extra-legal killings such as lynching were also
used as means to intimidate the perceived threat that Chinese labor and culture represented (Wei, n.d.; Zesch, 2012). For example, mob violence in Los
Angeles killed 18 Chinese in a single night of violence known as the Chinese
Massacre of 1871 (Johnson, 2011; Zesch, 2012). While several members of
the mob were convicted of crimes related to these deaths, their convictions
were overturned and none were ever retried for these deaths (Zesch, 2012).

Mexican and Latino populations, especially in the American Southwest,
have also experienced mistreatment by the criminal justice system and White
community. Urbina (2012) provides numerous examples of how Mexican and
Latino populations were systematically marginalized and faced barriers to equal
treatment both economically and legally. For example, the Texas Rangers were
often used to reinforce White dominance over Mexicans who were perceived
as a threat (Urbina, 2012). While different Latino populations have faced varying challenges depending upon the specific geographic and social context, legal
institutions and agents have been used to restrict or obfuscate their full integration into the existing community (Urbina, 2012). Marquart et al. (1994) noted
that while capital punishment, and especially extra-legal lynching, in Texas
was predominantly directed at African Americans, these tools have been used
by Whites against both Blacks and Hispanics. The threat of official or unofficial violence was often used to keep Blacks and Hispanics "in their place" and
to enforce a policy of exclusion from economic, political, and legal institu-

tions (Marquart et al., 1994). Table 9.2 shows the some differences and similarities between executions and lynchings.

#### Table 9.2 Executions versus Lynchings

|                     | Capital punishment | Lynching      |
| ------------------- | ------------------ | ------------- |
| Legal status        | Legal              | Illegal       |
| Carried out by      | Government         | Citizens*     |
| Number in US history| 16,508             | 4,749         |
| Years               | 1608–2013†         | 1882–1968††   |
| Most common victims | People of color    | People of color |

* Lynchings were often carried out with the assistance of government officials (e.g., police officers, sheriffs).

† Number obtained by combining Espy File data and current execution statistics, see DPIC, 2015a and DPIC, 2015e.

†† Data from Tuskegee Institute archives available at http://192.203.127.197/archive/handle/123456789/507.

It is clear that punishment, and the death penalty in particular, were used disproportionately against a variety of ethnic minorities throughout American history. Under certain contexts, this was the result of official and institutional discrimination. Elsewhere, this disparity was more episodic. Despite the disproportionate use of capital punishment against a wide variety of minority groups, the relationship between race and capital punishment in America is closely intertwined with the history and remnants of slavery, especially in the southern states. As noted earlier, those of African descent account for almost one-half of all legally sanctioned executions in the U.S since the earliest colonial times. Figure 9.1 shows the result of a lynching in the state of Indiana in 1930. When extra-legal lynching is included, this relationship becomes even stronger. Thus, the "peculiar institution" of slavery has had a lasting impact on the culture of the American South and the nature and use of capital punishment since that time (Friedman, 1993; Sellin, 1954; Wolfgang, 1974; Bowers, 1974; Marquart et al, 1994; Bressler, 2012).

### Slavery and Capital Punishment

Scholars have noted that is not mere coincidence that the vast majority of executions have taken place in former slave states (Allen & Clubb, 2008; Bowers, 1974). As Table 9.3 notes, 1,134 of the 1,397 executions in the United States since 1976 have taken place in the South (DPIC, 2015f). Of the ten states with

Figure 9.1. A Lynching in Indiana, 1930

Source: http://en.wikipedia.org/wiki/Lynching#mediaviewer/File:ThomasShippAbram Smith.jpg

the most executions, seven are southern states and two are considered border states (Oklahoma and Missouri). The five states with the largest number of executions are either southern or border states, and these account for almost 75% of all executions in the U.S. since 1977 (DPIC, 2015f).

Table 9.3 Executions by Region since 1976*

| Region | Executions |
|---|---|
| South | 1,137 |
| Midwest | 171 |
| West | 85 |
| Northeast | 4 |
| Total executions | 1,397 |

* From Death Penalty Information Center (2015f).

It is well documented that the criminal justice system of the southern states was used to officially and unofficially support slavery and, after the Civil War, segregation (Bressler, 2012; Friedman, 1993; see Bowers, 1974; Marquart et al., 1994). During the slavery era, the law was explicitly written to allow criminal punishment and executions for offenses committed exclusively by slaves (and Blacks more generally) or for which the penalties for slaves were considerably more severe than for White offenders (Allen & Clubb, 2008; Bowers, 1974). These **Slave Codes** were institutionalized efforts to increase penalties for slaves and Blacks to reinforce and protect White dominance (see Stampp, 1956; Friedman, 1993). In slave-era Virginia, for example, there were five capital offenses for Whites, while there were 70 capital offenses for Black slaves (Bowers, 1974). Whether the killing of a slave was a legally imposed penalty or an extra-legal lynching, it served an important function. As Friedman (1993) noted, "capital punishment was an important pillar of the southern social control system. Hanging a slave was a useful 'ritual' to impress blacks with the futility of violence against whites" (p.88).

While a justice of the peace could try a slave for a minor offense, the criminal courts were used for more serious violations of law (Friedman, 1993). Perhaps more importantly, a slave owner wielded considerable authority in punishing his slaves (i.e., property), including killing them under certain circumstances (Friedman, 1993). While the use of cruel and unusual punishments towards slaves was prohibited by statute in some slave states, the penalties for this were relatively modest and required the actual application of the law, which rarely took place in an official manner (Bressler, 2012; Friedman, 1993).

# The Post-Civil War South and Capital Punishment

The importance of legal executions and extra-legal lynching in the South did not diminish after the abolition of slavery (Oshinsky, 2010). After the Civil War, the Slaves Codes of the southern states were modified to avoid explicit conflict with the 13th and 14th Amendments' prohibition against slavery and the **Equal Protection Clause**. Often referred to as **Black Codes**, these laws were designed to reinforce and protect segregation in much the same way they previously protected slavery (Bowers, 1974; Marquart et al., 1994). For example, Johnson (1941) noted, "It is common knowledge that 'first degree burglary' is defined as a capital crime in several states as a threat to Negro offenders who enter a white residence after dark" (quoted in Bowers, 1974, p. 72). While the law did not distinguish a different penalty for White offenders, in the application of the law, prosecutors could choose to apply it disproportionately against

Blacks. Thus, official and unofficial actions taken by southern lawmakers, criminal justice agents, and many citizens were designed to maintain a *racial caste system* and to deny Blacks equal protection of the law supposedly granted via the 14th Amendment. Recall the argument by Michelle Alexander from Chapter 3 that mass imprisonment is America's current racial caste system.

One example of a criminal justice activity with negative consequences for Black defendants, capital or otherwise, was the selection of criminal juries. Throughout the United States, but particularly in the segregated south, official and unofficial strategies were used to exclude Blacks from juries, especially when the purported victim was White (Bright, 1995). The result, if not the explicit goal, was to reduce the likelihood that Black defendants would have their case heard by an "impartial jury" as guaranteed by the Sixth Amendment. Bright (1995) documents how government officials rigged jury lists to avoid having Blacks called for jury duty. Furthermore, when Blacks were called for jury service, prosecutors could strike Blacks from the jury pool during *voir dire* for "cause" justifications that were clearly pretexts for race. Worse, prosecutors could use their *peremptory challenges* to disproportionately eliminate potential Black jurors without justification, as noted in Chapter 7. These practices were most commonly used in interracial cases.

In addition, the legal representation provided for Black defendants, when provided at all, was frequently substandard and provided ineffective assistance of counsel (Bright, 1995; see *Powell v. Alabama*, 1932). Given the near absence of Blacks serving in any official criminal justice position in the segregated south, Black defendants in capital cases were frequently arrested and charged by White (male) police officers, judged by White jurors, had their sentence imposed by White judges, and requested executive clemency from White governors (Bowers, 1974; Bright, 1995). Under such circumstances, not surprisingly, the evidence indicates widespread bias in the treatment of Black offenders by the criminal justice system. The result was significant racial disparities in case outcomes, especially in the South, particularly in interracial crimes, and most notably for the crime of rape in which a Black male was accused of assaulting a White female.

There was considerable regional, state, and even local jurisdictional differences in the application of the death penalty. For example, Allen and Clubb (2008) provide an interesting discussion of regional differences in the use of capital punishment and lynching since colonial times. Nevertheless, nearly one-half of all legal executions between 1608 and 1945 took place in the South and another 13% in border states (Allen and Clubb, 2008). Furthermore, almost three-quarters of all legal executions of Blacks took place in the South and 90% of African Americans lynched were killed in the South. By the 20th century, the use of the death penalty and extra-legal lynchings were predominantly Southern practices. Although many states throughout the country had the death penalty until the late 1960s, most executions during the 20th century occurred in the southern and border states (Allen & Clubb, 2008). The southern states were unique in the sense that they defined the most crimes as capital offenses and were more likely to actually impose a death sentence for a non-homicide crime, especially rape and burglary, compared with other regions of the country (Bowers, 1874).

# Rape, Race, and the Death Penalty

The clearest evidence of racial bias in the use of capital punishment in American history was for the crime of rape. The Southern cultural abhorrence of notions of Black sexuality and the perceived threats of Black men towards White females ensured that such cases would be dealt with quite severely. Reported cases of Black assaults on White females were often surrounded by public outcry and the threat of mob violence. While rape was legally defined as a capital offense in many southern states irrespective of race, the imposition of a death sentence, and especially executions, were overwhelmingly for Black offenders and almost always for crimes against White victims (Allen & Clubb, 2008). Oshinsky (2010) noted that of the 455 persons executed for the crime of rape in the U.S. from 1930–1967, 90% were Black males convicted of raping White females. All known executions for rape during this period occurred in a southern or southern border state. Of the 553 known legal executions for rape between 1864–1967, all but six occurred in the South (Bowers, 1974). In North Carolina, for example, nearly nine in ten people executed in the 20th century for the crime of rape (which is no longer a capital offense) were Black males (see Table 9.4).

Table 9.4. Race and Executions for Rape in North Carolina, 1910–1961

|           | Black | White | Other |
|-----------|-------|-------|-------|
| 1910–1920 | 11    | 1     | 0     |
| 1921–1930 | 11    | 1     | 0     |
| 1931–1940 | 16    | 1     | 0     |
| 1941–1950 | 21    | 4     | 2     |
| 1951–1961 | 2     | 0     | 0     |
| Total     | 61    | 7     | 2     |
|           | (87%) | (10%) | (3%)  |

https://www.ncdps.gov/Index2.cfm?a=000003,002240,002327,002330,002335

Marvin Wolfgang conducted an early important study on the relationship between race, rape, and capital punishment. He examined 3,000 rape cases in 250 southern counties that occurred between 1945–1965 and found that Black males convicted of raping White females were 18 times more likely to receive a death sentence than other racial combinations (Wolfgang, 1974). A strong relationship between race and death sentences remained even after controlling for legally relevant factors. Wolfgang (1974) reported, "I find that none of the nonracial variables ... explain this sentencing differential. I therefore conclude that over at least a twenty year period there has been a systematic, differential practice of imposing the death penalty on blacks for rape, and most particularly, when the defendants are black and their victims are white" (p.120). It is worth noting that this study only included legal executions and did not consider lynching. Furthermore, the data in the Wolfgang study included cases after the Supreme Court's ruling in *Powell v. Alabama* (1932; discussed below) which imposed more rigorous requirements for providing counsel for criminal defendants in capital cases. It is likely that an even stronger relationship between and race and death sentences for rape would have been found with earlier data.

Even those skeptical of evidence purporting overt discrimination in present capital punishment systems (e.g., Kleck, 1981; Lane, 2010) have acknowledged the clear racial bias in the historical use of capital punishment for the crime of rape. The Supreme Court eventually ruled the use of the death penalty in non-homicide rape cases to be unconstitutional in *Coker v. Georgia* (1977). Critics note that the Court's ruling in *Coker* spoke little about racial discrimination in capital rape cases. Instead, the Court focused on Eighth Amendment concerns over whether the death penalty was proportional to the crime of rape and, therefore, violated notions of cruel and unusual punishment (Oshinsky, 2010). Despite this omission, there is clear evidence that the historical use of the death penalty, particularly in cases of rape, was closely interrelated with official and unofficial bias towards minorities and Blacks in particular.

## *Extra-legal Lynching, Capital Punishment, and Race*

To focus exclusively on the use of legally sanctioned executions is to overlook the unfortunate frequency of extra-legal lynching in America prior to the 1950s. Bowers (1974) describes **lynching** as "an act of the community against someone thought to have violated its most basic social mores" (p. 41). As such, lynching shared some common features with legal executions. Where lynching was relatively common, the distinction between these acts was often blurry (Marquart et al., 1994). Marquart et al. (1994) note that both lynching and legal executions frequently appear to have served similar functions—to reinforce and protect the existing social and racial caste system, especially in the western and southern regions.

There has been considerable scholarly debate over the relationship between lynching and legal execution (Oshinsky, 2010). While it is dangerous to engage in generalizations, it appears that in many areas, especially the South, a finding of guilt and the imposition of a legal death sentence was often an unofficial concession to prevent mob violence (Oshinsky, 2010). An early study on lynching noted, "In order to prevent a lynching, or to prevent further mob outbreaks after a lynching, peace officers and leading citizen often made promises which virtually precluded impartial court procedure" (Raper, 1933, as quoted in Marquart et al., 1994, p. 2). In addition to actual lynching, the perceived threat of a lynching appears to have affected how capital defendants were treated by the justice system. Neither of these worked to the advantage of minorities.

As Allen and Clubb (2008) demonstrated, lynching was not reserved for Blacks nor did it occur exclusively in the South. All regions of colonial and post-Civil War America experienced lynchings. There was considerable variation in the use of lynchings, against whom they were used, and the factors that contributed to such incidents (Allen & Clubb, 2008; Bowers, 1974; Marquart et al., 1994). For example, in the western region and states, lynchings were frequently, though not exclusively, the result of vigilante justice carried out by organized groups formed to deal with perceived threats and crime in areas where the official justice system was weak or limited. In the western and northeastern regions of the United States, it appears that lynching was predominantly used against Whites. This is in stark contrast to the American South and southern border states. However, lynching of Blacks and ethnic minorities (esp. Mexican, Chinese, Native Americans, and to a lesser extent, European ethnic groups) did occur in non-southern regions. The relatively small size of the non-Black minority populations in most regions resulted in lynching rates that were noticeably disproportionate to their presence in the population (Allen & Clubb, 2008).

Despite this, the South led the nation in both executing and lynching individuals (Allen & Clubb, 2008). The exact count of lynching in America is unknown, but one account found 4,749 lynchings between 1882–1968. Over 3900 (83%) of these lynchings occurred in the South or southern border states (Allen & Clubb, 2008). Urbina (2012) noted that, since 1882, almost 75% of all lynchings were against Blacks. These numbers do mask geographic differences. While 78% of Texas lynchings between 1886–1918 were of those from African descent, lynchings in other former Confederate states during this time were almost exclusively used against Blacks. In Alabama, for example, 97% of lynchings involved a Black victim (Marquart et al., 1994). Allen and Clubb (2008) conclude:

> After the Civil War, legal execution in the South and Border states was
> largely limited to offenses that involved the death of a victim and to
> rape and attempted rape. There was no such limitation where lynch-
> ing was concerned ... Presumed offenses against white women, in-
> cluding rape and attempted rape but also a number of lesser and often
> trivial offenses, were among the most common of these other rea-
> sons ... Lynching, in short, effectively negated restrictions on the legal
> use of the death penalty and made the death penalty an almost com-
> monplace event. In these terms, the South and parts of the Border re-
> gion lived up to their violent reputations. (pp. 90–91)

The National Association for the Advancement of Colored People (NAACP) was
largely created in response to the growing evidence of the frequency of lynching, especially in the South (Marquart et al., 1994). This organization's legal
defense unit would play a critical role in litigating some of the most important civil rights cases of the 20th century including numerous cases involving
capital defendants.

Research by Franklin Zimring (2003: 66) finds that the "states and the region
where lynching was dominant show clear domination of recent executions, while
those states with very low historic lynching records are much less likely than average to have either a death penalty or execution late in the twentieth century."
Zimring finds that the median number of executions in high lynching states is
24, versus zero in low lynching states. Zimring explains that: "The statistical
contrast between these two groups of states shows that they occupy the same
extreme positions on the distribution of two distinct varieties of lethal violence
in the United States separated by almost a century and the formal participation
of government authority in the killing" (p. 96). Two recent studies show relationships between: 1) county-level lynchings and murder rates; and 2) state
level-lynchings and executions. The authors of the second study suggest that executions have replaced lynchings as a means to deal with perceived racial threats
(Jacobs, Carmichael, & Kent, 2005; Messner, Baller, & Zevenbergen, 2005).

# Race and the Constitutionality
# of the Death Penalty

A detailed history of constitutional challenges to capital punishment, even
one that focuses exclusively on claims of racial discrimination, is beyond the
scope of the present chapter. Fortunately, several excellent reviews of death
penalty jurisprudence can be found (e.g., Latzer & McCord, 2011; Baldus,

Woodworth, & Pulaksi, 1990; Steiker & Steiker, 1995; 2014; Liebman, 2007; Bohm, 2012). The following discussion highlights several eras in judicial engagement with the issues of race and constitutionality of capital punishment and the major cases that have shaped the current status of the death penalty in contemporary America.

## *Pre*-Furman *Era*

Prior to the 1950s, the federal courts and the U.S. Supreme Court rarely interfered with state criminal justice matters. By early parts of the 20th century, however, the federal courts began to hear appeals challenging the constitutionality of state procedural matters in capital cases. The records of these cases highlighted significant problems facing capital defendants, especially for Black defendants in the South (Bowers, 1974). One of these cases in particular, *Powell v. Alabama* (1932), would eventually influence criminal procedural jurisprudence for a range of criminal matters. In *Powell* (also known as the Scottsboro Boys case), nine African-Americans were accused of raping two White females. The defendants were tried in three trials lasting one day each by an all-White jury. Each defendant was found guilty and all but one (a juvenile) were sentenced to death. While the Alabama court provided legal representation, the defendants' limited opportunity to meet with their attorneys and the lack of effort on their attorneys part prompted the Supreme Court to determine that the quality of that representation was constitutionally insufficient and that capital defendants must be provided counsel for the effective aid in preparing their defense (*Powell v. Alabama*, 1932, p. 71).

Additional court cases highlighted concerns about the constitutionality of criminal procedures prior to the 1960s, especially in capital cases. It is not a coincidence that many of these cases involved minority and Black defendants. In *Patton v. Mississippi* (1947), a Black defendant was convicted of capital murder after having his case heard by an all-White grand jury and trial jury. The defense provided evidence that the exclusion of Blacks was not coincidental but the result of an intentional effort to preclude Blacks from serving on criminal juries. In fact, no Black had served on a criminal jury in that jurisdiction for the previous 30 years. The Supreme Court ruled that the deliberative or systematic exclusion of Blacks from juries was a violation of the Equal Protection Clause. While an important case for criminal jurisprudence, critics have noted that, in practice, the ruling led to more subtle efforts to continue to minimize the presence of Black jurors, especially in cases with Black defendants and/or White victims (Bright, 1995; Bowers, 1974).

In *Fikes v. Alabama* (1957), a Black defendant was charged with burglary with intent to commit rape, a capital offense under Alabama law at the time.

The defendant was removed from the local jurisdiction and questioned at a state prison in isolation for several days without an opportunity to consult with family or counsel. The state used the confession that was made following his extensive questioning to obtain a conviction and the defendant was sentenced to death. Even though there was no evidence of physical force being used against the suspect, the Court ruled that the long periods of isolation and intensive questioning without access to counsel equated to an involuntary confession which violated due process.

Although these cases were important in identifying impermissible procedures and activities, scholars note that these rulings did not end unequal or constitutionally suspect treatment of criminal defendants in capital cases (Bright, 1995; Oshinsky, 2010). Many cases simply failed to come to light due to a lack of resources for appellate legal representation. In addition, criminal justice procedures were often modified in a manner to avoid explicit conflict with court rulings but that continued to deny due process and equal protection for criminal defendants, especially minority defendants (Bright, 1995; Oshinsky, 2010). Criminal justice actors had numerous ways to circumvent or bar full equal due process protections for minority defendants. Efforts to limit access to meaningful representation and an impartial jury were frequently the core of legal challenges to the death penalty for much of the 20th century (Baldus et al., 1990; Bowers, 1974). Many contend that these tactics, such as the use of preemptory challenges to exclude minority jurors, continue to be used today (Bright, 1995).

By the late 1960s, appellate litigation in capital cases, especially by the NAACP Legal Defense Fund, had essentially imposed a moratorium on executions in the United States (Bowers, 1974). Because executions were predominantly occurring in a limited number of states, pending appeals from convicted capital offenders in these states ensured that few executions would take place. Supreme Court cases such as *Witherspoon v. Illinois* (1968)—which ruled jurors who had concerns about the death penalty, but could still impose a death sentence, could not be intentionally excluded from capital juries—continued to place requirements on state death penalty procedures. Death penalty opponents, however, suffered a setback in *McGautha v. California* (1971), when the Court ruled that the death penalty did not violate the Eighth Amendment and that allowing unguided jury discretion and combined guilt and sentencing hearings did not violate due process (Oshinsky, 2010).

## Furman v. Georgia *(1972)*

With somewhat mixed signals from the Court about the constitutionality of capital punishment, the NAACP's legal team—which had taken responsibility for litigating the appeals of all capital cases in the federal courts—continued to identify cases that seemingly raised constitutional issues (Oshinsky, 2010). Finally, in a divisive 5–4 decision, the Court ruled in *Furman v. Georgia* (1972) that the death penalty, as currently practiced, was unconstitutional on 8th and 14th Amendment grounds. Each justice filed a separate opinion and the ruling remains the longest written opinion ever produced by the Court (Oshinsky, 2010).

The decision pertained to the case of William Henry Furman, who was convicted of the murder of a Coast Guard petty officer who was the father of four children and the stepfather of six others. Furman was a 25-year-old African American with an IQ of only 65 who killed his victim in a failed burglary attempt. Because Furman was an African American and a stranger, and his victim was a Caucasian and a family man who served in the military, Furman's chance of *not* receiving the death penalty was slim, especially in a southern state with a history of racial unrest.

Furman's attorneys argued to the Supreme Court that capital punishment in Georgia was unfair because capital trials essentially gave the jury unbridled discretion about whether to impose a death sentence on convicted defendants. Consolidated with *Furman* were two cases (*Jackson v. Georgia*, No. 69-5030 and *Branch v. Texas*, No. 69-5031) that dealt with death sentences imposed against African American men for rapes of Caucasian women, a crime which has been a primary source of discriminatory punishment in American history.

The majority opinion in *Furman* found the death penalty to be unconstitutional for different reasons. Some justices found the use of unguided discretion to be unacceptable while others were concerned about the disproportional executions of minorities and low status offenders. There was a core sentiment by the majority that the arbitrariness and capriciousness which seemingly plagued decision-making in capital cases was unconstitutional (see generally, Baldus et al., 1998; Oshinsky, 2010; Bowers, 1974). The dissent focused on judicial restraint and an unwillingness to invalidate a centuries old practice. That, the dissent argued, should be left to publicly elected legislatures and governors.

While the Court's ruling only overturned the death sentences of inmates in the two states from which the cases came (Georgia and Texas), "it effectively halted capital punishment in the United States" (Oshinsky, 2010, p. 54). Nearly 600 death row inmates had their sentences commuted to life imprisonment as a result of the ruling in *Furman*. However, as noted by Bowers (1974), "it did so without necessarily implying that the thousands of previous executions in America were unconstitutional. That is to say, the Court did not rule that capital punishment *per se* was unconstitutional, but only that it had *become* unconstitutional—cruel and unusual—as a result of the rare and arbitrary way in which it had recently been imposed" (p. 17, emphasis in original). As we shall see, Bowers was quite correct—the Supreme Court was not yet done with the death penalty.

## Gregg v. Georgia *(1976)*

The growing conservative political landscape of the 1970s and public concerns over rising crime rates lead to considerable criticism of the Court's ruling in *Furman*. As a result, states determined to keep the death penalty quickly revised their capital punishment statutes to comport with their interpretation of the Court's concerns. Given the diversity of the Court's opinion in *Furman*, it was unclear exactly how the states should proceed (Baldus et al., 1998). In general, states took one of two different strategies. The first was to remove discretion from the jury decision and to require a mandatory death sentence in cases that met statutorily defined criteria (Baldus et al., 1990; Oshinsky, 2010). The second strategy was to create a **bifurcated trial process** in which findings of guilt would be determined at one proceedings and then, if convicted, a separate hearing would be held to determine the appropriate penalty (i.e., a death sentence or not). Within a year of the *Furman* ruling, Georgia had revised its death penalty statutes and began sentencing convicted offenders to death. Several states quickly followed and death rows began to fill up once again (Oshinsky, 2010).

The *Gregg* case dealt with the crime of Tony Gregg, who was convicted of armed robbery and murder after killing two men who had picked up Gregg and fellow hitchhiker Floyd Allen. Gregg and Allen had been picked up in Florida and rode north toward Atlanta when the car broke down. Simmons was in possession of enough cash to purchase a new car; after purchasing this new car, the group picked up another hitchhiker who was let out in Atlanta. Apparently, Gregg and Allen decided to rob and kill the men after the other hitchhiker got out of the car. This hitchhiker, Dennis Weaver, contacted the police after reading about the murders in the newspaper. The next day, Gregg and Allen were arrested in North Carolina driving the victim's car and were in possession of the murder weapon.

Gregg's attorneys argued to the Supreme Court that the state's new guided discretion law was unconstitutional and asked the Court to overturn the death sentence. In 1977, the Supreme Court agreed to hear death penalty appeals for capital defendants sentenced in five states (NC, LA, FL, TX, and Gregg's cases from GA). Not surprisingly, all five cases emanated from southern states which were among the first to revise their statutes. The Court's 7–2 ruling in *Gregg v. Georgia* (1976) found that the bifurcated trial and penalty phase system and other provisions in Georgia, Florida, and Texas took sufficient steps to reduce arbitrariness in the imposition of the death penalty so that it was no longer un-constitutional (Baldus et al., 1998). Statutes that imposed a mandatory death sentence (North Carolina and Louisiana) on defendants convicted of a capital crime were ruled unconstitutional by a 5–4 vote. The majority opinion in these latter cases ruled that a mandatory death sentence did not offer the jury suffi-cient discretion to consider mitigating circumstances and unique factors of a case (Baldus et al., 1998). Only two justices, Brennan and Marshall, concluded that the death penalty was *per se* unconstitutional (Oshinsky, 2010).

As a result of the ruling in *Gregg*, the associated cases, and other cases that soon followed, the Supreme Court reauthorized states to impose and carry out death sentences. While the Court rulings suggested confidence in these proce-dures to reduce arbitrariness and racial disparities in the application of the death penalty, death penalty opponents and many social scientists were not convinced.

## McCleskey v. Kemp *(1987)*

Several years after the ruling in *Gregg*, the Legal Defense Fund of the NAACP funded a major study of Georgia's death penalty following *Gregg*. Commonly referred to as the "Baldus Study," the project was conducted by David Baldus, Charles Pulaski, and George Woodworth (see generally, Baldus et al., 1990; also Oshinsky, 2010). The researchers examined offenders convicted of mur-der or voluntary manslaughter following the enactment of the new death penalty statutes after *Furman* for a six-year period — over 2,000 defendants. In what has been highlighted as the most sophisticated study of capital pun-ishment at the time, the study controlled for over 200 legally relevant factors and examined several stages of the adjudication process (Gross & Mauro, 1989).

The study found that, after controlling for legally relevant factors, the race of defendants was not associated with death sentences in Georgia. However, those convicted of killing White victims were 4.3 times more likely to receive a death sentence than those convicted of killing Black victims. The pattern of **race-of-victim bias** was most pronounced in mid-range cases where there were nei-ther extensive aggravating nor mitigating circumstances and considerable discretion was left to decision-makers (Baldus et al., 1990). Furthermore, death sentences were far more likely in cases with Black defendants and White vic-tims than any other racial combination. The lawyers for Warren McCleskey, a Black man convicted of killing a White police officer in Georgia, used the re-sults of the Baldus study as evidence that Georgia's death penalty was still im-plemented in an arbitrary and discriminatory manner.

This case dealt with Warren McCleskey, who joined three accomplices to rob a furniture store. McCleskey, an African American man, secured the front of the store by rounding up customers and the manager, while his accomplices entered the store from the rear. A silent alarm was tripped and a White police officer entered the front of the store. The officer was hit with two shots, killing him. McCleskey, while under arrest for an unrelated offense, admitted to the robbery but denied the shooting. Two witnesses testified at trial that McCleskey admitted to the shooting and evidence suggested that at least one of the bullets came from the type of gun that McCleskey carried during the robbery. Thus, two aggravating factors were determined beyond a reasonable doubt, that McCleskey committed a murder during the commission of an armed robbery and that he killed a peace officer engaged in the performance of his duties. No mitigating factors were offered for evidence so the sentencing jury recommended death and McCleskey was sentenced to die by the judge.

McCleskey's attorneys argued to the Supreme Court that the administration of capital punishment in Georgia was racially biased against African Americans. In what has been described as one of the most controversial Supreme Court decisions of the 20th century (Gross, 2012; Bright, 1995; Powers, 2013), the Court ruled by a 5–4 vote that statistical evidence of a pattern of racial disparity is insufficient to rule a specific death sentence unconstitutional (Gross, 2012; Baldus et al., 1998). The Court ruled that evidence of a general statistical relationship between race and case outcome does not demonstrate that race affected the outcome *in this particular case*. In other words, defendants must be able to demonstrate that their race (or the race of the victim) negatively affected the outcome in their individual case. As scholars have noted, this is a difficult burden to demonstrate. Furthermore, statistical evidence of outcome disparity is sufficient in other areas of the law dealing with Equal Protection issues such as employment discrimination and voting rights cases (Baldus et al., 1998). Despite widespread criticism from social scientists, legal scholars, and death penalty opponents, *McCleskey* continues to guide courts' review of death penalty cases and has made it difficult to introduce statistical evidence of racial disparities from serving as the basis for challenges to capital punishment (see Gross, 2012; Bright, 1995; Baldus et al., 1998; Shatz & Dalton, 2013).

# Social Science Research and Evidence of Racial Disparities

As Bowers (1974) noted, the disproportionate application of punishment, such as the death penalty, may be the result of the differential application of the law or differential administration of justice. Under the former, the law is written in a manner that provides for legal mechanisms to target certain groups with enhanced penalties (e.g. penalties for crack vs. powder cocaine; see Tonry, 1995) or to create barriers to equal protection of the law. The **administration of justice** refers to the exercise of discretion from individuals at any stage of the adjudication process—from police investigation to a governor's use of his or her clemency power. If one or more of those legally authorized agents act in a manner that disproportionately affects persons with a particular status (whether intentional or not), the likelihood of racial disparities increases (Bowers, 1974).

In addition, some scholars distinguish *racial disparities* and *racial discrimination*. Although the concepts are closely related, contemporary social science research on sentencing and the death penalty typically uses the concepts separately. As first noted in Chapter 1, the term **disparity** is frequently used in empirical research that finds evidence of *differences* in case outcomes associated with one or more demographic characteristics such as race, gender, and or economic status. Difference, however, does not necessarily mean discrimination or unwarranted difference. Certain factors may be related to both case outcome and one or more demographic or other characteristics (often referred to as *extra-legal* factors). For example, Blacks disproportionately commit a variety of offenses, including homicide (Sampson & Lauritsen, 1997). Furthermore, Black defendants have, on average, more extensive prior criminal records than White offenders (Sampson & Lauritsen, 1997). Both of these may partially account for observed racial differences in case outcomes. Studies that fail to control for these factors can only speak of finding "unadjusted disparities" (see Baldus et al., 1990, 1998; Gross & Mauro, 1989). For this reason, it is critical that researchers control for as many legal and extra-legal factors as possible to rule out the possibility that some unobserved, but legitimate factor, might explain a finding of racial disparities.

The term **racial discrimination** is typically used to describe intentional, systematic, and/or widespread efforts to deny members of a minority group equal protection or due process of the law; different types of discrimination were noted in Chapter 1. Evidence of racial disparities is frequently used to support claims of racial discrimination. While some scholars are hesitant to draw explicit conclusions that these differences are necessarily the result of explicit racial bias and discrimination (Berk, Li, & Hickman, 2005; Robinson, 2008; Kleck, 1981; GAO, 1990), others have argued that there is sufficient statistical and case study evidence to support the conclusion that the criminal justice system, and capital punishment in particular, frequently operates in a racially discriminatory manner (Gross, 2012; Baldus et al., 1998; Robinson, 2008; Zatz, 1987). Furthermore, research on the role of *implicit bias* in decision making is highlighting the importance of *unconscious bias* in explaining evidence of racial disparities (see generally, Levinson & Smith, 2012, esp. Smith & Cohen, 2012). The terms **implicit bias** and **unconscious bias** refer to disparities that come about as a result of discriminatory beliefs people hold but do not know they hold; recall the theories of focal concerns and symbolic interactionism from Chapters 6 and 7.

The factors associated with the use of the death penalty is one of the most examined questions in criminal justice research (for reviews, see Grosso, O'Brien, Taylor, and Woodworth, 2014; Kleck, 1981; General Accounting Office, 1990; Gross and Mauro, 1989; Urbina, 2012). A dominant theme throughout much of this research is the extent to which race, both of the defendant and the victim, is related to decision making and case outcomes of capital defendants. Given the disproportionate number of Black defendants in the U.S. criminal justice system and the historical oppression and marginalization of Blacks in America, it is understandable why considerable public, legal, and scholarly attention has focused on the relationship between race and the death penalty.

Several early studies on race and capital punishment found considerable evidence of a relationship between a defendant's race and receiving death sentences and executions. For example, research by Magnum (1941), Johnson (1941), and Garfinkel (1949) all found evidence that, at least in the South, Black defendants were far more likely to receive a death sentence than Whites charged with similar crimes, especially for the crime of rape. Furthermore, evidence of racial disparities was most pronounced in cases where the defendant was Black and the victim was White. Not only were Blacks more likely to be sentenced to death, they were also more likely to be executed. Studies of executive clemency found that convicted Black offenders were far less likely to have their sentences commuted by a governor than White offenders (Ohio Legislative Service Commission, 1961; Wolfgang, Kelly, & Nolde, 1962).

Some have argued that the relationship between criminal justice outcomes and defendant race has been greatly diminished or eliminated (Wilbanks, 1987). Even critics of the death penalty acknowledge that since *Gregg v. Georgia*, racial disparities in the use of the death penalty have been reduced considerably (Baldus et al., 1998; Oshinsky, 2010; Sampson & Lauritsen, 1997). While there are numerous and tragic exceptions to this pattern, a variety of factors — including stronger constitutional protections for defendants and increased guidance in the exercise of discretion — appear to have been successful in reducing racial disparities in capital cases. Nevertheless, research continues to highlight and provide evidence of problems in the administration of justice, including the death penalty (Bright, 1005; Robinson, 2008; Chiricos & Crawford, 1995; Zatz, 1987).

A number of recent studies have examined sentencing disparities in the imposition of the death penalty (e.g., Baldus et al., 1990, 1998; Baldus, Woodworth, Grosso, and Christie, 2002; Hinson, Potter & Radelet, 2006; Paternoster & Brame, 2008; Phillips, 2008; Pierce & Radelet, 2002; Shatz & Dalton; Unah, 2009). In general, contemporary research on the death penalty indicates that the *defendant's* race is only marginally related to whether a murder results in a death sentence. Defendant characteristics most closely associated with a death sentence tend to be *aggravating factors*, such as defendant culpability, that are prescribed by law (Baldus et al., 1990, 2002; Jennings et al., 2014; Paternoster et al., 2003; Pierce & Radelet, 2002; ). There are some notable exceptions. For example, Baldus et al. (1998) found that juries in Philadelphia were significantly more likely to impose death sentences in cases with Black defendants. Additionally, Baldus, Grosso, Woodworth, and Newell (2012) found evidence of minority defendant disparity in the administration of the death penalty within the United States Armed Forces. Despite this, much research finds that race of defendant bias has been significantly reduced or eliminated in many jurisdictions (see Sampson & Lauritsen, 1997).

## Race of Victim Disparity

While research indicates that the race of the defendant is not statistically associated with capital punishment as it once was, the race of victim appears to continue to play a role in the outcomes of death penalty cases. Defendants who murder Whites are significantly more likely to be sentenced to death than defendants who murder Blacks (e.g., Baldus et al, 1990; Gross & Mauro, 1989; Hinson, Potter & Radelet, 2006; Paternoster et al., 2003, Williams & Holcomb, 2001; Pierce and Radelet, 2002; Vito and Keil, 1988; Thompson, 1997; Sorensen and Wallace, 1995; Unah, 2009). As noted earlier, the Baldus study widely cited in *McCleskey v. Kemp* (1987) found substantial race-of-victim effects even after controlling for a substantial number of legally relevant factors. In fact, those convicted of Whites were found to be 4.3 times more likely to have been sentenced to death. Numerous studies in a variety of jurisdictions have found similar results—those convicted of killing Whites (regardless of defendant race) are significantly more likely to be sentenced to death.

Has anything changed since this time? According to a recent study which examined every execution in the US from 1976–2013: "The single most reliable predictor of whether a defendant in the United States will be executed is the race of the victim" (Baumgartner, Grigg, & Mastro, 2015: 1). Further: "Blacks make up about half of the total homicide victims in the US though they represent only about 12 percent of the population. Yet, among convicted murderers who have been executed, only 15 percent of victims have been Black." This means that the group most likely to be murdered (African American males) is least likely to have its killers sentenced to death and executed, whereas killers of Whites are much more likely to be sentenced to death and executed.

Numerous possible explanations have been offered for these findings. One interpretation of this phenomenon is that Black victims are devalued by court actors and, hence, their murderers are viewed as less deserving of a death sentence. Since jury decisions appear to be influenced by whether the victim is perceived as "worthy" of a death sentence (i.e., whether their behavior contributed in some way to their victimization or if they were an "innocent" victim), *implicit bias* towards death victims could contribute to racially disproportional outcomes (e.g., Sundby, 2003; Smith & Cohen, 2012; Bowers, Sandys, & Brewer, 2004; but see Stauffer, Smith, Cochran, Fogel, & Bjerregaard, 2006). Stereotypes or implicit bias that Blacks are more likely to engage in illegal or morally questionable behavior may affect the perceived blameworthiness of the defendant, the perceived harm of a particular crime, and the credibility of the victim as a "victim" (Baumer et al., 2000; Myers, 1979; Smith & Cohen, 2012; Stanko, 1981–82). Still others have claimed that an unwillingness to seek the death penalty for Black victim cases, which predominantly involve Black offenders, is a reflection of community values in the Black community that are less supportive of the death penalty (e.g., Lane, 2012). Each of these can contribute to an underrepresentation of Black victim homicide cases among death sentences, even if a case meets the legal threshold for being death-eligible.

Another common finding from this research is that Black offender/White defendant cases are the racial combination most likely to receive a death sentence, even controlling for legally relevant factors (e.g., Baldus et al., 1990; Farrell & Swigert, 1986; Gross & Mauro, 1989; Williams et al., 2007; Radelet & Pierce, 1991; Thomson, 1996; Unah, 2009). Thus, in some cases, race of defendant is found to matter greatly. Explanations for this finding tend to focus on the perceived seriousness and harm of an offense that crosses racial boundaries (see Hawkins, 1987; LaFree, 1989; Spohn, 1994). **Interracial crimes** may be perceived as representing a significant deviation from social relations between racial groups. Beyond the criminal act itself, the violation of racial group interactions may influence a more severe response to reinforce social norms (Bowers et al., 2004).

Figure 9.2 illustrates that, since 1976, jurisdictions with the death penalty have executed 291 Black defendants for killing White victims, but only 31 White defendants who killed Black victims. Despite the fact that relatively few homicides or rapes involve White perpetrators and Black victims (see Baldus et al.,

**Figure 9.2. Executions from Inter-Racial Killings in the US, 1976–2014**

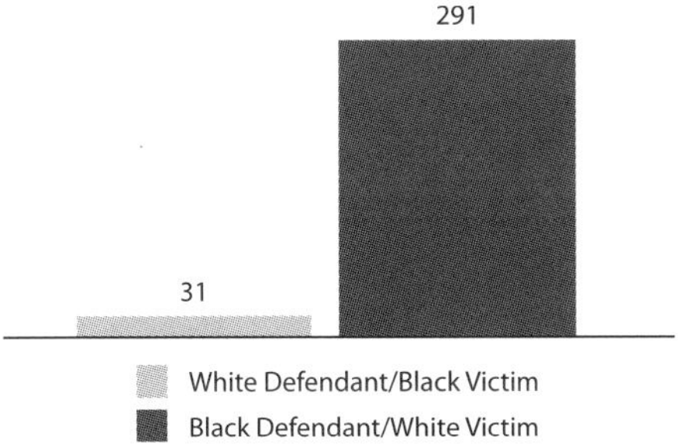

Source: http://deathpenaltyinfo.org/race-death-row-inmates-executed-1976#Vic
Used courtesy of the Death Penalty Information Center.

2002; LaFree, 1989; Pierce & Radelet, 2002; Spohn, 1994), there is little evidence of more severe treatment of interracial crimes in these cases. The harsher response to interracial crimes involving Blacks who victimize Whites provides additional support for the argument that race has a continuing influence on who is sentenced to death in America.

## White Female Victims

Homicide and death penalty research consistently finds that homicides with female victims are treated more severely than homicides with male victims (Baldus et al, 1990; Baumer et al., 2000; Farrell & Swigert, 1986; Gross & Mauro, 1989; Radelet & Pierce, 1991; Tomisch, Richards, & Gover, 2014; Vito, Higgins, & Vito, 2014). Explanations for these findings have varied. Some scholars have argued from a **chivalry hypothesis** that females are thought to require additional protections from society and that violent crimes against females are viewed as more harmful than similar crimes against males. More severe sentences for crimes with female victims have also been explained in terms of the perceived "innocence" of females and the "undeserving" nature of their victimizations (Myers, 1979; Williams, 1976), the perceived "defenselessness" of females (Gross & Mauro, 1989), and the perception that females are less likely to contribute to their own victimization (Farrell & Swigert, 1986).

More recently, scholars have examined the interaction between victim race and gender on the outcomes of capital and non-capital cases (Curry, 2010; Hinson et al, 2006; Holcomb et al, 2004; Phillips, 2012; Sommers, Goldstein & Baskin, 2014; Williams, Demuth & Holcomb, 2007; see generally, Tomisch et al., 2014). With some exceptions (e.g., Stauffer et al., 2006; Jennings et al.,

2014), research is increasingly identifying the importance of the interaction of a victim's race and gender in explaining racial disparities, consistent with the idea of *intersectionality* introduced first in Chapter 1. For example, in their study of death sentences in Ohio, Holcomb et al. (2004) found that White female victim cases were significantly more likely to result in a death sentence compared to any other victim race-gender combination. The authors posit that the relationship between race-of-victim and death sentence may be partially explained by the strong relationship between White female cases and death sentences.

Williams et al. (2007) reexamined the data used in the Baldus study to assess the impact of victim race-gender on case outcome. While the Baldus et al. (1990) data indicate that cases with female victims were more likely to result in a death sentence, the original authors did not seek to explain these results. Replicating the primary statistical model reported in *McCleskey,* Williams et al. (2007) found that cases with Black male victims were significantly *less* likely to result in a death sentence compared with other victim race-gender combinations. Importantly, cases with White female victims were almost 14.5 times more likely to receive a death sentence than cases with Black male victims, even while controlling for legally relevant factors (Williams et al., 2007). Furthermore, their study reported a hierarchy in the strength of the relationship between victim race-gender and case outcome. In particular, White female victim cases were significantly more likely than any other victim combination to result in the imposition of a death sentence. The authors suggested that a "White female effect" may exist in some jurisdictions and the strong relationship between White female victims and case outcome might account for more general disparity findings (see also Holcomb et al., 2004; Phillips, 2012; Tomisch et al., 2014).

# Future Issues and Considerations

The final section of this chapter examines several issues that may become increasingly relevant for American capital punishment, especially the racial dimensions of the death penalty. Obviously, these are not exhaustive, but they each have the prospects to result in official or unofficial changes in the use of the death penalty.

## *Increasing Diversity of U.S. Population*

This chapter has focused on the history and evidence of racial disparities in the application of death penalty with an emphasis on Black offenders. As the chapter noted, White ethnic minorities and Native Americans have experienced considerable discrimination and unequal protection of the laws in America. Social science, legal scholarship, and death penalty jurisprudence, however, has focused primarily on cases with Black, compared to White, offenders. For social science, the reasons often have to do with numbers. It is difficult to conduct meaningful statistical analyses on non-Black minorities due to their relatively small percentage of those sentenced to death in a particular jurisdiction compared to White and Black offenders.

The increasing diversity of the U.S. population raises potentially interesting questions about the death penalty. The Pew Research Center (2008) estimates that by 2050, Whites will no longer constituent a majority of the U.S. population. In particular, the Hispanic/Latino population in the United States is projected to increase from 14 to 29% of the total U.S. population (Pew Research Center, 2008). Historically, rapid changes in immigration and perceived threats to the status of the majority have been met with various efforts to marginalize and weaken minority groups. The impact of increasing population diversity in America is unclear. Current legal and institutional protections would seem to bar a return to overt discrimination, but this is not certain. Furthermore, it is possible that social anxiety associated with these changes could lead to further implicit bias (Levinson & Smith, 2012). The result could be an increase in outcome disparities throughout the criminal justice system, including capital punishment. Alternatively, increasing diversity of the population, especially the Hispanic/Latino population, might increase diversity among criminal justice agents and juries. While this would not necessarily result in an increasing sensitivity to concerns over equal protection or due process, it is a possible outcome in some communities. Of course, a combination of these or other outcomes is also possible. Regardless, it is quite plausible that, as American society becomes more ethnically diverse, the relationship between race and capital punishment will change in subtle or perhaps even more dramatic ways (see Urbina, 2008).

## *Innocence and Exonerations*

Another issue that may affect the status of the death penalty in America is the numerous exonerations of death row inmates, particularly since the mid-1990s. Since 1973, 150 persons sentenced to death have been released from prison due to sufficient evidence to prove the individual was factually innocent of the crime (DPIC, 2105b; 2004). Considerable media and academic attention has been given to such cases and the factors associated with false convictions in capital cases (Innocence Project, n.d.; Westervelt & Humphrey,

2001). In addition, scholars and death penalty opponents have noted the relationship between race and wrongful convictions. To date, over one-half (52%) of exonerations of death row inmates since 1973 have been of Black offenders and another 8% were Hispanic/Latino (DPIC, 2015). Thus, 60% of exonerated death row inmates since 1973 have been minorities.

The relationship is even stronger for DNA exonerations in capital and non-capital cases. Seventy percent (70%) of DNA exonerations have been of minorities (Innocence Project, n.d.). While a variety of factors have been identified that increase the likelihood of wrongful convictions, a major concern is that exonerated persons are frequently low status, minority individuals who often have diminished cognitive functioning (Parker, DeWees & Radelet, 2003; Scheck, 2014; Taslitz, 2006; Westervelt & Humphrey, 2001). For example, Temple (2009) chronicles the case of Bo Jones, a Black male who was falsely convicted of capital murder in the death of a White man and sentenced to death in North Carolina. He spent 13 years on death row and came within several days of being executed. If it had not been for the zealous efforts of his attorney, Ken Rose (among others), Bo Jones would still be on death row or would have been executed (see also Scheck, Neufeld, & Dwyer, 2003).

It is impossible to know how many wrongfully convicted persons are currently awaiting execution or the long-term impact of the "innocence movement" (Redlich, Acker, Norris & Bonventre, 2014). The frequency of these events and the close relationship with race may raise enough public and political attention to result in meaningful changes to how capital punishment is used in the U.S. There appears to be considerable evidence that the U.S. has executed a factually innocent person since *Gregg* (DPIC, 2015; Cohen, 2012). However, these cases have lacked the DNA evidence to unequivocally demonstrate factual innocence. As a result, they have not captured the public or political attention that such a case would likely generate. Many death penalty experts claim that, unfortunately, if such a case has not yet happened, it is simply a matter of time (Robinson, 2008). If it can be proven that a factually innocent person was executed, it could change national discourse and policy on capital punishment.

## Legislative Action and Racial Justice Acts

In response to the Supreme Court's ruling in *McCleskey*, death penalty reformers pushed for the passage of federal and state legislation to allow the consideration of statistical evidence of racial discrimination in capital cases (Alexander, 2014). Often referred to as **Racial Justice Acts**, such statutes allow the courts to assess whether race influenced the imposition of a death sentence in a particular case. In 1994, a federal Racial Justice Act was proposed and passed the House, but it failed to get further political support and no more progress has been made on that law (Alexander, 2014). Two states, Kentucky and North Carolina, have passed Racial Justice Acts. Each law differs in meaningful ways such as the specific requirements for offenders to receive relief and the type of relief available. In many regards, Kentucky's law is less favorable to offenders, while North Carolina's law was typically described as more progressive (for a specific discussion of the differences between these laws see Alexander, 2014; see also Powers, 2013).

To date, the Kentucky law has not yet led to an overturned death sentence and has only had a marginal effect on the death penalty in the state. The North Carolina Racial Justice Act, however, has resulted in the resentencing of four offenders from death to life without parole (Florshiem, 2014). Many death penalty experts and critics hailed the law as an opportunity to minimize the errors of the Court in *McCleskey* (Powers, 2013; Vidmar, 2012). The law, however, was not without its critics. In 2012, only three years after the law was passed, it was amended. Once the Republican Party gained control of the legislature and governorship, the Act was quickly repealed in 2014 (Florshiem, 2014; Alexander, 2014).

What is to be made of these developments? On the one hand, the passage of a Racial Justice Act, especially in a southern state, indicates a level of ambivalence and concern with the administration of the death penalty. On the other hand, such laws have passed in only two states, took one or more decades after the *McCleskey* ruling to be passed, and have been used to only modest (though meaningful) effect. Worse still, North Carolina's law was recently repealed. Viewed with an eye on the present, such laws seem to be too few, too weak, and too rarely used to overcome a historical and cultural pattern of racial discrimination and disparity in the administration of the death penalty. From another, more optimistic view, perhaps these are early indications that America is slowly, albeit too slowly, recognizing the difficult and troubling relationship between race and the administration of capital punishment.

# Conclusion

Capital punishment is meant to be the most severe punishment for the most severe crime (i.e., capital murder). Ideally, it is intended to reduce murder through incapacitation and deterrence, as well as serve justice by achieving retribution for family members of murder victims and society. Capital punishment is also meant to be applied solely based on legal factors such as the aggravated nature of the murder. In reality, the death penalty is rarely carried out, greatly inhibiting its crime prevention and justice functions. Further, the death penalty remains greatly impacted by extra-legal factors including race and ethnicity.

From the earliest years in America, the death penalty was characterized or even plagued by serious racial and ethnic biases, typically exercised against people of color. During slavery and the post-civil war south in particular, capital punishment as well as extra-legal lynchings were used by governments as well as citizens to maintain status quo power relations in society. While biases remain, it is the race of victim bias that appears to continue to plague capital punishment in America.

## Discussion Questions

1. What is capital punishment or the death penalty?
2. Define the terms lynching and mob violence.
3. Outline and discuss the major functions of capital punishment.
4. Compare and contrast the ideals of capital punishment with its realities.
5. Summarize how race and ethnicity have impacted capital punishment in US history.
6. What is the link between slavery and capital punishment, if any?
7. What is the relationship between lynching and capital punishment, if any?
8. How did race impact the imposition of death sentences for the crime of rape?
9. Summarize the major issues dealt with by the U.S. Supreme Court in the cases of *Furman v. Georgia*, *Gregg v. Georgia*, and *McCleskey v. Kemp*. Do you agree with the Court in these cases? Explain.
10. What is meant by the term race of victim bias?
11. What are implicit bias and unconscious bias and how do they impact capital punishment?
12. What is the chivalry hypothesis and how might it impact capital punishment?
13. Why might Americans be more likely to impose death sentences on killers of White females than on other groups?
14. How might the increasing diversity of the U.S. population and the discovery of innocent people on death row impact the death penalty?

## References

Baldus, D., Grosso, C.M., Woodworth, G., & Newell, R. (2012). Racial discrimination in the administration of the death penalty: The experience of the United States Armed Forces (1984–2005). *Journal of Criminal Law & Criminology, 101*(4), 1227–1336.

Baldus, D. & Woodworth, G. (1998). Race discrimination and the death penalty: An empirical and legal overview. In J. R. Acker, R.M. Bohm, & C.S. Lanier (Eds.), *America's experiment with capital punishment* (pp. 385–416). Durham: Carolina Academic Press.

Baldus, D.C., Woodworth, G., Grosso, C.M., & Christ, A.M. (2002). Arbitrariness and discrimination in the administration of the death penalty: A legal and empirical analysis of the Nebraska experience (1973–1999). *Nebraska Law Review, 88*, 486–753.

Baldus, D., Woodworth, G., & Pulaski, C. (1990*). Equal justice and the death penalty: A legal and empirical analysis.* Boston: Northeastern University Press.

Baldus, D., Woodworth, G., Zuckerman, D., Weiner, N.A., & Broffitt, B. (1998). Racial discrimination and the death penalty and the death penalty in the post-Furman era: An empirical and legal overview, with recent findings from Philadelphia. *Cornell Law Review, 83*, 1638–1770.

Baumgartner, F., Grigg, A., & Mastro, A. (2015). #BlackLivesDon'tMatter: Race-of-victim effects in US executions, 1976–2013. Forthcoming in *Politics, Groups, and Identities.*

Baumer, E.P., Messner, S.F., & Felson, R.B. (2000). The role of victim characteristics in the disposition of murder cases. *Justice Quarterly, 17*, 281–307.

Berk, R., Li, A., & Hickman, L. (2005). Statistical difficulties in determining the role of race in capital cases: A re-analysis of data from the state of Maryland. *Journal of Quantitative Criminology, 21*, 365–390.

Bohm, R.M. (2012). *The past as prologue: The Supreme Court's pre-modern death penalty jurisprudence and its influence on the Supreme Court's modern death penalty decisions.* Durham, NC: Carolina Academic Press.

Bowers, W.J., Sandys, M., & Brewer, T.W. (2004). Crossing racial boundaries: A closer look at the roots of racial bias in capital sentencing when the defendant is black and the victim is white. *DePaul Law Review, 53*, 1497–1538.

Cohen, A. (2012, May 12). Yes, America, we have executed an innocent man. *Atlantic Monthly.* Available at http://www.theatlantic.com/national/archive/2012/05/yes-america-we-have-executed-an-innocent-man/257106/.

Curry, T. (2010). The conditional effects of victim and offender ethnicity and victim gender on sentences for non-capital cases. *Punishment & Society, 12*(4), 438–462.

Death Penalty Information Center (2015a). *Executions in the U.S, 1608–2002: The Espy File.* Retrieved from www.deathpenaltyinfo.org/executions-us-1608-2002-espy-file.

Death Penalty Information Center (2015b). *Innocence and the death penalty*. Retrieved from http://www.deathpenaltyinfo.org/innocence-and-death-penalty#inn-yr-rc.

Death Penalty Information Center (2015c). *Causes of wrongful convictions*. Retrieved from http://www.deathpenaltyinfo.org/causes-wrongful-convictions.

Death Penalty Information Center (2015d). *Native Americans and the death penalty*. Retrieved from http://www.deathpenaltyinfo.org/native-americans-and-death-penalty.

Death Penalty Information Center (2015e). *Executions by year since 1976*. Retrieved from http://www.deathpenaltyinfo.org/executions-year.

Death Penalty Information Center (2015f). *Executions by state and region since 1976*. Retrieved from http://www.deathpenaltyinfo.org/number-executions-state-and-region-1976.

Death Penalty Information Center (2004). *Innocence and the crisis in the American death penalty*. Retrieved from http://www.deathpenaltyinfo.org/innocence-and-crisis-american-death-penalty#Sec04.

Farrell, R.A. & Swigert, V.L. (1986). Adjudication in homicide: An interpretive analysis of the effects of defendant and victim social characteristics. *Journal of Research in Crime and Delinquency, 23,* 349–369.

*Furman v. Georgia* (1972) 408 U.S. 238.

*Gregg v. Georgia* (1976) 428 U.S. 153.

Government Accounting Office (1990). *Death penalty sentencing research indicates pattern of racial disparities*. Washington, D.C.: Author.

Gross, S. & Mauro, R. (1989). *Death and discrimination: Racial disparities in capital sentencing*. Boston: Northeastern University Press.

Hinson, S., Potter, H., & Radelet, M.L. (2006). Race, gender, region, and death sentencing in Colorado, 1980–1999. *University of Colorado Law Review, 77,* 549–592.

Holcomb, J.E., Williams, M.R., and Demuth, S. (2004). White female victims and death penalty research. *Justice Quarterly, 21,* 877–902.

Innocence Project (n.d.). *Understand the causes*. Retrieved from http://www.innocenceproject.org/understand/.

Innocence Blog (2012, September 26). *What wrongful convictions teach us about racial inequality*. Available at http://www.innocenceproject.org/Content/What_Wrongful_Convictions_Teach_Us_About_Racial_Inequality.php.

Jacobs, D., Carmichael, J., & . Kent, S. (2005). Vigilantism, current racial threat, and death sentences. *American Sociological Review* 70: 656.

Jennings, W.J., Richards, T. N., Bjerregaard, B., Smith, M.D., & Fogel, S.J. (2014). A critical examination of the "White victim effect" and death penalty decision-making from a propensity score matching approach: The North Carolina experience. *Journal of Criminal Justice, 42,* 384– 398.

Johnson, J. Jr. (2011, March 11). How Los Angeles covered up the massacre of 17 Chinese. *LA Weekly* website retrieved from http://www.laweekly.com/ 2011-03-10/news/how-los-angeles-covered-up-the-massacre-of-18-chinese/.

Keil, T. & Vito, G. (1992). The effects of the *Furman* and *Gregg* decisions on black-white execution ratios in the South. *Journal of Criminal Justice, 20,* 217–226.

Kleck, G. (1991). [Review of *Equal justice and the death penalty: A legal and empirical analysis*]. *Contemporary Sociology, 20,* 598–599.

Kleck, G. (1981). Racial discrimination in criminal sentencing: A critical evaluation of the evidence with additional evidence on the death penalty. *American Sociological Review, 46,* 783–805.

Lane, C. (2010). The death penalty and racism. *The American Interest, 6*(2). Retrieved from http://www.the-american-interest.com/2010/11/01/the-death-penalty-and-racism/.

Latzer, B. & McCord, D. (2011). *Death penalty cases: Leading Supreme Court cases on capital punishment.* Amsterdam: Elsevier Publishing.

Levinson, J.D., & Smith, R.J. (2012). *Implicit racial bias across the law.* Cambridge: Cambridge University Press.

Liebman, J.S. (2007). Slow dancing with death: The Supreme Court and capital punishment, 1963–2006. *Columbia Law Review, 107,* 1–130.

*McCleskey v. Kemp* (1987) 481 U.S. 279.

Messner, S., Baller, R., & Zevenbergen, M. (2005). The legacy of lynching and Southern homicide. *American Sociological Review* 70: 633.

Ohio Legislative Service Commission (1961). *Capital punishment.* Staff Research Report (no. 46). Columbus, Ohio.

Parker, K. F., DeWees, M.A, & Radelet, M. (2003). Race, the death penalty, and wrongful convictions. *Criminal Justice, 18*(1), 48–54.

Paternoster, R. (1984). Prosecutorial discretion in requesting the death penalty: A case of victim-based racial discrimination. *Law and Society Review, 18,* 437–478.

Paternoster, R., & Brame, R. (2008). Reassessing race disparities in Maryland capital cases. *Criminology, 46,* 971–1007.

Paternoster, R., Brame, R., Bacon, S., Ditchfield, A., Biere, D., Beckman, K., et al. (2003). An empirical analysis of Maryland's death sentencing system with respect to the influence of race and legal jurisdiction: Final report. Found at www.urhome.umd.edu/newdsek/pdf/finalrep.pdf.

*Patton v. Mississippi* (1947) 332 U.S. 463.

Pew Research Center (2008). U.S. population projections: 2005–2050. Available at http://www.pewhispanic.org/2008/02/11/us-population-projections-2005-2050/

Phillips, S. (2008). Racial disparities in the capital of capital punishment. *Houston Law Review, 45*, 807–840.

Pierce, G.L. and Radelet, M.L. (2005). The impact of legally inappropriate factors on death sentencing for California homicides, 1990–1999. *Santa Clara Law Review, 46*, 1–46.

Pierce, G.L. and Radelet, M.L. (2002). Race, region, and death sentencing in Illinois, 1988–1997. *Oregon Law Review, 81*, 39–96.

*Powell v. Alabama* (1932) 287 U.S. 45.

Public Broadcasting Service (n.d.). *History detectives: Indentured servants in the U.S.* Available at http://www.pbs.org/opb/historydetectives/feature/indentured-servants-in-the-us/.

Raper, A.F. (1933). *The tragedy of lynching.* Chapel Hill, NC: University of North Carolina Press.

Radelet, M. & Pierce, G. (1991). Choosing who will die: Race and the death penalty in Florida. *Florida Law Review, 43*, 1–34.

Rizer, A.L. III (2002/2003). The race effect on wrongful convictions. *William Mitchell Law Review, 29*, 845–867.

Redlich, A.D., Acker, J.R., Norris, R.J., & Bonventre, C.L. (Eds.). (2014). *Examining wrongful convictions: Stepping back, moving forward.* Durham, NC: Carolina Academic Press.

Richards, T. N., Jennings, W.G., Smith, M.D., & Sellers, C., Fogel, S.J., & Bjerregaard, B. (2014). Explaining the "female victim effect" in capital punishment: An examination of victim sex specific models of juror decision-making. *Crime & Delinquency.* doi:10.1177/0011128714530826.

Robinson, M.B. (2008). *Death nation: The experts explain American capital punishment.* Upper Saddle River, NJ: Pearson/Prentice-Hall.

Sampson, R.J., & Lauritsen, J.L. (1997). Racial and ethnic disparities in crime and criminal justice in the United States. In M. Tonry (Ed.), *Ethnicity, crime, and immigration: Comparative and cross-national perspectives* (Crime and Justice, Volume 21) (pp. 311–374). Chicago: University of Chicago Press.

Scheck, B. (2014, April 2014). Stunning new case highlights how race bias corrupts juries. *Salon.* Available from http://www.salon.com/2014/04/15/barry_scheck_stunning_new_case_highlights_how_race_bias_corrupts_juries/ at Scheck, B., Neufeld, P., & Dwyer, J. (2003). *Actual innocence: When justice goes wrong and how to make it right.* New York, NY: New American Library.

Shatz, S.F. & Dalton, T. (2013). Challenging the death penalty with statistics: *Furman*, *McCleskey*, and a single county case study. *Cardozo Law Review*, 34, 1227–1282.

Smith, R.J., & Cohen, G.B. (2012). Capital punishment: Choosing life or death (implicitly). In J.D. Levinson, J.D. & R.J. Smith (Eds.), *Implicit racial bias across the law* (229–243). Cambridge: Cambridge University Press.

Sommers, I., Goldstein, J., & Baskin, D. (2014). The intersection of victims' and offenders' race/ethnicity on prosecutorial decisions for violent crimes. *Justice System Journal*, 35(2). DOI:10.1080/0098261X.2013.869153.

Sorenson, J. & Wallace, D. (1995). Capital punishment in Missouri: Examining the issues of racial disparity. *Behavioral Sciences and the Law*, 13, 61–80.

Spears, J. and Spohn, C. (1997). The effect of evidence factors and victim characteristics on prosecutors' charging decisions in sexual assault cases. *Justice Quarterly*, 14, 501–524.

Spohn, C. (1994). Crime and the social control of blacks: Offender/victim race and the sentencing of violent offenders. In G.S. Bridges and M.A. Myers (Eds.), *Inequality, crime, and social control* (249–268). Boulder: Westview Press.

Stampp, K. (1967). *The peculiar institution: Slavery in the Ante-Bellum South.* New York: Alfred A. Knopf.

Stanko, E.A. (1981–82). The impact of victim assessment on prosecutors' screening decisions: the case of the New York County district attorney's office. *Law and Society Review*, 16, 225–239.

Stauffer, A.R., Smith, M.D., Cochran, J.K., Fogel, S.J., and Bjerrgard, B. (2006). The interaction between victim race and gender on sentencing outcomes in capital murder trials: A further exploration. *Homicide Studies*, 10, 2, 98–117.

Steiker, C.S. & Steiker, J.M. (2014). Judicial developments in capital punishment law. In J.A. Acker, R.M. Bohm, & C.S. Lanier (Eds.), *America's experiment with capital punishment* (77–100). Durham, NC: Carolina Academic Press.

Steiker, C.S. & Steiker, J.M. (1995). Sober second thoughts: Reflections on two decades of constitutional regulation of capital punishment. *Harvard Law Review*, 109, 355–438.

Sundby, S.E. (2003). The capital jury and empathy: The problem of worthy and unworthy victims. *Cornell Law Review*, 88, 343–381.

Taslitz, A.E. (2006). Wrongly accused: Is race a factor in convicting the innocent. *Ohio State Journal of Criminal Law*, 4, 121–166.

Temple, J. (2009). *The last lawyer: The fight to save death row inmates.* Oxford, MS: University of Mississippi Press.

Thomson, E. (1997). Discrimination and the death penalty in Arizona. *Criminal Justice Review, 22*, 65–76.

Tonry, M. (1995). *Malign neglect: Race, crime, and punishment in America.* Oxford: Oxford University Press.

Tomsich, L., Richards, T.N., & Gover, A. (2014). A review of sex disparities in the "key players" of the capital punishment process: From defendants to jurors. *American Journal of Criminal Justice, 39*(4), 732–752.

Unah, I. (2009). Choosing those who will die: The effect of race, gender, and law in prosecutorial decision to seek the death penalty in Durham, North Carolina. *Michigan Journal of Race & Law, 15*, 135–179.

Urbina, M.G. (2012). *Capital punishment in America: Race and the death penalty over time.* El Paso, TX: LFP Publishing.

Vandiver, M. (1993). The quality of mercy: Race and clemency in Florida death penalty cases, 1924–1966. *University of Richmond Law Review, 27*, 315–345.

Vito, G.F., Higgins, G.E., & Vito, A.G (2014). Capital sentencing in Kentucky, 2000–2010. *American Journal of Criminal Justice, 39*(4), 753–770.

Wei, W. (n.d.). *The Chinese-American experience, 1857–1892.* Available from HarpWeek website at http://immigrants.harpweek.com/ChineseAmericans/1Introduction/BillWeiIntro.htm.

Westervelt, S.D., & Humphrey, J.A. (2001). *Wrongly convicted: Perspectives on failed justice.* Piscatawy, N.J.: Rutgers University Press.

Wilbanks, W. (1987). *The myth of a racist criminal justice system.* Monterey, CA: Brooks/Cole Publishing.

Williams, M.R., Demuth, S., & Holcomb, J.E. (2007). Understanding the influence of victim gender in death penalty cases: The importance of victim race, sex-related victimization, and jury decision making. *Criminology, 45*(4), 865–891.

Williams, M. & Holcomb, J. (2001). Racial disparity and death sentences in Ohio. *Journal of Criminal Justice, 29*, 207–218.

Wolfgang, M.E., Kelly, A. and Nolde, H.C. (1962). Comparisons of the executed and the commuted among admissions to death row. *Journal of Criminal Law, Criminology, and Police Science, 53*, 310–311.

Zatz, M. (1984). Race, ethnicity, and determinate sentencing, A new dimension to an old controversy. *Criminology, 22*, 147–171.

Zesch, S. (2012). *The Chinatown War: Chinese Los Angeles and the Massacre of 1871.* New York, NY: Oxford University Press.

Zimring, F. (2003). *The contradictions of American capital punishment.* New York: Oxford University Press.

# Chapter 10

# Race, Ethnicity, and Juvenile Justice

*by Jason Williams, PhD*

## Introduction

When most people think of issues in the *criminal justice system* (CJS), they rarely think about juveniles. The emphasis on identifying problems within the CJS focuses overwhelmingly on adults. Current debates within the *juvenile justice system* (JJS) hinge on punishment versus treatment. For example, some scholars have argued the need for evidence based responses (Guerra, Kim, & Boxer, 2008), while the system, as it is run now, advocates punitive solutions.

Moreover, the question of punishment is currently intertwined with a current and pressing debate known as **disproportionate minority contact** (DMC) which refers to the disproportionate amount of minority youth who come into contact with the juvenile justice system (JJS). Much of the research regarding DMC is situated around measures of contact and punishment about race. Many of these studies focus on specific areas of the juvenile justice as opposed to a full-scale analysis of the many components that make up the JJS and DMC. According to the Leadership Conference on Civil and Human Rights (2015), the racial disparities that characterize criminal justice in America affect young people deeply, and cause minority youth to be over-represented *at every stage of the juvenile justice system.*

This chapter will speak exclusively to concerns regarding juveniles within the JJS and race and ethnicity. First, a brief and comprehensive definition of what the JJS is will be offered. Then, the chapter will elaborate on the functions of the JJS. Third, the chapter will delve into the ideals of the American JJS. Next, the author explains the realities of American juvenile justice, along with some explanations for it.

# What Is Juvenile Justice?

The JJS is designed to respond to *criminal* and *delinquent* infractions committed by those who are underage or considered a juvenile under state law (usually those ages 17 years and under). The JJS is governed by state governments who hold absolute power to enact laws regarding juvenile crime and delinquency and what legally responsive measures are to be taken against those who find themselves accused of such behavior. As shown in Chapter 2, the JJS is based strictly on a philosophical doctrine known as **parens patriae,** adopted in 1838 as a result of *Ex parte Crouse* (Vito & Kunselman, 2012). The Supreme Court's decision cemented the use of parens patriae as a justification for intervening criminal and deviant matters concerning children. The philosophical doctrine—meaning, literally, "parent of the country"—dictates that the state has the legal and moral responsibility to intervene in cases when a child's biological parent(s) are unable to fulfill their parental responsibilities and when the child has become a nuisance to the community. The goal is for the court to focus on the best interests of children.

Prior to the adoption of the JJS, children faced the same kinds of punishment experienced by adults. The uniformity in juvenile and adult punishment was dominant before the reform era (pre 1820s), a time in which children were regarded as "little adults" who possessed *free will* and the same kinds of rational choices as adults. It is due to this logic that children were punished akin to adults. Such punishment, however, was not always supported by everyone.

For example, social activists and children advocates known as the **child savers** were steadfastly against equal punishment between adults and children. They believed that children needed to be reformed. Their efforts would later lead to radical changes in the administration of juvenile justice, thus changing the adjudication of minors from a penal process toward one of social welfare.

The community and political work of child advocates like the child savers eventually led to the creation of the **houses of refuge**. The first house of refuge was established in New York City in 1825. At this time, the creation of these spaces of refuge was seen as a major reform because previously juveniles were systematically mistreated and conceived as little adults. For example, prior to the reform era, many of the punitive responses to juveniles were primarily implemented against the poor.

In addition, there were also accounts of African American children being treated differently from their White peers (Ward, 2012). A keen example of this disparity is when the highest official for a Philadelphia house of refuge iterated, "It would be degrading to the white children to associate them with beings given up to public scorn" (Mennel, 1973, p. 17, as cited in Vito & Kunselman, 2012, p. 13).

The primary objective of the houses of refuge was to reform children away from deviant and anti-social behavior patterns. Children who were neglected and parentless were also sent to houses of refuge. Many of these houses were run by religious entities who utilized the teachings within their religious text to help guide the reformation of troubled youth. Aside from moral and behavioral change, oftentimes, these youth would be "sent out" on work details. These features would include farms, domestic care, and manual labor among many others. However, these details were not always beneficial to the well-being of the children as many of them were often abused and exploited, which almost always resulted in youth running away from their assignments.

Nevertheless, turning these youths over to the houses of refuge would eventually prove to be futile. Thus, through new reforms, the first juvenile court was born in Cook County, Illinois, in 1899. The court was mandated to adjudicate cases involving children ages 8–17. The development of this court was a brainchild of the child savers and other advocates whom although they believed in parens patriae; they also believed that the state had an essential role in the reformation and development of troubled juveniles.

The handling of juveniles would soon turn to one of systematic processes with a focus strictly on the needs of juveniles. Nevertheless, even with reform, decision-making regarding the handling of children is executed with ambivalent intentions.

## Functions of Juvenile Justice

The modern JJS is slightly similar to the adult CJS. However, the philosophy, which governs the JJS is staunchly different. For example, the role of the juvenile court is to act in the best interest of the child. There are five different kinds of minors who enter the JJS for various different reasons, as shown in Table 10.1. As you can see, the JJS is intended not just for young people who violate the law or special rules that apply just for them, but also to help children in great need of help.

---

### Table 10.1 Clients of the Juvenile Justice System

- **Delinquent children** enter the system as a result of engaging in law-breaking behavior.
- **Status offenders** are brought into the JJS for engaging in behavior that is considered unsuitable for children. Some examples of status offending are underage drinkers, runaways, and curfew violators.
- **Neglected children** enter the system as a result of parental neglect. Oftentimes these situations involve parents who are simply unable to provide economically, physically and emotionally for their children.
- **Dependent children** are those who have been abandoned and are in need of foster care.
- **Incorrigible children** are those who have behavior problems that are so beyond parental control that in order to address the problem holistically the court must become involved.

---

# Ideals of American Juvenile Justice

*Parens patriae* still profoundly influences modern day juvenile justice. Keeping with the notion that juveniles are to be cared for as opposed to stigmatized and harshly punished, the primary focus of the juvenile system is to institute rehabilitation. Instead of engaging in trials, youths attend hearings designed to be different from the usual adversarial processes experienced in the adult's system. These hearings are also closed from the public, as allowing them to be public can potentially bring unwarranted damage to juveniles. Another component of the juvenile system is *individualized justice*. The juvenile system is designed to reach children on their level and to respond in ways that fit each child's situation.

Furthermore, one of the foremost measures of the JJS is its focus on reducing labeling or stigma, as labeling can engender unwarranted pressure on children who come into contact with the courts. In addition, these separate courts are in place to prevent juveniles from being exploited or harmed by adults within the adult CJS. Table 10.2 illustrates some of the different terms used in the JJS and the adult CJS; many of these were first discussed in Chapter 2.

Table 10.2 Terms Used in Criminal and Juvenile Justice Systems

| Criminal Justice | Juvenile Justice |
| --- | --- |
| Crime | Delinquency |
| Arrest | Intake |
| Conviction | Adjudication |
| Sentence | Placement |

# Realities of American Juvenile Justice

In spite of the rhetoric of individualized justice and parens patriae of the juvenile court, the JJS has become more like the CJS in some important ways. This has largely happened over time, as the Supreme Court has issued some rulings that made the juvenile courts function more like adult courts. Among the cases included:

- *Kent v United States*, 383, US 541 (1966)—pertaining the case of 14-year-old Morris Kent, who was charged with robbery and rape after his fingerprints were found at the scene of a crime, and subsequently waived to the adult criminal court over objections of Kent's lawyer. The Court held that juveniles were entitled to hearing to determine whether waiving a juvenile case to adult courts was justified.
- *In re Gault*, 387 US 1 (1967)—dealing with the case of 15-year-old Gerald Gault, who was accused of making indecent phone calls to a neighbor while on probation for theft of a wallet, and where the police did not notify Gault or his parents of the charges against him, nor were sworn witnesses used against Gault and no record of the hearing were kept. The Court held that juveniles were entitled to due process rights including notice of charges, right to legal counsel, right against self-incrimination, and the right to confront accusers and cross-examine witnesses.

- *In re Winshop*, 397, US 358—involving a 12-year-old boy charged with stealing money from a purse and convicted in juvenile court by a preponderance of the evidence. The Court held that adjudication of delinquency, like a criminal conviction in an adult court, required proof beyond a reasonable doubt.

Due to cases such as this, one controversy that has emerged in juvenile justice is whether the juvenile courts ought to function like criminal courts. They do not fully, for the Court rules in *McKeiver v Pennsylvania*, 403 US 528, that juveniles are not entitled to full jury trials; yet the JJS has indeed become more like the adult criminal justice system over time. As one example, consider the claim of the Leadership Conference on Civil and Human Rights (2015):

> In the last decade, juvenile justice policy has increasingly blurred the distinctions between children and adults. Many states and the federal government have adopted laws that permit, encourage, or require youthful offenders to be tried as adults and ultimately transferred into adult prison populations. This ongoing erosion of the juvenile justice system we have known for a century is disastrous for juvenile offenders in general, but minority youths suffer most from this policy shift because they already bear the brunt of racially skewed law enforcement.

There are many other controversies within the JJS today; however, one of the foremost concerns is disproportionate minority contact (DMC). The **Office of Juvenile Justice and Delinquency Prevention (OJJDP)** (2012) refers to DMC as "the disproportionate number of minority youth who come into contact with the juvenile justice system" (p. 1). The OJJDP was created as a result of the *Juvenile Justice and Delinquency Prevention Act of 1974* (JJDP) whose purpose was to address the increase in juvenile delinquency and crime. As a result of DMC, in 1988 the OJJDP was authorized to mandate states participating in the program to address the problem. Consequently, states were encouraged to develop plans to reduce the disproportionate amount of minority youth in their respective jurisdictions.

In 1992, the demands to address DMC became a "core requirement" as nearly 30% of federal funding was tied to the States' commitment to addressing DMC. Moreover, in 2002 OJJDP was reauthorized to expand the core, thus including confinement and contact. However, despite these federal mandates and attempts at addressing DMC as it relates to every stage within the JJS, racial disparity continues to linger.

In addition, the OJJDP operationalizes the **Reduction Model** shown in Figure 10.1. The reduction model helps states to determine the extent to which

**Figure 10.1. DMC Reduction Cycle**

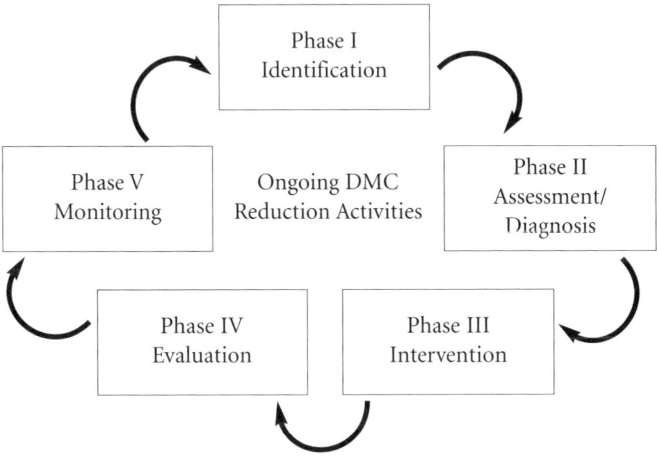

Source: http://www.ojjdp.gov/pubs/239457.pdf

DMC exists within their jurisdictions. It also provides a guide for states to initiate reduction strategies. The reduction model attempts to identify the degree to which disproportionality exists, which then leads to an assessment and an intervention. The next sections will examine the extent to which race may play a role in the administration of juvenile justice.

There are several processes and stages within the JJS within which researchers may study to determine the extent of DMC. However, the core areas of concern about DMC exist predominantly in disparities in intake, referrals to adult courts, and punishment. Another angle, on which to study the existence of these realities, is to examine the perceptions of juvenile justice, as perceptions often play a leading role in the administration of justice, as well as policy and procedural measures. Before moving on to these issues, it is important to note that major civil rights organizations, including the Leadership Conference on Civil and Human Rights (2015) have noted the serious issue of DMC:

> Racially skewed juvenile justice outcomes have dire implications, because the whole point of the juvenile justice system is to head off adult criminality. For example, one pillar of the juvenile justice system is the segregation of children from adult prisoners. Placing more black and Hispanic teenagers in adult prisons where they will come into contact with career criminals serves to incubate another generation of black and Hispanic criminals.

## Disparities in Intakes

There had been some arguments made by researchers alleging that the JJS is moving away from its original orientation based on therapeutics toward criminalization of youth. However, through the intake process one can ascertain the extent to which a paradigm change might be occurring within the JJS. One of the most important processes within both the adult and juvenile justice systems is the beginning of an adjudication. For example, the first stage of arbitration sets the stage for everything else. In fact, researchers have found that the inconsistencies in decision-making prior to court can have a devastating impact on the deposition phase (McCarthy, 1987; Wu, 1997).

In addition, research has found that **extra-legal factors** such as race, ethnicity and class have been found to be significant indicators of one's probability of preadjudication detention (Bishop & Frazier, 1996; Bortner & Reed, 1985; Secret & Johnson, 1997; Wu, Cernkovich & Dunn, 1997). Moreover, Bishop and Frazier (1996) found that factors such as gender and prior record are influential too.

Consistent with the idea of *intersectionality* first addressed in Chapter 1, some research has additionally suggested that African American delinquents are at a greater risk of detention when compared to other racial groups (Harms, 2002). Furthermore, after studying the phases of detention, Wordes, Bynum and Corley (1994) found that African American and Latino juveniles were more likely placed in custody. Wu (1997) concluded that one's detention status may have an impact on confinement at later stages of adjudication. The aforementioned studies are crucial because they explain official action that takes place at the intake stages of the JJS. Studies regarding intake dominantly show that there is a bias against the minority offender (Bishop & Frazier 1998; Dannefer & Schutt, 1982; Smith & Paternoster, 1990). There are many reasons for such bias; however, some research has found that family living status such as one coming from a single-parent home may have a negative impact on one's experience within the JJS (Pope & Feyerherm, 1990). Thus, since African American youth are more likely to come from single-parent homes they are also more liable to have their living experiences used against them.

Armstrong and Rodriguez (2005) while investigating contextual and individual characteristics on preadjudication detention decisions found that race, gender, and age had a profound impact on one's likelihood of being detained prior to adjudication. The researchers found that Hispanics were two and a half times more likely to be detained than Whites. In addition, they found that African Americans were one and a half more likely when compared to Whites to be detained. These findings correlate much of the literature that explains and confirms DMC. Thus, if minorities are more likely to be sent to preadjudication detention then typically they would face harsher punishments in the long run and spend a longer time navigating the system.

Some scholars have contended that racial stereotypes may play a role in the decision-making processes of court officers (Tittle & Curran, 1988), which is consistent with **symbolic threat theory**, a theory that asserts we will pay more attention to and fear people based on extra-legal factors such as race. Moreover, Bridges and Steen (1998) uncovered that probation officers' perceptions lead to disadvantaged outcomes for Black youth. They found that court officers were more likely to include individual characteristics and environmental attributes of White youth in the decision-making process. These disparities exist even in instances where youth of color and Whites are similarly situated (Bishop & Leiber, 2012).

Leiber, Peck and Beaudry-Cyr (2014), in a study that examined juvenile justice decision-making in a county with the largest amount of Blacks in Iowa, looked at the interrelationships between gender of probation officers and juvenile court detention and intake outcomes. First, they found that the race and sex of the offender and court officers are statistically significant. They reported that Blacks are 35% more likely to be recommended for detention and 26% more likely to be referred at intake when compared to similarly situated Whites. In addition, regarding drug offenses, they concluded that Whites were far less likely to be detained compared to similarly situated Blacks.

Furthermore, Bishop, Leiber and Johnson (2010), in a study that examined organization context, found that race was indeed significant during the intake processes for the juveniles in their sample. They suggested the JJS is a "nonsystem" (pg. 216), and that the decentralized nature of the system is the foremost and perhaps overlooked reason for inconsistences in juvenile justice outcomes. Within their study, the contextual variables were family structure and school status. As expected, they found that the contextual variables were significant. For example, youth who came from single parent homes as well as those who dropped out of school were significantly more likely to be referred to court. They also found compelling evidence of race and gender bias, for example, "the odds that an African American will be recommended for formal processing are over 50% higher than the odds for a White, whereas the odds that a male will be referred for formal processing are about 21% higher than those for a female" (p. 223).

In collaboration with the results from Bishop et al. (2010), it appears that prior records (Bishop, 2005; Farrell & Swigert, 1978) and implicit biases against minorities (see e.g., Chesney-Lind, 1977; Gaarder, Rodriguez, & Zatz, 2004) may play a role in the decision-making processes of court officers during pread-

## Figure 10.2 Overpolicing Minority Youth

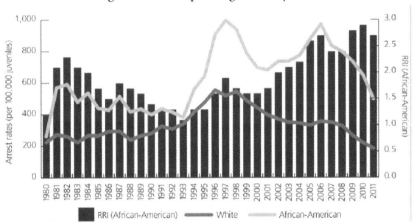

Source: http://sentencingproject.org/doc/publications/jj_Disproportionate%20Minority%20Contact.pdf

Used courtesy of The Sentencing Project.

judication, which ultimately becomes a self-fulfilling prophecy (Farrell & Swigert, 1978), thus making the stereotype a reality. However, neutral observers to such results may yield toward parens patriae as a means of justifying disparity within the system, thus alleging, perhaps, that minority children need more focus and discipline than their White counterparts. Prior research has shown the extent to which intake officers yield to contextual factors like *risk factors* during the decision-making process (Bridges, Conley, Engen, & Price-Spratlen, 1995; Farnworth, Frazier, & Neuberger, 1988). **Risk factors** refer to things that increase the odds of delinquent behavior.

According to a report by The Sentencing Project (2014), Black youth were nearly 270% more likely to be apprehended for the violation of curfew laws when compared to Whites. These disparities, which occur during preadjudication, may be the result of the over-policing of Black youth (see figure 10.2). Prior research has suggested the breaking of curfew laws could be due to contextual circumstances, such as family life and structure (Bishop et al., 2010).

Interestingly, the same trend of over-policing can be observed when scrutinizing arrest rates. The Sentencing Project (2014) purported that although there has been a drop in arrest rates nation-wide among all racial groups, Black youth continue to be two times more likely to be arrested compared to Whites (see figure 10.3). This stark contrast may suggest to some that there may need to be more comprehensive and possibly new measures to address the persistence of DMC.

## Figure 10.3. Arrest Disparities by Race

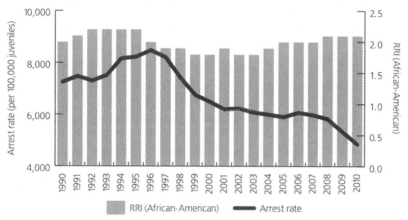

Source: http://sentencingproject.org/doc/publications/jj_Disproportionate%20Minority
%20Contact.pdf

Used courtesy of The Sentencing Project.

## *Disparities in Referrals to Adult Courts*

After *intake*—or what is referred to as *arrest* in the adult criminal justice system—things unfortunately seem to get worse. According to the Leadership Conference on Civil and Human Rights (2015):

> Over-representation of minority youths in the juvenile justice system increases after arrest. As a general matter, minority youths tend to be held at intake, detained prior to adjudication, have petitions filed, be adjudicated delinquent, and held in secure confinement facilities more frequently than their white counterparts.

Consider the issue of the rates at which juveniles are waived to criminal (adult) courts. The waiving of a youth to the criminal court can occur in three ways. First, there is concurrent jurisdiction that allows a prosecutor the discretion to charge a particular offender as an adult usually based on the severity of the offense. Next, there are statutory exclusion laws that mandate that certain crimes committed by juveniles are tried in criminal court. Last, there is *judicial waiver* that allows the juvenile court judges the authority to transfer juvenile offenders to the criminal court.

According to Puzzanchera and Addie (2014) in a report published by the OJJDP on juvenile cases waived to the criminal court "for every 1,000 peti-

Figure 10.4. Use of Judicial Waiver to Adult Courts

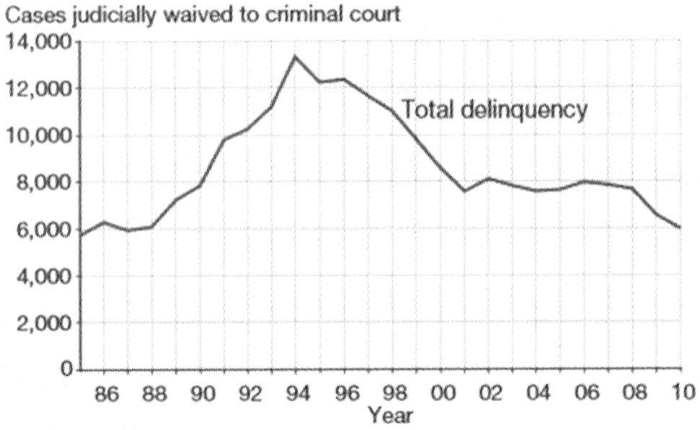

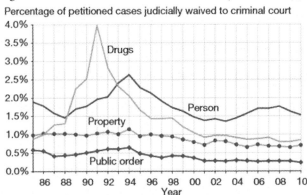

Source: http://www.ojjdp.gov/pubs/243042.pdf

Figure 10.5. Waivers to Criminal Court, by Offense Type

Source: http://www.ojjdp.gov/pubs/243042.pdf

tioned cases, 8 were waived to criminal court" (p. 1). In fact, the waiver peaked in the mid-90s at over 13,000 cases and then were lowered by a little over 50% in 2010 (see Figure 10.4) In addition, the overall peak was dominated by drug offenses as they were likely to be waived to criminal court more than any other offense from 1989–1992 (see Figure 10.5). Therefore, drug offenses during this period were considered more severe than the other recorded offenses with person offenses being the second most severe offense.

Puzzanchera and Addie (2014) purport that the primary differences in waivers are based on drug and personal offenses (see Figures 10.6 and 10.7). For example, regarding person offenses, in 1994 the likelihood of Black youth being waived was almost 1.5 times the probability of White youth. Regarding

**Figure 10.6. Waivers to Criminal Court, by Race (Personal Crime)**

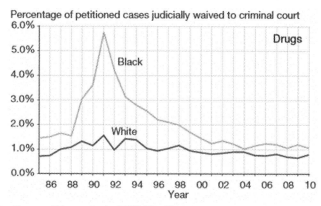

Source: http://www.ojjdp.gov/pubs/243042.pdf

**Figure 10.7. Waivers to Criminal Court, by Offense Type (Drugs)**

Source: http://www.ojjdp.gov/pubs/243042.pdf

drug offenses, in 1991 Black youth were waived nearly 6% more than White youth. The disparity observed in the figures bear caution about DMC and the policies and procedures enacted to halt the overrepresentation of minority youth within the justice system. Data show that "Black, Hispanic, and Asian-American youths are far more likely to be transferred to adult courts, convicted in those courts, and incarcerated in youth or adult prison facilities than white youths" (Leadership Conference on Civil and Human Rights, 2015).

The Leadership Conference on Civil and Human Rights (2015) concurs, noting that reviews of national statistics in reports released by the Youth Law Center that were prepared by researchers from the National Council on Crime and Delinquency "found substantial over-representation of minorities at all stages of the juvenile justice system, and noted that three out of every four youths admitted to adult prisons were minorities, despite the fact that the majority of juvenile arrests involved whites."

The discrepancies noted above are arguably linked to the "get tough" movement birthed from ambivalent crime policy from the 1980s onward (Shook, 2005). Crime and political debates surrounding the war on drugs and other crime issues brought about the punitive turn in American justice. Moreover, although much of this shift focused on the adult system, the JJS followed suit (see e.g., Beckett, 1997; Garland, 2001), which led to the use of the term "juvenile super predators" to describe those juveniles who were extreme threats to the community (Zimring, 1998).

The transferring of juveniles to adult court comes with lots of unintended consequences. In fact, Kurlychek and Johnson (2004, 2010) found that juveniles that are transferred to adult courts are treated more harshly than young adults. Moreover, this suggests that the transfer itself purports a higher level of dangerousness for those who are transferred to adult court, and this has tremendous implications for fairness within the justice system especially regarding race and ethnicity. With regard to bail and imprisonment, Steiner (2009) found that juveniles were more likely to be held on bail and imprisoned when compared to young adults.

## *Disparities in Punishment of Juveniles*

Outcomes in punishment are inextricably linked to processes at the beginning stages of the system (Bailey & Peterson, 1981; Chused 1973; Clarke & Kotch, 1980; McCarthy & Smith, 1986). For example, agents of the following entities have an enormous impact on the eventual punishment rendered to juveniles: social services, schools, family members, juvenile courts, and law enforcement. As mentioned throughout this chapter, agents within each of the aforementioned entities often rely (most times indirectly) on extra-legal factors (race, gender, stereotypes, etc.) to determine the trajectory of individual juveniles that come before them (see e.g., D'Angelo, Brown & Strozewski, 2013). The reliance on extra-legal factors in combination with legal factors often results in tremendous amounts of disparity. For juveniles, punishment is mostly identified via sentencing.

For example, Jordan and Frieburger (2010) examined the impact of race and ethnicity on the sentencing of juveniles in adult courts. Their study found a myriad of interesting intersectional results. They found that overall, Black juveniles were more likely to be sentenced to prison and jail as opposed to probation when compared to White youth. These findings tend to be consistent with research that examined the adult population as well (see, e.g., Spohn & Holleran, 2000; Steffensmeier & Demuth, 2000, 2006).

In addition, Jordan and Frieburger (2010) also found that being Black with a prior record increases the likelihood of being sent to prison; however, it was opposite for Whites. This shows a discrepancy in how judges may view previous records; this differential read of prior records could be aided by extra-legal and legal factors. This stage is naturally oppositional to most minority youth as they are likely to have a history of run-ins with the law as opposed to Whites, which can account for this disparity, consistent with the notion of *indirect effects* of race in punishment identified in Chapter 6. In addition, such disparity could be the result of judges seeing Black youth as more dangerous and therefore deserving of punishment, consistent with the theories of *focal concerns* and *symbolic interactionism* discussed in Chapters 6 and 7. Their results also indicated that although the Northeast was more accommodating to Blacks, Hispanics were more likely to receive prison. Hispanics were also likely to receive prison in the Midwest, which the authors contend is due to their small numbers in the heartland, which posits them as a threat to judges. They conclude by arguing that sentencing guidelines do very little toward preventing judges from utilizing extra-legal variables in their deliberations.

## Differences in Perceptions of Juvenile Justice

When it comes to perceptions of juvenile justice, very little research had been completed. However, Mears, Shollenberger, Willison, Owens, and Butts (2010) surveyed juvenile court practitioners to ascertain their perspectives on several juvenile justice processes. Their research provides an unheard inside view of those who work within the system. Their respondents include judges, prosecutors, public defenders, and court personnel. All respondents in their study were senior practitioners from the largest counties in the US.

Mears et al. (2010) purported that their most notable finding was the practitioners' contention that public support for rehabilitation ought to be a top priority. Their respondents believed strongly that rehabilitation of young offenders was the most efficient way of restoring the JJS. Of thirteen issues mentioned in their survey, the only issue that fell below 85% of support was DMC (76% support), thus suggesting that DMC is not that big of an issue (to their sample) perhaps. In addition, respondents indicated that the system is inadequate when addressing gender-specific programming for incarcerated juveniles. Respondents also put emphasis on the language barrier, thus indicating that youth, whose native language is other than English, tend to fare poorly in the system. Mears and company mention that although public support leans toward rehabilitative strategies, the results from their studies suggest that the system is oppositional to rehabilitation.

In addition, Mears et al. (2010) found that their respondents believed in reducing crime in the community as a prevention tactic. Furthermore, this suggests that the practitioners see a role in the community about combatting crime. There were some contrasts among respondents as well. These distinctions can best be understood via Packer's (1968) fictional models of criminal justice. Packer accentuated that **crime control** represented retribution while **due process** supported procedural rights. With regard to crime control vs. due process, Mears et al. (2010) found that prosecutors tend to favor crime control while public defenders believe in due process. To contextualize this distinction they purported that prosecutors also favored waiver laws and the reduced confidentiality in juvenile records for future prosecutions, and public defenders supported community oriented justice as an alternative to detention and current reentry programming.

Shockingly, Mears et al. (2010) expressed that there were some instances where practitioners disagreed with scientific evidence regarding individual policies. For example, regarding juvenile curfew policies, the researchers found that judges were more likely to believe that those policies are effective when, in fact, the evidence says otherwise. Such a finding suggests that practitioners may need to be trained in ways that allow them to effectuate evidence-based research into their daily duties.

In addition, Ward, Kupchik, Parker, and Starks (2011), in a similar study that surveyed juvenile probation officers from four Midwestern states, found that 70% of Blacks believed that DMC was a serious issue compared to only 41% of Whites and 39% of others (non-Black and White). These perceptions play a significant role in the current and aspirational plans of juvenile justice agencies and the players within the system. Moreover, they also found that officers, who prioritized punishment, are likely to support DMC over those who are likely to support alternatives, a result that was also found in the Mears et al. (2010) study. While most studies on perception consists of surveys given to the public, this section specifically summarized some attitudes of those who work in the system.

## Explanations

DMC indeed exists within the processes of juvenile justice, and there is evidence to suggest that DMC is a nation-wide crisis. Much of DMC is due to **differential involvement** (first defined in chapter 4) or the fact that minority youth are over-involved in crime, which then translates to DMC. Nevertheless, this overrepresentation in crime must be contextualized fully. For example, minority youth are more likely to come from poverty and dysfunctional communities and families that predispose them to criminality. Differential involvement of minority young people in crime can best be addressed by recognizing the roots of their involvement in crime, which are often economic.

In addition, differential treatment is also a factor that contributes to racial disparity within the JJS. For example, much of the evidence mentioned in this chapter pointed to two pictures of juvenile justice: one for children of color and one for Whites. Evidence of **differential treatment** (or *differential criminal selection*, as defined in Chapter 4) is further articulated through the differing perspectives of practitioners and other court workers who often rely on stereotypes when processing juveniles. Research continues to show the inability of court workers to rely strictly on legal factors. Thus, the continued use of extra-legal factors within the JJS will only sustain DMC.

The opinion of this author is consistent with that offered by the Leadership Conference on Civil and Human Rights (2015), who wrote:

> The disproportionate number of minority transfers to adult court *cannot be explained by the commission of more, or more serious, crimes* by minority youths. The JPI study found a 2.8-to-1 violent arrest ratio between minority and white youths—that is, for every white youth arrested for a felony, 2.8 minority youths were arrested. But after the felony arrest stage, the likelihood of minority youths being transferred to adult court as compared to white youths increased to 6.2-to-1. The ratio of adult court prison *sentences* increased even further: Minority youths arrested for violent crimes were seven times more likely overall to receive prison sentences from adult courts than white youths arrested for similar crimes. The numbers for black youth were particularly stark. As compared to a white youth who committed a violent crime, a black youth was 18.4 times more likely to be sentenced to prison by an adult court (Hispanics were 7.3 times more likely, and Asian-Americans 4.5 times more likely, than whites to be sentenced to a CYA facility by an adult court).

Thus, it seems that, as with the adult system, the further one looks into the JJS, the worse the problem of racial and ethnic disparities becomes.

# Conclusion

The non-system-like structure of the JJS nonetheless creates independence between agencies that breed corruption, inconsistencies, and disparity. The JJS is comprised of various organizations and actors that operate in distinct ways. For example, the role of the social worker is entirely different from the role of intake officers or the judge. Decentralization within juvenile justice processes must be addressed to ensure efficiency and equity within juvenile justice outcomes.

Moreover, although some measures have been taken to address DMC, evidence cited in this chapter has shown that practitioners within the JJS may not be privy to disparities. Practitioners may need to be educated and trained on the significance of reducing DMC and equalizing JJS. This can best be completed by using evidence-based policy as a mechanism of change within the JJS. Evidence-based policy would provide scientific solutions to the problems that exist within the JJS. Furthermore, with the use of evidence-based solutions, justice becomes more efficient and equitable.

As mentioned earlier, root causes of juvenile crime must be acknowledged. Minority youths over-involvement in crime should be addressed, but it must involve community-level interventions that would allow for these youths to be treated in the community. Non-intervention strategies must be pursued if DMC is ever to be alleviated. In addition, there need to be more studies focusing on the deterrent effect of waiver laws. Accountability needs to become a reality within juvenile justice processes, and individualized justice should return to the JJS. Restorative models of justice that include circumstantial contexts may be suitable for combatting DMC in the JJS too.

# Discussion Questions

1. What is juvenile justice?
2. What is parens patriae?
3. What is the significance behind *Ex parte Crouse*?
4. Explain the beliefs of the child savers.
5. What role did the houses of refuge play in the development of juvenile justice?
6. What are the functions of juvenile justice?
7. What is individualized justice and is it being pursued in contemporary juvenile justice?
8. What is DMC?
9. How does the reduction model help to rid DMC?
10. What are extra-legal factors?
11. Define Packer's models of criminal justice.
12. How do differential involvement and treatment impact juvenile justice?
13. What role do practitioners play in disparities?

# References

Armstrong, G. S., & Rodriguez, N. (2005). Effects of Individual and Contextual Characteristics on Preadjudication Detention of Juvenile Delinquents. *Justice Quarterly 22(4)*, 521–539.

Bailey, C. W., & Peterson, R. D. (1981). Legal versus extra-legal determinants of juvenile court dispositions. *Juvenile and Family Court Journal 32*, 41–56.

Beckett, K. (1997). *Making Crime Pay: Law and Order in Contemporary American Politics.* NY: Oxford University Press.

Bishop, D. (2005). The role of race and ethnicity in juvenile justice processing. In D. Hawkins, & K. Kempf-Leonard, *Our children, their children: Confronting racial and ethnic differences in American juvenile justice* (pp. 23–82). Chicago: The University of Chicago Press.

Bishop, D. M., & Frazier, C. E. (1988). The Influence of Race on Juvenile Justice Processing. *Journal of Research in Crime and Delinquency 25*, 242–263.

Bishop, D. M., & Frazier, C. E. (1996). Race effects in juvenile justice decision-making: Findings of a statewide analysis . *Journal of Criminal Law and Criminology 86(2)*, 392–413.

Bishop, D. M., Leiber, M., & Johnson, J. (2010). Contexts of Decision Making in the Juvenile Justice System: An Organizational Approach to Understanding Minority Overrepresentation. *Youth Violence and Juvenile Justice 8(3)*, 213–233.

Bishop., D., & Leiber, M. (2012). Race, ethnicity, and juvenile justice: Racial and ethnic differences in delinquency and justice system responses. In D. Bishop, & B. Feld, *Juvenile Justice* (pp. 445–484). NY: Oxford.

Bortner, M., & Reed, W. (1985). The preeminence of process: An examination of refocused justice research. *Social Science Quarterly 66(22)*, 413–425.

Bridges, G. S., & Steen, S. (1998). Racial disparities in official assessments of juvenile offenders: Attributional stereotypes as mediating mechanisms. *American Sociological Review 63*, 554–570.

Bridges, G., Conley, D., Engen, R., & Price-Spratlen, T. (1995). Racial disparities in confinement of juveniles: Effects of crime and community social structure on punishment. In K. Kempf-Leonard, C. Pope, & W. Feyerherm, *Minorities in juvenile justice* (pp. 128–152). Thousand Oaks: Sage.

Chesney-Lind, M. (1977). Judicial paternalism and the female status offender. *Crime & Delinquency 23*, 121–130.

Chused, R. H. (1973). The juvenile court process: A study of three New Jersey counties . *Rutgers Law Review 26*, 488–539.

Clarke, H. S., & Koch, G. G. (1980). Juvenile court: Therapy or control, and do lawyers make a difference? *Law and Society Review 14(2)*, 263–308.

D'Angelo, J., Brown, M. P., & Strozewski, J. (2013). Missouri: An Examination of the Relationship Between the Source of Referral to Juvenile Court and Severity of Sentencing Outcomes. *Criminal Justice Policy Review 24(4)*, 395–421.

Dannerfer, D., & Schutt, R. K. (1982). Race and Juvenile Justice Processing in Court and Police Agencies. *American Journal of Sociology 66*, 1113–32.

Farnworth, M., Frazier, C., & Neuberger, A. (1988). Orientations to juvenile justice: Exploratory notes from a statewide survey of juvenile justice decision makers. *Journal of Criminal Justice 12*, 477–491.

Farrell, R., & Swigert, V. (1978). Prior offense record as a self-fulfilling prophecy. *Law & Society Review 12*, 437–453.

Gaarder, E., Rodriguez, N., & Zatz, M. (2004). Criers, liars and manipulators: Probation officers' views of girls . *Justice Quarterly 21*, 547–578.

Garland, D. (2001). *The culture of control crime control and social order in contemporary society.* Chicago: : The University of Chicago Press.

Harms, P. (2002). *Detention in delinquency cases, 1989–1998.* Washington, D. C. : Office of Juvenile Justice and Delinquency Prevention.

Kurlychek, M. C., & Johnson, B. D. (2004). The Juvenile Penalty: A Comparison of Juvenile and Young Adult Sentencing Outcomes in Criminal Court. *Criminology 42(2)*, 485–517.

Kurlychek, M. C., & Johnson, B. D. (2010). Juvenility and Punishment: Sentencing Juveniles in Adult Criminal Court. *Criminology 48(3)*, 725–758.

Leadership Conference on Civil and Human Rights (2015). Justice on trial. Juvenile justice. Downloaded from: http://www.civilrights.org/publications/justice-on-trial/juvenile.html.

Leiber, M. J., Peck, J. H., & Beaudry-Cyr, M. (2014). When does Race and Gender Matter? The Interrelationships between the Gender of Probation Officers and Juvenile Court Detention and Intake Outcomes. *Justice Quarterly*.

McCarthy, B. R. (1987). Preventive detention and pretrial custody in the juvenile court. *Journal of Criminal Justice 15(3)*, 185–198.

McCarthy, B. R., & Smith, B. (1986). The conceptualization of discrimination in the juvenile justice process: The impact of administrative factors and screening decisions on juvenile court dispositions. *Criminology 24(1)*, 41–64.

Mennel, R. M. (1973). *Thorns and Thistles: Juvenile Delinquency in the United States 1825–1940.* Hanover: University of New Hampshire Press.

Mennel, R. M. (1973). *Thorns and Thistles: Juvenile Delinquents in the United States, 1825–1940, 1st Ed.* Lebanon: University Press of New England.

Office of Juvenile Justice and Delinquency Prevention. (2012). *Disproportionate Minority Contact.* Washington D.C.: U.S. Department of Justice. Retrieved from http://www.ojjdp.gov/pubs/239457.pdf.

Packer, H. L. (1968). *The limits of the criminal sanction.* Stanford : Stanford University Press.

Pope, C. E., & Feyerherm, W. H. (1990). Minority Status and Juvenile Processing: An Assessment of the Research Literature (Part I). *Criminal Justice Abstracts 22*, 327–335.

Secret, P. E., & Johnson, J. B. (1997). The effect of race on juvenile, justice decision making in Nebraska: Detention, adjudication, and disposition, 1998–1993. *Justice Quarterly 14(13)*, 445–478.

Shook, J. J. (2005). Contesting Childhood in the US Justice System. *Childhood 12(4)*, 461–478.

Smith, D. A., & Paternoster, R. (1990). Formal Processing and Future Delinquency: Deviance Amplification as Selection Artifact. *Law & Society Review 24*, 1109–31.

Spohn, C., & Hollerman, D. (2000). The imprisonment penalty paid by young unemployed Black and Hispanic male offenders. *Criminology 38*, 281–306.

Steffensmeier, D., & Demuth, S. (2000). Ethnicity and sentencing in U.S. federal courts: Who is punished more harshly? *American Sociological Review 65*, 705–729.

Steffensmeier, D., & Demuth, S. (2006). Does gender modify the effects of race—ethnicity on criminal sanctions? Sentences for male and female, White, Black, and Hispanic defendants. *Journal of Quantitative Criminology 22*, 241–261.

Steiner, B. (2009). The effects of juvenile transfer to criminal court on incarceration decisions . *Justice Quarterly 26(77)*, 77–106.

The Sentencing Project. (2014). *Disproportionate Minority Contact in the Juvenile Justice System.* Washington, D.C.: The Sentencing Project. Retrieved from http://sentencingproject.org/doc/publications/jj_Disproportionate%20Minority%20Contact.pdf.

Tittle, C. R., & Curran, D. A. (1988). Contingencies for dispositional disparities in juvenile justice. *Social Forces 67*, 23–58.

Vito, G. F., & Kunselman, J. C. (2012). *Juvenile Justice Today.* Upper Saddle River: Pearson.

Ward, G. K. (2012). *The Black Child-Savers: Racial Democracy and Juvenile Justice.* Chicago: The University of Chicago Press.

Ward, G., Kupchik, A., Parker, L., & Starks, B. C. (2011). Racial Politics of Juvenile Justice Policy Support: Juvenile Court Worker Orientations Toward
Disproportionate Minority Confinement. *Race and Justice 1(2)*, 154–184.

Wordes, M., Bynum, T. S., & Corley, C. J. (1994). Locking up youth: The impact of race on detention decision. *Journal of Research in Crime and Delinquency 31(2)*, 149–165.

Wu, B. (1997). The effect of race and juvenile justice processing. *Juvenile & Family Court Judges 48(1)*, 43–51.

Wu, B., Cernkovich, S., & Dunn, C. S. (1997). Assessing the effects of race
and class on juvenile justice processing in Ohio. *Journal of Criminal Justice 25(4)*, 265–277.

Zimring, F. (1998). *American Youth Violence.* NY: Oxford University Press.

# Chapter 11

# Summary and the Future

*by Matthew Robinson, PhD*

## Introduction

In this book, we've seen that there are clear relationships between race and ethnicity and crime and delinquency, as well as between race and ethnicity and criminal justice and juvenile justice practice. Although Americans believe in *liberty*, *equality*, and *happiness* for all (as laid out in the Declaration of Independence and the US Constitution, discussed in Chapter 1), and continue to strive to assure fairness in society so that "justice is blind," the research reported in this book shows that we still have a long way to go. Specifically, there is clear and convincing evidence that American criminal justice and juvenile justice practices remain significantly biased based on extra-legal factors including race and ethnicity which are not supposed to impact justice practices in the ideal world.

Of course, there are often conflicts between our ideals and real practice. So, whereas Americans prefer that government agencies such as law enforcement, courts, and corrections will treat all people equally—regardless of race, ethnicity, age, gender, and so on—there is significant evidence that criminal and juvenile justice systems continue in the 21st century to disproportionately impact (if not target) people of color, and especially young Black (and brown) men living in urban environments.

Contrary to popular belief, this reality does *not* begin with law enforcement. *Racial profiling* in policing is real, at least in some places (consistent with the notion of *contextual discrimination*, defined in the book as discrimination found in particular contexts or circumstances). Yet that police often target some people in some places more than others first and foremost stems from the criminal law (which defines certain acts and even certain people as more dangerous and worthy of justice system intervention) as well as media coverage of crime (which depicts some people and situations as more dangerous than others). Racial and ethnic disparities in criminal and juvenile justice system processing are thus *institutionalized*—meaning they are rooted in prominent American institutions.

This does not deny the reality of **individual discrimination**, which again refers to discrimination that results from the acts of particular individuals but is not characteristic of entire agencies or the criminal justice system as a whole. It's just that this kind of discrimination is easier to demonstrate as well as root out, whereas eliminating **institutionalized discrimination** requires making fundamental changes to US institutions.

In this chapter, the author summarizes the main findings of the book and then turn to the issue of the future. The main goal here is to provide a brief summary of the research presented in the book, as well as to suggest some reforms needed to bring about important change in America's criminal and juvenile justice systems.

# Race and Ethnicity Revisited

Recall that *ethnicity* is a real identifiable characteristic of a person or people which refers to place of origin (e.g., country of birth) and that signifies some shared cultural traits. However, *race* is socially a constructed characteristic assigned and ultimately embraced to a person or people based largely on skin color. Based on the color of people's skin—more so than on from what country they are born or their actual life experiences—people tend to categorize and even often judge others as if they share common traits passed down through genetics. Although the authors of this book acknowledge that the classification of people into racial categories is arbitrary and largely without biological basis, the designation of race has categories very real political, social, and economic effects.

As one example, in this book, you have seen that ethnicity and race have real and meaningful impacts on whether individuals are processed through our juvenile and criminal justice systems. That is, there are meaningful *disparities* or differences in justice processing across groups based at least in part of on the color of people's skin—which, over time and through American institutions such as the criminal law and the media, has been associated with differences in lifestyles and behavior according to different racial and ethnic stereotypes.

Research discussed in this book demonstrates that some *ecotypes*—groups of individuals that share adaptations to specific environments (e.g., inner-city Blacks)—are more likely to experience juvenile and criminal justice system involvement than other ecotypes. That is, it is largely *people of color*, and especially *minority groups*, that are most subjected to justice system intervention. For example, as shown in this book, Latinos and African Americans make up only about 25% of the US population, but together comprise about 60% of correctional inmates in America.

Of course, as noted in the book, there is a close relationship between race, ethnicity, and social class; people of color tend to have the lowest levels of income and wealth, and they also tend to suffer from higher rates of poverty and unemployment. Thus, disparities in juvenile and criminal justice might have as much to do with social class as they do with race and ethnicity. Whatever the case, the disparities in justice outcomes identified in this book are at least consistent with the arguments of scholars who posit that America's justice systems are either intentionally biased against people of color and the poor or at the least serve to function to oppress and control them in order to serve the interests of powerful groups in society (e.g., wealthy Whites). Such outcomes are clearly not consistent with the American ideals of liberty, equality, justice, and general happiness. Nor are they sustainable as America continues to become more diverse and less white.

The difference between the arguments of other scholars and the one presented here is that we are not saying the juvenile and criminal justice systems are intentionally biased against people of color, only that they undeniably most harm them. Our argument is that juvenile and criminal justice agencies serve the functions of controlling some segments of the population and serving limited interests, not that juvenile and criminal justice practices are intended to do so.

## The Problem in a Nutshell

In a nutshell, the problems identified in this book can be summarized this way: Race, ethnicity, and other extra-legal factors (e.g., social class) continue to impact juvenile and criminal justice processing, in spite of the ideal which holds that only legal factors should impact juvenile and criminal justice processes.

Without question, racial and ethnic disparities exist across all aspects of juvenile and criminal justice. More questionable is the degree to which these disparities are produced by differential involvement in delinquent and criminal behavior as well as the different forms of discrimination discussed above. As illustrated throughout this book, studies tend to show that different levels of offending cannot fully explain *disproportionate minority confinement* or over-representation of people of color in adult correctional facilities; offending that explains some over-representation is actually due to race or ethnicity per se but rather to the ecotypes of disadvantaged people that is economic and cultural in nature.

Thus, it is apparent that juvenile and criminal justice practices are characterized if not plagued by serious discrimination. Some of this is *individual* in nature; much of it is *contextual* or dependent on the context, situation, and place. These forms of discrimination are usually easily identifiable, making reform possible if not likely. Most troubling is the form of discrimination that has become part of American institutions such as the criminal law, the media, and criminal justice agencies themselves.

Research summarized in this book illustrates that there are biases against some groups in American society that are built into these institutions. Consider, for example, the criminal law, which criminalizes and identifies as serious only some harmful acts—those disproportionately committed by the poor and people of color. Then there is the media, which focuses our attention on some harmful acts more than others (e.g., street crime over corporate crime), and on some people under certain circumstances more than others (e.g., offenders who are of color and victims who are White). These institutions determine, first, which acts we focus on and which we don't, and second, which acts we think about and get concerned about and which we don't. That these institutions are controlled by powerful people, who are overwhelmingly White and wealthy, has been established and is without question.

This *institutionalized bias* is not only much harder to see, but it is also much more difficult to correct for that requires making changes to the institutions themselves. For example, if the law were made, voted for, and funded by groups demographically representative of the US population, it is likely but not certain that there would be less bias in the harmful acts we define as crime and as serious crime. Further, if the media were owned and operated by people demographically representative of the US population, it is likely but not certain that there would be less bias in the harmful acts we focus on in news and entertainment media. Yet assuring these outcomes would require organized and diverse efforts that could take decades to achieve. Think of how hard it would be and all it would take to diversify state legislatures and the US Congress. Think of all it would take to greater diversify media organizations. Later in the chapter, the author will attempt to lay out some preliminary ideas for achieving these reforms.

Then there are the problems within criminal justice organizations themselves, many of which were identified by the authors of this book. For example, research shows that:

1. The law is not written for, voted for, or paid for by people representative of the US population, assuring that the interests of a select group of people will be most represented by the law, and creating a bias against certain groups in society (i.e., young, poor people of color).
2. The juvenile justice system and criminal justice system focus almost exclusively on street crime, guaranteeing that especially poor males of color will fall under this jurisdiction.
3. The major focus of the US drug war is poor people of color.
4. Black and brown juveniles tend to receive harsher treatment than White juveniles by the juvenile justice system.
5. Young people of color are more likely than young White people to be harassed and targeted by the police.
6. Racial and ethnic profiling by the police does occur, at least in some jurisdictions.
7. People of color are more likely to have negative interactions with the police (including stops, being searched, being arrested, and having force and excessive force against them).
8. People of color are at times more likely than Whites to be denied bail, charged higher bail, charged with more serious crimes by prosecutors, and be given less favorable plea bargains. Also, when a criminal defendant is unemployed and thus poor, he or she is more likely to be detained in *preventive detention*, meaning he or she will be held in jail prior to trial rather than being released to his or her family.
9. Negotiated pleas tend to be biased against people of color, at least in some jurisdictions.
10. People of color are more likely to be removed from juries with peremptory challenges.
11. Jury decision-making is impacted by race and ethnicity, especially in cases with minority defendants and White victims.
12. Wrongful conviction is far more likely to impact African Americans and Latinos.
13. For at least some types of crimes, African Americans and Latinos tend to receive longer and tougher sentences than Whites.

14. The implementation of some sentencing policies (e.g., three strikes laws) is plagued by serious racial and ethnic disparities.
15. Both indirect and interactive effects of race and ethnicity are found in criminal sentencing.
16. Disparities exist in US correctional punishment, including probation, jail, and prison—poor, young men of color make up the majority of correctional clients.
17. Disparities based on race, ethnicity, social class, and even gender persist in capital punishment practice, so that killers of Whites (and especially African American men who kill White women) are more likely to be sentenced to death, and poor killers with inadequate defense attorneys are most prone to death sentences. Recall that the scholarship in this area is suggestive that the death penalty is plagued by *systematic discrimination*.

# Possible Reforms

Two types of reforms are justified by the findings of this book. First, there are those reforms that can be directed at individual agencies of criminal justice themselves—for example, reducing racial profiling in policing, increasing justice in the courts by forbidding the elimination of people from jury service through peremptory challenges, reducing the likelihood that racial discrimination will persist in capital punishment by increasing the representative nature of courtroom workgroups and juries. Second, there are those broader reforms that require changing who makes the law, votes for it, and pays for it, as well as how the media cover (and do not cover) delinquency and crime. Below the author outlines and discusses some reforms that would bring the realities of juvenile and criminal justice in line with America's ideals of liberty, equality, and happiness for all.

## *Police Reforms*

Beginning with the former type of reform and starting with the police, in order to achieve greater fairness in police outcomes, the processes that lead to disparities in stops, searches, arrests, excessive use of force, and so on, must be ceased. This means the differential level of focus on people of color and their communities must be stopped. To the degree that this focus results from greater calls for services and/or greater crimes in the communities where people of color live, one cannot reasonably expect this to occur. But intentionally targeting communities and/or people based on the color of people's skin is intolerable.

Similarly, racial and ethnic profiling must be prohibited by law. Of course, all people perhaps naturally over time learn to develop profiles as well as stereotypes of people based on the way they look, dress, and especially behave, consistent with symbolic interactionism, labeling theory, and the minority threat hypothesis. Yet, developing conceptions of dangerousness based on the color of one's skin or their nationality is not justifiable except for in cases where police are searching for a specific individual involved in a crime that has been described as being from a certain race or ethnicity.

Of even more importance than this is ending the explicit focus of police in the United States on street crimes and especially drug possession and dealing. The focus on these crimes—particularly drug crimes—has been found to directly produce disparities in criminal justice outcomes based on race, ethnicity, social class, and even gender. Street crimes can be quite serious, as in the case of murder and rape, but the harms produced by these crimes pale in comparison to the harms produced by white-collar and corporate crimes. Thus, greater law enforcement focus must be placed on such acts by powerful people which would logically reduce the focus on acts committed by people of color and simultaneously increase the focus on acts committed by Whites. Further, greater efforts must be made to prevent these crimes as well as the serious crimes of murder, rape, and so forth.

Beyond this, sensitivity and multicultural training for police officers is essential to overcome biases based on race and ethnicity. Officers must be reminded that their primary function is to protect and serve the community, both of which require treating all people as human beings; service must become the predominant purpose of policing, even more so than law enforcement (i.e., reacting to street crime).

This basic idea is supported by numerous criminal justice scholars as well as notable civil rights & social justice leaders and organizations. In the 1990s, a group of scholars formed the *National Criminal Justice Commission*, who pointed out that **community policing** is based on the notion that police "should serve residents in a neighborhood rather than simply police them" (Donziger, 1996: p. 160). Yet one significant problem with community policing is that many minority communities "feel both *overpoliced and underprotected*—overpoliced because the drug trade flourishes with the same vitality as before, and because police are often slow to respond to 911 calls from minority neighborhoods."

Legislators and policy-makers have placed more police in these neighborhoods on the basis of the belief that there is more crime there and that the presence of more police will reduce crime. The evidence from studies such as the now famous *Kansas City Patrol Study* (Kelling et al., 1974) and its replications

(Police Foundation, 1981) suggests that more police will not reduce crime. These studies found no evidence that patrol activities of police, whether proactive, reactive, or even absent, had any effects on crime rates. This is why the National Criminal Justice Commission concludes that "we need to learn how to police better before we add new police" (Donziger, 1996: 160, emphasis added).

Walker (2014) explains why adding more police will have no effect on crime rates. He argues that patrol will always be spread thin in a geographic area, so that its crime-preventive benefits will be minimal. He also suggests that many crimes are not suppressible by patrol because they happen in private areas between people who know one another. There is some research that suggests that adding more police to large cities will reduce street crime there, especially when patrols are directed at *hot spots of crime* (Sherman et al., 1997). The number of violent street crimes, as measured in the UCR, declined 34% between 1990 and 2000, and the number of UCR property crimes fell by 31%. During this time, the number of full-time officers increased 17%. Policing likely had something to do with these declines but scholars generally agree that police were not responsible for most of the declines.

Given this, it makes sense to use officers in a way that can make a difference—serving communities and the people who live there. Officers should be, first and foremost, friends to the people they serve, not occupying enemies to the people they police.

## Court Reforms

With regard to the courts, the biases in pre-trial process such as bail, plea bargaining, and charging in some jurisdictions can be best overcome by diversifying the courtroom workgroup. That is, it is necessary that people of color be better represented among those decision-makers whose discretion produces disparities based on extra-legal factors. Beyond this, all prosecutors and judges must be reminded in law school and through the professional organizations to which they belong that all people must be given *equal* access to justice in all forms, regardless of race, ethnicity, social class, gender, religion, and so forth. Fundamentally, this requires a rededication to doing justice and procedural rights/due process among all actors of the courtroom workgroups, especially its most powerful member—the prosecutor.

Standardizing bail based on offense seriousness alone would go a long way toward creating more equitable bail amounts across different populations. Outlawing plea bargaining, especially in serious crime cases, and requiring criminal trials—intended by Article III and the Sixth Amendment to the US Constitution, would also help alleviate differential access to plea bargains. And basing charging decisions solely on legal factors such as the amount of quality evidence of guilt and the nature of the offense(s) would reduce racial and ethnic disparities in charging decisions.

Peremptory challenges have no place in contemporary courts; they are part of US common law carried over from English legal traditions. We know that court officials such as prosecutors use race and ethnicity to exclude people from serving on juries, in spite of the fact that this is explicitly illegal. To achieve better representation of juries and more just court outcomes, peremptory challenges should be prohibited by law; prosecutors and defense attorneys will continue to use unlimited challenges for cause to eliminate jurors who have conflicts of interests, etc.

As for eliminating biases in the jury box among jurors themselves, this requires continued public education about the realities of crime, including who commits them and why. Reducing racism and ethnocentrism is not easy to accomplish, but it is possible and has been occurring over time.

Any move away from mandatory sentencing, three strikes laws, and truth-in-sentencing laws, will inevitably produce more just outcomes since these policies have been used to disproportionately harm people of color. States—even if driven largely by economic concerns—are beginning to abandon these practices, and this will result in more equitable and just sentencing outcomes.

As for differential sentencing outcomes across races and ethnicities, these will be best alleviated as young men of color are less likely to be arrested by the police for serious crimes, once the reforms stated above are adopted and implemented (because legal factors best predict sentencing outcomes). But after the point of arrest, sentencing disparities that arise from non-legal factors such as race and ethnicity are not tolerable in a nation whose people value liberty, equality, and happiness. Sentencing judges can simply sentence all like offenders to like punishments, and counties of states that discover unjust sentencing disparities must take action to correct them.

## Correctional Reforms

Most of the racial and ethnic disparities that exist in corrections arise out of problems in police and court practices. But the disparities that exist in capital punishment are intractable. Recall the claim by Walker, Spohn, & De-Lone, (2012) that American death penalty practice is consistent with *systematic discrimination*:

> Racial discrimination in the capital sentencing process is not limited
> to the South, where historical evidence of racial bias would lead one

to expect different treatment, but is applicable to other regions of the country as well. It is not confined to one stage of the decision-making process, but affects decisions made by prosecutors as well as juries. It is also not confined to the pre-*Furman* period, when statutes offered little or no guidance to judges and juries charged with deciding whether to impose the death penalty or not, but is found, too, under the more restrictive guided discretion statutes enacted since *Furman*. Moreover, this effect does not disappear when legally relevant predictors of sentence severity are taken into consideration. (p. 391)

The only true way to eliminate racial and ethnic biases in capital punishment is to abolish the death penalty, for states have been "tinkering with the machinery of death" for decades in order to make it fair and foolproof, but with no luck. Doing this will not eliminate racial and ethnic biases in criminal justice, but it will make sure no one dies as a result of them.

## *Larger Reforms*

As for the larger reforms noted above, the most fundamental problems with criminal justice stem from the biases that arise from the institutions of the law and the media. As shown in the book, lawmakers are not representative of the US population, voters are not representative of the US population (and most people do not regularly vote), and the money that determines elections does not come from people who are representative of the US population. Thus, it should not be at all surprising that studies find the law tends not to serve the interests of the people but rather serves the interests of elites in society who fund the law, as in an *oligarchy* rather than a democracy.

The criminal law is a special case, for the acts on which we direct most of our criminal justice attention have been defined as *crimes* and *serious crimes* for decades. Yet it remains true that lawmakers have always been non-representative of the US population. So, even though public opinion polls show that people generally agree with the behaviors legislated as crimes and serious crimes, studies also show that people would prefer to criminalize acts of elites when they are harmful and committed with culpability (Leeper Piquero, Carmichael & Piquero, 2008). That the harmful acts of wealthy individuals and corporations tend to be legal owes itself to the fact that the same people make the law and own the dominant means of communication in society. Our nearly exclusive focus on street crime—because of the law and the media—is one of the most significant sources of racial and ethnic biases in criminal justice.

Thus, racial and ethnic justice will not occur until people from all groups in society have ownership of the law and media. This requires increasing participation by people of color in lawmaking, voting, and funding the law, as well as diversifying ownership of the mainstream media sources that help determine our focus and the issues about which we are concerned. Numerous groups are doing just this, working to reform the criminal law, media, and criminal justice policy (e.g., mass incarceration, capital punishment). They include groups like the American Civil Liberties Union, Campaign for Effective Crime Policy, Crime Victims for a Just Society, Center for Justice and Reconciliation, Center for Restorative Justice and Peacemaking, Centre for Social Justice, Coalition for Federal Sentencing Reform, Crime Victims for a Just Society, Criminal Justice Policy Foundation, Death Penalty Information Center, Drug Policy Alliance, Families Against Mandatory Minimums, Free Press, Journey of Hope, Murder Victims Families for Reconciliation, National Center on Institutions and Alternatives, National Coalition to Abolish the Death Penalty, People of Faith Against the Death Penalty, Reclaim the Media, Restitution Incorporated, The Sentencing Project, Southern Poverty Law Center, Stop the Drug War, Stopviolence.com, Tolerance.org, Victim Offender Mediation Association, and more.

# Conclusion

Juvenile and criminal justice practices in the real world do not match American ideals of liberty, equality, justice, and happiness. In spite of our best efforts to eliminate disparities based on extra-legal factors such as race and ethnicity, disparities remain across all of juvenile and criminal justice practice. Extralegal factors impact justice processing independently (so that people of color are more likely to be arrested, convicted, and punished for some crimes) but they also interact to impact justice processing in ways that most impact young, poor men of color. Thus, the realities of US juvenile and criminal justice practices are impacted by numerous *extra-legal factors*, consistent with the reality of *intersectionality*.

In spite of the fact that ethnicity and race continue to impact juvenile and criminal justice practice, it is an undeniable fact that much progress has been made to make justice processes fairer. After all, we've come a long way since eradicating Native Americas, enslaving Africans, and subjugating women; we've progressed from the days of lynching and "separate but equal" facilities in society. As Americans have progressed, the realities of juvenile and criminal justice system processes have come closer and closer to our ideals.

This does not mean that it is inevitable that we will one day reach those ideals, only that it is likely. Change does not just occur in a vacuum, it requires work, struggle, and sacrifice to achieve. Pursuing reforms like those offered in this chapter is likely to expedite reaching America's justice ideals.

# Discussion Questions

1. Outline the major findings of the book with regard to the criminal law and the media.
2. Outline the major findings of the book with regard to the police.
3. Outline the major findings of the book with regard to the courts.
4. Outline the major findings of the book with regard to corrections.
5. Outline the major findings of the book with regard to capital punishment.
6. Which of the reforms identified in this book do you agree with/disagree with? Explain why.

# References

Donziger, S. (1996). *The real war on crime: The report of the National Criminal Justice Commission.* New York: HarperPerennial.

Kelling, G., Pate, T., Dieckman, D., & Brown, C. (1974). The Kansas City preventive patrol experiment: A summary report. Washington, DC: The Police Foundation.

Leeper Piquero, N., Carmichael, S., & Piquero, A. (2008). Research note: Assessing the perceived seriousness of white-collar and street crimes. *Crime and Delinquency, 54*(2), 291–312.

Police Foundation. (1981). The Newark foot patrol experiment. Washington DC: The Police Foundation.

Sherman, L., Gottfredson, D., MacKenzie, D., Eck, J., Reuter, P., & Bushway, S. (1997). Preventing crime: What works, what doesn't, what's promising. Washington, DC: U.S. Department of Justice, Office of Justice Programs, National Institute of Justice.

Walker, S. (2014). *Sense and nonsense about crime and drugs.* Beverly Hills, CA: Wadsworth.

Walker, S., Spohn, C., & DeLone, M. (2014). *The color of justice: Race, ethnicity, and crime in America.* Belmont, CA: Wadsworth.

# Index

Note: *f* indicates figure; *t*, table; and *n*, footnote.

official statistics. *See* crime data;
Uniform Crime Reports (UCR)
oligarchy, 63
over-representation, 205–6

*parens patriae*, 50, 274
parole, 49, 204. *See also* determinate
sentencing
passive force, 131
*Patton v. Mississippi*, 155, 251
*Pennsylvania, McKeiver v.*, 278
people of color, 12. *See also*
minority group
peremptory challenge, 156, 219,
221, 303
*Plata, Brown v.*, 207
plea bargaining, 49, 148–49,
153–54
number of convictions via, 149*t*
*Plessy v. Ferguson*, 150, 221
police, 48
attitudes toward, 129–30,
136–37, 162
behavioral expectations of, 117
code of ethics for, 114–16*t*
discretion of, 112, 115*t*
face-to-face contacts with,
122–23, 124–125*t*
functions of, 113–14, 113*t*,
114–15*t*
numbers of, 117–18
proposals for reforms of,
300–302
racial profiling by, 119–26
street crime and, 118–19
use of force by, 115, 130–35
Police-Public Contact Survey, 133,
134*t*
police shootings, lethal. *See* lethal
force

political action committee (PAC),
66–68
political donors, demographics of,
71–72*t*, 71–73
population demographics, U.S.,
12–17
in 2010, 12*t*
changes in, 13, 13*f*
death penalty and impact of
changing, 262–63
Hispanics and Latinos and, 14,
14*f*
poverty rate, by race and ethnicity,
18*t*
*Powell v. Alabama*, 246, 248, 251
prefrontal cortex, 34
pre-trial processes
disparities in, 150–57, 189–90,
190*f*
proposals for reforms of, 302–3
preventive detention, 23
prisoners
in jails, 203–4, 214
life without parole (LWOP) for,
216–18, 217*t*
in prisons, 204, 214–16
public perception of, 226
prisons, 204. *See also* correctional
system
female inmates in, 215–16
male inmates in, 214–15
probation, 49, 203, 213. *See also*
correctional system
probation revocation, 213
procedural law, 59
property crime(s)
demographics of offenders of,
45*t*
trends in, 38–39, 38*f*, 41–42,
41*f*

victimizations, violent and
  property, 41–42, 41*f*
victimless crime, 41
violence
    risk factors for, 101, 101*t*
    subculture of, 98
Violent Crime Control and Law
  Enforcement Act of 1994, 126
violent crime(s)
    demographics of offenders of,
      45*t*
    trends in, 38–39, 38*f*, 41–42,
      41*f*
voters, demographics of, 62–64

waiver, for juveniles, 52–53,
  283–86, 284*f*, 285*f*
war on drugs, 77, 177*t*, 181, 182
    arrests and, 39, 39*f*, 45*t*
    racial profiling and, 120–21
Wayne, Lil', 180

wealth, by race and ethnicity, 18*t*
*West Virginia, Strauder v.*, 155, 157
White, Byron, 156
white-collar crime, 32–33
    costs of, 32–33*t*
    harm caused by, 78
*Winshop, In re*, 278
*Witherspoon v. Illinois*, 252
women
    death penalty and female
      victims, 261–62
    inmates, 215–16 (*See also*
      inmates)
wrongful conviction, 159, 222–24.
  *See also* exonerations, death-row

youth. *See* delinquency; juvenile
  justice system

zone in transition, 15